PROCLAMATION
AND
PRESENCE

PROCLAMATION
AND
PRESENCE

OLD TESTAMENT ESSAYS IN HONOUR OF
GWYNNE HENTON DAVIES

EDITED BY
JOHN I DURHAM & J. R. PORTER

New Corrected Edition

MERCER UNIVERSITY PRESS
MACON, GEORGIA 31207

ISBN 0-86554-101-9

Proclamation and Presence
Originally published in Great Britain by SCM Press Ltd., London (© 1970),
and in the United States by John Knox Press, Atlanta, this New Corrected
Edition is published with the permission of SCM Press Ltd., and by arrangement
with John I Durham and J. R. Porter.

Proclamation and Presence
New Corrected Edition © 1983
Mercer University Press
Macon, Georgia 31207

Printed in the United States of America

All books published by Mercer University Press are produced on
acid-free paper that exceeds the minimum standards set by the
National Historical Publications and Records Commission.

Library of Congress Cataloging in Publication Data

Main entry under title:

Proclamation and presence.

Bibliography; p. xviii
Includes indexes.
1. Bible. O.T.—Criticism, interpretation, etc.—
Addresses, essays, lectures. 2. Davies, Gwynne Henton—
Addresses, essays, lectures. I. Davies, Gwynne Henton.
II. Durham, John I., 1933- . III. Porter,
J. R. (Joshua Roy), 1921— .
BS1171.2.P72 1983   221.6   83-17445
ISBN 0-86554-101-9

CONTENTS

I · OLD TESTAMENT HERMENEUTICS

II · THE HEXATEUCH

III · THE FORMER PROPHETS AND THE LATTER PROPHETS

Contents

ABBREVIATIONS

ABR	*Australian Biblical Review*
AFO	*Archiv für Orientforschung*
AJSL	*American Journal of Semitic Languages and Literatures*
AncB	The Anchor Bible
ANEP	*The Ancient Near East in Pictures Relating to the Old Testament,* ed. J. B. Pritchard
ANET	*Ancient Near Eastern Texts Relating to the Old Testament,* ed. J. B. Pritchard
AO	*Der alte Orient*
AOT	*Altorientalische Texte zum Alten Testament,* ed. H. Gressmann
ArOr	*Archiv Orientâlní*
ASAE	*Annales du service des antiquités de l'Égypte*
ASTI	*Annual of the Swedish Theological Institute in Jerusalem*
AThANT	Abhandlungen zur Theologie des Alten und Neuen Testaments
AV	Authorized Version
BASOR	*Bulletin of the American Schools of Oriental Research*
BBB	Bonner Biblische Beiträge
BDB	Brown, Driver and Briggs, *Hebrew and English Lexicon of the Old Testament*
BFChrTh	Beiträge zur Förderung christlicher Theologie
BH	*Biblia Hebraica*
BJRL	*Bulletin of the John Rylands Library*
BKAT	Biblische Kommentar: Alten Testament
BWANT	Beiträge zur Wissenschaft vom Alten und Neuen Testament
BZ	*Biblische Zeitschrift*
BZAW	Beihefte zur *Zeitschrift für die alttestamentliche Wissenschaft*
CambB	Cambridge Bible for Schools and Colleges
CBQ	*Catholic Biblical Quarterly*
CentB	The Century Bible

Abbreviations

DOTT	*Documents from Old Testament Times*, ed. D. Winton Thomas
EstBibl	*Estudios Bíblicos*
ET	English translation
EThL	*Ephemerides Theologicae Lovanienses*
EVV	English versions
EvTh	*Evangelische Theologie*
ExpT	*Expository Times*
FRLANT	Forschungen zur Religion und Literatur des Alten und Neuen Testaments
FuF	*Forschungen und Fortschritte*
GesK	Gesenius, Kautzsch, Cowley, *Hebrew Grammar*
GLECS	*Groupe Linguistique d'Études Chamito-Sémitiques*
HAT	Handbuch zum Alten Testament
HdO	*Handbuch der Orientalistik*, ed. B. Spuler
HKAT	Handkommentar zum Alten Testament
HSAT	Die heilige Schrift des Alten Testaments, ed. E. Kautzsch
HTR	*Harvard Theological Review*
HUCA	*Hebrew Union College Annual*
IB	*The Interpreter's Bible*, ed. G. A. Buttrick
ICC	The International Critical Commentary
IDB	*The Interpreter's Dictionary of the Bible*, ed. G. A. Buttrick
IEJ	*Israel Exploration Journal*
JAOS	*Journal of the American Oriental Society*
JBL	*Journal of Biblical Literature and Exegesis*
JCS	*Journal of Cuneiform Studies*
JEA	*Journal of Egyptian Archaeology*
JNES	*Journal of Near Eastern Studies*
JSS	*Journal of Semitic Studies*
JTS	*Journal of Theological Studies*
KeH	Kurzgefasstes exegetisches Handbook zum Alten Testament
KHC	Kurzer Hand-Kommentar zum Alten Testament
LXX	The Septuagint
Man. Disc. (1QS)	Manual of Discipline
MT	Masoretic Text
NRTh	*Nouvelle Revue Théologique*
OLZ	*Orientalistische Literaturzeitung*

Abbreviations

Or	*Orientalia*
OTS	*Oudtestamentische Studiën*
PEQ	*Palestine Exploration Quarterly*
Pesh	Peshitta
4Q Sl	*Serek Šîrôt ʿÔlat Haššabāt* (J. Strugnell, *SVT* 7 [1960], pp. 318–345)
Pss. Lam.	Psalms of Lamentation
RA	*Revue d'Assyriologie et d'Archeologie Orientale*
RB	*Revue Biblique*
R^D	Deuteronomic Redaction
RES	*Revue des Études Sémitiques*
RGG	*Die Religion in Geschichte und Gegenwart*, ed. K. Galling
RHR	*Revue de l'Histoire des Religions*
RSPhTh	*Revue des Sciences Philosophiques et Théologiques*
RSV	Revised Standard Version
SBT	Studies in Biblical Theology
SKG	Schriften der Königsberger Gelehrten Gesellschaft
SVT	*Supplements to Vetus Testamentum*
TBC	Torch Bible Commentaries
TDNT	*Theological Dictionary of the New Testament* (ET of *TWNT*), trans. and ed. G. W. Bromiley
ThLZ	*Theologische Literaturzeitung*
ThSt	Theologische Studien
ThT	*Theologisch Tijdschrift*
ThZ	*Theologische Zeitschrift*
Trierer ThSt	*Trierer Theologische Studien*
TWNT	*Theologisches Wörterbuch zum Neuen Testament*, ed. Gerhard Kittel and (later) G. Friedrich
VT	*Vetus Testamentum*
WdO	*Die Welt des Orients*
WC	Westminster Commentaries
ZA	*Zeitschrift für Assyriologie*
ZÄS	*Zeitschrift für Ägyptische Sprache und Altertumskunde*
ZAW	*Zeitschrift für die alttestamentliche Wissenschaft*

ZDMG	*Zeitschrift der deutschen morgenländischen Gesellschaft*
ZevE	*Zeitschrift für evangelische Ethik*
ZNW	*Zeitschrift für die neutestamentliche Wissenschaft*
ZThK	*Zeitschrift für Theologie und Kirche*

PREFACE

Proclamation and Presence was conceived, solicited, prepared and brought to publication as an expression of gratitude to an enthusiastic teacher of the Old Testament who has remained throughout his career a friend to Old Testament studies and Old Testament students. Those who have known Gwynne Henton Davies will be aware that two of his cardinal emphases have been the element of proclamation and the theology of the PRESENCE of God in the Bible. He has often lectured on 'the *kerygma* of the Old Testament' and 'the theocentric art of the Israelite', and he is not only a student but a practitioner of the art of proclamation.

It was therefore most gratifying to the editors of this volume that each of the fourteen essays, though the original letter of invitation specified only that the subject matter be limited 'to Old Testament topics related to the pre-exilic period', is in some way a direct exposition of one of these two emphases of Henton Davies' teaching.

We should like to express gratitude to a number of persons, first and foremost to all the contributors to this volume. The kind hospitality as well as the scholarship of Henton Davies is well known to scholars of many lands, and the editors desired to symbolize this by making the *Festschrift* an international production: eleven countries and five nationalities are represented by the contributors, and the co-editors represent the two countries with which Principal Davies' career has been most closely associated. It should be said also that the fourteen contributors represent a large number of colleagues and former students of Henton Davies who have warmly welcomed the preparation and publication of this volume.

The essays of Professors Cazelles, Eichrodt, Eissfeldt, de Vaux and Würthwein have been translated by the editors. In each case, we have submitted our translation to the appropriate contributor, but the editors take full responsibility for the final rendering. We record our appreciation for help given at one stage by Mr John Dunkley of the Department of French, and Mr W. P. Hanson of the Department of German, in the University of Exeter.

Special mention should be made of Mr Jack Lemons, Professor Durham's graduate assistant, for meticulous work on the indices and in checking the proofs, and the editors would like to thank most warmly, for valuable assistance at many points, their respective secretaries: Lady Bruce-Lockhart, of the University of Exeter, Mrs Norma Hash of Skipwith, Virginia, and Mrs Brenda Medlin of Wake Forest. Mrs Hash and Mrs Medlin, in addition, typed the final manuscript.

A final word of gratitude must go to the co-publishers of *Proclamation and Presence*: to the John Knox Press of Richmond, Virginia, who have encouraged the project almost from its inception, and to the SCM Press of London, who have produced the volume.

It is quite characteristic of Henton Davies that his first reaction upon hearing of the preparation of his *Festschrift* was 'But I don't deserve such an honour'. The overwhelming response of his many friends in many countries and the enthusiasm of the contributors to this volume have not even slightly borne him out. Thus this volume is offered to Gwynne Henton Davies, in respectful tribute to a student, a teacher, an expositor and a scholar of the Old Testament.

꿈 꿈 꿈

To the gratitude expressed above, there must now be added our warm appreciation to Mercer University Press, and particularly to Editor Edd Rowell, and Designer Margaret Jordan Brown, for the publication of this second and corrected edition of *Proclamation and Presence*.

JOHN I DURHAM & J. R. PORTER
March 1983

GWYNNE HENTON DAVIES
A BIOGRAPHICAL APPRECIATION

John I Durham

GWYNNE HENTON DAVIES was born on the nineteenth of February, 1906, in the Welsh town of Aberdare which lies in the basin north of the Merthyr Valley. His father was for most of his life an employee of a colliery near Aberdare, and at the time of Henton's birth was earning twenty-five shillings a week.

The formative influences upon the young Henton Davies were exerted by his father, a man of little formal learning, but dedicated to the welfare of his wife and two sons; by his mother, whose life was one of unremitting toil for her family; by an uncle who was an architect and a man of considerable erudition; by a form master in primary school who awakened in him a love of learning; and by the life of the Central Baptist Chapel, where he learned the freedom of the open forum, the meaning of prayer, the nature of worship and where he first experienced the ministry of great preaching.

In 1922, Henton qualified for university matriculation and was sent by his parents to Perse Grammar School, Cambridge, for two years of pre-university study with W. H. D. Rouse. Though these years were not entirely happy ones, they yet provided both a broadening of horizon and excellent training in the classical languages which were later to help shape his teaching of Hebrew.

In the winter of 1923/24, Henton Davies decided, at seventeen, that he would be a minister. His father had wanted him to study medicine; his mother, the law; but Henton stood firm in his decision. In 1924, he entered University College, Cardiff, to read Philosophy. In 1925, he was admitted also to the South Wales Baptist College, and in that year he changed from the Honours Course in Philosophy to the Honours Course in Hebrew. His teacher was Theodore H. Robinson, and this move brought him

xiii

into contact with a great tradition in Old Testament scholarship which was to have a profound effect upon him. In 1928, Henton took the B.A. with First Class Honours in Hebrew and Syriac and was awarded a Post Graduate Research Studentship in the University of Wales. This led, in 1929, to an M.A. with distinction for work on the 'Origin and Development of the Idea of Theocracy in Israel'.

From 1929 until 1931, Henton concentrated on the B.D. degree of the University of Wales. In 1931 he won a Dr Williams' Divinity Scholarship, and was so enabled to go up to Oxford, where he aspired to continue his Old Testament research. It was here that he became a student of H. Wheeler Robinson and so came into contact with a second great tradition in British Old Testament scholarship. Under the supervision of Principal Robinson and L. B. Cross, he submitted a B.Litt. thesis on 'The Covenant in the Old Testament' and was awarded that degree in 1933.

Hoping to complement his Oxford research with a study of the concept of covenant in rabbinic literature and in the New Testament, Henton journeyed to Marburg/Lahn in the autumn of 1933. He had hoped to study with Bialblocki, but discovered upon arrival that the Nazis had just removed the Jewish scholar from his post. His original plan frustrated, the young Davies spent two semesters in Marburg, attending the classes of Karl Budde and Rudolph Bultmann, and then returned to London to pursue rabbinics with A. Büchler of The Jews' College.

In 1935, Henton returned to the University of Wales in Cardiff, and completed his work towards the B.D. degree in Ecclesiastical History. It was awarded 'with distinction'. That same year, he was called as minister of West End Baptist Church, Hammersmith, in London, a pastorate which he occupied until 1938.

It was in the autumn of 1938 that Henton Davies came finally to the career for which he had so singularly prepared himself, when he accepted the Chair of Hebrew and Old Testament Studies in Bristol Baptist College, and along with it, in 1948, a special lectureship in Hebrew and Old Testament Studies in the University of Bristol. During this period in Bristol, which extended through the war years until 1951, Henton Davies became a member of the Society for Old Testament Study and so began an association which has done much to make him a friend of Old Testament scholars throughout the world.

When T. H. Robinson retired in 1946 from the secretaryship of the Society for Old Testament Study, Henton Davies and H. H. Rowley joined C. R. North as co-secretaries. Upon the withdrawal of Professor North in 1949, Davies became Home Secretary of the Society, and Rowley, the Foreign Secretary. Henton Davies served the Society as Home Secretary for fifteen years, during the period of its greatest growth. From 1961 to 1963, he served as Foreign Secretary, and in 1965 the Society elected him its President for 1966. Professor G. W. Anderson, in a Jubilee Year tribute to the Society in *Vetus Testamentum* (XVII, 1967, pp. 122–6), has aptly recognized T. H. Robinson, C. R. North, H. H. Rowley and Henton Davies as having 'exercised the most important influences on the development of the Society during the first half-century of its life'.

In 1951, Henton Davies became the first Professor of Old Testament Studies in the University of Durham, a chair which he occupied until he was elected eleventh Principal of Regent's Park College, a Permanent Private Hall of The University of Oxford, in 1958. During this same year, he was awarded the D.D. of the University of Glasgow and the M.A. of Oxford. While the seven years at Durham were in the main a time of Old Testament research and teaching, the years at Oxford since 1958 to this day have remained both this and also a period during which an ability for imaginative development and administration has been manifested.

Those who know Henton Davies best think of him not primarily as a theologian of the Old Testament, or a theorist in form-critical analysis, or a grammarian of Hebrew, or a specialist in textual studies – despite the fact that his abilities have been

A BIBLIOGRAPHY OF THE WRITINGS* OF
GWYNNE HENTON DAVIES

1942 'The Presence of God in Israel', in *Studies in History and Religion*, H. Wheeler Robinson *Festschrift*, ed. E. A. Payne. London: Lutterworth Press, 1942. Pp. 11–29.

1950 'The Yahwistic Tradition in the Eighth-Century Prophets', in *Studies in Old Testament Prophecy*, Theodore H. Robinson *Festschrift*, ed. H. H. Rowley. Edinburgh: T. & T. Clark, 1950. Pp. 37–51.

1953 *The Approach to the Old Testament*. An Inaugural Lecture delivered on May 15, 1953, to the Durham Colleges in the University of Durham. London: The Carey Kingsgate Press, 1953.

1955 'Select Bibliography of the Writings of Harold Henry Rowley', in *Wisdom in Israel and the Ancient Near East*, H. H. Rowley *Festschrift*, eds. M. Noth and D. W. Thomas. Supplements to *Vetus Testamentum*, III. Leiden: E. J. Brill, 1955. Pp. xi-xix.

'Contemporary Religious Trends: The Old Testament', *The Expository Times*, LXVII, 1 (Oct., 1955), pp. 3–7.

Co-editor with Alan Richardson of *The Teacher's Commentary*. London: SCM Press, 1955. Published in the U.S.A. as *The Twentieth Century Bible Commentary*, eds. Davies, Richardson, and C. L. Wallis, Harper and Brothers, 1956.

'The Literature of the Old Testament' and 'Exodus' in *The Teacher's Commentary*, s.v.

---

* Only books and contributions to journals, *Festschriften* and works of a composite nature are listed here, though Principal Davies has regularly contributed book reviews to a variety of periodical publications, most frequently to the annual *Book List* of the Society for Old Testament Study (since 1946) and to *The Expository Times* (since 1960).

With Alan Richardson, 'Genesis' in *The Teacher's Commentary*, s.v.

'The Clues of the Kingdom in the Bible', *Interpretation*, XIV, 2 (1955), pp. 155–60.

1956 'Commending the Old Testament', in *The Raven, A Magazine on Expository Preaching*. Issued by the British Council of Churches. No. 3, July, 1956.

1957 'Astonish', 'Remnant' in *A Theological Word Book of the Bible*, ed. Alan Richardson. London: SCM Press and New York: Macmillan Co., 1957, s.v.

1960 With A. B. Davies, *The Story in Scripture: A Shortened Text of the RSV*. London: Thomas Nelson and Sons, 1960.

1962 'Alms', 'Ark of the Covenant', 'Bamah', 'Beauty', 'Breastpiece (of the High Priest)', 'Chief Priest', 'Dancing', 'Dwarf' in *The Interpreter's Dictionary of the Bible*, vol. A–D, ed. G. A. Buttrick. Nashville and New York: Abingdon Press, 1962, s.v.

'Elder in the OT', 'Ephod (Object)', 'Footstool', 'Glory', 'High Place, Sanctuary', *ibid.*, vol. E–J, s.v.

'Kneel', 'Levitical Cities', 'Leviticus', 'Memorial, Memory', 'Mercy Seat', 'Mezuzah', 'Minister in the OT', 'Nethinim', 'Phylacteries', 'Pillar of Fire and of Cloud', 'Praise', 'Presence of God', 'Pulpit', *ibid.*, vol. K–Q, s.v.

'Sanctuary', 'Screen', 'Solomon's Servants', 'Sophereth', 'Swine', 'Tabernacle', 'Theophany', 'Threshold', 'Worship in the OT', *ibid.*, vol. R–Z, s.v.

'Deuteronomy' in *Peake's Commentary on the Bible*, eds. H. H. Rowley and M. Black. London and New York: Thomas Nelson and Sons, 1962. Pp. 269–84.

'Selection and Training of Candidates for the Ministry: The Baptist Churches in Great Britain', *The Expository Times*, LXXIII, 8 (May, 1962), pp. 228–30.

1963 'The Ark in the Psalms', in *Promise and Fulfilment*, S. H. Hooke *Festschrift*, ed. F. F. Bruce. Edinburgh: T. & T. Clark, 1963.

'Judges VIII 22–23', *Vetus Testamentum*, XIII, 2 (April, 1963), pp. 151–7.

1966 'The Holy Spirit in the Old Testament', *The Review and Expositor*, LXIII, 2 (Spring, 1966), pp. 129–34.

1967 *Exodus*. Torch Bible Commentaries. London: SCM Press, Fourth Impression, 1978.

'The Ark of the Covenant', *Annual of the Swedish Theological Institute*, V (1967), pp. 30–47.

Preaching the Lord's Supper. The London Baptist Preachers' Association Diamond Jubilee Lecture, 1967.

'A Welsh Man of God', *The Baptist Quarterly*, XXII, 7 (July, 1968), pp. 360-70.

Chapter III in *Breakthrough: Autobiographical Accounts of the Education of Some Socially Disadvantaged Children*, ed. Ronald Goldman. London: Routledge and Kegan Paul, 1968. Pp. 40-56.

1969 'Genesis' in *The Broadman Bible Commentary*, vol. I., ed. Clifton J. Allen. Nashville: The Broadman Press, 1969. Pp. 99-304.

1970 "Gerhard von Rad, *Old Testament Theology*" in *Contempory Old Testament Theologians*, ed. Robert B. Laurin. Valley Forge, Pennsylvania: Judson Press, 1970. Pp. 63-89.

With A. B. Davies, *Who's Who in the Bible*. Teach Yourself Series. London: The English Universities Press Ltd., 1970.

1975 *The Old Testament as a Whole*. The D. J. James lecture for 1975. Swansea, Wales: John Penny Press, 1975.

1981 "Amos—the Prophet of Re-Union", *The Expository Times*, XCII, 7 (April, 1981), pp. 196-200.

I

Old Testament Hermeneutics

1

The Limits of Old Testament Interpretation

Norman W. Porteous

ONE of the most valuable experiences it was my good fortune to have during the period of my university education was being shown for the first time what was involved in interpreting an ancient philosophical text. Plato's *Republic* was the text in question, and I remember well that my first instinctive reaction to the argument between Socrates and Thrasymachus in the first book was to do little more than describe it as clearly as I could, though the whole business seemed to me rather unreal and out of date and it did not occur to me that the author's problem could be a problem for me. And then, to my astonishment, if not also to my chagrin, I was most skilfully brought to see that I had been completely mistaken in my attitude to the text. Instead of supposing that my job was to reproduce an argument which was alien to my own processes of thought, I was invited to recognize that the ancient author was talking about something which, while it was relevant to his own world of thought, could also be of contemporary relevance, something still worth thinking about. It was certainly not that I was to read into his words something that was not there. Rather, as I was drawn into conversation with him, as it were, I found my thought becoming engaged with his thought and discovered that we could share a common concern for the truth. The ancient author did not indeed assume complete con-

3

trol, because sometimes I found myself in disagreement with him and learned to trust my own judgment and argue for my counter-position. And so the process went on and I learned clearly for the first time that an ancient mind and a modern mind could meet and converse, that, in spite of all the obvious differences of time and place, differences cultural and psychological, two universes of thought could merge to the extent that an object of thought and discussion could genuinely be the same for both. All this happened in a very short period of time and proved quite revolutionary; to that experience I date my intellectual coming of age. I do not in the least mean to imply that from that time I was able to maintain my part in the philosophic debate very skilfully – I was a mere tiro and fumbler – but at least I knew that for me the debate was on and that it was a real one. I had discovered – and perhaps I was rather slow in doing so – that one can have genuine encounter with the great minds of the past and really get involved, and so become alive in a new kind of way. Indeed to interpret a philosophical writer meant so to read him and expound him as to make it clear whether he had or had not the power to make one think; the mere repetition of his argument was not enough.

One can have a similar, though not identical experience when one is learning a foreign language and suddenly reaches the stage of being able to use it in an unselfconscious way to discuss with someone, whose language it is, a subject of common interest. One is no longer just translating laboriously what someone else is saying and being thankful that one can make some sense of it. The differences of language and modes of thought, not to speak of all the other circumstances which make a foreigner look foreign, become much less important than the exciting fact that a real conversation about something has become possible.

Now, there seems to me to be a certain analogy between the experiences I have been describing and what happens when we are seeking to interpret the Bible or rather the Old Testament which is our particular concern. The analogy, of course, should not be pressed too far in view of the very varied character of the Old

Testament material. But, when in each case we have made clear to ourselves, so far as we can, what the Old Testament writer is talking about, we should not refuse to allow ourselves, in whatever way seems appropriate in each case, to become involved in the writer's thought. It is a characteristic of the biblical writers that again and again they throw down a challenge and we should not be afraid to take it up. Thought should stimulate thought and, until it does so, it has not revealed its full quality and is, therefore, not adequately interpreted. Very often, of course, the thought of the writer fails to break through to our minds and we are left with something we cannot interpret in any genuine sense. The differences of the thought processes from our own are too great. We can describe up to a point, but we cannot really understand and so our own minds are not stirred to creative activity. But, when they are so stirred, what a difference it makes!

It seems to follow from all this that there is something not quite satisfactory about confining the interpretation of Scripture to description, any kind of involvement on the part of the interpreter being strictly excluded as improper to the correct carrying out of his task. As soon as one says this, however, one incurs the grave suspicion that one is trying to open the door to an uncontrolled process of reading into an ancient text answers to one's own questions and so missing the things that it may be trying to say. Indeed, when one remembers what fantastic interpretations have actually been foisted upon Scripture, one can have a great measure of sympathy with this suspicion and can readily understand those who take a rigid stand upon *Historismus* and exclude everything else from the exegete's task as doubtful intellectual gymnastics. After all, it may be argued, there is plenty for the biblical exegete to do if he confines himself to the historical study of the text he has to interpret. For, to do this adequately, it may be necessary for him to extend his view right to the horizon of the ancient writer's thought. Think how wide that horizon is in the case of the Second Isaiah. Then there is the writer's psychology to be examined, the vocabulary he uses to express his thought and the literary forms

5

in which his thought is cast. The exegete may go further still and compare what the author says with what other biblical writers have to say about the same topic. Is it unreasonable, it may be said, to ask him to limit himself and refrain from raising the question of truth, which might be the consequence of entering into conversation with the ancient writer? Indeed, when it comes to this business of conversation, does the modern interpreter not have the immediate advantage of being able only too easily to turn the supposed conversation into a monologue and to read into the text some point of view that he wants to affirm or deny?

It may be agreed that there is a real danger here. We may bring to an ancient author *our* questions and involve him in a debate which is alien to his concerns. At the same time I wish to hold to my point that, whatever the risk, one must not be afraid of becoming involved in the debate if one is really to understand and help others to understand what the biblical writer is talking about. It is obvious, however, that the intention of the writer must not be allowed to become submerged by one's own concern, so that the situation gets out of hand. Interpretation must remain interpretation of the text. There are limits to what it is permissible to do when one is expounding the meaning of a passage of Scripture.

It is, of course, impossible in a short paper to do much more than suggest some of the ways in which interpretation has passed beyond due limits so that the real intention of Scripture has been lost sight of. To make clear how one of the most serious of these misinterpretations has come about it is necessary to begin at a point at some distance from where the actual overstepping of the proper limit took place. As we all know, one of the greatest masters of the science of interpretation or hermeneutics was Schleiermacher, who suggested that the method of the interpreter of a text must consist in another kind of involvement than the one about which I have been speaking. Schleiermacher was very much aware of what may be called the mystery of individuality and of the difficulty of penetrating into another man's mind, especially when he is no longer alive and available for face to face conversation, but has to be understood on the basis of something which he has written or some work of art which he has produced. It may be added that Schleiermacher was especially concerned with the mystery of artistic production and tended to think of literary texts as examples of this. His suggestion was that, as the interpreter and the author to be interpreted share in a common humanity, there is the possibility of what he called divination through congeniality. How this divination takes place is suggested in one of the most subtle parts of Schleiermacher's hermeneutical theory. When, for example, I am trying to understand a piece of literature which reflects the experience of another man, I have to reproduce that experience to some extent within myself, so far as possible identifying myself with him, yet realizing all the time that it is his experience and not mine that is in question. This method of self-identification with another is, of course, the way in which we instinctively understand other people in the ordinary intercourse of life. In scientific interpretation, however, it is necessary to advance beyond what is instinctive. However skilful we are, use will have to be made of what is called the hermeneutical circle. Our understanding of what is before us will at first in all probability be very partial and we may have to commute backwards and forwards from part to whole and from whole to part until the whole jigsaw puzzle has been solved and the meaning of the whole is apparent. The operation is essentially the one we perform under examination conditions when we are trying to unravel the meaning of a difficult passage in a foreign language which has been set us for unseen translation. Incidentally the method of the hermeneutic circle in the interpretation of Scripture, useful as it is within limits, is liable to misuse when we assume a unity which does not in fact exist and overlook the variety of Scripture. This can happen especially when a dogmatic theory is imposed *ad extra*; but this can happen at the level of feeling also.

Schleiermacher, like his contemporaries de Wette and Fries, after the Kantian depreciation of feeling, reinstates it as an all-important element in religion. What has to be pointed out, however, is that Schleiermacher, while maintaining that it is through feeling that we succeed in bridging the gap which separates individualities, did not mean to lose sight of the intention of the writer whose work is being interpreted. In his early writings on the subject at any rate, he laid great emphasis on the importance of grammatical and philological analysis of the text. If I am not mistaken, however, his interest came to be transferred from the object of thought envisaged by the writer to something which Schleiermacher thought of as fundamentally an artistic production, an expression of life which could easily become isolated from the ultimate question of truth. The feeling may indeed be a feeling of absolute dependence but the reference of the feeling beyond itself can only too easily be replaced by interest in the feeling for its own sake.

Schleiermacher was too great a theologian to forget the divine authority that lay behind Scripture. What I wish to suggest, however, is that the effect of his emphasis on feeling and on religious experience led to a kind of reversal of the hermeneutical method, which has been alluded to, by which, instead of my experience providing the clue to that contained in the text to be interpreted, the experience of the other is used to enable me to reach fuller self-knowledge and to bring about the enrichment of my own religious emotions. That such self-knowledge and enrichment of feeling should come about is not necessarily a bad thing. What is undesirable is that the end result should be an undue concern with myself and with my own feelings to the exclusion of a proper concern for what the text says.

That something like this took place on a big scale is suggested by the tremendous development of the theology of religious experience during the nineteenth century and the growing interest in religious psychology. The Old Testament was valued as offering material for a history of Hebrew piety which, in line with Herder's enthusiastic welcome for the various types of human spirituality offered by the different national literatures, could be regarded as making its own specific contribution to the enrichment of life at a deep level. It was all a matter of the communication of religious emotion; little enough attention was paid to the fact that that was not what was surely the main concern of the biblical writers themselves, who, in much of what they wrote or recorded, were curiously indifferent to edification. Many of the psalms might indeed be a summons to rejoicing or might seek to evoke a mood of repentance, but even so such emotion had a reference away from itself. In interpretation there must be a recognition of a limit to this tendency to turn the intention of a writer upside down. The Bible is primarily about God and not about man, though if one considers what it says about God and what God says through it, we shall undoubtedly learn a great deal about man.

It is not difficult to see that the tendency to turn in upon oneself and one's own feelings points in the direction of the contemporary existentialist interpretation of the Bible with its insistence that biblical interpretation is essentially self-interpretation, that theology is anthropology. Existentialism does draw attention to a truth and we may learn from it, but its hermeneutical method oversteps a limit which ought to be observed. We must allow the text to start the conversation and we must ask of it the questions appropriate to it. What it has to say to us is more likely to be significant than what we would like it to say.

At this point in the discussion it may be helpful to remind ourselves of von Rad's opposition to regarding the Old Testament as providing the materials for a history of Hebrew piety and his insistence that the correct way to write an Old Testament theology – that is to interpret the Old Testament on the grand scale – is to ask what the Old Testament purports to be about. His claim, as we all know, is that it bears witness to certain decisive acts of God in history. Now, of course, von Rad's view of the matter has its weaknesses and these have led to a great deal of discussion, into the merits of which this paper will not enter. Although von Rad has devoted a considerable section on the Psalms to Israel's response, yet he does not make it sufficiently clear to what an extent the life of the simple Israelite was maintained by a personal attitude of piety and obedience to Yahweh's commands and so represented a 'lived' response to Yahweh's acts of salvation. Of course one is speaking only of a minority of the people, but nevertheless it is not to be overlooked. What must be pointed out, however, is that von Rad was on sound lines when he asked the question as to what the Old Testament was about, and it is at least significant that he has brought new life into what may be described as conversation with the Old Testament; the Old Testament is taken seriously as saying something which, not only was of concern long ago, but concerns us today and challenges us to creative thought and creative living. It does not merely represent an interesting but obsolete episode of human religious experience which at the best might perhaps serve to enhance our own religious emotions.

Von Rad then begins with what he believes to be the intention of Scripture and does not fly away immediately to something else. In other words he recognizes a limit to interpretation. The result is that he gives us in his writings some of the finest analyses and descriptions we have of the thought of various individuals and schools whose writings make up the Old Testament. He then goes on to ask us to see in the Old Testament a movement which consists in successive actualizations or layers of interpretation which Israel made of its experience. Incidentally a caveat has to be entered here, because, as von Rad skilfully removes the various layers of meaning going backwards in time, one is uncomfortably reminded of the process of peeling an onion; at the end of the process there might be nothing at all left! That by the way. What should be pointed out, however, is that in his interpretation of the movement in the Old Testament von Rad does recognize another limit by finding its culmination in the New Testament and by advocating the employment of what, rather hesitatingly, he calls a typological method – something very different from the kind of procedure that throws open the door to unlimited arbitrary interpretations which put a premium on ingenuity and are often based on what is purely accidental. In spite of much that has to be criticized in his method, von Rad does set a very definite limit to interpretation by relating the New Testament antitypes to the basic elements of Old Testament thought and the basic Old Testament institutions and rightly ignores fortuitous verbal coincidences. Indeed he is saying pretty much what H. H. Rowley says in his *The Unity of the Old Testament* when he draws attention to similar patterns of thought in the Old and New Testaments, or what John Bright says in his book *The Authority of the Old Testament*, when he claims that the Old Testament, in spite of all its variety, contains a basic theology to which the New Testament relates itself. It is true that von Rad emphasizes the variety of the theologies in the Old Testament; yet he sees them all as having a forward reference to the goal towards which the whole complicated history is moving. In some quarters, of course, he is criticized for seeing the Old Testament as open towards a future which promises its fulfilment and the transformation of human life – that is the point where opinions divide – but he cannot fairly be accused of following a method of interpretation which permits all manner of arbitrary attributions of meaning to the text. He may go too far, but he does recognize a limit and one cannot but be aware throughout that he is engaged in genuine conversation with the Bible about that to which he believes it to be bearing witness.

Probably no recent writer about biblical theology has done more than von Rad to make one aware of the ongoing movement of history and of the vital relation between Israel's developing thought and that history. He shows how the Old Testament bears witness to a living God – I prefer the word 'living' to 'acting' in this connection – who breaks in on men with his creative judgments just when they feel safest and are tempted to settle down in some fancied security and to shield themselves behind fixed beliefs. Extreme examples in the Old Testament of how dogma is challenged are the books of Job and Ecclesiastes. Even the most irreproachable dogma has to be challenged, in order that faith may be kept alive, faith in a living God who wills that men should find their only security in him. Von Rad makes one feel that Hebrew history throughout the formative period right up to the rise of Christianity was self-interpreting, the literature coming into existence as a witness to the events through which God was dealing with his people.

As the history moved on, however, a tendency began to make itself manifest which, though perhaps inevitable, had momentous consequences for the eventual interpretation of the Old Testament. It will be remembered that Martin Noth has given a closely argued account of what happened to Hebrew law when it lost its close, vital connection with the ongoing history of the covenant people and came to be regarded as an authority in its own right. Perhaps it is the almost inevitable result of the formation of a canon that this should happen. Yet the primary purpose behind the formation of a canon is to ensure that a religion remains true to type, not to provide an answer to every question that may be asked about belief or conduct. Yet it was precisely this subjection of the Torah to the vast system of Rabbinic casuistry that gradually came about through the progressive inclusion of Hebrew law in the canon. It came to be regarded as something static, its development only possible through the ingenuity of the ways in which it was applied to cover every aspect of Jewish life. No longer was it thought of as reflecting the moving history of the Covenant people, a conception which would have acted as a barrier to restrain the kind of interpretation that was now felt to be necessary.

Now, it is no part of the intention of this paper to criticize an interpretative method which served Judaism well and to which its survival as a distinctive religious system is probably due. If history forced Judaism into a backwater, the world, nevertheless, owes much to the men who found a way of preserving values which the world could ill afford to lose. That things might have happened otherwise should not blind us to what was in fact achieved. But the new religion which arose in the main stream of history, namely Christianity, made the mistake of taking over from Judaism a method of interpretation which was unsuited to its character. The time came very speedily – we can see the beginnings of the change in the pages of the New Testament itself – when the whole Bible, Old Testament and New Testament alike, ceased to be thought of as primarily witness to the classic events by which God had awakened faith and formed and disciplined a people for himself, and, although its original character could not be completely ignored, came to be regarded as something very like a legal document with unquestioned authority over men's thoughts and actions. One might say that here a very drastic limitation was placed upon the interpreter of Scripture, but, because it was the wrong kind of limitation, the way was opened for almost unlimited misinterpretation. Unfortunately the means were not yet available to recover what had earlier in the creative period been the instinctive understanding of the nature of the biblical witness, and so the freedom of interpretation which Christianity might have made possible was replaced by another kind of freedom which resulted from slavery to the *litera scripta*.

Misunderstanding of the nature of Scripture led on the one hand to the violent protest of Marcion who, as we all know, rejected the Old Testament wholesale and bowdlerized the New, while on the other hand the orthodox rushed to the defence of the Bible, and in particular of the Old Testament, by the method of the elaborate allegorization of Scripture. It was supposed by the orthodox – who did not enquire too carefully where they got it – that dogma, *their* accepted dogma, ought to control the interpretation of Scripture, upon which a false unity was imposed.

Once again, as in the case of Judaism, a wall was built round a religion which restricted the creative freedom it might have had and encouraged a freedom it would have been better without. It was only with the Reformation in the persons of its greatest champions – and even so only to a partial extent – and, after an interval, with the development of modern historical criticism, that the Bible was again allowed to speak for itself. That process of recovery was not without its vicissitudes. History seldom takes a straight course. Moreover the faithful have shown an under-

standable reluctance to let the Bible speak for itself through fear
that it should not say what they thought it ought to say. Indeed,
they are partly justified in their reluctance by the tendency on the
part of many biblical scholars to advocate pure *Historismus* as the
only permissible method of interpretation. Paradoxically we have
seen how the hermeneutical method of Schleiermacher pointed in
two directions, to *Religionsgeschichte* on the one hand and to
Existentialism on the other. The answer to both these one-sided
methods of interpretation is a proper emphasis on the Word of
God as mediated in and through Scripture. But just here a
word of caution is necessary. In all interpretation a limit must be
observed, the limit set by the intention of the biblical writer or
rather of the biblical witness. The unlimited use of typology and
allegory, where they are imposed upon the original meaning and
are not part of it, can lead to an avoidance of the challenge of
Scripture and the adoption of a spectator attitude. We should
loyally accept the limit set by the text and then enjoy the freedom of
conversation with it which can lead to something truly creative.
It is not permissible, when a writer is obviously talking about something quite specific, to argue that he must really be meaning
something different. Of course the end result of the freedom
claimed by the allegorist working in the interests of orthodoxy is
the imposition upon Scripture of a dull monotony. By the way, even
St Paul went off the rails on one occasion when he commented on
the text 'Thou shalt not muzzle the ox that treadeth out the corn'
by saying that God could not possibly be concerned about animals,
forgetting the last verse of the book of Jonah and what the Sermon
on the Mount has to say about sparrows! If we are to use Scripture
we must use it according to its own intention.

It is perfectly true that in the course of the Christian centuries
a remarkable variety of exegetical methods has emerged. They must
all be studied by those qualified to do so, as they all have their
historic importance. This does not mean, however, as is sometimes
maintained even today, that they are all equally valid. Much of
what goes for interpretation is patently arbitrary and throws light

on the minds of those who put it forward or on the period which produced it rather than on the Scripture it is supposed to elucidate. Furthermore a great deal of Scripture has, in the course of the ages, come to be used liturgically and there can be no objection in principle to this, especially when we remember that a great deal of Scripture was originally liturgical in character. But, because a scriptural passage receives a certain meaning in its liturgical use, that meaning must not without more ado be taken as legitimate interpretation of the original passage. No responsible Old Testament scholar would feel that his interpretation of certain passages must be determined by Handel's use of them in the *Messiah*, even though he would not wish to ban that marvellous oratorio!

The contention of this paper, then, is that, in view of what we now know about the character of the Bible – and we are thinking particularly of the Old Testament – the interpreter has no option but to accept the limit set by the intention of the biblical witness and start from what is really there. He need not, however, set a limit to what Scripture may then proceed to do to him. This is because Scripture bears witness to the living God who takes a hand in the conversation that ensues.

The intention of the biblical witness may not be easy to discover and it must certainly not be isolated from its context in any artificial way. This paper started with an account of how conversation could take place with a Platonic dialogue. The very fact that it was a dialogue made it natural to enter into the conversation. The material offered by the Bible, however, is very varied in character and that is what justified the form-critical treatment which has proved so fruitful of results in the modern period. But, while the witness is varied, it remains witness – witness to the living God. The interpretation of a philosophical text when it leads to genuine philosophical discourse can be profoundly exciting. Scriptural interpretation should be even more exciting, because, in dealing with the Old Testament and the New, we have to do with life under the judgment and promise of God. The Bible contains a strange mixture of the Word of God and the word of man – the presence of the latter as faithful response, as misunderstanding, as defiance, as prayer, as thanksgiving and so on must be fully recognized – but it is just this very character which makes conversation possible and forces us to see things we might otherwise miss. Indeed the very things, which on aesthetic or moral or religious grounds we might wish were not there, may mirror something in ourselves which brings us under judgment and at the same time points us to him who can fulfil as well as judge.

There is no need to force a false unity on Scripture, since the only complete unity is to be found in the purpose of God who deals creatively with all the infinite variety to be found among men. We must seek to discover the character of the text of Scripture before us by all the means at our disposal, remembering humbly that wisdom was not born with us and will not die with us. But, if we cannot anticipate the better methods of the future, neither must we fail to learn from the mistakes of the past. We are limited by what we believe the text to mean as men living in the present historical situation. It is just in that situation that Scripture can challenge us to furious thought in the presence of the living God to which it bears witness. But, if we fail in courage and stop short with the *litera scripta* instead of going on where the conversation would lead us, we are likely to be left with a statement which is essentially dead and that way lies the heresy of verbal inspiration. Speech points beyond itself and the process of interpretation must include genuine engagement with the thought expressed. God meets us in the words of Scripture, in the words of men who spoke thus and thus, but to misinterpret these words into a static law is to refuse the tremendous challenge of conversation with the living God who is the only ultimate authority and this leads ultimately to a kind of idolatry. Do not let us refuse the freedom which under God may be ours. A dangerous freedom no doubt, but danger is an element in the contingencies of history in which we find ourselves and it is not for us to avoid the decisions God requires of us and complain that he ought to have made them unnecessary. One can run away from the difficulties of Scripture or one can accept them and be led on by them to creative interpretation.

POSTSCRIPT

I have discovered an affinity, in spite of certain places where I would have reservations, between my thinking and that of Professor Markus Barth in his courageous book *Conversation with the Bible*, published in 1964. In writing the first draft of this paper I borrowed from him the word 'conversation' to describe the interpretative activity I had in mind. When I read the book itself later, I was surprised and delighted to find that he was championing the kind of interpretative freedom (though not licence) for which I have been arguing for years. There *must* be an alternative to the crypto-legalism in biblical interpretation which mars so much theological debate.

My contention is, in brief, that the legalistic method of interpretation leads inevitably either to casuistry (as for example, in Rabbinic Judaism) or to some form of allegorizing or making the text mean what it obviously does not mean. Against these erroneous methods of interpretation we must set the limit of the original meaning of the text so far as we can recover it and then have creative conversation with it, always remembering that the purpose of the conversation is to make audible to us the Word of the living God and that the word of man can, by God's grace, become his Word to us.

II

The Hexateuch

2

What do we know about Moses?*

Geo Widengren

OF the great founders of religion Moses is certainly one of the
least known and therefore most enigmatic figures. This statement
may sound astonishing to the ear of one who is not an expert in
Old Testament literature and source criticism. But every scholar
who has tried to make his way through the mass of traditions
preserved in the books of Exodus, Leviticus, Numbers and Deuteronomy knows that the endeavour to sift the evidence in order to
get hold of some tangible historical facts leaves us with a most
unpleasant feeling of uncertainty. No wonder then that the great
historian Eduard Meyer, to whom we owe the most penetrating
analysis of the beginnings of the people of Israel, nearly banished
the man Moses whom we know from the domain of historical
reality.[1] Because of the lack of historical reality in Moses, Eduard
Meyer said, no one had been able to depict Moses as a concrete
individual, to treat him as a real historical figure.[2]

* I would like to express my thanks to my colleague Dr A. Carlson,
with whom I discussed the problems treated in this article, and who has
drawn my attention to the articles of Albright and Lohfink. For stylistic
revision I warmly thank Professor John I. Durham.

[1] Eduard Meyer, *Die Israeliten und ihre Nachbarstämme* (Halle:
Martin Niemeyer, 1906), p. 451, n. 1: '*Den Mose, den wir kennen, ist . . .
nicht eine geschichtliche Persönlichkeit.*'

[2] *Es hat denn auch (abgesehen von denen, die die Tradition in Bausch und
Bogen als geschichtliche Wahrheit hinnehmen) noch niemand von denen, die ihn
als eine geschichtliche Gestalt behandeln, ihn mit irgend welchem Inhalt zu*

In his radical denial of the historical individuality of Moses Eduard Meyer has had both predecessors and successors. Our intention is not to give a survey of those scholars who shared or still share his opinion on this subject.[3] Eduard Meyer is quoted here because his investigations belong to the fundamental contributions to Old Testament scholarship – a fact not always recognized among Old Testament scholars.[4]

What is attempted in the following pages is the presentation of what might be called a minimum interpretation of available facts, that is, a skeleton of historical evidence which in my opinion stands the test of a critical evaluation of the literary sources. This investigation was begun without any presuppositions whatsoever, except that I was strongly impressed by the arguments presented by Meyer and after him by Noth.

I

We start by emphasizing a rather astonishing fact mentioned by Martin Noth, among others.[5] Moses is hardly mentioned by

---

erfüllen, ihn als eine konkrete Individualität darzustellen oder etwas anzugeben gewusst, was er geschaffen hätte und was sein geschichtliches Werk wäre.' *Ibid.*

[3] The short monograph of R. Smend, *Das Mosebild von Heinrich Ewald bis Martin Noth* (Tübingen: J. C. B. Mohr [Paul Siebeck], 1959), gives some orientation, but is unsatisfactory in so far as it hardly discusses non-German scholarship – an ever recurring fault in Old Testament monographs published in Germany. On some important points this work has to be supplemented.

[4] It calls for notice that such a book as that of Herbert F. Hahn, *The Old Testament in Modern Research* (London: SCM Press and Philadelphia: Muilenberg Press, 1956), has very little to say about Eduard Meyer, and actually nothing about his real importance. H. Gressmann, whose book *Mose und seine Zeit* (Göttingen: Vandenhoeck & Ruprecht, 1913) was dedicated to Gunkel and Meyer, apparently did not always understand the greatness of Meyer. A praiseworthy exception among contemporary scholars is Eduard Nielsen, *Shechem: A Traditio-Historical Investigation*, 2nd rev. ed. (Copenhagen: G. E. C. Gad, 1959).

[5] Cf. M. Noth, *Überlieferungsgeschichte des Pentateuch*, 2nd printing (Stuttgart: W. Kohlhammer, 1960), pp. 172–5.

name or alluded to by the great prophets (excepting Hosea). We pass in review the relevant passages in prophetic literature.

Hosea does not mention Moses by name but his allusion to him is unequivocal:

> And by a prophet Yahweh brought Israel up out of Egypt, and by a prophet was he kept (Hos. 12.14 [EVV, v. 13]).

It surely calls for notice that Moses in this passage is called a prophet, נָבִיא, the earliest datable instance of the application of that name to Moses.[6]

Hosea was active from about 750 to 722 BC in the Northern Kingdom. To the Southern Kingdom of much the same period we are carried with the prophet Micah,[7] who says:

> For I brought thee up from the land of Egypt, and from the house of bondage I rescued thee, and I sent before thee Moses, Aaron and Miriam (Micah 6.4).

In this case, however, it is quite possible that the reference to Moses, Aaron and Miriam is a later prosaic addition.[8] At any rate this passage does not reflect the earliest strata of tradition, in which, as we shall see, Aaron and Miriam are not found.

[6] Some commentators, however, think that this passage is spurious. If such is the case, Deut. 34.10 may be earlier, though W. F. Albright thinks the reference in Hosea is earlier even than Hosea. See his *Samuel and the Beginnings of the Prophetic Movement* (Cincinnati: Hebrew Union College Press, 1961), p. 9.

[7] For the date of Micah, cf. G. W. Anderson, *A Critical Introduction to the Old Testament* (London: G. Duckworth, 1959), pp. 157f.; C. Steuernagel, *Lehrbuch der Einleitung in das Alte Testament* (Tübingen: J. C. B. Mohr [P. Siebeck], 1912), ¶ 132, 1, p. 623.

[8] This is the opinion of J. M. P. Smith, *A Critical and Exegetical Commentary on Micah*, ICC (Edinburgh: T. & T. Clark, 1928), p. 121: 'This is a supplementary note by some reader, as is clear from its prosaic form.' That a casual reader would have made this addition is not very probable and later commentators seem to accept this passage as authentic. For our problem the question of authenticity is not too important as will be made clear subsequently, but it should be observed that the influence of Pentateuchal tradition in the later part of the Micah passage suggests that the reference is not authentic.

To the period just prior to the exile we are taken with Jeremiah. In a prose section he gives the following revelation:

> Then Yahweh said to me: 'Even were Moses and Samuel to stand before me, I would still have no heart for this people' (Jer. 15.1).

Here Moses and Samuel are mentioned together as the two great figures of the past who might intercede with God for the people. Apparently they are placed on the same footing, a fact which is surely striking.

We may leave aside such a passage as Mal. 4.4, where 'the Law of Moses' is mentioned as given on Mount Horeb. This notice is clearly inspired by a later strand in tradition, does not possess any independent value, and is moreover rather late.[9]

We move instead to the passages in the Psalms where Moses is mentioned, and we are immediately struck by the fact that Moses is mentioned only eight times; of these references, three fall within the same psalm.

The reference to Moses in the title of Ps. 90 can be completely ignored, for the name of Moses as the author of this psalm has no more value than other such attributions.[10]

Moses and Aaron are mentioned together in Pss. 77.21 (EVV, v. 20); 105.26; and 106.16; in each case, Moses and Aaron are apparently mentioned on equal terms, which seems quite remarkable. Still more significant is Ps. 99.6, where Moses, Aaron and Samuel are mentioned together as invoking the name of Yahweh. This passage recalls Jer. 15.1, where Moses and Samuel are both mentioned as intercessors before God.[11]

It is only in Ps. 103.7 and Ps. 106.23, 32 that Moses is given the

[9] Malachi is generally dated between 470 and 450 BC, cf. Anderson, *op. cit.*, p. 170.

[10] Cf. Sigmund Mowinckel, *Psalmenstudien VI: Die Psalmdichter* (Amsterdam: P. Schippers, 1961, reprint of Oslo: Kristiania, 1924), pp. 1, 3. The article of H. Bückers, 'Zur Verwertung der Sinai Traditionen in den Psalmen', *Biblica* 32 (1951), pp. 401–22, does not deal with the problem under consideration here.

[11] This has been observed by Noth, *op. cit.*, p. 173, n. 449.

position he occupies in the oldest strata of prose traditions. Thus Ps. 103.7 says of Yahweh:

> He made known his ways to Moses,
> to the children of Israel his acts.

That is to say God has revealed his ways to Moses, who in Pentateuchal tradition prayed to God to make his ways known to him. There can be no doubt about the fact that we have in Ps. 103.7 a reference to Ex. 33.13.[12]

In Ps. 106.23, there is reference to Moses' appearance as a mediator between God and the people and Moses' success in appeasing the divine wrath. This is generally recognized as a clear allusion to Deut. 9.25f.[13]

In v. 32 of the same psalm there is an allusion to another famous episode during the wanderings in the desert, that is, that of Meribah. This too is a reference to Pentateuchal traditions, as related in Num. 20.12, but it also shows an influence of Deuteronomic language.[14] As a whole, however, this psalm testifies to the influence exercised by Pentateuchal traditions. Not without reason, it has been called 'a rhymed chronicle'.[15]

An additional fact calls for special notice: the absence of any association of Moses with the law said to be promulgated by him. Psalm 119 mentions the *Torah* not less than twenty times, but Moses is not mentioned at all, and still less of course 'the Law of Moses', תּוֹרַת מֹשֶׁה. This circumstance, not at all emphasized in the pertinent literature, would seem to demand an explanation.

[12] Cf. Ex. 33.13a: וְעַתָּה אִם־נָא מָצָאתִי חֵן בְּעֵינֶיךָ הוֹדִעֵנִי נָא אֶת־דְּרָכֶךָ, and Ps. 103.7a: יוֹדִיעַ דְּרָכָיו לְמֹשֶׁה.

[13] Cf. the commentaries on the Psalms and Noth, *op. cit.*, pp. 172f.: '*offenbar schon eine literarische Abhängigkeit von der Pentateucherzählung,* . . .'

[14] The commentaries refer to Deut. 1.37 and 3.26 respectively where, however, the expressions used are בִּגְלַלְכֶם and לְמַעַנְכֶם respectively, and not בַּעֲבוּרְכֶם; cf. e.g., F. Baethgen, *Die Psalmen*, HKAT (Göttingen: Vandenhoeck & Ruprecht, 1897), p. 318, where this difference is left unnoticed.

[15] Cf. Fr. Buhl, *Psalmerne oversatte og fortolkede* (Copenhagen, 1900), p. 680.

It is also striking that in the several psalms alluding to the great events associated with the Exodus and the wanderings in the desert, there is no reference to the involvement of Moses. As an *instar omnium*, we may single out Ps. 105.

In the historical books of the Old Testament outside the Penta-teuchal tradition Moses is mentioned by name in the following passages: I Sam. 12.6, 8; I Kings 2.3; 8.9, 53, 56; II Kings 14.6; 18.4, 6, 12; 21.8; 23.25; Ezra 3.2; 6.18; 7.6 and Neh. 8 *passim*.

In several of these passages we meet with the expression we missed in the Psalms, namely 'the Law of Moses', תּוֹרַת מֹשֶׁה. This designation is found in I Kings 2.3, II Kings 14.6 and 23.25, Ezra 3.2 and 7.6. In Neh. 8.1 we come across the fuller expression סֵפֶר תּוֹרַת מֹשֶׁה, 'the book of the Law of Moses', and in Ezra 6.18, the corresponding Aramaic expression סְפַר מֹשֶׁה. In II Chron. 23.18 and 30.16 and also in the very late passage in Dan. 9.11, 13, we find תּוֹרַת מֹשֶׁה.

It is of importance to try to ascertain the date of the three pass-ages in the Books of Kings, the only pre-exilic writing where the expression in question is found. Of these, I Kings 2.3 is a passage 'interpolated with general Deuteronomic phraseology'.[16] This passage then, as dependent upon Deuteronomy and the tradition behind it, is of no relevance for our problem.

I Kings 8.9, 53, 56 are also clearly a result of later, chiefly Deuteronomic, editorial activity. Redactors added the prayer of Solomon (vv. 14–61)[17] and glossed the true tradition about the

---

[16] John Gray, *I & II Kings* (London: SCM Press and Philadelphia: Westminster Press, 1963), p. 95. Cf. J. A. Montgomery and H. S. Gehman, *A Critical and Exegetical Commentary on the Books of Kings* (Edinburgh: T. & T. Clark, 1951), p. 87. For references to Deuteronomic language cf. C. F. Burney, *Notes on the Hebrew Text of the Book of Kings* (Oxford: Clarendon Press, 1903), pp. xiii–xv. For סֵפֶר תּוֹרַת מֹשֶׁה, cf. N. Lohfink, 'Die Bundesurkunde des Königs Josias', *Biblica* 44 (1963), p. 286.

[17] Cf. Gray, *op. cit.*, pp. 190, 213f.

installation of the ark (vv. 1–11).[18] Accordingly, these passages may be considered dependent upon Pentateuchal traditions.

The passage, II Kings 14.6, agrees in wording with I Kings 2.3, where we also meet with the expression 'the Law of Moses':

I Kings 2.3	II Kings 14.6
according to what is written in the Law of Moses	according to what was written in the Book of the Law of Moses

Both passages betray their Deuteronomic origin and Gray rightly speaks of the 'Deuteronomic compiler' who commented upon the incident mentioned in II Kings 14.1–6. The whole section has been labelled 'the Deuteronomic introduction'.[19]

The passage in II Kings 18.4, 6 likewise belongs to a Deuteronomic introduction (to the reign of Hezekiah)[20] and v. 12 is a Deuteronomic comment on the fate of Israel.[21]

II Kings 21.8 is said to be a 'Deuteronomic homily'[22] while II Kings 23.25 is completely dependent upon the spirit of Deuteronomy – its context has with reason been called 'the Deuteronomic account of Josiah's Passover'.

To sum up: no pre-exilic passage independent of the Pentateuchal tradition speaks of 'the Law of Moses'. It must be said indeed that this expression has been introduced into the Books of Kings exclusively because of Deuteronomic influence.

The situation therefore is that the expression 'the Law of Moses' is lacking in the Psalms, lacking in prophetic literature, and lacking in all historical literature, except in passages where a Deuteronomic influence is to be observed. This implies that pre-exilic Israel, except as far as Pentateuchal tradition is concerned, did not at all know the concept and expression 'the Law of Moses'. This circumstance, together with the very scarce attestation of the name of Moses in pre-exilic writings outside the Pentateuch, is even more remarkable if we compare the very strong position

[18] *Ibid.*, p. 191 and above all Burney, *op. cit.*, pp. 104–9.
[19] Gray, *op. cit.*, p. 546.   [20] *Ibid.*, p. 607.
[21] *Ibid.*, p. 610.   [22] *Ibid.*, p. 675.

occupied by David.[23] It looks indeed as if David was possessed of much more importance for Israelite religion than Moses. How is this fact to be explained? Was Moses really so insignificant as Meyer and Noth want us to believe?

II

In order to answer or at least to try to answer these questions we must see what part of the Pentateuchal tradition can stand the test of reasonable historical criticism and to which places and tribes of Israel these traditions may be attributed.

We shall consider briefly in the remainder of this essay the following items: (1) the name of Moses; (2) the family of Moses; (3) the tomb of Moses; (4) Moses as a Levite; (5) the position of Moses in relation to Israel; (6) the local origin of the traditions about Moses; (7) historical conclusions.

1. The *name of Moses* in Hebrew is מֹשֶׁה, in Greek Μωυσῆς, corresponding to an Egyptian form of the verb *mśi*, 'to bear, give birth to', either so that it simply means 'child', *mś*, or so that it is a hypocoristic form of a theophorous name where the divine element is suppressed: cf. such theophorous names as *Ḥar-mose*, 'Horus is born'. By contrast, the authentic Hebrew names of the two nurses of Moses show them to be later additions to the older tradition, in which the real Egyptian name of Moses was preserved.[24]

2. Concerning *the father-in-law of Moses* we find in Judg. 1.16 and 4.11 an old tradition where this father-in-law is said to be a member of the Kenite tribe. This tradition is so much more

[23] David is mentioned about thirty times by the pre-exilic prophets and twelve times in the Psalms apart from the references in the titles.

[24] Our opinion is diametrically opposed to that of Noth, who thinks that it is quite normal to give an Egyptian name to an Israelite, cf. *op. cit.*, p. 175. That this is not the case is shown by the fact that Egyptian names are very scarce in the Old Testament and are actually limited to priestly families. Cf. further Meyer, *op. cit.*, p. 450.

valuable because it is independent of the Pentateuchal tradition.
Judges 1.16 reads: וּבְנֵי⟨חֹבָב הַ⟩ קֵנִי חֹתֵן מֹשֶׁה עָלוּ.

In LXX, Codex Alexandrinus: Καὶ οἱ υἱοὶ Ιωβαβ τοῦ Κιναίου
πενθεροῦ Μωυσῆ ἀνέβησαν. The passage (Judg. 4.11) also mentions
the tradition that the name of the father-in-law of Moses was
Hobab. Noth has probably found the correct explanation of the
relation between these two passages.[25]

This tradition agrees with Num. 10.29: 'And Moses said to
Hobab the son of Reuel the Midianite, Moses' father-in-law',
where the ambiguous expression is cleared up by Judg. 4.11.
From both passages we can see that the notice given in Ex. 2.18,
according to which the wife of Moses was the daughter of Reuel,
must be wrong. It is evident that in this place we should read:
וַתָּבֹאנָה אֶל⟨חֹבָב בֶּן⟩ רְעוּאֵל אֲבִיהֶן in accordance with Num.
10.29.[26] The father-in-law of Moses was not Reuel, but Hobab ben
Reuel.

[25] Cf. Noth, *op. cit.*, p. 185, with n. 475. See also the reconstruction
of the text proposed by C. F. Burney, *The Book of Judges*, 2nd ed.
(London: Rivingtons, 1930), p. 14. Against MT and the versions, Burney
eliminates 'the sons of', thus keeping only Hobab. That such a reconstruction is impossible to accept is self-evident. Meyer, *op. cit.*, p. 90, n. 2,
wanted to eliminate from Judg. 4.11 the words 'of the sons of Hobab, the
father-in-law of Moses'. We should, however, distinguish between
transmitted text and original tradition.

[26] Hugo Gressmann, *op. cit.*, p. 235, n. 1, wants to eliminate 'the
father-in-law of Moses' in Judg. 1.16 and 4.11 as *'falsche Glosse'* and to
change 'Hobab, the son of Reuel' in Num. 10.29 into 'Jethro'. Such
drastic changes show a complete lack of method. B. Baentsch, *Exodus-
Leviticus-Numeri*, HKAT (Göttingen: Vandenhoeck & Ruprecht, 1903),
p. 15, assumes Reuel in Ex. 2.18 to be a later gloss and this 'solution' is
accepted by Gressmann, *op. cit.*, p. 16, n. 1 and – though somewhat
hesitatingly – by Noth, *Das zweite Buch Mose, Exodus* (Göttingen:
Vandenhoeck & Ruprecht, 1959), p. 24 (ET: *Exodus, A Commentary*
trans. J. S. Bowden [London: SCM Press and Philadelphia: Westminster
Press, 1962], p. 37), where it is said that the father-in-law of Moses is
called Reuel in two passages: Ex. 2.18 and Num. 10.29. However, as we
have already stated, the father-in-law of Moses in Num. 10.29 is explicitly
called Hobab ben Reuel. A final point is that the reference to him as a
Midianite instead of Kenite in Num. 10.29 is a later harmonizing insertion.

Against the conclusion that Hobab ben Reuel was a Kenite Meyer has objected that the references in Num. 10.29 and Judg. 1.16 (and thus obviously Judg. 4.11 too, though it is not mentioned by Meyer) have been created by the attachment of the Kenites to Israel, which was motivated in turn by the tradition about Hobab the Kenite, the father-in-law of Moses. Meyer finds support for his hypothesis that the Midianite priest (Jethro) has been replaced by Hobab the Kenite in the fact that the Midianite priest (in 'J') is much older and '*sagengeschichtlich ganz anders begründet*'.[27] This statement, however, seems unacceptable because the tradition in Judg. 1.16, 20 is indeed very old, independent of Pentateuchal tradition, and probably older than that tradition; else there could hardly have been any reason to preserve it in spite of its deviation from the 'J' tradition.

On the other hand we have to admit, on the basis of literary criticism and analysis of traditions, that there was no unanimous tradition concerning the name of the father-in-law of Moses. Irrespective of how we assign the names of Jethro and Hobab to the older strata of tradition ('JE'), it is an irrefutable fact that the oldest traditions knew with certainty only that the father-in-law of Moses was either from the tribe of the Midianites (later called Jethro) or the Kenites (Hobab).[28]

We are left in equal uncertainty about the wife (or wives) of

[27] Cf. Meyer, *op. cit.*, pp. 90f.

[28] This conclusion is accepted by the modern representatives of literary criticism; cf. Noth, *Das zweite Buch Mose, Exodus*, p. 25 (ET: p. 37). Whether the name Jethro is to be assigned to 'J' or to 'E' would seem to be a disputed point. Meyer, *op. cit.*, p. 89 with n. 2, assumes that in Ex. 3.1 the name Jethro belongs to the original tradition of 'E' whereas the designation 'the priest of Midian' is added from 'J'. Noth on the other hand thinks that in the same passage the name Jethro is added, whereas 'the priest of Midian' belongs to the original tradition; cf. *Das zweite Buch Mose, Exodus*, p. 22 (ET: p. 36), where obviously 2.16 is supposed to belong to 'J'. Noth is in conflict here also with Baentsch, *op. cit.*, p. 18, who is of the opinion that the expression 'the priest of Midian' belongs to 'J', whereas in intact 'E'-traditions only the title 'the father-in-law of Moses' is used. Noth, *Überlieferungsgeschichte des Pentateuch*, p. 201, is certain, however, that the name Jethro does not belong to the original tradition.

Moses. The tradition which refers to the priest of Midian as his father-in-law associates with him as his wife Zipporah, the daughter of the priest of Midian (Ex. 2.21). This name belongs to the 'animal' names and means 'Birdie'.[29] In itself such a name is of common Semitic occurrence, irrespective of antiquity, and may well belong to the Mosaic period.[30] As has been repeatedly pointed out, however, it is highly uncertain how reliable this tradition may be, for we have already seen that the tradition about Hobab the Kenite as a father-in-law of Moses is at least as well attested as the Midianite priest who (probably in later traditions) receives the name Jethro. Moreover, there is the curious tradition, of which only a fragment is preserved in Num. 12.1, that Moses had a Cushite wife. With Noth we see ourselves forced to the conclusion that it is very unlikely that Moses had three different foreign wives. On the contrary, the original and authentic tradition most probably only knew that Moses had a non-Israelitic wife. The attempt to solve the problem of her origin was made in three different ways[31] by different circles of traditionists. We therefore conclude with Noth that Zipporah is not an individual historical figure, but simply the 'outlandish' wife of Moses as an individualized type.

Pentateuchal tradition gives Aaron as the brother and Miriam as the sister of Moses. The name 'Aaron' may be of Egyptian origin, for it seems impossible to present any Hebrew etymology.[32] That Aaron originally had nothing to do with Moses – at least as

[29] For 'animal names' cf. Noth, *Die israelitischen Personennamen* (Stuttgart: W. Kohlhammer, 1928), p. 230.

[30] For the explanation of the name Zipporah cf. Noth, *Überlieferungsgeschichte des Pentateuch*, pp. 201f. I cannot find this name in Noth, *Die israelitischen Personennamen*, p. 230, or in the index, p. 256, where it should be indexed.

[31] Cf. Noth, *Überlieferungsgeschichte des Pentateuch*, p. 185.

[32] Cf. Noth, *Die israelitischen Personennamen*, p. 63 with a reference to G. Kerber, *Die religionsgeschichtliche Bedeutung der hebräischen Eigennamen des A.T.* (Freiburg i. B.: J. C. B. Mohr, 1897), pp. 76f. I. Hösl, 'Zur orientalischen Namenkunde: Maria-Moses-Aaron', *Serta Monacensia*, Franz Babinger *Festschrift*, eds. H. S. Kissling and A. Schmaus

his brother – is generally acknowledged. Exodus 15.20 may be mentioned in support of this contention, for there Miriam is introduced as 'the sister of Aaron', demonstrating that Moses, at the time when this tradition got its fixed form, did not belong to Aaron and Miriam as their brother.[33]

We omit in this connection any consideration of the 'P' traditions to concentrate on the older strata of tradition, and here we meet with some curious references. In Ex. 17.8–13, Aaron together with Hur assists Moses when the Israelites conquer the Amalekites by supporting Moses' hands when he holds his staff stretched out. This fact has been thought to be indicative of the prominent role Aaron and Hur originally played in this account – thus these two figures, in the oldest authentic tradition, had presumably been the leaders in the battle.[34] It is not sure, however, that this hypothesis is well founded; for it could be argued that Aaron and Hur are here degraded to the role of assistants – not of Moses, who after all does not fight at all, but of Joshua who actually conducts the battle. Aaron's role here – together with that of the enigmatic Hur, of whom very little is known except that he appears in the company of Aaron – rather agrees with his general task as Moses' assistant.

Aaron appears again in Ex. 24.14 together with Hur as the deputy of Moses. Neither here nor in Ex. 17.10, 12 does Aaron take precedence over Hur, which shows that Aaron, in these older strata of tradition, occupied a much more modest position than in later traditions.[35]

(Leiden: E. J. Brill, 1952), p. 85, interprets the name as *'ʒrn*, 'great is the name (of God)'. That explanation, however, would imply that the Hebrew tradition had completely lost the correct pronunciation of this name, for Old Egyptian *rn*, 'name', is either *ran* or *ren* (in different dialects) in Coptic.

[33] Cf. Noth, *Überlieferungsgeschichte des Pentateuch*, p. 195, n. 499. It is moreover typical that in the infancy legend where the sister of Moses appears (Ex. 2.4, 7), she remains completely anonymous; cf. Baentsch, *op. cit.*, p. 138 (on Ex. 15.20), who, however, does not draw any conclusions from this fact.

[34] Cf. Noth, *Überlieferungsgeschichte des Pentateuch*, p. 196.

[35] The disappearance of Hur in Ex. 32, leaving the field to Aaron alone, is certainly due to the recent date of this tradition, where we meet with a

In Ex. 18.12 Aaron appears with the elders of Israel taking part in the sacrificial meal prepared by the father-in-law of Moses. Here Aaron is clearly subordinate to Moses. If, however, we examine the preceding passages where the elders of Israel are mentioned, we will find that Aaron is not introduced at all, but that only Moses and the elders are mentioned together. For that reason it is highly probable that Aaron was introduced later in Ex. 18.12 as accompanying and in a way leading the elders.[36] Indeed, there is everywhere in Pentateuchal tradition a clear tendency to push Aaron forward at the side of Moses as much as possible – and that not only in 'P', but also in the strata of tradition called 'E'; e.g., Ex. 24.1ff., where the appearance of Aaron obviously is secondary.[37] The figure of Aaron in 'P' has in fact acquired such an importance that we must ask ourselves why this development has taken place. This question, however, is more adequately answered in connection with a discussion of the position occupied by Moses, and we must therefore postpone the treatment of this problem.

From the brother Aaron we pass to the sister Miriam, who perhaps also carries an Egyptian name.[38] It has already been stated that in Ex. 15.20 she is introduced as a sister of Aaron (and as a 'prophetess') but not as a sister of Moses. This implies that Miriam has no association with Moses in the oldest traditions, and this conclusion is confirmed by the appearance in the infancy-legend, Ex. 2.4, 7f., of a sister of Moses who is completely anonymous. This tradition apparently did not know any name for Moses' sister. It might of course be argued that Moses had more

definite tendency (on which I hope to say more in my forthcoming work, 'Oral Tradition and Written Literature'). From the fact of the disappearance of Hur I would therefore be inclined to draw some conclusions other than those of Noth, *Überlieferungsgeschichte des Pentateuch*, p. 196, n. 501.

[36] Cf. *ibid.*, p. 196.   [37] So also *ibid.*

[38] Cf. L. Koehler and W. Baumgartner, *Lexicon in Veteris Testamenti Libros* (Leiden: E. J. Brill, 1958), p. 567, with a reference to A. H. Gardiner, 'Egyptian Origin of Some English Personal Names', *JAOS* 56 (June, 1936), pp. 194f. Egyptian names composed with *mri*, to love, are rather common.

than one sister, but the facts adduced at any rate demonstrate that Miriam was very loosely attached to Moses, and this moreover only in later traditions.[39] It is curious to note that in later polemical traditions Miriam appears together with Aaron in opposition to Moses; so Num. 12. The controversies of later times, as reflected in this passage, are no more clear than the earlier accounts.[40] We may say finally that Miriam seems to be a historical figure, probably of southern Judaean extraction, to judge from the fact that her tomb is said to be found in Kadesh.[41]

We pass then to the parents of Moses. In the introduction to the infancy-legend it is stated that a man of the house of Levi took as his wife a Levite woman. Of this marriage, Moses was born. It calls for notice that in true saga manner the parents of Moses are anonymous.[42] In two other passages, however, Pentateuchal tradi-

---

[39] Cf. also Noth, *Überlieferungsgeschichte des Pentateuch*, pp. 197, 199.

[40] Cf. *ibid.*, p. 199.

[41] I do not understand why Noth (*ibid.*, p. 200) rejects the tradition now found in Num. 20.1, where we read: 'The children of Israel, the whole congregation, came into the desert of Zin in the first month . . . and the people dwelt in Kadesh, and Miriam died there, and was buried there.' Here it is explicitly stated that Miriam was buried at Kadesh – in a tradition generally ascribed to 'E', but certainly preserved as shaped by the 'P' circle of traditionists. Noth's statement that Miriam '*in der Wüste Zin, die . . . irgendwo zwischen dem "Skorpionenaufstieg" und Kades gesucht werden muss, gestorben und begraben ist*' is incomprehensible to me. And further, if we accept the tradition about the tomb of Moses (cf. below) why should we not accept the tradition about the tomb of Miriam? They would seem to have the same historical value – or lack of value.

[42] The text causes some difficulty for ויקח את־בת־לוי means 'he took the daughter of Levi' (sc. as his wife), which is difficult to understand from a chronological point of view. For the translation cf. A. Dillmann, *Die Bücher Exodus und Leviticus*, 3rd ed. (Leipzig: S. Herzl, 1897), p. 18; here also there is comment on whether the names really were unknown to this traditionist or whether possibly he had names transmitted to him other than those given in the genealogies. See further for this problem Baentsch, *op. cit.*, p. 10, and the following note. Another difficulty lies in the fact that while according to Ex. 2.1 Moses obviously was the first child born of the marriage, nevertheless he has an elder sister in Ex. 2.4; cf. e.g., Baentsch, *op. cit.*, p. 9. It is obvious that we are dealing with traditions of different ages and from different circles of traditionists.

tion offers us a genealogy of Moses, namely Ex. 6.14–25 and Num. 26.57–60. Here the parents are provided with personal names: the father is called Amram and the mother Jochebed. The name of the father causes no difficulty. It means 'עָם (i.e., the Divine Uncle) is elevated', and is a theophorous name of high antiquity. The name of the mother on the other hand has been the subject of much discussion and some scholars look at it with suspicion.[43] It is the second[44] element that causes some difficulty, for כֶּבֶד is not easy to interpret.[45] However, the LXX has the form Ιωχαβεδ, i.e., יוֹכָבֶד, and if this form belongs to an authentic tradition, both parents would carry theophorous names constructed after a manner to be found in the oldest strata – names built of divine subject + perfect verb which in time lose their literal significance.[46] Such names are actually among the oldest types of theophorous names in Israel,[47] and this fact speaks for the authenticity of both names, provided we read יוֹכָבֶד. This fact of course does not mean that we can say with any certainty that the genealogies presented in Ex. 6.14–25 and Num. 26.57–62 in the document 'P' inspire confidence. On the contrary, they exhibit so many difficulties and uncertainties[48] that they possess no more historical value than the genealogies we find in abundance in Arabic literature.[49]

[43] Cf. Noth, *Die israelitischen Personennamen*, p. 111, and even Baentsch, *op. cit.*, p. 50.

[44] As for the first element, 'The view that this name is a compound with יה has been questioned, but remains the view least open to objection', says G. B. Gray, *Studies in Hebrew Proper Names* (London: Adam and Charles Black, 1896), p. 156.

[45] Cf. Baentsch, *op. cit.*, with reference to E. Nestle, *Die israelitischen Eigennamen* (Haarlem: F. Bohn, 1876), p. 78. Noth, *Die israelitischen Personennamen*, p. 111, does not think it impossible that we have before us an otherwise unknown *qatl*-form of the root כבד.

[46] Cf. Noth, *Die israelitischen Personennamen*, pp. 17ff.

[47] Cf. *ibid.*, pp. 20ff., and for עם as a theophorous element, pp. 76ff.

[48] Cf. Baentsch, *op. cit.*, pp. 48–50; H. H. Rowley, *From Joseph to Joshua* (London: Oxford University Press, 1950), pp. 70ff.

[49] Cf. R. A. Nicholson, *A Literary History of the Arabs* (Cambridge: Cambridge University Press, 1930), p. xx.

We are in a far better position when we come to one son of
Moses: Gershom. About him we have some traditions outside the
Pentateuch against which we can check the Pentateuchal tradition.
Gershom is born to Moses by his wife Zipporah, Ex. 2.23. This
Gershom had a son, Jonathan, who was a priest to the tribe of
Dan after the settlement in Canaan, Judg. 18.30.[50] 'The mention
of the name of the priest ... is undoubtedly ancient, and must
emanate from one of the old narratives', Burney has written.[51]

That the priestly family of Dan carried its ancestry back to
Gershom, the son of Moses, that much is certain. From that fact
Noth concludes that we have in the Pentateuchal reference an
influence of northern Israelite tradition.[52] Because there are no
other such claims of descent from Moses registered among priestly
families, it would seem quite legitimate to assume that Moses
had a son, Gershom, from whom the priests of the Danites des-
cended. The other son of Moses mentioned in Pentateuchal
tradition, Eliezer, is an altogether nebulous figure of whom
nothing can be said with any probability.[53]

[50] Cf. Burney, *The Book of Judges*, pp. 434f., and, for the whole story,
pp. 408–17 (where Burney assumes a double strand of narrative; this
seems to me quite improbable).

[51] *Ibid.*, p. 415.

[52] Cf. Noth, *Überlieferungsgeschichte des Pentateuch*, p. 202. For Noth
the son Gershom is the starting-point in the creation of the tradition
about the Midianite wife Zipporah. According to him Gershom was
associated with Moses before the Midianite wife, who belonged to the
Southern traditions and who then was made the mother of Gershom.
Actually there is a real link between the two stories which I cannot find
noted in literature – though undoubtedly this point must have been
observed. Judges 17.7 says of Jonathan ben Gershom: והוא לוי והוא
גר־שם, 'and he was a Levite who dwelt there as a *gēr*'. Here we have a
pun on the name Gershom, and the same word-play is implied in Ex.
2.22, where it is said that Moses called his son Gershom, ויקרא את־שמו
גרשם כי אמר גר הייתי בארץ נכריה. In this passage the LXX actually has
Γηρσαμ ('mit Eintragung des *a* aus שָׁם in den Namen selbst', as Baentsch,
op. cit., p. 16, observes). The traditions in Judg. 17.7 and Ex. 2.22
accordingly belong to the same circle of traditionists.

[53] Cf. Ex. 18.4, cf. I Chron. 23.15, 17 and 26.25. Cf. Noth, *Die israelitischen Personennamen*, p. 38, n. 1 and p. 154.

36

3. The tradition about the *death and burial* of Moses is accepted by Noth as the only sure criterion of the historical existence of Moses.[54] While this may be disputed there is at any rate no special reason to reject the authenticity of the reference in Deut. 34.6, with its exact geographical localization of the tomb of Moses – any more than in the case of Miriam's tomb,[55] which, however, does not mean, of course, that this particular account has any special historical value.

4. Jonathan ben Gershom ben Moshe is said in Judg. 17.7 to be a *Levite*. This statement presents us with the problem of the relation between Moses and the Levites. The genealogies in Ex. 6 and Num. 26 tell us that Moses belonged to the tribe of Levi. We have already expressed our opinion about the value of such genealogies, but we still have the statement in Ex. 2.1 that the father of Moses was a man of the tribe of Levi who married a Levite woman. The unanimity of tradition on this point is thus established by these references in addition to those in Judg. 17.7, 9, 11; 18.30 which call Jonathan ben Gershom ben Moshe a Levite.[56]

What does this term 'Levite' mean? With some scholars, both past and present, it could certainly be argued that in Mosaic times there was no secular tribe Levi.[57] The term לוי has been

---

[54] Cf. *ibid.*, pp. 186–9, and cf. H. Ringgren, *Israelite Religion*, trans. D. E. Green (London: S.P.C.K. and Philadelphia: Fortress Press, 1966), p. 38 with n. 37.

[55] Cf. above, p. 34, n. 41.

[56] Meyer, too, considers Moses a Levite, *op. cit.*, p. 78, n. 2, emphasizing the fact that tradition is unanimous on this point.

[57] Cf. Nielsen, *op. cit.*, pp. 264ff., esp. pp. 272–7, where he concludes that there never was such a tribe. A. Lods, *Israël des origines au milieu du VIIIième siècle* (Paris: Editions Albin Michel, 1949), p. 512, points out that Levi might be a common designation for priests. Ringgren, *op. cit.*, pp. 29, 37f., leaves the problem open. I would prefer to say that when the Levites appear in a truly historical context they are nothing but priests. I do not think it is possible to state whether they were at the outset something else, but I can agree with G. W. Anderson, *The History and Religion of Israel* (London: Oxford University Press, 1966), pp. 78f., that 'it seems to be neither impossible nor improbable that there was in fact one tribe of Levi, which, at an early period, came to specialize in cultic functions'. The arguments presented by Nielsen, however, deserve careful attention.

associated with the South-Arabic priestly category *lawi'u* mentioned in the inscriptions of Al-ʿOla, a Minaean colony in Northern Arabia.[58] The term 'Levite', as used of Aaron in Ex. 4.14, clearly denotes *only* a priest, as has been pointed out several times.[59]

That Moses was a Levite in our period means not that he had exclusive rights of sacrifice, but that it was he who communicated the will of the Godhead in the form of a תּוֹרָה. Moses *qua* Levite was a proclaimer of תּוֹרוֹת.[60] These were communicated by the Levites by means of the Urim and Tummim, as Deut. 33.8–10 explicitly states:[61]

[58] Cf. F. Hommel, *Aufsätze und Abhandlungen I* (München: H. Lukaschik, 1892), pp. 30f.; Meyer, *op. cit.*, pp. 88f. (with some hesitation); G. Hölscher, *Die Propheten* (Leipzig: J. C. Hinrichs, 1914), p. 102; H. Grimme, *Muséon* 37 (1924), pp. 169ff.; W. F. Albright, *Archaeology and the Religion of Israel*, 2nd ed. (Baltimore: The Johns Hopkins Press, 1946), pp. 109, 204f. The inscriptions (quoted by Hölscher *in extenso*) are accessible in *Répertoire d'Épigraphie Sémitique* 3351, 3356, 3357, 3603. The term *lw'* denotes a person dedicated to the service of a deity. The etymology from *lawā*, 'to be attached to', would therefore seem the most acceptable. R. de Vaux, *Ancient Israel, Its Life and Institutions*, trans. J. McHugh (London: Darton, Longman and Todd and New York: McGraw-Hill, 1961), pp. 369–71, however, rejects any connection with the term *lw'* as a possible explanation of the Hebrew term. 'If anyone borrowed the word *lewy*, it was the Minaeans, who modified the sense of the term and gave it a feminine which did not exist in Hebrew.' This last statement, however, is extremely forced, because the use of the feminine form shows the root *lw'* to be a living one in Minaean dialect; further, it is more natural to suppose a common Semitic origin of the root *lw'*.

[59] Cf. Lods, *op. cit.*, p. 512, and for older literature, e.g. Baentsch, *op. cit.*, p. 31.

[60] For the priest as communicating oracles cf. e.g., Hölscher, *op. cit.*, pp. 105f., and for a comparison with Moses, pp. 107ff., esp. p. 117. In general cf. J. Begrich, *Die priesterliche Tora*, BZAW 66 (Berlin: Verlag Alfred Töpelmann, 1936), pp. 63–88.

[61] For the implications of this problem cf. Meyer, *op. cit.*, pp. 51ff. The passage in question has been treated by F. M. Cross and D. N. Freedman, 'The Blessing of Moses', *JBL* 67 (Sept., 1948), pp. 191–210, esp. pp. 203f. Their conclusion that vv. 8–10 are later additions has been contested by Nielsen, *op. cit.*, p. 270, n. 2, who points out that according to their own criteria for ancient poetry (lack of *nota accusativi*, definite article and אֲשֶׁר), at the most only vv. 8b–9a could be regarded as additions

Thy Tummim and Thy Urim to Thy devoted man,
  whom Thou didst prove at Massah,
    with whom Thou didst contend at the waters of Meribah.
Who saith of his father and of his mother:
  'I have not seen them,'
neither does he acknowledge his brethren nor know his sons.
  For they guard Thy dictate
    and observe Thy covenant.
  They teach Jacob Thy judgments
    and Israel thy תּוֹרָה.

Nothing then is more easily understood than that Moses, as a Levite, gave to the children of Israel the תּוֹרֹת communicated to him by Yahweh.

This conclusion would *a priori* render it probable that the Ten Commandments are ultimately of Mosaic origin. This has of course been asserted by many scholars, among them Rowley, who has devoted a careful investigation to this problem.[62] After the illuminating treatment of this question by Nielsen, who found a most probable setting in life of the Ten Commandments, it would, however, be very difficult to maintain more than a very general Mosaic inspiration of some of the commandments.[63] We are

---

of a more recent period. The text itself does not present any difficulties, and the deviations of the LXX are easy to explain. Pesh. tends to confirm MT. For the translation I have generally followed A. R. Johnson, *The Cultic Prophet in Ancient Israel*, 2nd ed. (Cardiff: University of Wales Press, 1962), p. 6.

[62] H. H. Rowley, 'Moses and the Decalogue', *BJRL* 34 (1951), pp. 81–118 (in revised form, this essay appears in *Men of God: Studies in Old Testament History and Prophecy* [London and New York: Thomas Nelson and Sons, 1963], pp. 1–36), where we also get a careful survey of earlier treatments of this subject.

[63] Cf. E. Nielsen, *De Ti Bud* (Copenhagen, 1965), p. 114, where only the possibility of a Mosaic origin of the general content of the Ten Commandments is admitted. The local origin of this law as North-Israelite was also advocated by Nielsen. The author has further surveyed the most modern literature on the subject and devoted much care to form-critical analysis. Nielsen's book is accessible also in an English translation, *The Ten Commandments in New Perspective*, SBT, 2nd series 7, trans. David Bourke (London: SCM Press, 1968), from *Die Zehn Gebote* (Copenhagen: Prostant apud Munksgaard, 1965), p. 139.

certainly not in a position to prove their Mosaic origin, but must be content to speak of a possible Mosaic inspiration.

The position of Moses *qua* Levite is thus easily defined. He acts as a lawgiver and priest, and this position of his is conspicuous everywhere in the preserved traditions. As proclaimer of the divine תּוֹרֹת he could also well be characterized as a prophet, נָבִיא, and the reference in Hos. 12.14 (EVV, v. 13) may therefore be, from this point of view, an authentic saying of Hosea, reflecting the reputation of Moses in later generations in the Northern Kingdom.

5. As is well known, Pentateuchal tradition also depicts Moses as the great *leader of his people*. That the authenticity of such traditions has been seriously contested is equally well known.[64] There are, however, two passages in close connection with this tradition, though from a formal point of view found outside it, which must be mentioned: namely Josh. 9.24 and Judg. 1.20.

The first passage makes the inhabitants of the Canaanite town of Gibeon refer to the fact that Yahweh had ordered Moses to conquer the whole land and exterminate all its inhabitants. That this is a Deuteronomic addition is quite certain,[65] and the safest course to take therefore is not to draw any conclusions from it.

The case is rather different with the second passage, Judg. 1.20. Though Noth has not mentioned this passage in his survey of Old Testament references to Moses, it is yet a passage which deserves some attention. It runs as follows: 'And they gave Hebron to Caleb, as Moses had said, and he dispossessed from thence the

---

[64] Cf. Eduard Meyer and Martin Noth.

[65] Cf. W. Rudolph, *Der 'Elohist' von Exodus bis Josua*, BZAW 68 (Berlin: Verlag Alfred Töpelmann, 1938), p. 203 and M. Noth, *Das Buch Josua*, HAT, 2nd ed. (Tübingen: J. C. B. Mohr [P. Siebeck], 1953), p. 59. In his *Überlieferungsgeschichte des Pentateuch*, p. 175, Noth was far more positive ('*es könnte sich um eine ziemlich alte Aussage handeln*'). As early as 1895, in the *Polychrome Bible* (London: James Clark & Co.,) the editor of the 'Book of Joshua', W. H. Bennett, attributed this reference to the Deuteronomic expansions.

three sons of Anak.' This tradition agrees in its first part with the tradition in Num. 14.24, 30, but it may be accepted as belonging to the oldest strata of the Book of Judges.[66] There was obviously an ancient tradition that Moses had promised the Calebites Hebron in return for the services rendered him and the Israelites by their eponymous ancestor. Here Moses already appears as the authoritative leader who disposes freely of the cities his people are to conquer. That much is of importance to our problem, the more so because this tradition is partly independent of Pentateuchal tradition.[67] It would thus seem to be evident that the oldest strata of tradition depict Moses as the leader of the people.

We cannot enter here upon a discussion of how Moses appears in other respects in the oldest strata of Pentateuchal tradition, for this task would imply a complete re-examination of the results arrived at by literary criticism. Instead we turn to the relationship of Moses to Aaron. It is difficult to say whether Aaron is a historical figure or not. The traditions about him in the Pentateuch, especially in 'P', are so strongly tendentious in purpose that it seems next to impossible to extricate from them any authentic historical facts.

It is easier to say what Aaron really stands for. The expressions בְּנֵי־אַהֲרֹן and בֵּית אַהֲרֹן denote the priests during the time of the monarchy. The בְּנֵי־אַהֲרֹן are called כֹּהֲנִים in Lev. 1.5 (7), 8, 11, etc., i.e., in the document 'P'. They are priests by profession. But they undoubtedly belong to a period much later than that with

---

[66] Cf. Burney, *The Book of Judges*, p. 20 (where he ascribes this passage to 'J' in accordance with ideas hardly accepted today). It calls for notice that Num. 14.24 is also an old tradition, hesitatingly ascribed by Baentsch, *op. cit.*, p. 528, to 'E'. He also refers to the other passages where this tradition appears, e.g. Josh. 14.9 (on which cf. Noth, *Das Buch Josua*, pp. 83–85).

[67] This point should be developed further, though there is no space to do so in this article. It should be noticed that in both Judg. 1.20 and Josh. 14.9; 15.13, Hebron is mentioned as associated with Caleb. Perhaps Num. 14.24 is based upon these more concrete notices.

41

which we are concerned.[68] The same is true, to an even higher degree, of the expression בֵּית אַהֲרֹן; it appears in some psalms whose date, while disputed, is certainly comparatively late.[69] It may be a designation of the priests in the time shortly before the exile – and thereafter. Aaron is here nothing more than the eponymous ancestor of the Aaronites, and his historical existence is for that reason more than uncertain, as we have said above.[70] He represents above all the claim of certain priestly families in Jerusalem.[71]

6. That Moses was in some way attached to the *oasis Kadesh Barnea* has been the opinion of many scholars since the days of Wellhausen. The older strata of tradition place in Kadesh some of the events with which Moses is associated.[72] Here it was that Israel wanted to celebrate the pilgrim festival for which permission to leave Egypt was asked of Pharaoh. In the original tradition, of which only traces are left, Moses led Israel to this place. It is possible to recover the following fragments:[73]

[68] The expression בְּנֵי־אַהֲרֹן is attested in the Holiness Code, Lev. 17–26. With A. Bentzen, *Studier over det zadokidiske praesteskabs historie* (Copenhagen, Festschrift Københavns Universitet, 1931), pp. 14f., I would be ready to assume that this designation belonged to the Holiness Code from the time of its redaction – in any case to a period much later than Moses.

[69] Cf. Pss. 115.10, 12; 118.3; 135.19. This last psalm shows association with Pentateuchal tradition, but the division there between the 'House of Aaron' and the 'House of Levi' demonstrates at least that v. 19 is of a date later than Josiah's reform.

[70] Cf. Meyer, *op. cit.*, pp. 92f.; Noth, *Überlieferungsgeschichte des Pentateuch*, p. 196, *'eine einigermassen farblose Erscheinung'*.

[71] Cf. Johannes Pedersen, *Israel III-IV* (Copenhagen: Brammer og Korch, 1940), pp. 283–6, on Num. 16–17 and the implications of that story.

[72] Cf. J. Wellhausen, *Prolegomena zur Geschichte Israels*, 6th ed. (Berlin: G. Reimer, 1905), pp. 341f.; Meyer, *op. cit.*, pp. 60ff. Accepted also by Rowley, *From Joseph to Joshua*, p. 104.

[73] Cf. Meyer, *op. cit.*, pp. 61f. I cannot find that Noth has made any serious attempt at reconstructing this chain of traditions, cf. *Überlieferungsgeschichte des Pentateuch*, pp. 76, 127–9, 242f. and *Exodus: A Commentary*, trans. J. S. Bowden (London: SCM Press, 1962), pp. 127ff. (where Kadesh is not mentioned). G. Beer, *Exodus*, HAT (Tübingen: J. C. B. Mohr [P. Siebeck], 1939), has obviously missed completely the importance of Kadesh.

Ex. 5.1–3 (combination of two traditions; Ex. 3.18 is a secondary reference)
Ex. 15.22+25b (continuation of Ex. 14.31)
Ex. 17.1b–7
Num. 20.2–12 (same tradition as preceding, but shaped in 'P').

This tradition is the oldest and the authentic tradition. It shows that there was in Kadesh a Yahweh-sanctuary where the Hebrew tribes celebrated their חַג. Here Moses officiated as a priestly Levite, here also he gave the תּוֹרָה to the tribes of Israel, Ex. 18. I can see no reason to doubt the historicity of this tradition.

More difficult to solve is the problem of Moses' leadership at the Exodus. If Moses actually was associated with the emigration from Egypt, how are we to explain the fact that Amos, speaking of the Exodus, says that God brought Israel out of Egypt, but makes no reference at all to Moses (2.10, 3.1)? Yahweh brought the בְּנֵי־יִשְׂרָאֵל, their whole מִשְׁפָּחָה, up from the land of Egypt.[74] Why is Moses as leader not mentioned here? On the other hand, we have seen already that Hosea (12.14, EVV, v. 13) emphasizes Moses' role as 'the prophet' when God brought Israel up from Egypt.[75] In the Psalms also we miss a reference to the position occupied by Moses at the Exodus. Not even in Ps. 81.11 (EVV, v. 10) is Moses mentioned, in spite of the fact that this passage explicitly refers to God as having brought Israel up from Egypt. We have found already that Moses is referred to in a few psalms, probably of exilic and post-exilic date; but never as the man who led Israel out of Egypt. If Moses actually carried out this great deed, why is his leading role in this event hardly mentioned at all by later

[74] For possible connections with written Pentateuchal tradition, cf. O. Procksch, *Geschichtsbetrachtung und geschichtliche Überlieferung bei den vorexilischen Propheten* (Leipzig: J. C. Hinrichs, 1902), pp. 110f. For the name Israel, cf. G. A. Danell, *Studies in the Name Israel in the Old Testament* (Uppsala: Appelbergs, 1946), pp. 110ff.
[75] For Moses as a prophet, cf. Procksch, *op. cit.*, p. 126, where he refers to Deut. 34.10. He also discusses other possible connections with Pentateuchal tradition.

The Hexateuch

generations? This question we shall try to answer below, but first we must say a few words about Sinai.

We have stated that all the facts indicate that in the oldest strata of tradition, Kadesh was the focus of the traditionist's interest. Indeed, the expedition of the Israelites to Sinai was probably absent in the oldest strata.[76] Later, however, the Sinai-traditions got the upper hand, and the Kadesh-traditions were pushed into the background.[77] Originally, as is shown by the ancient poem in Deut. 33, Yahweh went to Kadesh from Sinai where he had his dwelling-place,[78] being the God of Sinai, זֶה סִינַי.[79]

The Kadesh-traditions were associated with the Southern tribes – for obvious reasons.[80] But the traditions about Moses and Mosaic institutions were spread above all among the Central tribes, Ephraim and Manasseh, 'Israel' in its restricted meaning.[81] As a special place where a circle of traditionists may have collected the traditions about Moses Gressmann postulates Shechem, pointing out Shechem's importance for Covenant and Law.[82] Eduard Meyer has argued on the other hand that the Southern traditions about Moses were accepted by the Central and Northern

[76] Cf. Wellhausen, op. cit., pp. 349ff.

[77] Ibid., p. 351: 'Mit offenbarer Absicht wird namentlich Kades möglichst in den Hintergrund gedrängt.'

[78] Especially emphasized by Meyer, op. cit., p. 60, after the hints given already by Wellhausen. So also E. Auerbach, Moses (Amsterdam: G. J. A. Ruys, 1953), pp. 74ff. There is no space to list points of agreement and disagreement with this stimulating book. The difference in method here is too great for an appropriate comparison. For a lucid review, cf. O. Eissfeldt, Kleine Schriften, III (Tübingen: J. C. B. Mohr [P. Siebeck], 1966), pp. 240–55, esp. p. 253.

[79] Cf. Judg. 5.5 and note the following scholars: H. Grimme, 'Abriss der biblisch-hebräischen Metrik', ZDMG 50 (1896), p. 573 with n. 1; H. S. Nyberg, 'Deuteronomion 33, 2–3', ZDMG 92 (1938), p. 338, n. 1; W. F. Albright, From the Stone Age to Christianity, 2nd ed. (Baltimore: The Johns Hopkins Press, 1946), p. 199.

[80] The Levites as the priests of Kadesh are associated with the Southern tribes, cf. Meyer, op. cit., p. 85.

[81] Ibid., 'Aber die Leviten bringen ihre heimischen Anschauungen und die auf Mose zurückgeführten Traditionen mit und halten an sie fest.'

[82] Cf. Gressmann, op. cit., p. 386.

44

tribes after having been transmitted to them by the Levites.[83] Some aspects of this reconstruction are rather uncertain, but one fact would seem to remain sure: the traditions about Moses were preserved in Northern Israel.

This line of research has been carried on by Nielsen, who has pointed to other indications of a northern origin of Mosaic traditions, e.g., the firm connection between Yahweh and Sinai, which is mentioned in a number of passages, both in ancient poems and in prophetic stories of Northern provenance.[84] He has also stressed the fact that such a tradition as Ex. 18.1ff., where Moses is instructed by his Midianite father-in-law, could hardly represent 'an originally Southern tradition' because the contact between Israel and Midian was effected in the tribe of Ephraim and on both sides of the river Jordan, involving the Central and Northern tribes.[85] The importance of the stay of the Central tribes in the territory east of Jordan is further stressed.

It also calls for notice, finally, that the Deuteronomic traditions are from the Northern Kingdom, as has been made increasingly clear in modern research.[86] Here, obviously, we have other strata of strong Mosaic traditions.

7. Let us then sum up some of the conclusions we are able to draw from the evidence available both within and outside Pentateuchal tradition.

The prophets have very little to tell us about Moses. Among pre-exilic prophets only Hosea, Micah and Jeremiah mention his name or allude to him, a fact in itself indicating his importance

---

[83] Cf. Meyer, *op. cit.*, pp. 82ff.

[84] Cf. Nielsen, *Shechem, A Traditio-Historical Investigation*, pp. 350f. He does not mention Gressmann among his references, but refers instead to Luther, Meyer, Sellin, and Luckenbill; note p. 347. Cf. also *De Ti Bud*, p. 114 (ET: p. 139) (the Mosaic traditions are most firmly rooted among the Joseph tribes in the Northern Kingdom).

[85] Cf. Nielsen, *Shechem, A Traditio-Historical Investigation*, p. 355.

[86] Cf., in an older generation, the works of, e.g., Welch and Oestreicher and in the next generation after them, e.g., A. Alt, 'Die Heimat des Deuteronomiums', *Kleine Schriften*, II (Munich: C. H. Beck, 1953), pp. 250–75. A recent discussion is found in Lohfink, *op. cit.*, pp. 492–4.

to them. Jeremiah, further, was strongly influenced by the Deuteronomic tradition, as Rowley has shown.[87] When Jeremiah speaks of how Yahweh brought Israel out of Egypt he does not use the *hiphil* of the verb עלה, but the characteristic Deuteronomic expression, הוציא.[88] Though Micah, in a verse that only may be authentic (6.4c), uses as do Hosea and Amos the expression העלה, he shows himself dependent, as we have seen, upon the fully developed Pentateuchal tradition.

The prophets, with the exception of Hosea, belonged to Judah. Their silence about Moses is for that reason easy to explain. They were not acquainted with Northern traditions before the time of Jeremiah, who received these traditions in their Deuteronomic shaping. A supplementary proof is the silence about Jerusalem in the Northern Kingdom.[89]

The Psalms too are mainly of Southern, i.e., Jerusalemite, origin, though some Northern psalms have been incorporated in the biblical Psalter. Even so, the whole collection has been transmitted to us in a Jerusalemite redaction. The insignificant role played by Moses in the cultic poetry of the Jerusalem temple in pre-exilic times is thus quite understandable.

The figure of Moses was thus taken into the Southern Kingdom thanks chiefly to Deuteronomic circles, through whom also Moses found his way into the historical books of Deuteronomic inspiration.

According to our analysis, then, the importance of Moses is

[87] Cf. H. H. Rowley, 'The Prophet Jeremiah and the Book of Deuteronomy', *Studies in Old Testament Prophecy*, T. H. Robinson *Festschrift*, ed. H. H. Rowley (Edinburgh: T. and T. Clark, 1950), pp. 157–74, esp. pp. 167ff.

[88] I have counted about twenty-one passages where the verb הוציא is used whereas העלה is used only in Deut. 20.1.

[89] Cf. M. Noth, 'Jerusalem und die israelitische Tradition', *Gesammelte Studien zum Alten Testament* (Munich: Chr. Kaiser Verlag, 1960, pp. 172–87; ET: 'Jerusalem and the Israelite Tradition', *The Laws in the Pentateuch and Other Studies* trans. D. R. Ap-Thomas [Edinburgh: Oliver and Boyd, 1966 and Philadelphia: Fortress Press, 1967], pp. 132–44).

quite unaffected by the insignificant role he plays in literature of Southern origin in pre-exilic times. The main facts of his life as well as his position as the leader of Israel may at least be partially extricated from the mass of legendary traditions about him, in part through a careful use of rare references to him outside Pentateuchal tradition. To exceed the minimum interpretation of evidence about Moses, as it is presented in this article, would demand a new examination of Pentateuchal tradition. This is certainly a task for future research.[90]

[90] When undertaking that task one has to bear in mind the fact rightly emphasized by Rowley, *From Joseph to Joshua*, p. 106: '. . . that while the J narrative displays a special interest in the traditions of Judah and the E narrative in those of Ephraim, both are corpora of traditions of all the tribes. Both appear to have been compiled after the traditions had been fused in the period of the early monarchy.' He further states, on p. 107: 'The conflation is unhistorical, but the separate traditions may be accepted as genuinely historical. Our only difficulty is to disentangle them.' I am afraid, however, this is no small difficulty.

3

The Revelation of the
Divine Name YHWH

Roland de Vaux

IT may seem useless or presumptuous to take up once again a problem which has been treated so often. In these pages, however, we do not claim to add yet another solution to those which have already been put forward: our intention is merely to note the developments and the new perspectives to which recent studies have given rise and to offer this essay in tribute to Professor G. Henton Davies who was concerned with the revelation of the divine name in his recent commentary on Exodus.[1]

According to the Yahwist tradition, the invocation of the name Yahweh goes back to the origins of humanity, to the time of Enosh, son of Seth (cf. Gen. 4.26). Consequently the Yahwist account of the apparition to Moses in Midian retains only the theophany at the burning bush, Ex. 3.1–5, and the mission of Moses, Ex. 3.16–20.

According to the Elohist tradition of Ex. 3.6, 9–15, God revealed to Moses the meaning of the name Yahweh, by which he wished henceforth to be invoked.[2] In order to bring this tradition into

---

[1] G. Henton Davies, *Exodus*, TBC (London: SCM Press, 1967).

[2] The attribution of this to the Elohist has recently once again been called into question, cf. especially S. Mowinckel, 'The Name of the God of Moses', *HUCA* 32 (1961), pp. 121–33; *Erwägungen zur Pentateuch Quellenfrage* (Trondheim: Universitets forlaget, 1964), p. 64 (the text is

harmony with that of the Yahwist, it is sometimes said that Moses did not receive the revelation of the name Yahweh, which he already knew, but merely an explanation of it.[3] This is to weaken the import of the text, for v. 15 is part of the ancient account[4] and is explicit: Yahweh is a new name.

This is even more clearly affirmed by the Priestly tradition, which transfers the scene to Egypt (Ex. 6.2–13). God reveals himself under the name Yahweh, which was unknown to the Patriarchs and which was to replace the name El Shaddai by which they had invoked him.

I. THE FORM OF THE NAME

In effect, Yahweh was always to be solely and exclusively the name of the God of Israel. This name is used in two forms in the Bible: the long form יהוה – which is nearly always used – and the short form יה, used in the liturgical acclamation הַלְלוּיָה and occasionally in poetry. In the composition of proper names of

---

from J): A. Besters, 'L'expression "Fils d'Israel" en Exod. 1–14', *RB* 74 (1967), pp. 321–55, especially pp. 328–33 (the text is from J, with modifications by a priestly redactor who is responsible for v. 15 in particular).

[3] This solution is imposed particularly on those who deny the existence of an independent Elohist tradition, such as S. Mowinckel, 'The Name of the God of Moses', *HUCA* 32 (1961), p. 126, or on those who reject all documentary criticism, such as M. H. Segal, 'The Revelation of the Name JHWH', *Tarbiz* 12 (1940–41), pp. 97–108 (Hebrew); *The Pentateuch, its Composition and its Authorship, and Other Biblical Studies* (Jerusalem: The Magnes Press, 1967), pp. 4–8. An argument which seems conclusive to certain scholars is that the mother of Moses bears a name compounded with Yahweh, יוֹכֶבֶד. But this name is given only by late genealogies: cf. Ex. 6.20; Num. 26.59, and it is not certain that it contains the name Yahweh, cf. M. Noth, *Die israelitischen Personennamen* (Stuttgart: W. Kohlhammer, 1928), p. 111; L. Koehler and W. Baumgartner, *Lexicon in Veteris Testamenti Libros* (Leiden: E. J. Brill, 1953), p. 372.

[4] Cf. M. Noth, *Exodus*, trans. J. S. Bowden (London: SCM Press and Philadelphia: Westminster Press, 1962), p. 43; G. Fohrer, *Überlieferung und Geschichte des Exodus*, BZAW 91 (Berlin: Verlag Alfred Töpelmann, 1964), p. 40.

people the divine name assumes shortened forms: -יְהוֹ, -יוֹ, -יְ, at the beginning and יְהוּ-, יָה-, at the end.[5] Although the question remains a matter for argument, the long form is primitive. It is this form which, standing alone, is used almost exclusively in the Bible and it is this form which Ex. 3.14 is attempting to explain. Outside the Bible the name of the God of Israel is יהוה on the stele of Mesha in the ninth century BC, on an eighth century seal,[6] in the ostraca of Tell Arad at the end of the seventh century,[7] often in the letters of Lachish[8] at the beginning of the sixth century, and in *graffiti* which may also well be pre-exilic.[9] The short form has been read on a potsherd from Samaria, dating from the eighth to the seventh centuries BC as ליה,[10] and on a potsherd from Meggido, dating from the seventh century, as ליו;[11] but these readings are uncertain. The two letters יה on post-exilic

[5] Outside the Bible -*yw* is also found on ostraca and seals.
[6] Cf. F. M. Cross, 'Yahweh and the God of the Patriarchs', *HTR* 55 (Oct., 1962), p. 251.
[7] Cf. Y. Aharoni, 'Hebrew Ostraca from Tel Arad', *IEJ* 16 (1966), pp. 1–7.
[8] The two examples of *Yhw* in the Lachish letters which A. Murtonen cites in *A Philological and Literary Treatise on the Old Testament Divine Names* אל, אלוה, אלהים and יהוה, Studia Orientalia 18, 1 (Helsinki, 1952), p. 43, are faulty readings made by the first editor.
[9] Cf. J. Naveh, 'Old Hebrew Inscriptions in a Burial Cave', *IEJ* 13 (1963), pp. 74–92.
[10] Cf. G.A. Reisner and C. S. Fisher, *Harvard Excavations at Samaria* (Cambridge: Harvard University Press, 1924), p. 238, n. 35 and pl. 55b (though it is possible that the three letters form the termination of a theophorous name lost when the sherd was broken). Another example of *lyh* in Aramean script, proposed by E. J. Sukenik, 'Potsherds from Samaria, Inscribed with the Divine Name', *PEQ* (Jan., 1936), pp. 34–37 (cf. S. A. Birnbaum 'Ostraca: Sherds with Letters in Aramaic Script', J. W. Crowfoot and others, *Samaria-Sebaste III: The Objects from Samaria* [London: Palestine Exploration Fund, 1957], p. 28), must be discarded.
[11] Cf. H. G. May, 'An Inscribed Jar from Megiddo', *AJSL* 50 (1933–34), pp. 10–14; R. S. Lamon and G. M. Shipton, *Megiddo I* (Chicago: University of Chicago Press, 1939), pl. 115, 5. But the reading *wāw* is very doubtful.

official stamps do not represent the divine name[12] but are an abbreviation of יהד, the name of the province of Judea in the Persian and Hellenistic period.[13] The short form יהו is constant, save on one occasion (יהה), in the Elephantine papyri, but the ostraca from the same site always have יהה.[14] The long form is therefore the older and more frequent form in sources outside the Bible. Moreover a contraction of the long form is more readily explained philologically than the lengthening of a short one.

As to the pronunciation of the name, we know that the Massoretes provided the divine name with the vowels of אֲדֹנָי , 'my lord', which is to be read in place of the tetragrammaton. The pronunciation *Yahweh* is based on the etymological interpretation given in Ex. 3.14, on the analogy of the Amorite names *Yawi-ilā*, *Yawi-Addu*, *Yawi-Dagan*, which we shall examine later, and on the Greek transcriptions Ιαουε and Ιαβε. A pronunciation *Yahwo*[15] had already been proposed and has recently been competently defended. This pronunciation can invoke in its support the Elephantine form יהו which would be pronounced *Yaho*, the abridged forms which the divine name takes in personal names, the transcription Ιαω in certain Fathers of the church and in Diodorus Siculus 1.94, and the names Ιαω and Ιαο on gnostic gems, on amulets and in magical papyri of the first five centuries of our era. This argument from Greek transcriptions is the most striking, but it loses its force when it is noted that Ιαω, originally at least, was possibly nothing more than a mechanical transcription of the Hebrew יָ, and so provides no proof of a pronunciation

---

[12] *Contra* L. H. Vincent, 'Les épigraphes judéo-araméennes postexiliques', *RB* 56 (April, 1949), pp. 286–91.

[13] Cf. Y. Aharoni, 'Excavations at Ramat Rahel, 1954', *IEJ* 6 (1956), pp. 148f.; *Excavations at Ramat Rahel* (Rome: Universita Degli Studi/ Centro di Studi Semitici, 1962), pp. 6, 30; (1964), pp. 20, 44.

[14] Cf. A. Dupont-Sommer, 'Le syncrétisme religieux des Juifs d'Eléphantine d'après un ostracon araméen inédit', *RHR* 130 (1945), pp. 22–23; *Semitica* II (1949), p. 34.

[15] Cf. W. Vischer, 'Eher Jahwo als Jahwe', *ThZ* 16 (1960), pp. 259–67.

Yao.[16] All things considered the pronunciation *Yahweh*, which is commonly accepted, is preferable.

II. THE NAME YAHWEH OUTSIDE ISRAEL?

Nevertheless this divine name, which was new to Israel and was to remain her exclusive property, could have existed previously elsewhere, and evidence has been sought for it before the time of Moses outside Israel.[17] At one time the ancient Babylonian names *Yaum-ilum* or *Yawum-ilum*, which were translated 'Yahweh is God', were quoted; there is also evidence for the shortened form *Yaum*. But it is now recognized that *Yaum* is the independent pronoun 'mine'.[18]

[16] Likewise *'Iaῄ* in Origen, *Selecta in Psalmos*, *Ps. ii*, J. P. Migne, *Patrologiae Graecae* (Paris, 1857–66), vol. XII, 1104, is only a transcription of *Yah*.

[17] The work of A. Murtonen, *The Appearance of the Name YHWH outside Israel*, Studia Orientalia 16, 3 (Helsinki, 1951), taken up again in *A Philological and Literary Treatise on the Old Testament Divine Names* (cf. above n. 8), pp. 44–54, needs correcting and completing at several points. The name *Aḥi-yawi*, which had been read on a tablet of Taanach (fifteenth century BC), should be read *Aḥi-yami*, cf. W. F. Albright, 'A Prince of Taanach in the Fifteenth Century B.C.', *BASOR* 94 (April, 1944), p. 20. I do not take into account the names of Azriya'u of Ya'udi (Samal) under Tiglath-pileser III and of Ya'ubidi (also called Ilubidi) of Hamath under Sargon II: they date from considerably after the time of Moses and reflect an Israelite influence.

[18] Cf. I. J. Gelb, B. Landsberger, A. L. Oppenheim, E. Reiner *et al.*, *Chicago Assyrian Dictionary* (Chicago: The Oriental Institute, 1964), s.v. *ja'um*, with references, and B. Landsberger, 'Solidarhaftung von Schuldnern in den babyl.-assyrischen Urkunden', *ZA* 35 (1924), p. 24, n. 2; J. Lewy, 'Studies in Akkadian Grammar and Onomatology', *Or* 15 (1964), pp. 362 and 393; W. von Soden, 'Jahwe "Er ist, Er erweist sich" ', *WdO* 3, 3 (1964–66), p. 178. Recently, H. Cazelles, 'Mari et l'Ancien Testament', *XVᵉ Rencontre Assyriologique Internationale*, Liège, 1966 (Paris, 1967), pp. 73–90, especially pp. 82–86, has explained the name of Yahweh itself by this personal pronoun: 'Yaw (Yaum)' would mean 'Mine'. But (*a*) the pronoun *yaum* is proper to Akkadian and does not exist in West-Semitic, and (*b*) this does not explain the long form 'Yahweh'.

It was thought that a god *Yw* had been discovered in a mythological text from Ras Shamra, in which the God El says: 'The name of my son *yw.-ilt* ...'[19] Although this reading has been contested, it is beyond doubt;[20] but the text is obscure and full of lacunae. A connection with Yahweh, proposed by the original editor, is still admitted as possible by certain specialists in Ugaritic,[21] but it is either rejected or considered very uncertain by others.[22] In any case this supposed divine name does not appear again anywhere else in the Ras Shamra texts. As this poem speaks immediately afterwards of the god *Ym* = Yamm, the god of the sea and rivers well known at Ras Shamra, it is possible that *Yw* is a different spelling or the component part of an epithet of this god. But it would be even more difficult to establish an equation between Yamm and Yahweh,[23] and if the primitive form of the divine name is the long form *Yhwh*, the possibility of a borrowing is exluded.

This long form has been compared to the element *Yawi-*, or *Yaḥwi-*, in the Amorite proper names *Yawi-ilā*, *Yaḥwi-ilā*, *Yawi-Addu*, *Yawi-Dagan* and *Yaḥwi-Nasi*. We shall ourselves use these names to shed light on the etymology, form and meaning

[19] C. Virolleaud, *La Déesse 'Anat* (Paris: P. Geuthner, 1938), tablet VI AB iv 14 = Cyrus Gordon, *'nt*, pl. x in *Ugaritic Textbook* (Rome: Pontificium Institutum Biblicum, 1965), p. 255 = *Corpus* Herdner no. 1, see A. Herdner, *Corpus des tablettes en cunéiformes alphabétiques découvertes à Ras Shamra-Ugarit de 1929 à 1939* (Paris: P. Geuthner, 1963).

[20] Herdner, *op. cit.*, p. 4.

[21] Thus Gordon, *op. cit.*, Glossary no. 1084, p. 410; J. Aistleitner, *Wörterbuch der ugaritischen Sprache*, 2nd ed. (Berlin: Akademie Verlag, 1965), no. 1151.

[22] To mention only recent works, cf. J. Gray, 'The God YW in the Religion of Canaan', *JNES* 12 (1953), pp. 278–83; *The Legacy of Canaan*, 2nd ed. (Leiden: E. J. Brill, 1965), pp. 180–4; M. Pope, 'Syrien: Die Mythologie der Ugariter und Phönizier', *Wörterbuch Der Mythologie*, part I, vol. I: *Götter und Mythen im vorderen Orient*, ed. H. W. Haussig (Stuttgart: Ernst Klett Verlag, 1965), pp. 291f.

[23] In spite of A. Murtonen, *A Philological and Literary Treatise on the Old Testament Divine Names*, pp. 90–92; E. C. B. MacLaurin, 'YHWH, The Origin of the Tetragrammaton', *VT* 12 (1962), pp. 449–51.

of the name Yahweh. But recently an attempt has been made to see in them the actual name of the God of Israel. They should, it is claimed, be translated: 'El (or Addu, or Dagan . . .) is Yahweh', and they would thus imply the adoption of a god Yahweh by the Amorites at the beginning of the second millennium BC and his assimilation to their own particular gods.[24]

This explanation is unlikely. These names belong to the numerous class of Amorite names formed of a verb and a divine name. In the present case, the problem is to determine which verbal root is used and in what tense.[25] In effect, Accadian does not know ה and does not generally transcribe it, although sometimes it expresses it by *ḫa*. The forms, *Yawi-N.* and *Yaḫwi-N.*, could therefore contain the same root *hwy*, 'to be'. But Accadian also does not know *ḥa*, which it generally transcribes by *ḫa*, but which it occasionally omits. The two names could therefore contain the root *ḥwy*, 'to live'. As for the verbal form, Amorite seems to have retained from general Semitic the simple *Qal*, with the forms **yaqtal*, **yaqtil* and **yaqtul* for completed action (perfect-present) and the forms **yaqtalu*, **yaqtilu* and **yaqtulu* for uncompleted action (imperfect-future); the forms of the causative (*Hiphʿil*) are respectively **yaqtil* and **yaqtilu*. But, for verbs of the **yaqtil* type in the simple *Qal* and for verbs with the third radical *w/y*, the spelling does not permit any distinction between the simple and the causative.

Leaving aside the uncertainty on the point of the aspect (perfect-present or imperfect-future), several translations of these names are therefore theoretically possible: 'N. lives' or 'N. gives life', 'N. exists' or 'N. brings into existence'. Furthermore, the divine name can be in the vocative: 'He (the child) exists, o N.' or 'He (the child) lives, o N.' Finally, it is possible that a distinction

[24] Cf. A. Finet, 'Iawi-Ilâ, roi de Talḫayûm', *Syria* 41 (1964), pp. 117–42, especially pp. 118–22.

[25] Cf., most recently, H. B. Huffmon, *Amorite Personal Names in the Mari Texts* (Baltimore: Johns Hopkins Press, 1965), pp. 70–72; W. von Soden, *op. cit.*, pp. 179–81.

should be drawn between two series of names: *Yaḥwi-N.* formed with the root *ḥwy*, 'to live', and *Yawi-N.* formed with the root *hwy*, 'to be'. In the framework of Amorite onomastic, where other names are formed with the root *ḥwy* and where the causative is frequently used, and bearing in mind also the more frequent transcription of *ḥ* by *ḫ* in Accadian, the most probable explanation of *Yaḥwi-N.* is 'N. gives life', which is very appropriate as a name given to a new-born child.

If *Yawi-N.* is different and contains the root *hwy*, 'to be', it would be the only Amorite name formed with this root, but it would have an equivalent in the Accadian names *Ibašši-Ilum*, *Ibašši-Ilāni*, *Ibašši-Adad*. And, in its stative form, *Baši-Ilum*, which means 'the god, the gods, Adad exist', it is neither a simple statement of fact nor a confession of faith, but a grateful homage to the god who has shown himself as existing and active.[26] Following this, *Yawi-N.* would mean 'N. exists' rather than 'N. brings into existence', though this latter does, however, remain possible. In any case, the elements *Yaḥwi-* and *Yawi-* are not a divine name.

The only name, outside the Bible and prior to the exodus, which one could legitimately compare with Yahweh is *Yhwꝫ*, which appears as one of the 'Shasu lands' in a geographical list of the time of Amenophis III in a temple at Soleb (Nubia)[27] and in a copy of that list in a temple at Amara West (Nubia) from the reign of Ramses II.[28] 'Shasu' is a generic name given by the

[26] Cf. J. J. Stamm, *Die akkadische Namengebung* (Leipzig: J. C. Hinrichs Verlag, 1939), p. 179.

[27] J. Leclant, 'Fouilles et travaux en Egypte et au Soudan, 1961–62, II: Fouilles au Soudan et découvertes hors d'Egypte', *Or* 32 (1963), p. 203; 'Les fouilles de Soleb . . .', *Nachrichten der Akad. der Wiss. in Göttingen*, Phil.-Hist. Klasse, 13 (1965), pp. 205–16; R. Giveon, 'Toponymes ouest-asiatiques à Soleb', *VT* 14 (1964), pp. 239–55; and in *Fourth World Congress of Jewish Studies*, Papers, I (Jerusalem, 1967), p. 193; S. Herrmann, 'Israel in Ägypten', *ZAS* 91 (1964), pp. 63ff.; 'Der alttestamentliche Gottesname', *EvTh* 26 (1966), pp. 281–383.

[28] See the list from 'Amara West', which will be edited by H. W. Fairman, *Amara West, I, the Temple*. Provisionally, cf. B. Grdseloff, 'Edôm

Egyptians to the Bedouin living east of their frontier in Sinai, Southern Palestine and Southern Transjordan. The only Shasu name which can be identified in these lists is the 'Shasu' land *S'rr*, obviously Se'ir = Edom. Thus *Yhw3*, as *S'rr*, must be here a geographical name, the name of a region or of a place, or an ethnic name, the name of the group living in that region. It might also have been the name of the god worshipped in that region or by this group, but this is a mere hypothesis. What remains – and it is very important – is that, in a region with which the forefathers of Israel had so many connections, there was, as early as the middle of the second millennium BC, a geographical or ethnic name very similar, if not identical, with the name of the God of Israel.

In conclusion it is possible – it is even likely, given its archaic form – that the divine name *Yhwh* existed outside Israel before Moses, but we have as yet no conclusive proof of this.

III. THE ETYMOLOGY AND MEANING OF THE NAME YAHWEH

We must surely reject an Egyptian etymology, which was propounded almost a century ago and which has recently been taken up again and developed.[29] On this view, the name would be composed of two Egyptian words: *Yah*, the god 'moon' and *we3*, 'one'. We must also reject explanations deriving the name from

---

d'après les sources égyptiennes', *Revue de l'Histoire Juive en Egypte*, I (1947), pp. 79–83; S. H. Horn, 'Jericho in a Topographical List of Ramesses II', *JNES* 12 (1953), p. 201; K. A. Kitchen, 'Some New Light on the Asiatic Wars of Ramesses II', *JEA* 50 (1964), p. 67; H. H. Rowley, 'Moses and Monotheism', *From Moses to Qumran: Studies in the Old Testament* (London: Lutterworth Press and New York: Association Press, 1963), pp. 53f.

[29] N. Walker, *The Tetragrammaton* (West Ewell, England, 1948); 'Yahwism and the Divine Name "Yhwh"', *ZAW* 70 (1958), pp. 262–5; 'Concerning Ex. 34.6', *JBL* 79 (1960), p. 277; 'The Riddle of the Ass's Head, and the Question of a Trigram', *ZAW* 75 (1963), p. 226. An Egyptologist has criticized this position, cf. J. Vergote, 'Une théorie sur l'origine égyptienne du nom de Yahweh', *EThL* 39 (1963), pp. 447–52.

Indo-european, where *Dyau-s*, which became Zeus in Greek and Ju-piter in Latin, would have become *Yaw* in Hebrew;[30] or those deriving it from Hurrian, where *Ya* would mean 'god' and would have been lengthened by the Hurrian sufixes *-ha* or *-wa*;[31] or finally those which seek an origin in the undeciphered writing from the Indus Valley dating from the third millennium BC where, it is claimed, mention is made of a god *Yaé* or *Yaue*.[32]

It is clearly in the Semitic field that we must search. There the name has been explained as a cultic exclamation, formed from the interjection *ya*, which is current in Arabic, and from the personal pronoun *huwa*, 'he': thus, *Ya-huwa*, 'O he', which would be at the root of the long form *Yhwh* as well as at that of the short form *Yhw*.[33] In fact, the personal pronoun of the third person appears to be used at times in the Bible as a substitute for, or an equivalent of, the divine name.[34] Thus the proper name אֲבִיהוּא is parallel to the names אֲבִיָּה, אֲבִיָּהוּ, אֲבִיאֵל. Similarly אֱלִיהוּא (also written אֱלִיהוּ) is equivalent to אֱלִיָּהוּ and אֱלִיָּה. In the same way מִיכָהוּ (without the final א, but cf. אֱלִיהוּ) is comparable to מִיכָאֵל, מִיכָיָה and מִיכָיָהוּ. Lastly, the name יְהוּא is composed of the abbreviated divine name *Yo-* (which changed to *ye-* before the sound *u*) and the pronoun הוּא. Deutero-Isaiah frequently uses the formula אֲנִי הוּא, 'I he', that is, 'I am he' (Isa. 43.10, 13; cf. also 41.4;

---

[30] Cf. E. Littmann, 'Review of *Le Inscrizioni Antico-Ebraiche Palestinesi, raccotte e illustrate* by David Diringer', *AFO* 11 (1936), p. 162.

[31] Cf. J. Lewy, 'Influences hurrites en Israel', *RES* (1938), pp. 49–75, especially pp. 55–61.

[32] Cf. B. Hrozny, 'Inschriften und Kultur der Proto-Inder von Mohenjo-Daro und Harappa, II', *ArOr* 13 (1942), pp. 1–102, especially pp. 52ff.

[33] Cf. M. Buber, *Moses* (Oxford: East and West Library, 1946 and New York: Harper Torchbooks, 1958), pp. 49f. and above all S. Mowinckel, 'The Name of the God of Moses', *HUCA* 32 (1961), pp. 121–33, especially pp. 131–3.

[34] So Mowinckel, 'The Name of the God of Moses', *HUCA* 32 (1961), and Hans Kosmala, 'The Name of God (YHWH and HÛ')', *ASTI* 2 (1963), pp. 103–6. Cf. also N. Walker, 'Concerning HÛ' and 'ANÎ HÛ' ', *ZAW* 74 (1962), pp. 205f.

48.12, possibly 52.6 [cf. Deut. 32.39]); compare also Ps. 102.28 (EVV, v.27), וְאַתָּה הוּא, 'thou art he'. At Qumran, in a paraphrase of Isa. 40.3, the tetragrammaton is replaced by הוּאהָא,[35] and the Rabbis were to use הוּא in the same way. Outside Israel, but still in Semitic circles, the *dhikr* of the Moslem confraternities consists in the indefinite repetition of the divine name in different forms; in particular, *Allah-hu* followed by an epithet, or simply *Huwa*, 'he'.[36]

The following observations can be made. In the proper names cited, the personal pronoun definitely refers to God and means that this God, Elohim or Yahweh, is the God of him who bears the name. Thus אֲבִיהוּא means 'he is my father', אֱלִיהוּ, 'he is my God', מִיכָאֵל, 'who is like him (God)?' and יְהוּא, 'he is Yahweh'.[37] Likewise the Moslem invocation means 'he is Allah'. But it is impossible to say that הוּא is a divine name, or even, properly speaking, that it is a substitute for one; in הוּא יְ., הוּא is obviously not a substitute for Yahweh. In the biblical texts quoted, this idea of a personal God evolves to that of the one God, cf. especially Isa. 43.10, Deut. 32.39, and of the God who remains always the same, cf. especially Isa. 41.4; 48.12; Ps. 102.28 (EVV, v. 27); cf. also Job 3.19 where in Sheol 'the small and the great are הוּא, "the same" '.[38] In Isa. 52.6, the translation should be 'It is I who . . .', cf. 51.9 'It is thou who . . .'.

[35] Man. Disc. 8.13 and cf. 3.17, 25; 4.25, where הוּאהָ takes the place of 'God'.

[36] Cf. L. Gardet, '*dhikr*', *Encyclopédie de l'Islam*, new ed. (Leiden: E. J. Brill, 1965), vol. II, pp. 223–6; 'Un problème de mystique compàrée: la mention du nom divin (*dhikr*) dans la mystique musulmane', *Revue Thomiste* 52 (1952), pp. 642–79, especially p. 633.

[37] Cf. Noth, *Die Israelitischen Personennamen*, pp. 143 f. Cf. the Ugaritic name *hw'il* = *Huwa'il*, 'He is El (God)', C. Virolleaud, *Le Palais Royal d'Ugarit* II, Mission de Ras Shamra, vol. VII, ed. C. F. A. Schaeffer (Paris: Imprimerie Nationale et Librarie C. Klincksieck, 1957), p. 132, no. 104, line 7.

[38] This is the meaning which the *Lexicon* of Koehler-Baumgartner gives to all these texts. Compare Mal. 3.6: 'I am Yahweh, I do not change.'

It is far more likely that the name contains a verbal root and, according to the spelling, this root should be *hwh*, the ancient *hwy*. There was a root הָוָה (הוֹא) in Hebrew with the sense 'to fall'. The verb is used once, Job 37.6, and from it derive two substantives; הַוָּה, 'destruction' and הֹוָה , 'disaster'. There is ample evidence for this root in Arabic, where *hwy* means 'to fall' or 'to throw down', and on account of this an attempt has been made to explain the name Yahweh as the god of storms, thunder and lightnings.[39] In Arabic there is also a root *hwy* with the sense of 'to love, to act with passion', and Hebrew contains a corresponding substantive, הָוָה, meaning 'desire'. Yahweh would then be he who loves and acts with passion, 'the Passionate One'.[40] But the verb is not employed in Hebrew, which uses a related form אָוָה, 'to desire', and the substantive הַוָּה, which is rare (cf. Micah 7.3; Prov. 10.3; 11.6), always has the pejorative sense of 'lust'. Moreover, these two hypotheses seem to involve an improper usage of Arabic in which the meaning of ancient roots has in fact undergone a great development and diversification.

Almost all recent authors derive the name *Yhwh* from the north-western Semitic root *hwy*, 'to be'. There is perhaps evidence of it in Amorite, as we have seen, in the proper names of the *Yawi-ilā* group, and it may also have existed in Ugaritic.[41] However, the normal root which signifies 'to be' in both Amorite and Ugaritic is *kwn* and this is the only one attested in the Canaanite of the Amarna letters and in Phoenician. In Accadian, the phonetic equivalent *ewu/emu* means 'to turn oneself into', 'to become like',

[39] So, earlier, P. de Lagarde, J. Wellhausen; cf. also H. Bauer and P. Leander, *Historische Grammatik der hebraischen Sprache* (Hildesheim: Georg Olms Verlagsbuchhandlung, 1962), vol. I, p. 24, n. 2.

[40] Cf. S. D. Goitein, 'YHWH The Passionate', *VT* 6 (1956), pp. 1–9.

[41] In a quadrilingual lexicon which remains as yet unedited, opposite Sumerian, Accadian and Hurrite words meaning 'to be', we find the Ugaritic *hwy*, cf. C. Virolleaud, *Comptes-Rendus du GLECS*, vol. VIII, p. 66; C. H. Gordon, *Ugaritic Textbook*, Glossary no. 754b. But note the reservations of F. M. Cross, *HTR* 55 (Oct., 1962), p. 254, n. 124, on this reading.

which in the causative is 'to turn into', 'to make like'. But the root is current in Aramean and its dialects, from the oldest inscriptions[42] right down to biblical and post-biblical Aramean, as well in Nabatean, Palmyrenian and Syriac, in the forms *hwh*, *hw'* and *hwy*. In biblical Hebrew the use of the Aramaic root *hwh* is exceptional,[43] cf. Gen. 27.29; Isa. 16.4; Eccles. 2.22; 11.3; Neh. 6.6. The first reference occurs in an old, poetic text which could have retained the primitive form; in the other cases *hwh* is an Aramaism. In fact, the verb became היה in Hebrew. In this case, then, the name Yahweh would have preserved the archaic form of the root. It remains to determine in what grammatical form it is found there.

Some have tried to explain the name as a participle, and support for this has been found in some odd turns of phrase in the Phoenician inscription of Karatepe (eighth century BC), where a verbal form *yqtl* is followed by the independent pronoun of the first person. This is taken as a causative participle with a preformative *y* instead of the normal *m*. The name Yahweh would then mean 'he who supports, maintains, establishes'.[44] But this explanation is unacceptable[45] and the Karatepe forms are generally interpreted as infinitives followed by the personal pronoun.[46] Such an infinitive, without the determining pronoun, could never have become a proper name.

A case has also been made out for seeing in *Yhwh* a descriptive

---

[42] References in Ch. F. Jean and J. Hoftijzer, *Dictionnaire des Inscriptions Sémitiques de l'Ouest* (Leiden: E. J. Brill, 1965), p. 63.

[43] Cf. M. Wagner, *Die lexikalischen und grammatikalischen Aramaismen in alttestamentlichen Hebräisch*, BZAW 96 (Berlin: Verlag Alfred Töpelmann, 1966), p. 45.

[44] Cf. J. Obermann, 'The Divine Name YHWH in the Light of Recent Discoveries', *JBL* 68 (1949), pp. 301–23; 'Phoenician yqtl 'nk', *JNES* 9 (1950), pp. 94–100; 'Survival of an Old Canaanite Participle and its Impact on Biblical Exegesis', *JBL* 70 (1951), pp. 200–9, and elsewhere.

[45] Cf. G. R. Driver, 'Reflections on Recent Articles', *JBL* 73 (1954), pp. 125–31.

[46] Cf. J. M. Solá-Solé, *L'Infinitif Sémitique* (Paris: H. Champion, 1961), pp. 110–18.

substantive formed with the prefix *ya*, and certain analogous formations in Hebrew have been cited in support, e.g., יַחְמוּר, a kind of antelope (the 'red'); יַלְקוּט, the shepherd's wallet (the 'receptacle'); יַנְשׁוּף, a bird, perhaps the screech owl[47] (the 'blower'); יָרִיב, the adversary at law (the 'plaintiff'). Yahweh would then be described as 'The One who Is', 'The One who Exists'.[48] But this type of substantive is extremely rare, and can be explained as a substantified verbal imperfect;[49] this is, in fact, the explanation for the name Yahweh to which we shall adhere.

There exist in Hebrew certain personal names which may be explained in this way by a verb finite in form, and which are not hypocoristica as the names Jacob(-el) and Isaac(-el) certainly are. This explanation could be put forward for the names of Esau's sons, יְעוּשׁ and יַעְלָם (cf. Gen. 36.5, 14, 18), and for those of a descendant of Judah, יִדְבָּשׁ (I Chron. 4.3), and a descendant of Issachar, יִבְשָׂם (I Chron. 7.2). There would be nothing extraordinary in a divine name being formed in this fashion. The pre-Islamic Arabs worshipped a god *Yaġuṯ* (the name is identical with that of Esau's son יְעוּשׁ), 'he helps', and also a god *Yaʿuq*, 'he prevents (misfortune)'.[50] It remains to decide whether the name Yahweh contains the verb 'to be' in the simple form 'he is' or in the causative form 'he causes to be'.

[47] Cf. G. R. Driver, 'Birds in the Old Testament: I. Birds in Law', *PEQ* (April, 1955), p. 15.

[48] Cf. L. Koehler, 'Jod als hebräische Nominal prefix', *WdO* I (1950), pp. 404–5; Koehler and Baumgartner, *Lexicon*, pp. 357a, 369a; G. Beer, *Hebräische Grammatik*, vol. I, 2nd ed., rev. by R. Meyer (Berlin: Walter de Gruyter, 1952), ¶40, 3.

[49] So W. von Soden, *op. cit.*, p. 182.

[50] Cf. J. Wellhausen, *Reste arabisches Heidenthums*, 2nd ed. (Berlin: G. Reimer, 1897), pp. 19–24; M. Höfner, 'Die Stammesgruppen Nord- und Zentralarabiens in vorislamischer Zeit', *Wörterbuch der Mythologie*, *op. cit.*, pp. 478f.; T. Fahd, *Le panthéon de l'Arabie centrale à la veille de l'hégire* (Paris: Maisonneuve, 1968), pp. 191–7.

A certain number of authors favour this second solution.[51] The form *Yahweh*, they say, is a causative (*yaqtil*); the simple form would be *Yihweh* (*yiqtol*) and the name would therefore mean 'he causes to be', 'he is the creator'. The short form *Yahu* would be the corresponding jussive. To this, the objection has been raised that such an idea was too abstract and philosophical for so early a period,[52] or that it does not correspond with the biblical notion of God.[53] These objections are invalid. They deny to Israel notions which had long been widespread among the people who surrounded her. But the philological objections are more serious.

In this hypothesis the name Yahweh is compared with the Amorite names *Yaḥwi-ilā* and *Yawi-ilā*, which are regarded as causatives. But we have already seen that it was impossible to distinguish, from the spelling alone, between the simple and causative forms of verbs with a weak third radical. The passage of the preformative *ya-* to *yi-*, of *yaqtul(u)* to *yiqtol*, which characterizes Hebrew, had not yet come about in Amorite, at least not in proper names.[54] It is true that this change was in process in Ugaritic and in the Canaanite of the Amarna letters and that it finally occurs in classical Hebrew. But this preformative *ya-* could, in the name Yahweh, be a mark of archaism, as in the use of the root *hwh* instead of the root *hyh*. It has also been pointed out that in Hebrew the verb הָיָה is never used in the causative and

---

[51] Cf. especially, W. F. Albright, 'Contributions to Biblical Archaeology and Philology, 2. The Name Yahweh', *JBL* 43 (1924), pp. 370–8; *From the Stone Age to Christianity*, 2nd ed. (Baltimore: Johns Hopkins Press, 1946), pp. 197–9; 'Review of *L'épithète divine Jahvé Sᵉba'ôt: Étude philologique, historique et exégétique*, by B. N. Wambacq', *JBL* 67 (1948), pp. 379f.; 'Jethro, Hobab and Reuel in Early Hebrew Tradition', *CBQ* 25 (1963), p. 10, and his disciples, especially D. N. Freedman, 'The Name of the God of Moses', *JBL* 79 (1960), pp. 151–6; F. M. Cross, *op. cit.*, p. 253.

[52] Cf. among others Mowinckel, 'The Name of the God of Moses', *HUCA* 32 (1961) p. 128.

[53] So von Soden, *op. cit.*, p. 182.

[54] Cf. H. B. Huffmon, *op. cit.*, p. 64, cf. n. 25.

that other roots are used to mean 'to make', 'to create';[55] but this is unconvincing since Aramaic and Syriac regularly use the causative of *hwy/hw'*. The strongest objection to this hypothesis is that it necessitates a correction of the text (Ex. 3.14) which gives the explanation of the name Yahweh. To this problem we shall return.

We consider then that the most likely solution is that the name Yahweh is formed from the root הוה/הוי, used in the imperfect of the simple form, and that it means 'he is'. But, in Hebrew, this root had become היה and the vocalization of the verbal form had been modified: the name cannot be explained from the Hebrew which we know. This causes some difficulty for the interpretation given in Ex. 3.14, and this gives us good reason for presuming the name to be pre-Israelite, although we have seen that, so far, it is not certainly attested outside Israel before the time of Moses.

IV. THE BIBLICAL INTERPRETATION OF THE NAME YAHWEH

But what we are above all concerned with is the interpretation given to this name in the theophany at the burning bush, Ex. 3.13–15:

> [13] Then Moses said to God, 'If I come to the people of Israel and say to them, "The God of your fathers has sent me to you," and they ask me, "What is his name?" what shall I say to them?'
>
> [14] God said to Moses, 'אֶהְיֶה אֲשֶׁר אֶהְיֶה'. And he said, 'Say this to the people of Israel, "אֶהְיֶה has sent me to you." '
>
> [15] God also said to Moses, 'Say this to the people of Israel, "יהוה, the God of your fathers, the God of Abraham, the God of Isaac and the God of Jacob has sent me to you": this is my name for ever, and thus I am to be remembered throughout all generations.'

This is the only explicit explanation of the divine name in the Bible. It is in keeping with the philological interpretation which

[55] This is the principal objection raised by W. Eichrodt, *Theology of the Old Testament*, vol. I, trans. John Baker (London: SCM Press and Philadelphia: Westminster Press, 1961), p. 187.

we have advocated, for it recognizes in the name the simple imperfect of the root 'to be'. Those who postulate a causative sense are forced to presume that the primitive formula was אַהְיֶה אֲשֶׁר יִהְיֶה: 'I cause to be what comes into existence.'[56] And for this restoration they can call upon Egyptian parallels such as 'he is the one who makes exist that which will exist' in a hymn to Amenhemet III,[57] or the invocation to 'him who makes everything exist' found several times in the great hymn to Amon.[58] Alternatively one could simply change the vocalization to אַהְיֶה אֲשֶׁר אַהְיֶה: 'I cause to be that which I cause to be, I create that which I create.'[59] The formula would have been corrected when the old causative of הָיָה became obsolete. But, since philology does not enable us to establish the causative sense of the name Yahweh, to correct the Massoretic text in order to make it conform to a hypothesis is totally arbitrary. It is the text itself which must be explained.

At a first reading one has the impression of witnessing the formation of the divine name. God is the One who Is. Speaking of himself he cannot say 'he is', which would be tantamount to recognizing a Being other than himself. He must say 'I am', and it is 'I am' who will send Moses. But Moses cannot say 'I am', since he is not the One who Is: he says, therefore, 'he is'.

But the text is obviously overweighted. In v. 13 Moses asks the name of the God of the fathers; v. 14 does not give the answer, since the God of Israel was never called אֶהְיֶה. The answer is

---

[56] Cf. P. Haupt, 'Der Name Jahwe', *OLZ* 12 (1909), col. 211–14; W. F. Albright, 'Contributions to Biblical Archaeology and Philology, 2. The Name Yahweh', *JBL* 43 (1924), pp. 376f.; *From the Stone Age to Christianity*, p. 198.

[57] On a stele in the Cairo Museum, cf. M. Kamel, 'The Stela of Seḥetep-îb-rēʿ in the Egyptian Museum', *ASAE* 40 (1940–41), pp. 209–29, see p. 217.

[58] *ANET*, 2nd ed. (Princeton University Press, 1955), pp. 365–7.

[59] D. N. Freedman, 'The Name of the God of Moses', *JBL* 79 (1960), pp. 152f.

given in v. 15: the name of the God of the fathers is Yahweh. Moreover, there are certain repetitions: '[14] God said . . . And he said . . . [15] God also said. . . .' It appears that v. 15 is basic, that v. 14a has been added to provide an explanation of the name and that v. 14b, which uses the same words as v. 15 except for אֶהְיֶה instead of יהוה, is a link between the name itself and the explanation of it.[60] It thus appears that the name Yahweh – whatever its original meaning may have been – came to Israel from outside and was then explained and given a new religious sense.[61]

What is the explanation which is given? In Hebrew, the ancient form for completed action (perfect-present), *yaqtul*, has disappeared and been replaced by the *qatal* and the *wayyiqtol*, the form for uncompleted action (imperfect-future), *yaqtulu*, has become *yiqtol*. Whatever the solution to the thorny problem of the 'tenses' or 'aspects' of the Hebrew verb,[62] the use of the verb הָיָה is sufficiently clear. The *yiqtol* of the verb הָיָה as an active verb, 'to happen, to become', is sometimes used to express the frequentative past, as in Num. 9.16, 20f.: 'and so it was', more rarely for the frequentative present, as in Eccles. 1.9: 'what will continue

[60] Following M. Noth, *Exodus*, p. 43, against those who hold v. 15 to be secondary. But v. 14 represents an early development of the Elohist tradition, as Noth says; it is not a late gloss as B. D. Eerdmans claims in *Alttestamentliche Studien* (Giessen: Alfred Töpelmann, 1910), pp. 12–14. The text of Ex. 3.14 was already known to Hosea, cf. below.
[61] See W. Zimmerli, *Gottes Offenbarung* (Munich: Chr. Kaiser Verlag, 1963), p. 280; R. C. Dentan, *The Knowledge of God in Ancient Israel* (New York: The Seabury Press, 1968), pp. 131 and 257, n. 7.
[62] Cf. C. Brockelmann, *Hebräische Syntax* (Neukirchen: Verlag der Buchhandlung des Erziehungsverein, 1956), pp. 37–45, with references to previous works; F. Rundgren, *Das althebräische Verbum: Abriss der Aspektlehre* (Stockholm: Almqvist and Wiksell, 1961), and the review by R. Meyer, *OLZ* 59 (1964), col. 117–26; A. Sperber, *A Historical Grammar of Biblical Hebrew* (Leiden: E. J. Brill, 1966), especially pp. 587–92. The work of O. L. Barnes, *A New Approach to the Problem of the Hebrew Tenses* (Oxford: J. Thornton and Son, 1965), throws little light on the question.

to be'. The *yiqṭol* of הָיָה as a stative verb, 'to be', always has a future sense, 'he will be'.[63] According to normal Hebrew usage, the formula would therefore mean 'I shall be who I shall be', and it is thus that both Aquila and Theodotion rendered it: ἔσομαι ὅς ἔσομαι.

It has recently been affirmed that this is the correct meaning.[64] In the preceding verses God says to Moses, 'I will send you . . . that you may bring forth my people, the sons of Israel, out of Egypt' (Ex. 3.10). And later, 'I will be with you' (Ex. 3.12). A little further on, on two occasions, God says to him 'I will be with your mouth' (Ex. 4.12, 15). In this context of salvation and promise, the name Yahweh would mean that God will always be present with Israel. The same perspective is found again in the Priestly account of the revelation of the divine name, 'And I will take you for my people, and I will be your God; and you shall know that I am Yahweh your God, who has brought you out from under the burdens of the Egyptians' (Ex. 6.7). The formula, 'I will take you for my people, and I will be your God', was to become a summary of the Covenant and it is particularly frequent in Jeremiah and Ezekiel.[65]

We shall see that these ideas of presence, promise and covenant are indeed embodied in the theophany of Ex. 3, but it seems difficult to allow that, in Ex. 3.14, אֶהְיֶה should be translated by a future. In all the parallel texts which have been cited, 'I shall be' is determined by an addition. One can say: 'I shall be this or that, I shall be with . . . like . . . for . . .', but one cannot say absolutely 'I shall be' in the first person, as this would suggest that the

---

[63] Cf. P. Joüon, *Grammaire de l'hebreu biblique*, 2nd ed. (Rome: Institut Biblique Pontifical, 1947), paras. 111 *i* and 113*a*.

[64] Cf. R. Abba, 'The Divine Name Yahweh', *JBL* 80 (1961), pp. 320–28.

[65] The texts are collected by K. Baltzer, *Das Bundesformular* (Neukirchen: Verlag der Buchhandlung des Erziehungsvereins, 1960), p. 46; J. L'Hour, *La Morale de l'alliance* (Paris: J. Gabalda, 1966), p. 35. Cf. R. Smend, *Die Bundesformel* (Zurich: EVZ-Verlag, 1963), pp. 5ff.

speaker does not yet exist. It is quite true that the formula 'I shall be who I shall be' is so determined, but this is the explanation of the name, which is itself absolute, and cannot be translated by 'I shall be'. It would seem that this future is only an apparent one, and that it originates from the effort made to interpret the old name Yahweh by the same Hebrew grammatical form, although that form no longer expressed the completed action (perfect-present) of the ancient *yaqtul. It is this sense which should be retained here rather than that of normal Hebrew usage. It is thus that the LXX understood it, 'Εγώ εἰμί, as do almost all modern translations.

The formula of Ex. 3.14 employs a stylistic device which is sometimes incorrectly termed 'paranomasia'.[66] Linguistically, paranomasia is the juxtaposition of words which, though they show a certain similarity, either etymological or merely formal and external, do not have the same sense.[67] In this verse, it is a case of the repeated use of the same root with the same sense, and what interests us is the use of the same verb in the same person both in the principal clause and also in the dependent relative clause. This is a stylistic device in which Arab authors particularly indulge, but which is common to the Semitic languages and which serves several purposes.[68] The device is found several times in Hebrew where it is used to express something undetermined: 'Send him whom you will send' (Ex. 4.13); 'Bake what you will bake and boil what you will boil' (Ex. 16.23); 'They went whithersoever they went' (I Sam. 23.13); 'I go whither I go' (II Sam. 15.20); 'Sojourn wherever you can sojourn' (II Kings 8.1), etc.

[66] Cf. P. Joüon, *op. cit.*, para. 158 *o*; H. Reckendorf, *Über Paranomasie in den semitischen Sprachen* (Giessen, 1909).

[67] Cf. J. Marouzeau, *Lexique de la terminologie linguistique* (Paris: Paul Geuthner, 1933). It is in this correct sense that the word is understood in the case of Hebrew by I. M. Casanowitz, *Paranomasia in the Old Testament* (Boston, 1894) and E. König, *Stilistik, Rhetorik, Poetik* (Leipzig: Dieterich'sche Verlags, Theodor Weicher, 1900), pp. 291ff.

[68] Cf. H. Reckendorf, *op. cit.*, pp. 156f.; T. C. Vriezen, "Ehje 'Ašer 'Ehje', *Festschrift Alfred Bertholet*, ed. W. Baumgartner and others (Tübingen: J. C. B. Mohr [Paul Siebeck], 1950), pp. 498–511.

According to certain authors,[69] this undetermined sense could well be that of the formula used in Ex. 3.14. 'I am who I am', 'I am that I am' would be an evasive answer. Yahweh would be refusing to reveal the mystery of his being: he is the Unnameable, the Incomprehensible, the Indeterminable. A comparison is sometimes made with the scene at the Jabbok, where Jacob asks the name of the mysterious being with whom he is wrestling, and this being replies: 'Why is it that you ask my name?' (Gen. 32.30).[70] When Manoah puts the same question, Yahweh's angel replies, 'Why do you ask my name, seeing it is wonderful?' (Judg. 13.18). But precisely in these two cases the divinity is refusing to give his name, whereas in Ex. 3.13–15, he is revealing it: this name is Yahweh. The formula must therefore have a positive sense. The conclusion is all the more certain if, as we have shown, v. 15 is original and v. 14 secondary. The formula 'I am who I am' is not an evasive answer, but an attempt at explaining the divine name which has been revealed, and this explanation must of necessity be positive.

Furthermore, the same stylistic device can also express totality or intensity. Thus, 'I will be gracious to whom I will be gracious and will show mercy on whom I will show mercy' (Ex. 33.19), means 'I am indeed he who is gracious and shows mercy'. 'I will speak the word which I will speak, and it will be performed' (Ezek. 12.25) means 'All my words will be performed'. 'When they came to the nations, wherever they came, they profaned my holy name' (Ezek. 36.20) means 'Among all the nations where they came they profaned my name'. One can draw a parallel between this intensive meaning and a remarkably similar Egyptian expression. In the Instructions to his son Meri-ka-re',

[69] A. M. Dubarle, 'La signification du nom Iahweh', *RSPhTh* 35 (1951), pp. 3–21, with references to previous works; G. Lambert, 'Que signifie le nom divin YHWH?', *NRTh* 74 (1952), pp. 897–915, and with variations, O. Eissfeldt, 'Jahwe, der Gott der Väter', *ThLZ* 88 (1963), cols. 481–90, esp. col. 483.
[70] This parallel is developed by O. Eissfeldt, 'Jakobs Begegnung mit El und Moses Begegnung mit Jahwe', *OLZ* 58 (1963), cols. 325–31.

at the end of the third millennium BC, the Pharaoh Akhthoës, speaking of his victories over the Bedouin who were threatening the frontiers of Egypt, says 'I am while I am'.[71] This is an affirmation that he exists and that he acts with power.

We should perhaps go a step further. A century ago A. Knobel and E. Reuss translated our text: 'I am he who is',[72] by analogy with the rule of Hebrew syntax that, when the subject of the principal clause is in the first or second person, the corresponding word in the relative clause is in the same person.[73] Recently, this translation has again been adopted and supported by fuller arguments.[74] A comparison has been drawn between 'I am Yahweh who (i.e., *I*) brought you from Ur of the Chaldeans' (Gen. 15.7) and the stereotyped phrase: 'I am Yahweh your God, who (i.e., *I*) brought you out of the land of Egypt' (cf. Ex. 20.2; 29.46; Lev. 19.36; 25.28; Deut. 5.6, etc.). Also, 'Are you the man who (i.e., *you*) came from Judah?' (I Kings 13.14) and 'It is I who (i.e., *I*) have sinned and done very wickedly' (I Chron. 21.17). If Ex. 3.14 had for its text אֶהְיֶה אֲשֶׁר יְהְיֶה, one would not hesitate to translate 'I am he who is', and one can hold that this is the sense which the writer had in mind, since he wished to explain the name Yahweh as the verb 'to be' in the third person; but this syntactical rule prevented his saying it. This is the sense which the LXX translators, who understood Hebrew, retained: Ἐγώ εἰμί ὁ ὤν.

Whether one accepts the translation 'I am he who is', or whether one adheres to the more current 'I am that I am', the formula

[71] *ANET*, 2nd ed., p. 416 (l. 95); cf. A. Alt, 'Ein ägyptisches Gegenstück zu Ex. 3.14', *ZAW* 58 (1940), pp. 159f.
[72] Cf. A. Knobel, *Kurzgefasstes exegetisches Kommentar zum AT. Die Bücher Exodus und Leviticus* (Leipzig, 1857); E. Reuss, *La Bible* (Paris, 1879).
[73] Cf. C. Brockelmann, *op. cit.*, ¶153 a.
[74] E. Schild, 'On Exodus iii 14 – "I am that I am" ', *VT* 4 (1954), pp. 296–302; J. Lindblom, 'Noch einmal die Deutung des Jahwe-Namen', *ASTI* 3 (1964), pp. 4–15. But see the reservations of O. Eissfeldt, 'Äh°yäh °ašär 'ah°yäh 'Ēl 'ōlām', *FuF* 39 (1965), pp. 298–300.

still explains the name Yahweh in terms of the verb 'to be'. One must take care not to introduce into it the metaphysical notion of Being in itself, of aseity as elaborated by Greek philosophy. However, it is not certain, though it is sometimes said, that the LXX translation already reflects the influence of Greek thought, and we shall come to the LXX interpretation without any such supposition. But the influence of Greek thought is manifest in the Wisdom of Solomon, where the whole creation is contrasted with 'he who is' (cf. Wisd. Sol. 13.1). This metaphysical sense was developed by the mediaeval scholastics and is still retained in some Old Testament 'Theologies'.[75] Such a notion is foreign to the biblical mentality, for which 'to be' is first and foremost 'to exist' – in the terms of existentialist philosophy, a *Dasein*. But this existence, this *Dasein*, is realized in many different ways, and there is a danger of loading the formula of Ex. 3.14 with all the potentialities of existence and, finally, of including in it the whole biblical teaching about God.[76]

We shall not review all the proposed solutions, both ancient and modern, but simply accept the usual meaning of the verb הָיָה and its function in the Hebrew language. In the phrase אֶהְיֶה אֲשֶׁר אֶהְיֶה, the relative clause אֲשֶׁר אֶהְיֶה is the predicate of אֶהְיֶה; as are many relative clauses, this one is the equivalent of a participle. Again, we adhere to the LXX translation. With another verb and

[75] Cf. P. Heinisch, *Theology of the Old Testament*, trans. W. Heidt (Collegeville, Minnesota: The Liturgical Press, 1950), pp. 55–57; F. Ceuppens, *Theologia Biblica*, vol. I, 2nd ed. (Rome: Taurini, Marietti, 1949), pp. 27, 30.

[76] Cf. C. H. Ratschow, *Werden und Wirken. Eine Untersuchung des Wortes hajah als Beitrag zur Wirklischkeitserfassung des Alten Testaments* (Berlin: A. Töpelmann, 1941), p. 81; T. Boman, *Hebrew Thought Compared with Greek*, trans. J. Moreau (London: SCM Press, 1960 and Philadelphia: Westminster Press, 1961), p. 49, for whom Ex. 3.14 means that there is no other *hayah* like the *hayah* of God which includes at one and the same time 'being' and 'becoming', 'existence' and 'action'. Cf. the incisive criticism of this approach by J. Barr, *The Semantics of Biblical Language* (London: Oxford University Press, 1961), pp. 68–72, although he does not refer specifically to our text.

in a different context, Hebrew would use the personal pronoun אֲנִי followed by a participle. But the participle of הָיָה is never used, and the first אֶהְיֶה takes the place of אֲנִי because the explanation plays on the etymology of the name Yahweh and the verb had to be given prominence. Now if we replace the relative clause by the divine name (which its purpose is to explain), it will be seen that the formula of Ex. 3.14 is equivalent to אֲנִי יהוה, 'I am Yahweh'.

This expression[77] occurs repeatedly in the parallel Priestly account (cf. Ex. 6.2, 6, 7, 8) and is also very frequent in the Priestly source in the Pentateuch in general, in particular in the 'Holiness Code', and in Deutero-Isaiah and Ezekiel. But it is already found in the Yahwist (cf. Gen. 15.7; 28.13) as well as in the Elohist (Ex. 20.2); and in Hosea it occurs with reference to the revelation of the divine name in Ex. 3, 'I am Yahweh your God from the land of Egypt' (Hos. 12.10 [EVV, v. 9]; 13.4).

In sum, the best rendering of the formula of Ex. 3.14 is 'I am He who Exists'. Yahweh is the God whom Israel must recognize as really existing.[78] The exegesis of this verse could stop there, and we must remember that the text is intended to give us an explanation of the divine name and not a definition of God.

But, for a Semite, a proper name is itself a definition of the person who bears it, and one might ask what meaning the Elohist writer gave to the name Yahweh when he explained it as 'He who Exists'. The enquiry should not begin from a philosophy of Being, nor from the possible uses of the Hebrew verb הָיָה, nor from the general biblical concept of God. It must start from the immediate context or from near at hand in the same source, and it can extend to embrace the rest of the Elohist tradition, but not beyond.

[77] Cf. W. Zimmerli, 'Ich bin Jahwe', *Geschichte und Altes Testament*, A. Alt *Festschrift* (Tübingen: J. C. B. Mohr, 1953), pp. 179–209; K. Elliger, 'Ich bin der Herr – euer Gott', *Theologie als Glaubenswagnis*, K. Heim *Festschrift* (Hamburg: Furche-Verlag, 1954), pp. 9–34.
[78] Cf. J. Lindblom, *op. cit.*, p. 12.

As to the context, immediately before the revelation of the name God calls Israel his people (Ex. 3.10); it is this people which Moses is to bring out of Egypt (Ex. 3.11), and God will be with Moses for this purpose (Ex. 3.12). When the Elohist source resumes after the revelation, Yahweh says to Moses: 'I will be with your mouth' (Ex. 4.12), and again: 'I will be with your mouth and with his (Aaron's) mouth' (Ex. 4.15). According to Ex. 4.22f., which there is no reason to deny to the Elohist,[79] Moses is to say to Pharaoh: 'Thus says Yahweh, "Israel is my first-born son . . . let my son go." ' Yahweh, then, is 'with Moses'. Already the God of the Fathers had been with Abraham (Gen. 21.22 [E]); with Isaac (Gen. 26.3, 28 [J]) and with Jacob (Gen. 28.15; 31.3 [J]).

It was a personal or family relationship, he was the father's God. Now Yahweh is with Moses for the service of the people, and it is with the people that Yahweh is united in a remarkable way. Israel is his people, his first-born son. The care of the people is of prime importance: Yahweh sends Moses to lead them out of Egypt and orders Pharaoh to let them go, and it is for their good that he reveals his name. The consequence is implicit: Israel must recognize that Yahweh is for her the only one who exists and the only saviour. This is not a dogmatic definition of an abstract monotheism, but the injunction of a practical monotheism,[80] and henceforth Israel will have no other God but Yahweh. Furthermore, the fundamental article of the people's faith is already included in this revelation: it is Yahweh who will bring the people out of Egypt, compare Ex. 3.9–11 with Deut. 26.5–9. And last, the way is paved for the Covenant: Israel becomes the people of God.

We meet these ideas again in a more explicit form, in the same Elohist tradition, in connection with the theophany at Mount Horeb, which complements that of the burning bush and is foreshadowed in it; cf. Ex. 3.12 and Ex. 3.1. It is on Mount Horeb,

[79] Cf. G. Fohrer, *Überlieferung und Geschichte des Exodus*, BZAW 91 (Berlin: Verlag Alfred Töpelmann, 1964), p. 41.
[80] So Lindblom, *loc. cit.*; G. W. Anderson, *History and Religion of Israel* (London: Oxford University Press, 1966), p. 37.

through the medium of Moses, that Yahweh solemnly joins himself to his people by means of a covenant of which the Decalogue is the charter. The proclamation of the Decalogue begins with 'I am Yahweh', and we have already noted how this corresponds with the formula of Ex. 3.14, and goes on to recall God's act of deliverance, 'I am Yahweh your God, who brought you out of the land of Egypt' (Ex. 20.2; first announced in Ex. 3.9f.). The first commandment is: 'You shall have no other gods before me' (Ex. 20.3). Yahweh demands an exclusive worship, for he is a 'jealous God' (Ex. 20.5). He is the only one who Exists. In Ex. 33,[81] Moses asks Yahweh to reveal to him his דֶּרֶךְ, his mode of being (Ex. 33.13), and Yahweh replies: 'I will proclaim before you my name "Yahweh"; and I will be gracious to whom I will be gracious, and will show mercy on whom I will show mercy' (Ex. 33.19). This seems to be parallel to Ex. 3.14, with its use of the same stylistic device. The commentary on this declaration is to be found in Ex. 34.6, where it is not easy to decide to which source the verse belongs: 'Yahweh passed before him (Moses), and proclaimed, "Yahweh, Yahweh, a God merciful and gracious ... " '

If we consider the Elohist tradition as a whole and what differentiates its doctrine from that of the Yahwist tradition,[82] we can distinguish the following elements in the revelation of Ex. 3.9–15: the special interest accorded to the people, the awareness of the transcendence and mystery of God, and the manifestation and activity of God realized through the medium of Moses.

One might also call upon Hosea as a witness to the Elohist

[81] Scholars generally do not attempt to distinguish between J and E in this chapter and M. Noth, *Überlieferungsgeschichte des Pentateuch*, 2nd ed. (Stuttgart: W. Kohlhammer Verlag, 1960), p. 33, n. 114, does not detect any traces of E there. But H. Seebass does find traces of E in the verses that I refer to and draws attention to their similarity to Ex. 3.13f., which anticipates and summarizes the Sinai tradition, cf. his *Mose und Aaron: Sinai und Gottesberg* (Bonn: H. Bouvier and Co. Verlag, 1962), pp. 18f., 23f.; *Der Erzvater Israel und die Einführung der Jahweverehrung in Kanaan*, BZAW 98 (Berlin: Verlag Alfred Töpelmann, 1966), pp. 58, 61.

[82] Cf. L. Ruppert, 'Der Elohist – Sprecher für Gottes Volk', *Wort und Botschaft*, ed. J. Schreiner (Würzburg: Echter-Verlag, 1967), pp. 108–17.

tradition.[83] In his work one can find several reminiscences of, and a kind of commentary on, the theophany at the burning bush. He speaks of Moses as a prophet (Hos. 12.14 [EVV, v. 13]), which recalls Ex. 4.12, 15, cf. 16, and is taken up again in Deut. 18.15. He places in Egypt the beginning of faith in Yahweh: 'I am Yahweh your God from the land of Egypt . . .' (Hos. 12.10 [EVV, v. 9]), and from this he draws the inference: 'I am Yahweh your God from the land of Egypt: you know no God but me, and besides me there is no saviour' (Hos. 13.4). Since the time in Egypt, Yahweh has called Israel his son (cf. Ex. 4.22), but the more he so called him, the more this son sacrificed to the Baals (Hos. 11.1f.). Hosea contains the only explicit reference to the formula of Ex. 3.14 which can be found in the whole of the Old Testament: 'Call his name לֹא עַמִּי, for you are not my people and for you I am not, לֹא אֶהְיֶה' (Hos. 1.9).[84] The parallel with לֹא עַמִּי makes לֹא אֶהְיֶה into a proper name: just as 'my people' in Ex. 3.10 becomes 'Not-my-people', so אֶהְיֶה in Ex. 3.14b becomes לֹא אֶהְיֶה. Israel's infidelity has broken the covenant which the theophany at the burning bush foreshadowed and which was concluded on Mount Horeb. But this covenant will be restored: instead of calling the Israelites 'Not-my-people', they will be called 'Sons of the living God' (Hos. 2.1 [EVV, 1.10]).

Illuminated thus by its context and placed in the setting of the Elohist tradition, the explanation of the divine name in Ex. 3.14 can be interpreted as follows: Yahweh is the only real 'Existing

---

[83] Cf. O. Procksch, *Das nordhebräische Sagenbuch. Die Elohimquelle* (Leipzig: J. C. Hinrichs Verlag, 1909), pp. 248–55; S. Herrmann, *Die prophetischen Heilswartungen im Alten Testament*, BWANT V, 5 (Stuttgart: W. Kohlhammer Verlag, 1965), p. 108.

[84] Cf. H. W. Wolff, *Dodekapropheton, I. Hosea*, 2nd ed. (Neukirchen: Verlag der Buchhandlung der Erziehungsvereins, 1965), pp. 23f.; E. Jacob, *Osée*, etc. (Neuchâtel: Delachaux and Niestlé, 1965), p. 22. The correction 'I shall not be *your* God', adopted by many critics and recently by A. Weiser, *Die Propheten: Hosea*, etc., 2nd ed. (Göttingen: Vandenhoeck and Ruprecht, 1967) and R. Smend, *op. cit.*, p. 38, n. 73 is supported by only a few minuscules of the LXX.

74

One'. This means that he is transcendent and remains a mystery for man. But he is active in the history of his people Israel, and this people must recognize him as its only God and its only saviour. The narrative of Ex. 3.9–15 underlines at the same time the continuity of this faith with that of the fathers and also the novelty expressed by the divine name thus interpreted. It is by its adherence to that faith that the people of Israel will come into being as a nation, and it is on that faith that its religion will be founded. Israel will be united by belief in a God who has no sacred history, such as have the mythological gods, because he is simply, totally and forever the Existing One, but also one who, at the same time, directs the course of human events.

He is a God who reveals himself not in the natural phenomena of the cycle of the seasons, as do the gods of fertility and vegetation, but who shows himself in events which follow one another in time and which he directs towards a goal. This is a religious concept totally different from those which the Hebrews had known in Egypt, and from those which they were to find in Canaan. The historian of religions cannot help but be struck by this extraordinary novelty, while the believer will see in it the intervention of God. Exodus 3.14 contains in embryo the developments which the progress of revelation will draw from it, and, in the perspective of faith, the profound meaning which theologians have read into it is justified. Without going outside the Bible, 'I am he who exists' finds its echo and its commentary in the last book of the Scriptures: ' "I am the Alpha and the Omega," says the Lord God, who is, and who was, and who is to come, the Almighty' (Rev. 1.8).

4

The Deuteronomic Legislator — a Proto-Rabbinic Type

J. Weingreen

THE title of this paper will indicate my involvement in a wide field of study which I term 'the continuity of tradition from Old Testament to early Rabbinic times'. Briefly, my overall interest is to demonstrate that certain Rabbinic religious institutions, modes of legislation, types of exposition of the sacred Scriptures and folklore, the evolved forms of which are found in the literature of the *Mishna*, are already discernable, in rudimentary form, in the Masoretic Hebrew Old Testament. It is not essential for our general purpose to attempt to place the conclusions of this broad study within a fixed and concise chronological framework. One may say, however, that such Rabbinic-type processes are compatible with the crystallizing or maturing of social, political and religious institutions in ancient Israel and may well have been operative in the Davidic or Solomonic periods. This paper is confined to the phenomenon of Deuteronomic literary and legislative activity which, according to the generally accepted critical view, falls within the latter portion of the pre-exilic period of Israel's history. Furthermore, this study will deal with a special kind of legislative process which is usually recognized as being Rabbinic in character and therefore generally designated as such. However, it is not necessarily, on that account, to be regarded as being of Rabbinic origin. On the contrary, my purpose is to demonstrate that this kind of legislative machinery could be traced back to much earlier antecedents and, in fact, was already employed by the Deuteronomic legislator. By pointing out a direct line of continuity in a legislative method from the Deuteronomist to the Mishnaic Rabbis, the extreme antiquity of the Rabbinic tradition will have been established. A final point to be mentioned in these introductory remarks is that this paper is based on the results of earlier studies of mine and reference to these will be made as the theme unfolds.

My starting-point is a paper which I read to the World Congress of Jewish Studies, held in Jerusalem in 1965. The subject was Saul and the Habiru',[1] and the purpose of this study was to restore a lost page of early Israelite history. The main conclusion arrived at was that, in the initial stages of Saul's reign, the *Habiru* had actively involved themselves in the crucial struggle which was waged between the Israelites and the Canaanites for the mastery of the land of Canaan. By adopting the simple principle, already familiar to scholars, of reading *Habiru* for the Hebrew term עִבְרִי[2] and applying it wherever that term occurred in the Masoretic Hebrew text of I Samuel, and with an occasional restoration of this term with the aid of the LXX, the conclusion was reached that the *Habiru* were a third military force which appeared on the scene at this time. However, it is not relevant to my present purpose to summarize the arguments I produced in that paper or to mention the new renderings which flowed from them. My immediate interest is the final phase of that paper which dealt with the law of the עֶבֶד עִבְרִי, as laid down in Ex. 21.2ff. The RSV, following the traditional interpretation, translates the text thus: 'When you buy a Hebrew slave, he shall serve six years, and in the seventh he shall go out free, for nothing.' The rendering 'a Hebrew slave' is misleading, in view of the identification of the term

[1] Fourth World Union of Jewish Studies, Papers, vol. 1 (Jerusalem, 1967), pp. 63–66.
[2] Julius Lewy, 'Origin and Signification of the Biblical Term "Hebrew"', *HUCA* 28 (1957), pp. 1–13.

עִבְרִי with *Habiru*. I fully endorsed the view, so convincingly expressed by Julius Lewy, that this law referred, not to an Israelite slave bought by a fellow Israelite, but to a *Habiru* who had bound himself to the service of an Israelite.[3] It is now well known that the traditional mode of life of the *Habiru* was such that, in times of peace when there was no call for their enlistment as mercenary soldiers, they would often voluntarily enter serf-like service for a limited period.[4] The law in Ex. 21 was designed to fix and regulate the terms of such *Habiru* service under an Israelite master.

We may now move on to consider this law, as it appears in a revised version in Deut. 15.12ff., and to try to understand the reasons or motives for its modification at the hands of the Deuteronomic legislator. He was placed in an awkward dilemma regarding the relevance of this law of Ex. 21 in his day. By this time, not only had the *Habiru* disappeared from the scene as a class of society but, apparently, all knowledge of their former existence had been lost. By now the term עִבְרִי in the Old Testament had come to mean Israelite. This identification, apparently, was reinforced by such Pentateuchal references as 'Abram the עִבְרִי' (Gen. 14.13) and 'the God of the עִבְרִים' (Ex. 5.3), the latter being parallel with an earlier description, 'Yahweh, the God of Israel' (Ex. 5.1). The assumption that biblical texts in which the term עִבְרִים occurred were to be understood as relating to the Israelites or, in some instances, to their forebears posed a serious problem to the Deuteronomic legislator. Leviticus 25.39ff. lays down the terms by which an impoverished Israelite may enter into the service of a fellow Israelite, but it expressly prohibits the reduction of an Israelite bondman to the status of a slave – 'You shall not make him serve as a slave' (v. 39) and 'they shall not be sold as slaves' (v. 42). Slaves could be acquired from the surrounding nations or

[3] Julius Lewy, *op. cit.*, pp. 3f.
[4] Cyrus H. Gordon, *The Living Past* (New York: The John Day Co., Inc., 1941), p. 161.

from resident aliens (vv. 44–46a), but not from among the Israelites. It followed, then, that even though the term עִבְרִי in the law of Ex. 21 was taken to designate an Israelite – and for this identification compare the renderings of both Targum Onkelos and Jonathan עבדא בר ישראל – yet, in the light of Lev. 25 this regulation could not be interpreted as having any reference to an Israelite slave acquired by a fellow Israelite. On the other hand, the law of the עֶבֶד עִבְרִי was on the divine statute book and could be neither erased nor ignored.

In this dilemma only one solution was possible for the Deuteronomic legislator. He had to modify the law of Ex. 21 by interpretation in such a way as to achieve two significant results. First, this interpretation had to be designed so as to eliminate any suggestion that it dealt with the enslavement of an Israelite by another Israelite, even for a limited period. Secondly, it was essential to make this Exodus law conform with, and extend the provisions of, other existing related laws, such as those which recognized the propriety and, therefore, regulated the terms of service entered into by an Israelite bondman or bondwoman under an Israelite master. A distinction in thought, if not in language, had to be made between the status of a bondman and that of a slave. A male Israelite could voluntarily become the bondman of a fellow Israelite through the exigencies of poverty (Lev. 25.39ff.) or compulsorily, as the penalty to be paid by a convicted robber who had not the means to make the statutory restitution (Ex. 21.37 [EVV, 22.1]; 22.3 [EVV, v. 4], which properly belongs to the former passage). In the case of a female, the law in Ex.21.7ff. lays down the conditions whereby an Israelite may sell his daughter into the service of another Israelite. The harmonization of the law of the עֶבֶד עִבְרִי of Ex. 21 with those just cited was an imperative need and this was finally achieved by the simple method of giving practical expression to their re-interpretation of this law by rewriting the statement of the law in the Deuteronomic version. This new version now appeared as a development of, or advancement upon, existing laws concerning the entry of an Israelite into the service of another Israelite.

Before attempting to illustrate how the Deuteronomic legislator achieved his objective, it will be instructive to see first how the later Rabbinic authorities dealt with this awkward situation. What will emerge from this examination will be that they too were faced with the same dilemma as their Deuteronomic predecessor and that they had to employ methods of interpretation analogous to his in order to achieve a harmonization of seemingly conflicting laws. In this connection it is interesting to note that the mediaeval Jewish commentator Rashi surprisingly raises the question as to whether or not the term עֶבֶד עִבְרִי in Ex. 21.2 is to be understood as meaning 'the slave of an Israelite', as opposed to the inadmissible rendering 'an Israelite slave'. Furthermore, Ibn Ezra, while insisting that the designation עִבְרִי in this connection must necessarily refer to an Israelite, nevertheless mentions the view, which he rejects, that it could denote a non-Israelite descendant of the patriarch Abraham who, according to tradition, was known as an עִבְרִי because of his descent from his ancestor עֵבֶר. This interpretation would identify the עִבְרִי slave as being either an Ishmaelite or Edomite. The fact that alternative interpretations of the term עֶבֶד עִבְרִי were in circulation sufficiently to attract attention suggests some uncertainty and uneasiness about the correct identification of the subject of the law in Ex. 21.2. However, both these commentators are agreed that the formula כִּי תִקְנֶה, 'When you buy or acquire', used in Ex. 21.2 carries with it the implication that purchase or acquisition can be secured only by means of a legal process to be effected by authorized law officers, acting as the law demands. This line of casuistic argument produced the interpretation that the law in Ex. 21 deals specifically with the case of a convicted thief who did not possess the means of making the prescribed restitution. He is, in consequence, sold into service for a limited period by the court authorities. Targum Jonathan bears

out this interpretation by rendering the Hebrew עבד עבד תקנה כי
as ארום תיזבון בגנבותיה לעבדא בר ישראל, 'when you acquire an Israelite bondman because of his theft', thereby giving expression to the official Rabbinic exposition of this law. The point I
am trying to bring home is this. Because the Levitical law would not
tolerate the enslavement of an Israelite by a fellow Israelite, the interpretation of the law in Ex. 21.2 had, of necessity, to flow from
the premiss that it could have no reference to an Israelite slave, in
spite of the identification of the term with Israelite. They were,
consequently, forced to relate it to the convicted Israelite thief
who defaulted in the matter of the prescribed restitution. This kind
of manipulative interpretation of legal texts does not represent a
late phenomenon developed by the Mishnaic Rabbis. It was
already in operation at the time of the Deuteronomist and reflects
changed sociological conditions which brought such modifications
into effect.

Let us now examine this law, as it is represented in its revised
form in Deut. 15.12ff. The RSV translation of this text is: 'If
your brother a Hebrew man, or a Hebrew woman, is sold to you,
he shall serve you six years and in the seventh year you shall let
him go free from you. And when you let him go free from you,
you shall not let him go empty-handed. You shall furnish him
liberally out of your flock, out of your threshing floor and out of
your wine press.' It seems to me that this rendering, the conventional one, does not accurately represent the Hebrew thinking and
continuity underlying this Hebrew passage. If I may paraphrase
the intent of this text I would say that the correct understanding
of it is 'If your brother an עִבְרִי (i.e., an Israelite) sells himself to

you (i.e., in accordance with the provisions of Lev. 25.39ff.) and, in
parenthesis, this applies also to a Israelite bondwoman (in accordance with the law in Ex. 21.7) and this bondman serves you for six
years and you let him go free in the seventh year (i.e., as laid down
in Ex. 21.2) then, when you set him free, do not let him go empty-
handed, but furnish him liberally with livestock, grain and wine.'

This passage is in two parts. There is, first, an introductory portion which states the special circumstances with which the legislator is dealing and this is followed by the introduction of the new law appertaining to these circumstances. This is the pattern of the legislation in both Ex. 21 and Lev. 25. In the former the text states that it is dealing with the situation in which an Israelite has acquired a *Habiru* slave – 'When you acquire a *Habiru* slave' – and then it proceeds to fix the limitations and other conditions of his service – 'six years shall he serve and in the seventh he shall go out free for nothing.' Similarly the Leviticus text first refers to the accepted practice of an impoverished Israelite selling himself into the service of a fellow Israelite – 'And if your brother becomes poor beside you and sells himself to you' – and then it proceeds to enunciate the law applicable to such a situation – 'you shall not make him serve as a slave. He shall be with you as a hired servant.' The text in Deut. 15 follows this twofold pattern, as we have stated above.

We see, then, that the legislator in Lev. 25 protects the impoverished Israelite bondman from being exploited as a slave, while the one in Deut. 15 directs that the master must make adequate provision for his bondman's material well-being after his liberation. We noted that the RSV correctly translates וְנִמְכַּר in the Leviticus text as 'and he sells himself'. It seems to me that this same word in the form יִמָּכֵר in the Deuteronomy text, dealing with the same situation, should likewise be understood to mean 'if (he) should sell himself' and not 'if (he) is sold to you'. This understanding of the word יִמָּכֵר is borne out by the *Mishna Kiddushin* I, 2, which enacts that an עִבְרִי bondman may be acquired either by money or by writ – עבד עברי נקנה בכסף ובשטר – the writ implying a written document containing some such legal phrase as 'Behold I am sold to you'.[5]

---

[5] *The Mishnah*, ed. and trans. Herbert Danby (London: Oxford University Press, 1933), p. 321, n. 13. Note that both Targum Onkelos and Targum Jonathan render the Hebrew יִמָּכֵר by יזדבן, 'sell himself'.

The Deuteronomic Legislator—a proto-Rabbinic Type

A number of interesting points emerge from an examination of the amended law, as it appears in Deut. 15, reflecting a Rabbinic-type mode of exposition of established pentateuchal legal texts, as employed by the Deuteronomic legislator. First, the formula כִּי תִקְנֶה, 'when you buy or acquire', of the original law of Ex. 21 is abandoned and is replaced by the phrase כִּי־יִמָּכֵר, 'if (he) sells himself', in the Deuteronomy version. In this way he associates the Exodus law with the one in Leviticus concerning the terms of service by an impoverished Israelite. As one might expect, the Talmudic Rabbis in *Kiddushin* 14b discuss the differences in terms of service between one who sells himself voluntarily through poverty and the convicted thief who is sold by the court against his will. However, the tendency to associate apparently different legalistic texts and to adduce subsidiary regulations from this association is well attested in Rabbinic literature. Secondly, the Deuteronomist extends the application of this law to the female, whom he designates as the עִבְרִיָּה. The inclusion of the bondwoman in this law points to the operation of a principle of Rabbinic exposition known as לרבות, that is, to include by extending the scope of the law.[6] The Deuteronomic legislator is consistent, for in Deut. 15.17 he directs that the practice of boring the ear of a bondman who refuses his freedom is to be applied also to the bondwoman – 'and also to your bondwoman shall you do like-wise'. It is true that there much confusion is developed as a result of the Deuteronomic recasting of Exodus law and the attempt to harmonize it with the other regulations mentioned. Leviticus 25 directs that the impoverished Israelite who enters the service of another Israelite must remain with him till the year of release, whereas Deuteronomy fixes the period as six years, as in Ex. 21.2. Furthermore, the only way by which a female Israelite becomes a bondwoman is by her being sold into service by her father. All

[6] J. Weingreen, 'Exposition in the Old Testament and in Rabbinic Literature', *Promise and Fulfilment*, S. H. Hooke *Festschrift*, ed. F. F. Bruce (Edinburgh: T. and T. Clark, 1963), pp. 195f.

these contradictory elements give the Rabbis much scope for casuistic discussion, as evidenced by *Kiddushin* 14b and the mediaeval Jewish commentators. However, the expository principle לרבות may be said to be at least as old as the age of the Deuteronomist and could be much older, since its application suggests that it was already an established principle of exposition.

We have seen, then, that the Deuteronomic legislator, when faced with two contradictory laws, was forced to find some kind of harmony between them which would make them complementary to each other. It appears that an appeal to another Rabbinic-type rule of exposition justified juridically the alteration of the original law. It is a well known device in Rabbinic disputation, when faced with the dilemma of dealing with two contradictory scriptural passages, that a third must be found to harmonize them.[7] This device was carried to an extreme by the Chronicler when he was faced with two conflicting accounts of the same event. It will be recalled that I Sam. 17.49–51 describes the slaying of the Philistine giant Goliath by the youthful David, while II Sam. 21.19 attributes this feat to a certain Elhanan. The latter passage is re-written in I Chron. 20.5 and in this Elhanan is credited with the slaying of Goliath's brother whose name, by a further distortion of the text, turns out to be Lahmi. This latter example may be regarded as a link in the chain of continuity in an expository procedure stretching from the Deuteronomist through the Chronicler and on to the Mishnaic Rabbis, exemplifying the tradition that the harmonization of contradictory texts should be attained by the formulation of a third version.

What is significant in this connection is that, though the Deuteronomic and Mishnaic methods of exposition may, in some instances, have much in common, their respective attitudes towards the existing written text differ radically and this calls for

[7] One of the thirteen rules of scriptural exposition formulated by Rabbi Ishmael is: 'when two texts contradict each other, [we cannot determine the sense] until a third text is produced which reconciles them.'

some comment. The Rabbinic authorities were constrained by the limiting factor of the reverence in which they held the text as divinely inspired and, therefore fixed and immutable; that is to say, it could never be subjected to any alteration in wording. Flexibility in and extensions of the implications of the text, as they understood them, could be achieved only by the employment of an elaborate system of guiding rules of exposition. They thus achieved their legislative aims by means of external interpretation, leaving the texts they were handling unaltered and unimpaired. The analogy, if you will, with regard to authorized scriptural readings is the system of the *K^ethib* and *Q^ere*. It is not surprising, then, that they should have formulated their approach to the study of the Scriptures in the maxim מאי תורה מדרש תורה – 'What is Torah? It is the exposition of the Torah' (*Kiddushin* 49a). The Deuteronomist, however, and, indeed the Chronicler, had no such compunction, for when he found it necessary to promote modifications in existing laws, he actually changed the wording of the text, with alterations, additions and omissions, to attain his objectives. Apart from the general consideration that such deviations may reflect changed social conditions and evolved religious thinking in the age of the Deuteronomist, they were often inspired by worthy motives. One is drawn to the conclusion, in fact, that the Deuteronomic legislation, with regard to the status of an Israelite bondman, marked an advance in enlightened and humane government. The provision made in Deut. 15.13f. for the material well-being of the freed Israelite bondman after his six years of service seems to justify this judgment.

If I understand the mind of the Deuteronomic legislator aright, I would suggest that the directive that the master provide his freed Israelite bondman with the basic material means of starting a new life of economic independence flows from a Rabbinic type of reasoning which has its roots in a scriptural legal text. It will be recalled that Lev. 25.39f. states that the impoverished Israelite who sells himself into the service of another was not only to be spared the rigours of serfdom, but he was to be treated as a hired servant. It is to be noted that, following upon the above directive to the master with regard to his freed bondman, the Deuteronomic writer exhorts the master in the following words: 'It should not be hard for you when you let him go free, for at half the cost of a hired servant he has served you six years' (Deut. 15.18). It looks as if this statement is based upon the Leviticus text, where the status of the Israelite bondman is defined as that of a hired worker. The implication which the latter text would carry would be that, on the completion of his six years of service, the freed bondman would be entitled, morally and legally, to some accumulated wages.

One further incidental point may be of some relevance in this discussion. It was noted earlier that the official Rabbinic interpretation of the law in Ex. 21 confined it to the case of a convicted robber and did not follow the Deuteronomist in associating it with that of an impoverished Israelite who became a bondman. What is of significance in this study is not that there should necessarily be agreement in the conclusions reached by the Deuteronomic legislator and the later Rabbis, but that their approach to the study of sacred legal texts exhibits similar characteristics, thus reinforcing the thesis of a direct line of continuity in tradition from the former to the latter.

At this stage in our study it may be useful to make mention of the view of literary critics that the influence of the Deuteronomist is to be found in the writings of the prophet Jeremiah. It is of no direct interest to our main theme to attempt to determine the exact nature of this influence. For our purpose it is sufficient to note that, in at least one of his oracles, the prophet is represented as endorsing a Deuteronomic law. In Jer. 34.9ff. the prophet denounces the inhumanity displayed by some Israelite masters towards their Israelite (i.e., עִבְרִי) bondmen and bondwomen. He describes how they had, at first, complied with the terms of the covenant which king Zedekiah had made with the people, providing for the release of their fellow Israelites who had become bondpeople, but they had later repudiated this undertaking and had

86

forceably brought them back into their service. In his protest against this cruel duplicity he is represented as quoting the actual wording of the Deuteronomic version of this law, thereby displaying his public support for it.

I now refer to a short study of mine which appeared in *Vetus Testamentum* in 1966, in which I considered the case of the wood-gatherer.[8] Briefly, the text narrates that a man found gathering wood on the Sabbath was brought before Moses for judgment. He, in turn, is represented as referring the case to divine adjudication, which condemned the man to death (Num. 15.32–36). I suggested that, by the act of gathering wood on the Sabbath, this man had exposed himself to the charge of intent to light a fire. The question to be decided, then, was (1) whether this act was to be construed as expressed intent to profane the Sabbath and (2) whether proven intent carried with it the same penalty as the actual committing of the crime. I now offer an alternative solution. It seems to me possible that the question was whether or not the gathering of wood was to be considered work and, therefore, prohibited on the Sabbath. It is to be noted that, though the prohibition of work on the Sabbath is stated several times in the Pentateuch, it was necessary to determine which forms of activity were to be classed as work. Exodus 39.21 prohibits farm work on the Sabbath and Ex. 35.3 the kindling of fire, while Jer. 17.21f. adds the carrying of burdens. These are to be regarded, not as additional Sabbath observance laws, but as examples of the kind of activity which is to be described as work and, therefore, forbidden on the Sabbath.[9] The *Mishna Sabbath* 7.2 lists thirty-nine forms of activities forbidden on the Sabbath and the above mentioned three scriptural examples are included in them. There seems to me to be no doubt that there were many more activities

[8] J. Weingreen, 'The Case of the Woodgatherer (Numbers XV 32–36)', *VT* 16 (July, 1966), pp. 361–4.

[9] J. Weingreen, 'Oral Torah and Written Records', *Holy Book and Holy Tradition*, edd. F. F. Bruce and E. G. Rupp (Manchester: University of Manchester Press, 1968), pp. 54–67.

than the three given which came under the category of work in biblical times. Doubtful cases would be referred to the judicial authorities as, I now suggest, was the incident of the wood-gatherer. In the application of the general law prohibiting work on the Sabbath to a specific instance, there is also a continuous line of progressive legal tradition from biblical to Rabbinic times.

If the explanation I now offer that the gathering of wood on the Sabbath was pronounced as being work, then the death penalty which followed would be expected. This solution is reinforced by some further considerations. (1) The Talmudic Rabbis were at pains to convince themselves that the wood-gatherer was, in fact, engaged in physical work, for they insert into this account the theory that he was caught trying to uproot trees.[10] (2) This kind of activity on the Sabbath is forbidden in the *Mishna Sabbath* 18.1, which states: 'Bundles of straw, bundles of branches and bundles of young shoots may be removed from their place, if they had been put in readiness (before the Sabbath) as cattle fodder; but if not, they may not be removed.' (3) Three cases brought to Moses were referred by him to divine judgment. They are (*a*) the case of the daughters of Zelophehad, who claimed the right of inheritance in the absence of male heirs (Num. 27.1ff.), (*b*) the case of the blasphemer (Lev. 24.10ff.) and (*c*) the case of the wood-gatherer. It is to be noted that, following upon the divine ruling, new laws were promulgated only with regard to the two former cases whereas, following the incident of the wood-gatherer, no new regulation was made. The explanation for the enactment of new laws, following upon the verdicts given in the cases of the daughters of Zelophehad and the blasphemer, may be that these cases presented unprecedented situations which could be expected to recur. A new law was, therefore, necessary. The absence of any fresh legislation following upon the verdict against the wood-gatherer may be accounted for by the fact that his case was not understood as presenting the court with a novel situation but, rather, with another form of activity on the Sabbath, and the question

[10] *Sabbath*, 96b.

before the court was whether or not this activity was to be pronounced as work. That is to say, his case is an example of court proceedings to determine whether or not the accused had been guilty of the violation of an existing law.

Once again, for our immediate purpose, there is nothing to be gained by becoming involved in the problem of allocating the narratives here quoted to specific strands and thus to place them in some kind of chronological scheme, as if they followed a firm pattern of evolution. It would be sufficient to say that, if the narrative of the wood-gatherer is to be assigned to the Priestly School, this kind of judicial process is surely much older. One might even argue that the citing of farm work as an example of activity prohibited on the Sabbath in Ex. 34.21, which is assigned by literary critics to the Yahwist, points to a pre-Deuteronomic period in which the judicial authorities in Israel laid down the kinds of activity forbidden on the Sabbath. It was, apparently, a continuing process. Even taking the findings of literary critics into account, one must bear in mind that the strands which they date do not represent the inauguration of literary processes but their culmination, and presuppose a history.

In presenting the attitude of the Deuteronomic legislator in this paper, the implication has been not that he was an innovator but, rather, the developer of already existing and effective legalistic processes. The recognition that Rabbinic-type processes may be detected in pre-Deuteronomic strands will support this view. I feel justified, therefore, in maintaining that the operation of such methods is compatible with the maturing of Israel's political, social and religious institutions, that is to say, it may even go back as far as the Davidic or Solomonic era.

5

Gilgal or Shechem?

Otto Eissfeldt

FIVE stories in the Old Testament appear to have as their setting
on the one hand Shechem or Mount Ebal and Mount Gerizim
which lie near the town, and on the other hand Gilgal near Jericho.
In the first place, the command of Moses to his people in Deut.
11.29–32 to set the blessing on Mount Gerizim after their arrival
west of the Jordan, but to set the curse on Mount Ebal (v. 29),
contains references which much more readily suggest that Gilgal
is where the action should take place.

The second instance is found in Deut. 27, the patch-work
nature of which is generally recognized,[1] in the section vv. 11–13,
which is a parallel to the above passage. Here Moses charges his
people that after the crossing of the Jordan six tribes shall take up
a position on Mount Gerizim to bless the people, and the six
remaining tribes shall stand on Mount Ebal to curse them. The
juxtaposing of Shechem and Gilgal is admittedly not so clear here
as it is in 11.29–32, but the reference in 27.12 to 'when you have
passed over the Jordan'[2] much more easily fits Gilgal, which

[1] In the analysis of Deut. 27 it is generally agreed that there are in this
chapter four different complexes, namely vv. 1–8, vv. 9f., vv. 11–13 and
vv. 14–26. There is by no means general agreement, however, about
which hands were at work in these passages.

[2] This and other similar expressions can perhaps be placed side by
side with the Deuteronomic formula 'the place which the LORD will
choose, to make his name dwell there': both these formulations still do
not name the place to be chosen and have, therefore, to limit themselves
only to a general indication of it. Just as in Deuteronomy Jerusalem is

was near to the Jordan, than Shechem, which lay much further inland.

Thirdly, there is the command of Moses to the representatives of Israel in Deut. 27.1–8 that on crossing the Jordan they should set up large stones west of the river, cover them with plaster, write all the words of the Law on them, build an altar of unhewn stones, and offer sacrifices on it. The time reference 'and on the day you pass over Jordan' (v. 2), and the similar expressions in v. 3 and v. 4, again suggest Gilgal, which is near the Jordan, whereas in v. 4 Mount Ebal is named as the scene of the action and in v. 5 'there' refers back to this statement, thus clearly indicating the region of Shechem. The fourth example, which occurs in Josh. 8. 30–35, is the account of how the command of Moses was carried out by Joshua. On the one hand Mount Gerizim and Mount Ebal are mentioned as the scenes of the action (v. 33), but in the same verse the Ark of the Lord is mentioned, better fitting Gilgal[3] than Shechem.

Fifthly, in Josh. 24.1–Judg. 2.9, there is the story of Joshua pledging Israel just before his death to the exclusive veneration of Yahweh at Shechem and also the account of his death there. In this section, the references in Judg. 1.1 'After the death of Joshua the people of Israel inquired of the LORD, "Who shall go up first for us against the Canaanites, to fight against them?" ' and Judg. 2.1 'Now the Angel of the LORD went up from Gilgal to Bochim', together with other evidence, seem to be remnants of a narrative which suggests not Shechem but Gilgal as the scene of Joshua's leave-taking and death. This last case, which deserves and requires special treatment, will not be discussed here so that in

---

suggested, so also the indication in Deut. 27.1–8 and Josh. 8.30–35 of some point west of the Jordan, as the place for the altar in accordance with the command of the Book of the Covenant or the stones inscribed with the Deuteronomic Law, could suggest Gilgal. At any rate in Josh. 3–7; 10.6, 7, 9, 15, 43; 14.6; Judg. 2.1 Gilgal plays an important role.

[3] According to Josh. 3–7; 9.14 the Ark is permanently situated in Gilgal until, according to Judg. 2.1, where 'the Angel of the LORD' represents an ideological development of the Ark, it leaves this place.

what follows we shall be dealing only with Deut. 11.29–32;
Deut. 27.11–13; Deut. 27.1–8 and Josh. 8.30–35.[4]

I

Deuteronomy 11.29–32 reads:

[29] And when the LORD your God brings you into the land which
you are entering to take possession of it, you shall set the blessing on
Mount Gerizim and the curse on Mount Ebal. [30] Are they not
beyond the Jordan, west of the road, towards the going down of the
sun, in the land of the Canaanites who live in the Arabah over against
Gilgal, beside the oak of Moreh?[5] [31] For you are to pass over the
Jordan to go in to take possession of the land which the LORD your
God gives you; and when you possess it and live in it, [32]you shall be
careful to do all the statutes and the ordinances which I set before you
this day.

Here in v. 29 Gerizim and Ebal are named specifically as the
bearers of the blessing and the curse, the blessing for those who

---

[4] Cf., in addition to the Introductions to the Old Testament and the
commentaries on Deuteronomy and Joshua, Emanuel Albers, *Die
Quellenberichte in Josua I–XII* (Bonn, 1891); Otto Eissfeldt, *Hexateuch-
Synopse* (Leipzig: J. C. Hinrichs, 1922, 2nd ed., 1962); Johannes Hempel,
Die Schriften des Deuteronomiums (Leipzig: R. Voigtländer, 1914);
Johannes Hollenberg, 'Die deuteronomischen Bestandteile des Buches
Josua', *Theologische Studien und Kritiken* 47 (1874), vol. I, pp. 462–506;
Heinrich Holzinger, *Einleitung in den Hexateuch* (Freiburg and Leipzig:
J. C. B. Mohr, 1893); Paul Kleinert, *Das Deuteronomium und der
Deuteronomiker* (Leipzig: Velhagen and Klasing, 1872); Abraham
Kuenen, 'Bijdragen tot de Critiek van Pentateuch en Jozua. V: de
godsdienstige vergadering bij Ebal en Gerizim', *ThT* 12 (1878), pp. 297–
323; Eduard Nielsen, *Shechem: A Traditio-Historical Investigation*,
2nd rev. ed. (Copenhagen: G. E. C. Gad, 1959); Martin Noth, *Überlieferungsgeschichtliche Studien: Die Sammelnden und Bearbeitenden
Geschichtswerke im Alten Testament*, SKG (Halle: Max Niemeyer Verlag,
1943); Rudolf Smend, *Die Erzählung des Hexateuch auf ihre Quellen
untersucht* (Berlin: Georg Reimer, 1912); Julius Wellhausen, *Die Composition des Hexateuch und der historischen Bücher des Alten Testaments*,
3rd ed. (Berlin: Georg Reimer, 1899).

[5] Reading אֵלוֹן for אֵלוֹנֵי, 'oaks' or 'terebinths'.

observe the Law of Yahweh and the curse for those who break it. Verse 30 also, even though the reference 'west of the road, towards the going down of the sun' cannot, unfortunately, be interpreted with absolute certainty, contains the words 'beside the oak of Moreh' which are quite clearly a geographical reference to the region of Shechem; at least the comparison of this passage with Gen. 12.6; 35.4 and Judg. 9.37 would suggest this. However, 'in the land of the Canaanites who live in the Arabah over against Gilgal' can obviously refer only to the region of Gilgal near Jericho.

In Deut. 11.30, therefore, geographical references stand side by side which refer partly to Shechem and partly to Gilgal. Before any attempt is made to explain this, it is important first of all to examine the two sections, Deut. 27.1–8 and Josh. 8.30–35 which are similar to the passage 11.29–32 in that they also narrate events that apparently occur in two places, on the one hand in Shechem, and on the other in Gilgal. First, however, a word about Deut. 27.11–13.

II

Deuteronomy 27.11–13, which is parallel in content to 11.29–32, reads:

> [11] And Moses charged the people the same day, saying, [12] 'When you have passed over the Jordan, these shall stand upon Mount Gerizim to bless the people: Simeon, Levi, Judah, Issachar, Joseph and Benjamin. [13] And these shall stand upon Mount Ebal for the curse: Reuben, Gad, Asher, Zebulon, Dan, and Naphtali.'

The juxtaposition of Shechem and Gilgal is admittedly not so clear here as in 11.29–32, but the reference 'when you have passed over the Jordan' in Deut. 27.12, which more clearly fits Gilgal than Shechem, contrasts with the overall picture in 27.11–13, where Gerizim and Ebal are specifically named as the scene of action.

III

Deuteronomy 27.1–8 reads:

[1] Now Moses and the elders of Israel commanded the people, saying, 'Keep all the commandment which I command you this day. [2] And on the day you pass over the Jordan to the land which the LORD your God gives you, you shall set up large stones, and plaster them with plaster; [3]and you shall write upon them all the words of this law, when you pass over to enter the land which the LORD your God gives you, a land flowing with milk and honey, as the LORD, the God of your fathers, has promised you. [4] And when you have passed over the Jordan, you shall set up these stones, concerning which I command you this day, on Mount Ebal, and shall plaster them with plaster. [5] And there you shall build an altar to the LORD your God, an altar of stones; you shall lift up no iron tool upon them. [6] You shall build an altar to the LORD your God of unhewn stones; and you shall offer burnt offerings on it to the LORD your God; [7] and you shall sacrifice peace offerings, and shall eat there; and you shall rejoice before the LORD your God. [8] And you shall write upon the stones all the words of this law very plainly.'

IV

Joshua 8.30–35 tells the story of how this command is carried out by Joshua. It reads:

[30] Then Joshua built an altar in Mount Ebal to the LORD, the God of Israel, [31]as Moses the servant of the LORD had commanded the people of Israel, as it is written in the book of the law of Moses, 'an altar of unhewn stones, upon which no man has lifted an iron tool'; and they offered on it burnt offerings to the LORD, and sacrificed peace offerings. [32] And there, in the presence of the people of Israel, he wrote upon the stones a copy of the law of Moses, which he had written. [33] And all Israel, sojourner as well as home born, with their elders and officers[6] and their judges, stood upon opposite sides of the ark before the Levitical priests who carried the ark of the covenant of the LORD, half of them in front of Mount Gerizim and half of them in front of Mount Ebal, as Moses the servant of the LORD had commanded at the first, that they should bless the people of Israel. [34] And afterward he read all the words of the law, the blessing and the curse, according to all that is written in the book of the law. [35] There was

---

[6] But for וְשֹׁטְרִים, read וְשֹׁטְרָיו, 'their officers'.

not a word of all that Moses commanded which Joshua did not read before all the assembly of Israel, and the women, and the little ones, and the sojourners who lived among them.

V

In the four sections discussed above, Deut. 11.29–32; 27.11–13; 27.1–8 and Josh. 8.30–35, there is evidence therefore that the events narrated take place in Shechem, whereas other references suggest Gilgal. Before an attempt can be made to explain this, we must make clear the origin, on the one hand of Deut. 27.1–8 and Josh. 8.30–35, which recount the command and its implementation and so belong together, and on the other of Deut. 11.29–32 and 27.11–13. The references in Deut. 27.1–8 and Josh. 8.30–35 to an altar which in any case is situated elsewhere than 'the place which the LORD will choose, to make his name dwell there' – to use the language of Deuteronomy – correspond to Ex. 20.24–26:

> [24] 'An altar of earth you shall make for me and sacrifice on it your burnt offerings and your peace offerings, your sheep and your oxen; in every place where I cause my name to be remembered I will come to you and bless you. [25] And if you make me an altar of stone, you shall not build it of hewn stones; for if you wield your tool upon it you profane it. [26] And you shall not go up by steps to my altar, that your nakedness be not exposed on it.'

This parallel suggests an altar of a pre-Deuteronomic kind; but on the other hand the references to the writing on large plastered stones of the law of Moses, which must be the basic part of our present Deuteronomy, presuppose a knowledge of that law-book. This state of affairs is best explained by assuming that the details common to both sections concerning an altar of unhewn stones stem from an editor who wished in this way to link the Book of the Covenant with the oldest narrative of the Hexateuch; and that these additions, which primarily served this particular purpose, were used two hundred years later by an editor who considered Deuteronomy as the standard law to link the originally independent Deuteronomy with the older Hexateuch. The

95

repetitions and irregularities that are found in both Deut. 27.1–8 and Josh. 8.30–35 can be taken as a clear indication that, at one time or another, several hands participated in the creation of the two levels that are present.

Deuteronomy 11.29–32 and Deut. 27.11–13 differ from Deut. 27.1–8 and Josh. 8.30–35. The two former passages basically refer only to the proclamation of the blessing and the curse which come at the end of the primitive Deuteronomy, that is, the basic form of Deut. 28–30. Here an old tradition seems to have been used, according to which Mount Ebal and Mount Gerizim, lying in the vicinity of Shechem, were the settings for liturgies of curses and blessings. Evidence for this tradition is provided above all by the curse dodecalogue in Deut. 27.14–26, which apparently has originally nothing to do with its context but has only received its present position because the scene of the events in which it is set is placed at Mount Ebal and Mount Gerizim.

Thus it can be said of the two pairs of stories, Deut. 27.1–8; Josh. 8.30–35 and Deut. 11.29–32; 27.11–13, that the first group originally linked only the Book of the Covenant with the pre-Deuteronomic Hexateuch narrative and was set in Gilgal, but was transformed by a secondary development into a link with Deuteronomy; whereas the second group is concerned with the proclamation of the blessing and the curse with which the Deuteronomic law is concluded, and is set at Mount Gerizim and Mount Ebal. Yet both these groups were similar, in that the proclamation of blessing, in the case of the obedience of Israel to the Law, and of curse where the Law was broken, had basically the same aim as the erection in Gilgal of an altar in accord with the directions of the Book of the Covenant and the replacement of the altar by large stones on which the Deuteronomic Law was written. This resulted from the adaptation and supplementation of the original pre-Deuteronomic material of Deut. 27.1–8 and Josh. 8.30–35. That is, both these stories recognize the Book of the Covenant and Deuteronomy.

Thus it is already clear that the two pairs of stories have had a mutual influence on one another and that their settings, originally different, were no longer kept sharply apart. In Deut. 11.29–32, to the original 'Mount Gerizim' and 'Mount Ebal' in v. 29 (the originality of which is quite certain even though the rest of this verse is doubtful) was added in v. 30 'in the land of the Canaanites who live in the Arabah over against Gilgal'.

In Deut. 27.11–13, where otherwise Mount Ebal and Mount Gerizim are named as the scene of the action, 'when you have passed over the Jordan', more appropriate to Gilgal, is added. While in Deut. 11.29–32 and Deut. 27.11–13 Shechem or its mountains Ebal and Gerizim appear to be original, in Deut. 27.1–8 and Josh. 8.30–35, as far as we can recognize from these contradictory and uneven passages, it is evidently Gilgal that is the scene of the action, as is suggested by 'when you have passed over the Jordan' in Deut. 27.2, 3, 4, and 'on opposite sides of the ark before the Levitical priests who carried the ark of the covenant of the Lord' in Josh. 8.33. The mention of 'on Mount Ebal' in Deut. 27.4 and the word 'there' in vv. 5 and 7 in reference to Mount Ebal, as well as 'on Mount Ebal' in Josh. 8.30 and 'there' in Josh. 8.32 and 'half of them in front of Mount Gerizim and half of them in front of Mount Ebal' in 8.33, quite clearly presuppose that Shechem is the scene of the action.

As has already been suggested, this mixing of Gilgal and Shechem in the passages under discussion may be explained by the fact that the erection of an altar complying with the demands of the Book of the Covenant, and thus implying a recognition of that law-book, as well as the writing of the Law of Moses, namely Deuteronomy, on the large stones, in the last analysis mean the same as the proclamation in solemn liturgy of the blessing that results from the observance of this Law and the curse that comes when it is broken. The juxtaposition of distinct and mutually exclusive geographical references in the four passages under discussion here should not simply be equated, forthwith, with the similar confusion in Deut. 1.1f. where in order to determine the position of Moses more accurately in Transjordan, seven or eight places are named which in fact lie on the road from Horeb to the mountain of Seir mentioned in v. 2. In this latter case, we are clearly dealing with a quite mechanical mistake, whereas in the former important factual considerations have caused the confusion.

Thus it is also quite conceivable that an editor should find that the commands given by Moses in Deut. 11.29–32 and 27.11–13 to speak the blessing on Mount Gerizim and the curse on Mount Ebal, the realization of which is indeed not expressly reported, were in fact carried out in Josh. 8.34f.: 'And afterward he read all the words of the law, the blessing and the curse, according to all that is written in the book of the law', and that he thereafter underlined this interpretation of the passage by his subsequent additions to it.

VI

I should now like to consider a little further why the editor who produced the basic form of Deut. 27.1–8 and Josh. 8.30–35 in order thereby to link the Book of the Covenant, Ex. 20.24 (22) – 23.12 (33), with the pre-Deuteronomic Hexateuch narrative, in fact chose Deut. 27.1–8 and Josh. 8.30–35 for his additions. It is first of all important to remember here that at the time when this editorial activity was undertaken, say around the middle of the eighth century BC, neither D nor P, that is, neither Deut. 1–30 nor Ex. 25–31; 35–40; Lev. 1–27; Num. 1.1–10.28; parts of 10.29–16. 35; 17–19; parts of 20–25; 26–31; parts of 32, 33–36, belonged in fact to the Hexateuch. Thus Deut. 27.1–8 and Josh. 8.30–35 were not so far removed from the Book of the Covenant, with which it was the original intention of these two sections to link the Hexateuch narrative.

In the case of Josh. 8.30–35, which expressly names Mounts Ebal and Gerizim in the vicinity of Shechem as the scene of the story, it is particularly striking that this region was still in the undisturbed possession of the Canaanites and thus the impression is given that a great festival is being celebrated in the land of the enemy. In addition to this, the narrative in Josh. 9.1–3, which follows on from 8.30–35, refers to the conquest of Jericho and Ai by the Israelites but makes no reference to the story in 8.30–35; that is, it passes over 8.30–35 and links up with 6.1–8.29. As far as this latter point is concerned, since we are dealing with an editorial addition – and that at any rate is clear from 8.30–35 – it is quite understandable that the continuity is disturbed. If, however, we accept that the original form of Josh. 8.30–35, and likewise Deut. 27.1–8, basically presuppose not the region of Shechem as the scene of the action, but Gilgal near Jericho, then it can and will become quite clear that Gilgal is meant[7] as the first settlement of Israel west of the Jordan after the crossing of the river – where, in accordance with the demands of the Book of the Covenant, an altar was set up.

The stories contained in Josh. 1.1–8.29, which as a whole take only about ten days – that is, they deal basically with a sequence of events that hang closely together – tell of measures which are to help Israel obtain a bridgehead west of the Jordan. One of these measures is the attack on Jericho and on Ai. Only after this has been brought to a successful conclusion and Jericho and Ai have fallen into the hands of the Israelites is an unassailable Israelite bridgehead west of the Jordan successfully set up. Now the battles of conquest can begin. This bridgehead has its centre in Gilgal and is indeed not only a military centre, in that it is Joshua's head-quarters, but also, through the presence there of the Ark, it is a cultic centre, since the cultic activities which are narrated in Josh. 3–6; 7.6; 9.6, 14; Judg. 2.1 are quite clearly connected with the Ark. The acquisition of the Jordan crossing by Israel therefore is in fact only completed by the conquest of Jericho and Ai and it is indeed understandable that an editor who wished to strengthen the validity of the Book of the Covenant in the region west of the Jordan by an altar set up there after the crossing of the river should

---

[7] Cf. above pp. 90f., note 2.

introduce the report of the building of this altar,[8] that is, the basis of Josh. 8.30–35, into the Hexateuch narrative that he had before him. It is similarly clear that a later editor, wishing in a similar way to legitimize Deuteronomy, which for him was the decisive authority, should for his purpose substitute the stones with the Law of Moses in the place of the altar.

VII

The observation that the sections considered above in Deut. 11.29–32, 27.1–8, 11–13 and Josh. 8.30–35 contain references which suggest Mount Ebal and Mount Gerizim near Shechem as the scene of the action, along with others which would appear to suggest rather Gilgal near Jericho as the place where the events occur, is almost two millennia old. One of the first to make this suggestion was Eusebius (*ca.* AD 260 to 339) in his Greek *Onomasticon of Biblical Place Names* (translated into Latin by Jerome, *ca.* AD 345 to 420), specifically in his comments on Deut. 11.29–30 and Josh. 4.19[9] which read, in the Latin text of Jerome:

> Gebal mons in terra repromissionis, ubi ad imperium Moysi altare constructum est. sunt autem iuxta Iericho duo montes uicini contra se inuicem respicientes, e quibus unus Garizin alter Gebal dicitur. porro Samaritani arbitrantur hos duos montes iuxta Neapolim esse, sed uehementer errant: plurimum enim inter se distant, nec possunt inuicem benedicentium siue maledicentium inter se audiri uoces, quod scriptura commemorat.
>
> Garizin mons super quem steterunt hi qui maledicta resonabant iuxta supra dictum montem Gebal.
>
> Golgol, quae et Galgal, iuxta quam montes esse scribuntur Garizin et Gebal. Galgal autem locus est iuxta Iericho, *errant igitur Samaritani, qui iuxta Neapolim Garizin et Gebal montes ostendere uolunt, cum illos iuxta Galgal esse scriptura testetur.*

[8] Just as the Book of the Covenant is introduced by a statement concerning the altar, so also Deuteronomy (Deut. 12) and the Holiness Code (Lev. 17) begin with a similar injunction. The altar command therefore sometimes represents the whole Law.

[9] Erich Klostermann, *Eusebius Werke*, vol. III, first half: *Das Onomastikon der biblischen Ortsnamen* (Leipzig: J. C. Hinrichs'sche Buchhandlung, 1904), pp. 65, 67ff.

Galgala, haec est quam supra posuimus Golgol, ad orientalem plagam antiquae Ierichus cis Iordanem, ubi Iesus secundo populum circumcidit et pascha celebrauit ac deficiente manna triticeis panibus usus est Israel. in ipso loco lapides quoque, quos de alueo Iordanis tulerunt, statuerant. ubi et tabernaculum testimonii fixum multo tempore fuit. cecidit autem in sortem tribus Iudae. et ostenditur usque hodie locus desertus in secundo Ierichus miliario, ab illius regionis mortalibus miro cultu habitus. sed et iuxta Bethel quidam aliam Galgalam suspicantur.

Of a similar nature is what Procopius of Gaza (*ca.* AD 464 to 528) says in his commentary on Deut. 11[10] concerning the position of Mount Ebal and Mount Gerizim in Deut. 11.29–32, as well as II. Reland's remarks in his *Palestina ex monumentis veteribus illustrata* I-II, 1714, pp. 503f, where he reproduces Procopius. In the essay by Abraham Kuenen mentioned on p. 92, n. 4, an essay written in 1878 but well worth reading today, the author reproduces on p. 316 the section repeated by his compatriot Reland from Procopius[11] together with Reland's own comments. He says with regard to this that, in accordance with Reland's opinions, the introduction, which Reland attacks, of Mount Ebal and Mount Gerizim in the sections under discussion needs no further refutation. Yet it retains its significance, because it shows how embarrassing for the interpreter is an uncritical trust in the historical accuracy of Josh. 8.30–35. Already on p. 315 Kuenen maintains 'We are here not in the realm of reality but in the realm of a freely creating imagination'.

[10] Procopii Gazaeae, *Commentarii in Deuteronomium* (J.-P. Migne, *Patrologiae Cursus Completus Series Graeca Prior.* Tomus LXXXVII, Pars Prima, 1865, col. 894–991), col. 906f.

[11] In the essay by Abraham Kuenen, *op. cit.* (see above, p. 92, note 4), for '*Jerome, Comment, ad. Deut. XI*', on page 316, line 14 and note 1, should be read 'Procopius of Gaza, *Comment. ad. Deut. XI*'.

6

The Succession of Joshua

J. Roy Porter

IN the Pentateuch and the book of Joshua, there are a number of
passages which describe in different ways the designation of
Joshua as Moses' successor, and the nature of the work he is
appointed to perform. The number and variety of such descriptions show that this was an important element in the Pentateuchal
tradition about Joshua. Indeed, if Noth is correct, it is the oldest
surviving element in that tradition in the Pentateuch as we have
it – in contrast to at least some material in the book of Joshua –
for he argues that only in the original form of Num. 27.15–23 is the
figure of Joshua genuinely and originally at home in a pre-Deuteronomic and pre-Priestly passage.[1] The traditions dealing with

[1] In his *Überlieferungsgeschichte des Pentateuch* (Stuttgart: W. Kohlhammer Verlag, 1948), p. 193, Noth holds that in its existing form
Num. 27.15–23 is part of the P narrative work, but that it must depend
on older and pre-Deuteronomic traditions, since it does not suit the
interests of P, which was not concerned with any narrative of the conquest
of Palestine, cf. also *ibid.*, p. 16. That this passage indeed enshrines
ancient conceptions will be argued in the following pages, but such a
view can hardly be based on Noth's premises. In the first place, Num.
27.15f. says nothing about the conquest and occupation of Palestine as
Joshua's function, unlike, for example, Deut. 21.1–8, which Noth
describes, not quite correctly, as 'parallel in content', *ibid.*, p. 193: it is
concerned solely with Joshua's leadership of the nation in succession to
Moses. Indeed, Noth himself makes precisely this point in his *Überlieferungsgeschichtliche Studien*, I (Halle: Max Niemeyer Verlag, 1943),
p. 191. Secondly, while Noth is certainly correct in stating that P's
special interest is the statutes and ordinances which constituted Israel

the appointment of Joshua as Moses' successor have been discussed in part by K. Möhlenbrink[2] and, as far as the specifically Deuteronomic material is concerned, by N. Lohfink.[3] Combining their discussions, two basic blocks of material may be distinguished:

1. Num. 27.12–23[4] + Deut. 34.9,[5] in connection with which Num. 32.28 and 34.17 have also to be considered.
2. Deut. 31.1–8,[6] 14f., 23 and Josh. 1.1–9, with which Deut. 1.38; 3.21f., 28 are clearly connected.

---

as a community at Mount Sinai, *ibid.*, pp. 205f., and even that these are 'timeless', *ibid.*, p. 209, yet for P they are also embodied in *continuing* institutions, such as the priesthood. Thus the transmission of certain offices, for example, those of the priests and Levites, must be provided for. Numbers 27.15f. secures this in the case of the ruling authority of Moses, alongside whom stands the priestly Aaron, in P's view, and it is therefore in no way discordant with the over-riding concern of the P complex.

[2] K. Möhlenbrink, 'Josua im Pentateuch', *ZAW* 59 (1943), pp. 49–56.

[3] N. Lohfink, 'Die deuteronomistische Darstellung des Übergangs der Führung Israels von Moses auf Josua', *Scholastik* 37 (1962), pp. 32–44. Cf. also his 'Der Bundesschluss im Land Moab', *BZ* n. f. vol. 6 (1962), pp. 32–56.

[4] The reasons for holding that the whole of this pericope is concerned with the appointment of Joshua as Moses' successor will be discussed below.

[5] At this point, it does not greatly matter whether we see this verse as the direct continuation of Num. 17.12–23, with many scholars, or, with Möhlenbrink, *op. cit.*, p. 52, as an independent recapitulation of the original form of the passage in Numbers. Probably the first alternative is preferable, since, as will be argued later, the theme of the people's obedience forms an important element in the description of Joshua's succession.

[6] It is frequently claimed, cf. Möhlenbrink, *op. cit.*, p. 52, Noth, *Überlieferungsgeschichtliche Studien*, I, p. 39, that only vv. 2, 7, 8 and possibly v. 1 are original to this section. This is true in the sense that the language properly belongs to the installation of an individual, i.e., Joshua, and is only secondarily transferred to 'all Israel'. But whether the passage ever actually existed without vv. 3–6 is much more doubtful. Noth argues that these verses are additions partly because some of them have the singular rather than the plural form of address, and partly because they anticipate vv. 7f. But the alternation of singular and plural verbs is too common a characteristic of Deuteronomy to provide any sound criterion for the division of sources; cf. the comments of A. R. Johnson, *The One and the Many in the Israelite Conception of God*, 2nd

We may begin by considering this second block, representing the Deuteronomic tradition. The important contribution made by Lohfink is his clear demonstration that the passages in question are not simply exhortations addressed to Joshua, but that they represent a regular formula for the installation of a person into a definite office. This formula has three members which receive a very distinct and precise shape in the linguistic usage of the Deuteronomic school:

(*a*) Encouragement of the person addressed, expressed by the phrase חֲזַק וֶאֱמָץ, cf. Deut. 31.7 (cf. v. 6), 23; Josh. 1.6, 7, 9. Cf. also the related phrases אֹתוֹ חַזֵּק, cf. Deut. 1.38 and וְחַזְּקֵהוּ, cf. Deut. 3.28. In close connection with this particular expression occur other pairs of words with similar meanings, such as ירא and חתת, cf. Deut. 31.8; ערץ and חתת, cf. Josh. 1.9; ירא and ערץ, cf. Deut. 31.6; cf. לֹא תִירָאוּם, Deut. 3.22.[7]

---

ed. (Cardiff: University of Wales Press, 1961), p. 12. With regard to the second point, the section is carefully constructed so that it refers both backwards, to earlier passages in Deuteronomy, and forwards, by transferring the words spoken to Joshua to the nation also. Thus v. 3b is not an anticipation of v. 7, as Noth holds, but a clear reminiscence of Deut. 3.28 and indicated as such by the phrase 'as the Lord has spoken', while vv. 4f. follow on from the mention of Joshua with an adaptation of the words addressed to him at Deut. 3.21f. Other instances in an installation ceremony of a closely similar address to the individual, on the one hand, and to a group, on the other, such as is represented here in v. 6 and vv. 7f., are found elsewhere, cf. especially I Chron. 22.6–16, 17–19, and it thus seems advisable to treat the section as a unity.

[7] Lohfink, cf. 'Die deuteronomistische Darstellung ...', *Scholastik* 37 (1962), p. 37, n. 27, thinks that these further word-pairs indicate a Deuteronomic expansion of the original formula, under the influence of the well-known Deuteronomic *Gattung* of the 'war-sermon'. This may be so, but it is noteworthy that similar twin verbs occur, along with the principal expression, in accounts of installations which, as Lohfink himself recognizes (cf. *ibid.*, p. 39), do not derive from the Deuteronomic passages but reflect an actual current practice. So, ירא and חתת occur at I Chron. 22.13; 27.20; II Chron. 32.7. But in any case, as will become clear later, these installation formulae clearly varied in the exact details of their wording and we can no longer recover an 'original' form, if indeed such a thing ever existed.

(*b*) Statement of a task or function, introduced by כִּי אַתָּה, cf. Deut. 31.7, 23; Josh. 1.6. Cf. also כִּי הוּא, Deut. 1.38; 3.28.

(*c*) Assurance of the divine presence and help, expressed either in a double-member statement, cf. Deut. 21.8b (cf. v. 6); Josh. 1.5, or in a single-member one, cf. Deut. 31.23; Josh. 1.9; Deut. 3.22b.

Although this formula receives such clear expression in the Deuteronomic tradition, it is not itself confined to that tradition: this is shown by the fact that D. J. McCarthy, quite independently of Lohfink, has demonstrated that there exists elsewhere in the Old Testament a formula for 'investing an officer', in which he finds exactly the same three elements that have been discussed above.[8] Lohfink[9] also calls attention to this point and a combination of the references given by the two scholars produces the following additional list of passages as evidence for the formula in question: II Sam. 10.12; Hag. 2.4; Ezra 10.4;[10] I Chron. 22.6–13, 16; 28.2–10, 20; II Chron. 19.8–11; 32.6–8. To these may be added at least such passages as Josh. 7.1; 10.24f.;[11] I Chron. 22.17–19; II Chron.

---

[8] D. J. McCarthy, *Treaty and Covenant* (Rome: Pontifical Biblical Institute, 1963), pp. 143f., no. 6.

[9] 'Die deuteronomistische Darstellung . . .', *Scholastik* 37 (1962), p. 39.

[10] This is perhaps the weakest example and is hardly more than a somewhat distant adaptation of the formula.

[11] Lohfink, 'Die deuteronomistische Darstellung . . .', *Scholastik* 37 (1962), p. 38, would not include this passage, because he considers it represents a speech of a leader in the Holy War, rather than a formula of admission to office: the two *Gattungen* had features in common, which led to their confusion in the Deuteronomic circle. But Lohfink is not consistent here, for II Sam. 10.12, which he takes as his basic instance of the formula, is just as much a war-speech. Nor is Josh. 10.24f. addressed to the whole people, as he claims, but אֶל קְצִינֵי אַנְשֵׁי הַמִּלְחָמָה and the three basic elements are present in it, if not in the same order as in Deuteronomy and Joshua: so, (*a*) encouragement, v. 25a; (*b*) statement of function, v. 24b; (*c*) assurance of divine help, v. 25b. It is similarly instructive to compare II Chron. 15.2–7, which could be described as admission to a task (the extirpation of idolatry), with II Chron. 20.14–17, which could be described as a war-speech, for, in both of these, traces of

19.5–7. It will be seen that the pattern of the formula is not exactly uniform and its distinctive wording in the Deuteronomic material represents only one variant of it. Sometimes (*b*) precedes (*a*),[12] and the elements of encouragement (*a*) and assurance (*c*) can be expressed in different ways, although it is worth noting that (*a*) almost invariably has the form of two imperatives joined together by *wāw*.[13] Nevertheless, the fundamental structure seems clear enough to permit us to speak of a definite form of installation to an office or function in this case.

If, then, the formula under consideration is not necessarily the creation of the Deuteronomic school, it is necessary to go on to enquire from where that school derived it and what are its original setting and background. As the survey of its occurrences has shown, it could be used on a variety of occasions and as a means of admitting to a number of different functions. Thus, to discover the background of its Deuteronomic usage, we have first to discover its purpose and occasion in Deuteronomy and Joshua and then to see what parallels to this can be found elsewhere in the Old Testament. The answer to the first question can hardly be in doubt: the formula is used on the occasion of the transfer of the leadership of the nation from Moses to Joshua and its purpose is to install Joshua into the same office that Moses had held.[14]

the formula under discussion can be discerned, even though this does not constitute the *Gattung* for these passages in their existing form, cf. J. M. Myers, *II Chronicles*. Anc B (New York: Doubleday and Company, 1965), pp. 88, 115. Thus (*a*) encouragement is represented by II Chron. 15.7a; 20.15b, 17b, (*b*) statement of task, by II Chron. 20.16 and probably II Chron. 15.7b, and (*c*) assurance of divine help, by II Chron. 15.2, יהוה עִמָּכֶם and II Chron. 20.17c. At this point, we are only concerned with indicating the formula and not with its *Sitz im Leben*, a problem which will be considered later.

[12] E.g., in the passages from I and II Chron.

[13] A possible exception is Hag. 10.4, cf. Lohfink, 'Die deuteronomistische Darstellung . . .', *Scholastik* 37 (1962), p. 39, n. 33.

[14] That Joshua is depicted in the canonical Old Testament tradition, which in this context is predominantly Deuteronomic, as the successor of Moses, is universally recognized: cf. e.g., R. Bach, 'Josua', *RGG³*, vol. 3, p. 872 and, for convenient lists of biblical passages illustrating the point,

When the Deuteronomic version of the formula is examined from this point of view, there emerge other features in it, in addition to the ones already noted, which can be seen to be significant pointers towards its character and *Sitz im Leben*, not least because of their occurrence in what appear to be related passages elsewhere in the Bible. We may call attention to five such features.

I

First, the words of installation are described as a solemn charge, expressed by the *Pi'ēl* of the root צוה.[15] The significance of this word is that, in this particular setting, it indicates admission to a clearly defined office, as its use in the description of the ceremony in Num. 27.12f., where very interestingly it occurs twice, vv. 19, 23, clearly shows.[16] Thus it is found in conjunction with the installation formula when such a definite office is in question, the kingship,[17] judgeship,[18] or a position of authority in the

cf. E. M. Good, 'Joshua son of Nun', *IDB*, vol. E–J, p. 996 and B. D. Napier, *Song of the Vineyard* (New York: Harper and Row, 1962), pp. 125f.

[15] Cf. Deut. 31.14, 23; Josh. 1.9; Deut. 2.21–28. Although the word צוה is not found in Deut. 31.7, the use of the root קרא there, which occurs with צוה in similar contexts (cf. Deut. 31.14; I Chron. 32.6) probably indicates the same idea.

[16] For the sense of the root in Num. 27, cf. N. H. Snaith, *Leviticus and Numbers*, CentB, new ed. (London: Thomas Nelson and Sons, 1967), p. 311.

[17] I Kings 2.1; I Chron. 22.6. The fact that in this latter passage Solomon is designated the temple-builder implies his succession to the throne, since to build the temple was one of the most important prerogatives of ancient Near Eastern kings. For this in Israel, cf. G. Widengren, *Sakrales Königtum im Alten Testament und im Judentum* (Stuttgart: W. Kohlhammer Verlag, 1955), pp. 14–16. Thus the play on בית as meaning both 'temple' and 'dynasty' in II Sam. 7 rests on a fundamental concept of the monarchical pattern and provides no evidence for a secondary transformation of an original text, as has been widely accepted since the basic study of the chapter by L. Rost, *Die Überlieferung von der Thronnachfolge Davids* (Stuttgart: W. Kohlhammer Verlag, 1926), pp. 47–74. Similarly, if I Chron. 22; 28–29 are to be understood as an account of

[18] Cf. II Chron. 19.9.

public works' system.[19] Elsewhere, when the installation formula is used with reference to less specific functions, the root צוה is not found with it. Further, this root suggests the action of someone in authority who transfers his power to another, either wholly in the case of his successor, or partly in the case of a subordinate.[20] Thus the occurrence of צוה in the passages under discussion indicates that the installation formula in them has its background in the royal practice and administration of the Judaean monarchy, with which the outlook of at least the Deuteronomic history, where the Deuteronomic presentation of Joshua really belongs, is closely linked.[21] More particularly, in view of the fact that it is the

---

the transmission of kingship from David to Solomon, there is no need to cut out from these chapters, as incompatible with their main concern, the sections in which Solomon is commanded to build the temple, as is proposed by K. Baltzer, *Das Bundesformular* (Neukirchen: Neukirchener Verlag, 1960), pp. 79–84. Also in the light of these considerations, we should be cautious about regarding II Sam. 7.13 as a later addition to the chapter, in spite of the majority of scholarly opinion, such as is recently represented, for example, by J. Schreiner, *Sion-Jerusalem Jahwes Königssitz* (Munich: Kösel Verlag, 1963), pp. 98f.

[19] Cf. 1 Chron. 22.17. Since David's words are addressed to כָּל שָׂרֵי יִשְׂרָאֵל they can hardly mean that these men were to take part in the actual labour of building the temple. Rather, we should see here the appointment of these 'leaders' to supervisory positions over the public labour force, corresponding to the manner in which this was in fact organized during the reign of Solomon, for the construction of the temple, cf. I Kings 5.13–18, especially v. 16; and 9.23.

[20] This would be the situation with reference to the appointment of judges at II Chron. 19.8f., for the king was the fount of justice in Israel, cf. E. R. Goodenough, 'Kingship in Early Israel', *JBL* 47 (1929), pp. 169–205. The point is clearly brought out in such passages as Ex. 18.14–26 and Deut. 1.9–18, where Moses, like the Israelite king, seems to represent the νόμος ἔμψυχος.

[21] Cf. Noth, *Überlieferungsgeschichtliche Studien*, I, p. 137; G. von Rad, 'The Deuteronomic Theology of History in I and II Kings', *The Problem of the Hexateuch and other Essays*, trans. E. W. Trueman Dicken (Edinburgh and London: Oliver and Boyd and New York: McGraw-Hill, 1966), pp. 214–21. Von Rad believes (p. 218) that the Deuteronomic history's 'messianic' view of King David represents a great change from the theological outlook of the book of Deuteronomy itself. But the

transfer of authority from Moses to his successor that is in question, it is from the practice that marked the transmission of the
royal office from one king to another that the Deuteronomic
presentation would seem to be derived.

II

Secondly, there is the close connection of the installation formula
in its Deuteronomic setting with an exhortation to keep the law
of Moses and even with a reference to the actual book of the law,
In particular, in Josh. 1.7 the first element of the formula occurs.
to be followed immediately by a warning to Joshua to act according
to the law of Moses and a command to him, v. 8, to study continually סֵפֶר הַתּוֹרָה הַזֶּה. Noth[22] holds that Josh. 1.7–9 is a later addition to the original text and Lohfink[23] agrees that these verses are
an intrusion in the formula proper, although he is compelled to
make an exception for the last clause of v. 9, since this is necessary
to provide element (c). Yet both these authors emphasize how fully
these verses correspond to the Deuteronomic theological interests
and, in support of this observation, we may point to the fact that
warnings about keeping the law and directions for reading and
preserving the book of the law are found immediately following
the descriptions of Joshua's appointment in Deut. 31.[24] However,

---

dichotomy must not be pushed too far, in view of the considerable
evidence that Deuteronomy depicts Moses as the prototype of the
Davidic king, cf. J. R. Porter, *Moses and Monarchy* (Oxford: Basil
Blackwell, 1963), pp. 23–27.

[22] Cf. *Überlieferungsgeschichtliche Studien*, I, p. 41, n. 4 and his *Das
Buch Josua*, 2nd ed. (Tubingen: J. C. B. Mohr [Paul Siebeck], 1953),
pp. 28f.

[23] Cf. 'Die deuteronomistische Darstellung . . .', *Scholastik* 37 (1962),
pp. 36–38.

[24] Cf. Deut. 31.9–13, 23–29: the evidence is all the clearer when it is
recognized that vv. 16–22, which interrupt the original connection
between v. 15 and v. 23, are a very late insertion, cf. Noth, *Überlieferungsgeschichtliche Studien*, I, p. 40. G. Widengren, 'King and Covenant', *JSS* 2
(1957), p. 13, relying on the use of the second person singular in the

it is by no means certain that we ought to view this feature simply as a specifically Deuteronomic expansion of an originally pre-Deuteronomic formula, for we have a mention of the need to observe the law in other passages in the Old Testament where the formula is found.[25] It can of course be argued that these passages are either in fact Deuteronomic or are following a Deuteronomic model: I Kings 2.3f. is almost universally held to be Deuteronomic and G. von Rad[26] has cogently argued that the speeches in the books of Chronicles, of which I Chron. 22.11–13 obviously forms part, are closely related to the sermonic hortatory material characteristic of the Deuteronomic school. It may readily be admitted that the language and formulation of I Kings 2.3f. are Deuteronomic and even, though with much less certainty, that the speeches in Chronicles are in what von Rad has called 'the Deuteronomic-Levitical tradition'. But the possibility still remains open that the Deuteronomic combination of the installation formula with an exhortation to keep the law springs from an actually existing and regular practice, just as we have seen the formula itself does. For we note that the passages outside Deuteronomy and Joshua, where the combination of installation formula and law occurs, are

verse, thinks that v. 11 may originally have been addressed to Joshua, in which case it would parallel the custom of the Israelite king's reading of the law. The suggestion is interesting but unfortunately the reason for it is untenable, cf. above, note (6): we have, e.g., exactly the same feature in the speech to the Levites in vv. 26, 27a, which can hardly be addressed to Joshua.

[25] Cf. I Kings 2.2–4; I Chron. 22.11–13: cf. also I Chron. 28.7. It may be noted that the first two of these passages contain a specific reference to the law given by Moses, and this leads one to ask whether כָּל הַתּוֹרָה in Josh. 1.7 may not be original, in spite of the opinion of the great majority of commentators, cf. most recently J. Gray, *Joshua, Judges and Ruth*, CentB, new ed. (London: Thomas Nelson and Sons, 1967), p. 50. The argument from the following מִמֶּנּוּ is not decisive in view of such passages as Ex. 25.15; Lev. 6.8; 7.18; 27.9; Judg. 11.34.

[26] Cf. 'The Levitical Sermon in I and II Chronicles', *op. cit.*, p. 268 and in general, his *Das Geschichtsbild des chronistischen Werkes*, BWANT 54 (Stuttgart: W. Kohlhammer Verlag, 1930). Cf. also W. Rudolph, *Chronikbücher* (Tübingen: J. C. B. Mohr [Paul Siebeek], 1955), pp. xiv–xv.

concerned with the succession of a new king to the throne, and thus point in the same direction as the use of the root צוה discussed above. There is a good deal of evidence for the close association of the king and the law[27] and for the view that this connection was forged at his enthronement. Here we may refer to an important and much discussed verse, II Kings 11.12. For our present purpose, it is not of great importance to decide whether the עֵדוּת referred to here are the Mosaic Tablets of the law or a royal protocol on the Egyptian model, for even von Rad,[28] who takes the latter view, emphasizes that the word is virtually synonymous with בְּרִית so that thus the עֵדוּת would contain the provisions of the divine covenant with the dynasty. But the descriptions in the Old Testament of the Davidic covenant show that by it the king was bound to keep Yahweh's law and that the prosperity and even the continuance of the dynasty depended upon this, cf. especially Ps. 89.29–38; 132.11f.[29] It is thus entirely appropriate that when Joshua succeeds he should be exhorted to keep the law and admonished that his success depends on his doing so:[30] this fits in perfectly with the use of the installation formula at the accession of a king, provides further evidence for the background of the Deuteronomic presentation of the transfer of leadership from Moses to Joshua, and indicates how this should be understood.

There are further considerations which support such an opinion.

[27] Cf. the fundamental works of Widengren, cited above in notes 17 and 24, and J. R. Porter, *op. cit.*, pp. 11–13.

[28] Cf. 'The Royal Ritual in Judah', *The Problem of the Hexateuch and other Essays*, pp. 227f.

[29] This reference is particularly significant in the present context if Ps. 132 is part of a liturgy to commemorate the inauguration of the Davidic dynasty, cf. J. R. Porter, 'The Interpretation of 2 Samuel vi and Psalm cxxxii', *JTS* n.s. 5 (1954), pp. 167–9. Cf. also H.-J. Kraus, *Worship in Israel*, trans. G. Buswell (Oxford: Basil Blackwell and Richmond: John Knox Press, 1966), pp. 183–8.

[30] Cf. Josh. 1.7f. Cf. G. Östborn, *Tōrā in the Old Testament* (Lund: Hakan Ohlssons Boktryckeri, 1945), p. 65.

It has often been noted, and it is indeed obvious, that by far the closest parallel to what Joshua is commanded to do in Josh. 1.7f. is what the king is commanded to do in Deut. 17.18–20[31] and this in itself is an indication that the Deuteronomist describes Joshua in royal terms. What has not generally been remarked is that, according to Deut. 17.18, the king is to acquire a copy of the law immediately on his accession, for this is the meaning of the phrase כְּשִׁבְתּוֹ עַל כִּסֵּא מַמְלַכְתּוֹ.[32] Thus Joshua is pictured as

---

[31] That the 'law of the king' in Deut. 17.14f. has in view a real situation, that it is not directed against the monarchical institution and that vv. 18–20 are an integral part of it have been shown by A. Caquot, 'Remarques sur la "loi royale" du Deuteronome', *Semitica* 9 (1959), pp. 21–33. Cf. also the comments of Widengren, 'King and Covenant', *JSS* 2 (1957), p. 15, and of J. R. Porter, *Moses and Monarchy*, p. 25. *Contra*, cf. E. W. Nicholson, *Deuteronomy and Tradition* (Oxford: Basil Blackwell and Philadelphia: Fortress Press, 1967), p. 93, who, however, does not appear to know the above-mentioned studies. The arguments tentatively put forward by G. von Rad, *Deuteronomy*, trans. D. Barton (London: SCM Press and Philadelphia: Westminster Press, 1966), p. 119, for regarding vv. 18f. as a later addition are extremely weak; (1) no doubt in these verses Deuteronomy is thought of as a literary document but it had become so in Judaean circles – and it is the practice of the *Judaean* monarchy which, we hold, these verses reflect – at least before the time of Josiah, as von Rad (*ibid.*, pp. 27f.) and Nicholson (*op. cit.*, pp. 101f.) both admit; (2) if it is stated that 'v. 20 is better understood as the direct continuation of v. 12', we have to ask to what, in that case does the מִצְוָה of v. 20 refer, and it should be noted that, in Deuteronomy, the word often indicates precisely the whole Deuteronomic law, cf., e.g., Deut. 8.1; 15.5. O. Bächli, *Israel und die Völker. Eine Studie zum Deuteronomium* (Zürich: Zwingli Verlag, 1962), pp. 187f., interprets Deut. 17.18f. as showing the king having responsibility for reading and interpreting the law, a function which belonged to him throughout the monarchical period. In the course of his discussion, Bächli calls attention to the exercise of this function in the cases of Joshua and, significantly, Solomon, cf. especially I Kings 8.14f. B. Lindars suggests that the word מצוה in Deuteronomy 'is to be connected with the function of the king in promulgating law', cf. 'Torah in Deuteronomy', *Words and Meanings*, D. Winton Thomas *Festschrift*, eds. P. Ackroyd and B. Lindars (Cambridge: University Press, 1968), p. 128.

[32] For this interpretation, cf. especially I Kings 2.12; II Kings 13.13; also I Kings 1.46; 3.6; II Kings 11.19; I Chron. 28.5.

coming into possession of a copy of the law when he succeeded Moses, just as the king was to do when he succeeded to the throne. It may even be that there is some significance at Josh. 1.8 in the use of the demonstrative pronoun זֶה, which also occurs similarly in Deut. 17.18f. The expressions סֵפֶר הַתּוֹרָה הַזֶּה or הַתּוֹרָה הַזֹּאת are otherwise confined to the book of Deuteronomy. Apart from Deut. 1.5 and 4.8, where the הַזֹּאת is proleptic, referring, as the latter passage shows, to the הַחֻקִּים וְהַמִּשְׁפָּטִים of either 5.1f. or 12.1f., these expressions indicate an actual document, usually a book written, or read, by the people[33] or the priests and elders[34] or Moses himself.[35] Possibly, then, behind Josh. 1.8 lies the practice of handing over an actual document to the king at his accession, as at II Kings 11.12, although it may well be the case that the Deuteronomic writer has transformed this into סֵפֶר הַתּוֹרָה הַזֶּה in pursuit of his particular interest. As a further parallel between Joshua and the picture of the king in Deut. 17 attention may be called to Josh. 8.30–35. This passage is clearly Deuteronomic and, indeed, from the literary point of view it is constructed from various passages in the book of Deuteronomy,[36] but there are important deviations from what is said in Deuteronomy,[37] and it is necessary to ask the reason and purpose of these. They cannot all be discussed here, but from the standpoint of the present enquiry, it may be observed that it is Joshua who builds the altar and writes out the law, while it is the whole people who are commanded

---

[33] Cf. Deut. 27.3, 5f., 8, 26.   [34] Cf. Deut. 31.11f.

[35] Cf. Deut. 31.9, 24, 26; 32.46. Nothing is said as to who wrote the law in Deut. 28.58, 61; 29.21, 29; 30.10, though probably we are to understand that it was Moses, but in any case it is a written book that is in question.

[36] Primarily, Deut. 27.4–8, but cf. also Deut. 27.11–14; 29.10; 30.1; 31.9–13. For a valuable discussion of Josh. 8.30–35, cf. S. Mowinckel, *Psalmenstudien*, V (Amsterdam: Verlag P. Schippers, 1961), pp. 97f.

[37] Some of these are listed in E. Nielsen, *Shechem: A Traditio-Historical Investigation*, 2nd rev. ed. (Copenhagen: G. E. C. Gad, 1955), p. 77.

to do it in Deuteronomy;[38] and perhaps Joshua even offers the sacrifices.[39] Similarly it is Joshua who reads the law, while Deuteronomy envisages this as the function of the priests and elders.[40] It would now be widely accepted that the passage in Josh. 8 is based, however remotely in its present form, on an actual festival at Shechem,[41] which probably involved (as vv. 33f. suggest) a covenant-renewal ritual and which is to be connected with the ceremony described in Josh. 24. Possibly, therefore, the part played by Joshua here reflects the part played by the king in the festival during the monarchical period, while the presentation in Deuteronomy comes from the exilic period, when the kingship had come to an end.[42] For elsewhere, we find that kings, in their capacity as head of the cult, build altars,[43] read the law,[44] and offer sacrifices.[45] Further, v. 32 says that Joshua inscribed a copy of the law of Moses אֲשֶׁר כָּתַב. These last words

---

[38] Cf. Deut. 27.3, 5f., 8.

[39] LXX reads the singular in v. 31, ἀνεβίβασεν. If this is original, MT may represent an example of dittography, יעלו being influenced by the following עליו. The words וַיִּזְבְּחוּ שְׁלָמִים would then be a gloss, when the change had taken place, perhaps added under the influence of Ex. 24.5.

[40] Cf. Deut. 31.11.

[41] Cf. e.g. W. Beyerlin, *Origins and History of the Oldest Sinaitic Traditions*, trans. S. Rudman (Oxford: Basil Blackwell, 1965), p. 43.

[42] The chapters of Deuteronomy which contain the material under consideration are extremely difficult to analyse with respect to the date and character of the material in them. However, the edition – or editions – of 'Deuteronomy' which they represent may well come from the exilic period. Cf. O. Eissfeldt, *The Old Testament, an Introduction*, trans. P. Ackroyd (Oxford: Basil Blackwell and New York: Harper & Row, 1965), p. 233.

[43] Cf. I Sam. 14.35 (Saul); II Sam. 24.25 (David); I Kings 6.20 and 9.25 (Solomon); I Kings 12.33 (Jeroboam); I Kings 16.32 (Ahab); cf. also II Kings 16.10f. (Ahaz).

[44] Cf. II Kings 23.1–3.

[45] Several of the passages cited above in note 43 speak of the king sacrificing. For kings sacrificing עֹלוֹת וּשְׁלָמִים cf. also I Sam. 13.9f.; II Sam. 6.17.

are usually omitted, following LXX, as a gloss, and their subject is considered to be Moses; but it could equally well be Joshua, referring to a book of the law which he himself had *already* written.[46] Joshua would thus be depicted as having done what the Israelite king was commanded to do in Deut. 17.18. The case is somewhat different with Josh. 24.25f., but once again a custom typical of ancient Near Eastern kingship lies in the background. Here Joshua inserts his own statutes and ordinances into the book of the law. This presents a close parallel to what is known of the ancient Mesopotamian law-codes, which were basically a promulgation of old traditional regulations by the sovereign, but to which he might add his own decrees designed to safeguard the traditional laws and to bring them up to date. There is evidence that Israelite kings did the same thing and thus Joshua's action in these verses represents his promulgation of the law in accordance with royal practice.[47]

The connection, then, between the installation formula and the the law in Josh. 1 can be seen to be very close, once it is realized that the Deuteronomic tradition is drawing on the particular type of installation ceremony represented by the accession of a king, and indeed this combination is itself a pointer to such a background. In concluding this part of the discussion, attention may be drawn to another possible example of the connection of law and enthronement, which also again suggests that the linking is not a creation of the Deuteronomic school but a concept already extant which it adopted and adapted to its own outlook. It has been suggested that the position of Ps. 1, which invokes a blessing on the one who keeps the law, just before Ps. 2, which is part of a royal enthronement festival, is not fortuitous,[48] and that they

---

[46] Cf. the somewhat ambiguous translation of RSV.

[47] For a discussion, which cannot be repeated here, of the significance of the promulgation of the law by Mesopotamian and Israelite kings, cf. J. R. Porter, *Moses and Monarchy*, pp. 15, 24.

[48] Cf. E. Nielsen, 'Some reflections on the History of the Ark', *SVT* 7 (1960), p. 71.

belong together as a part of the liturgy for the king's accession.[49] Psalm 1 certainly has mythological features, especially the 'tree' and the 'streams of water', which appear elsewhere as part of a widespread royal ideology.[50] It might therefore have the function of setting before the new king an ideal of royal behaviour,[51] which consisted in faithful obedience to the law, and of reminding him that only by so doing could he hope to prosper. It would thus correspond very closely to the words of David to Solomon and of Yahweh to Joshua, as they enter their new office,[52] and the combination of Pss. 1 and 2 would be exactly parallel to the pattern of exhortation to keep the law and installation formula in the passages we have been dicussing. Another context in which the combination of law and enthronement appears is perhaps also significant. In Ps. 93.5, one of the psalms celebrating the accession of Yahweh to his royal throne, occur the words עֵדֹתֶיךָ נֶאֶמְנוּ מְאֹד[53] and, if Weiser's view is correct,[54] the so-called Enthronement Psalms were part of the liturgy of a covenant-

[49] Cf. M. Bič, 'Das erste Buch des Psalters: Eine Thronbesteigungsfestliturgie', *La Regalità Sacra*, R. Pettazzoni *Festschrift* (Leiden: E. J. Brill, 1959), pp. 316–32, especially p. 320.

[50] Cf. G. Widengren, *The King and the Tree of Life in Ancient Near Eastern Religion* (Uppsala: A.-B. Lundequistska Bokhandeln, 1959), and E. O. James, *The Tree of Life* (Leiden: E. J. Brill, 1966), especially pp. 1–31 and pp. 93–128.

[51] Cf. I. Engnell, 'Planted by the Streams of Water', *Studia Orientalia Johanni Pedersen Dicata* (Copenhagen: Einar Munksgaard, 1953), pp. 85–96.

[52] Compare especially the mention of the observance of the law, followed by וְכֹל אֲשֶׁר־יַעֲשֶׂה יַצְלִיחַ, Ps. 1.3, with the same feature followed by לְמַעַן תַּשְׂכִּיל אֵת כָּל־אֲשֶׁר תַּעֲשֶׂה, I Kings 2.3, אָז תַּצְלִיחַ, I Chron. 22.13, and אָז תַּצְלִיחַ אֶת־דְּרָכֶךָ וְאָז תַּשְׂכִּיל, Josh. 1.8. For the connection of ideas between Ps. 1 and Josh. 1, cf. also R. A. Carlson, *David, the Chosen King* (Uppsala: Almqvist and Wiksell, 1964), p. 243, n. 1.

[53] עדות here, as frequently in the Psalter, means Yahweh's laws as forming a single corpus, cf. G. Widengren, *Sakrales Königtum* ..., p. 94, n. 69.

[54] Cf. A. Weiser, *The Psalms*, trans. H. Hartwell (London: SCM Press and Philadelphia: Westminster Press, 1963), pp. 35–52.

renewal festival, which would include the reading of law. Of course, Yahweh here is the one who gives the law, not the one who keeps it, but, *mutatis mutandis*, the same pattern of law and installation is found in connection with the divine king as with the earthly monarch. Further, in another Enthronement Psalm, Ps. 99.6f., there is a curious and not very clearly motivated reference to three great figures of the past who kept Yahweh's testimonies and statutes. In the light of the above discussion, this should perhaps be understood as an indirect exhortation to the congregation, and perhaps especially to the king,[55] to observe the law, by reminding them that this has been the distinguishing mark of their famous predecessors. We may possibly also understand that this element was related to, if not derived from, the similar exhortation at the accession of the human king.

III

The examination thus far has tended to suggest that the features of the Deuteronomic presentation of the succession of Joshua find their closest parallel in a passage not mentioned by Lohfink or McCarthy, namely in David's speech to Solomon in I Kings 2.1ff., which, in view of the facts already discussed, is to be interpreted as a formal handing over of authority from the old king to the new. This passage may be analysed as follows:

(*a*) Solemn charge, v. 1: *Pi'ēl* of צוה.

(*b*) Encouragement, v. 2: חָזַקְתָּ וְהָיִיתָ לְאִישׁ.

(*c*) Exhortation to keep the law, v. 3.

(*d*) Assurance of divine help, v. 4.

---

[55] For the special place of the king in the Enthronement Festival, cf. S. Mowinckel, *The Psalms in Israel's Worship*, trans. D. R. Ap-Thomas (Oxford: Basil Blackwell and New York: Abingdon Press, 1962), vol. I, pp. 128f., and for the probable influence of the enthronement of the earthly king on the festival of Yahweh's enthronement, cf. Weiser, *op. cit.*, p. 63.

(e) Statement of task, v. 5, introduced by וְגַם אַתָּה.[56]

Clear traces of the same pattern may be discerned in I Chron.
22–23.1; 28–29, chapters which, as K. Baltzer has shown,[57] represent the transmission of the royal authority from David to Solomon, and are thus a parallel to, or an expansion of, 1 Kings 2.1ff.
Thus:

(a) I Chron. 22.6: *Piʿēl* of צוה.
(b) I Chron. 22.13b; I Chron. 28.10b, 20b.
(c) I Chron. 22.12, 13a. Cf. I Chron. 28.7; 29.19a.
(d) I Chron. 22.16b; I Chron. 28.20c. Cf. I Chron. 22.11a.
(e) I Chron. 22.7–12, esp. v. 11, עַתָּה; I Chron. 28.10a, עַתָּה.
   Cf. I Chron. 29.19b.

What is important in both these sets of passages is the appearance of the exhortation to keep the law, which seems to be a mark
of the installation formula only when this is employed for a king,
since it is not found when the formula is used for admission to
another office. Hence the occurrence of this element in Josh.
1.1–9 is significant as indicating the original royal background of
the account of Joshua's installation there.

At this point, we should notice a feature which also occurs both
in the case of Solomon and in the case of Joshua, the fact that the
successor assumes office immediately on the death of his prede-

---

[56] Lohfink may be correct, 'Die deuteronomistische Darstellung . . .',
Scholastik 37 (1962), p. 39, in thinking that element (b), encouragement,
may sometimes consist of a single verb. He calls attention to Hag. 2.4,
where וַעֲשׂוּ certainly appears to represent element (e), and to II Sam.
10.12, where וְנִתְחַזַּק may do so, although here it could be held that v. 11
represents the mention of the task. If Lohfink is to be followed, then, in
the above analysis וְהָיִיתָ לְאִישׁ should be considered as the statement of
the task, so that the scheme would be confined to vv. 1–4. Whichever
alternative is preferred does not seriously affect the argument for the
presence of a definite pattern in I Kings 2.1ff.

[57] K. Baltzer, *Das Bundesformular*, pp. 79–84.

cessor[58] and that this occurs without any break or interruption. This in itself constitutes a notable difference from the succession to the charismatic leadership, where, in the Deuteronomic pattern of the book of Judges, there is always an interval between the death of one judge and the raising up of another.[59] It is, however, peculiarly characteristic of the monarchical institution in the Ancient Near East that it was dynastic, so that it was greatly concerned with securing a clearly regulated and uninterrupted succession in the royal office, especially of course from father to son,[60] and it was just this which distinguished it from other types of political organization, not least from the old charismatic rulership.[61] It need hardly be pointed out that the parallel is not exact since Joshua was not the son of Moses,[62] but there is much

[58] Cf. Deut. 31.2, which, in view of Deut. 34.7, implies Moses' imminent death; Josh. 1.2; I Kings 2.2a; I Chron. 23.1.

[59] I Sam. 8.1 (cf. 12.2) is not Deuteronomic but probably is based on an old local tradition, cf. Noth, *Überlieferungsgeschichtliche Studien*, I, p. 97. In any event, it represents an exceptional case and is commonly understood precisely to reveal an attempted advance from the genuinely old institution of the judgeship, cf. e.g. H. W. Hertzberg, *I & II Samuel*, trans. J. S. Bowden (London: SCM Press and Philadelphia: Westminster Press, 1964), p. 71.

[60] To give a single example from the immediate environment of Israel, this concern is very prominent in the Ugaritic legends of Keret and Aqhat, cf. G. R. Driver, *Canaanite Myths and Legends* (Edinburgh: T. & T. Clark, 1956), especially pp. 5, lines 28ff.; 8, lines 46ff. As for the Old Testament, this concern is basic in II Sam. 7, a passage which reveals perhaps more clearly than any other the nature of Israel's royal ideology, cf. vv. 11b–16, 25–29.

[61] This is shown by the fact that it is precisely the question of regular hereditary succession that is at issue when the introduction of kingship in Israel is proposed, cf. Judg. 8.22f.

[62] On the other hand, the intimate association of Joshua with Moses during the wilderness period should be noted. It seems clear that Joshua did not belong originally in most of the traditions concerning this period in which he now appears (cf. Beyerlin, *op. cit.*, pp. 48f.). We may wonder whether he has not been introduced largely for the purpose of being designated as Moses' successor, cf. Beyerlin's comment on Ex. 17.8f., *op. cit.*, p. 16, so that his relationship to Moses is patterned on that of the king to the young heir-apparent. Thus he is described as a נַעַר and he is

associated in the direction of the community during Moses' lifetime (cf. Num. 32.28; Deut. 32.44) with what could be called 'rights of succession', cf. Num. 34.17, as was the case with Solomon and David, cf. I Kings 2.35, Abijah and Rehoboam, cf. II Chron. 11.22, and Jotham and Azariah, cf. II Kings 15.5b. In this capacity Joshua is regularly designated as מְשָׁרֵת, cf. Ex. 24.13; 33.11; Num. 11.28 and this word is

used of him in connection with his installation as Moses' successor at Josh. 1.1. First, it may be observed that this term, or the root, is most frequently used of servants in the royal administration, cf. II Sam. 13.17f.; I Kings 1.4, 15; 10.5; Prov. 29.12; Esth. 1.10; 2.2; 6.3; I Chron. 27.1; 28.1; II Chron. 9.4; 17.19; 22.8; interestingly, the noun is employed of heavenly agents in contexts where Yahweh is pictured in royal imagery, cf. Pss. 103.21 (cf. v. 19); 104.4 (cf. vv. 1–3). But, secondly, the word is also used of Elisha's chief servant, cf. II Kings 4.43; 6.15 and of Elisha himself in the same capacity *vis-à-vis* Elijah, cf. I Kings 19.21, and it has therefore been suggested that the closest parallel to the relationship between Moses and Joshua is the one between Elijah and Elisha, so that Joshua's succession, like Elisha's, would be to the prophetic office (cf. M. de Buit, *La Sainte Bible: le livre de Josué* 2nd ed. [Paris: Editions du Cerf, 1958], p. 10). Certainly this was how the matter was viewed in later Jewish tradition, cf. Ecclus. 46.1. But there is no indication in the canonical traditions about him that Joshua acted as a prophet. Further, it may be asked whether the legend of Elisha as the successor of Elijah, which has some curious features, has not itself been influenced by motifs which really belong to the royal sphere: (1) In the words of J. Gray, *I & II Kings* (London: SCM Press and Philadelphia: Westminster Press, 1963), p. 366, referring to I Kings 19.16, 'there is no other case of the conferring of prophetic authority by anointing'. But before the exile the rite of anointing was confined to the installation of kings, and even if the expression is intended, in the case of Elisha, to be understood in a figurative sense (cf. O. Eissfeldt, *Könige*, HSAT I, 4th ed. [Tübingen: J. C. B. Mohr, 1922], p. 329), it would still be necessary to give full weight to the background whence it is derived. (2) The 'mantle' which plays so important a part in conferring his position on Elisha, cf. I Kings 19.19b; II Kings 2.13f., is properly a robe of state, commonly worn by kings (cf. for the evidence J. A. Montgomery and H. S. Gehman, *The Books of Kings*, ICC [Edinburgh: T. & T. Clark, 1951], p. 316). (3) The ascension of Elijah, cf. II Kings 2.11, which also plays a vital part in the designation of Elisha as his successor, cf. v. 10, again probably has a royal background, cf. G. Widengren, 'The Ascension of the Apostle and the Heavenly Book', *Uppsala Universitet Årsskrift* (Uppsala: A.-B. Lundequistska Bokhandeln, 1950), pp. 7–24, and, especially in regard to the feature of the heavenly chariot, cf. H. P. l'Orange, *Studies on the Iconography of Cosmic Kingship in the Ancient World*, Inst. for Sammenlignende Kulturforskning (Oslo: H. Aschehoug & Co., 1953), pp. 48–79.

in the account of the transfer of office from one to the other which suggests features of the more properly dynastic succession and which leads to the conclusion that in this respect Moses and Joshua are depicted as prototypes of the Israelite King.

As further possible support for this contention, reference may be made to the narrative of the choice of Saul as king in I Sam. 9–10. Whatever may be said of the original background and significance of these chapters, their present setting in the Deuteronomic history is the succession of Saul to the office of Samuel,[63] in view of the latter's imminent decease.[64] The element of encouragement, (*b*), seems to be clear in I Sam. 10.7a, and that of the assurance of divine help, (*d*), in I Sam. 10.7b. We may find the statement of the task, (*e*), in I Sam. 10.1b and the solemn charge, (*a*), in the words of I Sam. 9.27.

Again, the recurrence of several of the main features of the formula in the case of a king who is succeeding to the 'judgeship'[65] of his predecessor confirms what has already been noted as the probable source of the same features in the succession of Joshua.

That the leadership of Moses, as this is pictured in Deuteronomy, was considered to involve a continued succession to the office he had held has recently been emphasized by M. G. Kline, who does not hesitate to use the adjective 'dynastic' to describe

---

If this is so, the undoubted similarities between the two groups Moses-Joshua and Elijah-Elisha reflect a common royal pattern. For the general possibility of features borrowed from kingship in the call and appointment of prophets, cf. Widengren, 'The Ascension of the Apostle and the Heavenly Book', *Uppsala Universitet Arsskrift*, p. 33, n. 3.

[63] This is shown by the repeated use of the word שפט to describe the function of the new king in I Sam. 8, a feature rightly stressed by Hertzberg, *op. cit.*, p. 72.

[64] I Sam. 8.1, 5; 12.2.

[65] The extent to which Saul's kingship was viewed as the continuation of the old charismatic leadership of the 'judges', of which Samuel was the last, has been stressed above all by A. Alt, cf. his *Essays on Old Testament History and Religion*, trans. R. A. Wilson (Oxford: Basil Blackwell and New York: Doubleday and Co., 1966), pp. 188–92 and 243f., but he seriously underestimates the new, and distinctively monarchical features, in Saul's royal authority.

this succession.[66] But, as has already been seen, this concept really belongs to the sphere of royal ideology rather than to the charismatic leader, whom Moses and Joshua are usually supposed to exemplify. Indeed, Kline himself comments: 'It may be observed in passing that Deuteronomy's interest in the perpetuity of Yahweh's rule and specifically its concern with the security of the dynastic succession is a mark of the profound unity between the Deuteronomic and Davidic covenants.'[67] That is, the closest parallel to what we have in Deuteronomy with regard to the succession of Joshua is to be found in the royal Davidic covenant, where the security of the succession and the continuation of the royal house forever is one of the major concerns.[68]

Again, however, this depicting of the succession element in the office of Moses in terms of the Davidic covenant can be seen to be much older than the Deuteronomic presentation. We may take as our starting-point some comments of M. L. Newman in his discussion of the 'J' tradition in Exodus.[69] He refers to Ex. 34.27 for Yahweh making a covenant with Moses, just as he did with the Davidic king,[70] and to the expression לְעוֹלָם in Ex. 19.9a, which, together with the synonym עַד עוֹלָם, is used elsewhere at least twenty times in connection with Yahweh's promise of the continuation of the Davidic dynasty, and which, in Newman's view, suggests 'the establishment of a dynastic office of covenant

---

[66] Cf. M. G. Kline, *The Treaty of the Great King* (Grand Rapids: W. B. Eerdmans Publishing Co., 1963), pp. 35–40.

[67] *Ibid.*, p. 38. Möhlenbrink, *op. cit.*, p. 54, had already noted how sharply the narratives of Joshua's succession distinguish him from the line of charismatic leaders.

[68] Cf. especially Ps. 132.11f. and the comments of Aubrey R. Johnson, *Sacral Kingship in Ancient Israel*, 2nd ed. (Cardiff: University of Wales Press, 1967), pp. 23–25, and Ps. 89.35–38 and the comments of G. W. Ahlström, *Psalm 89* (Lund: C. W. K. Gleerups Förlag, 1959), pp. 50f.

[69] Cf. M. L. Newman, *The People of the Covenant* (New York: Abingdon Press, 1962), pp. 50f.

[70] Further evidence for this is supplied by Ex. 34.10a; 32.10b; Num. 14.12b. For a discussion of these passages, cf. J. R. Porter, *Moses and Monarchy*, p. 17, n. 52.

mediator'. It is true that, in Newman's view, this was intended to refer to the establishment of a *priestly* dynasty, in which 'the succession was traced from Moses to Aaron to Aaron's sons, Nadab and Abihu'.[71] But to such an interpretation there are at least two cogent objections. First, Newman bases his view on the fact that Aaron, Nadab and Abihu share in the eating of the covenant meal, that is in the making of the covenant, at Ex. 24.1f.; 9–11.[72] But so do the seventy elders, who can hardly be thought of as representing a priestly dynasty, and there seems no reason for importing the idea of the establishment of a priestly succession into the Exodus passage at all. Secondly, there seems no evidence in the biblical sources that Aaron was expected to succeed to the office of Moses and, according to tradition, he did not but died before him.[73] Still more is this true of Nadab and Abihu who, again according to tradition, died before Aaron[74] and were expressly excluded as the transmitters of the priestly line.[75]

As has been noted, the only successor to Moses known to the Old Testament is Joshua and it is significant that in Josh. 24, one of the passages where his figure seems to be rooted more firmly in the tradition,[76] he is found acting as the mediator of a covenant, and in this chapter there is even the suggestion of a particular covenant, as in the case of Moses, with Joshua and his family.[77] Thus the argument of Newman, with its emphasis on the parallels between the covenant with Moses and that with David, again points to Joshua as Moses' successor in the royal pattern.

Further, there is much evidence that the Israelite king was responsible for maintaining and renewing the covenant,[78] and

[71] Newman, *op. cit.*, p. 132. [72] *Ibid.*, p. 51.
[73] Cf. Num. 20.28. [74] Cf. Lev. 10.1–3.
[75] Cf. I Chron. 24.2.
[76] This was first demonstrated by A. Alt, 'Josua', *Kleine Schriften*, I (Munich: C. H. Beck, 1953), pp. 191f.
[77] This may be indicated by Josh. 24.15b.
[78] Cf., above all, Widengren, 'King and Covenant', *JSS* 2 (1957), pp. 1–32, and the suggestive comment of J. Bright, *A History of Israel*

the influence of royal practice may even be discerned in Josh. 24. Behind the conclusion of the covenant in that passage seems to lie the formula of Deut. 26.17–19, according to which, on the one hand, Yahweh declares that Israel is his people, and, on the other, the people declare that Yahweh is their God. On the basis of such passages as II Kings 2.17; 23.3, G. Fohrer has concluded that this formula is a reflection of the terms of the covenant concluded between God and his people by the king.[79] Thus, whatever the precise origin of the material in Josh. 24 in its present form, we again see Joshua fulfilling the same function that was ascribed both to Moses and to the Davidic king.

Evidence for the presence of a pattern derived from royal practice in the accounts of Joshua's succession may also perhaps be found in another direction. Royal features in the patriarchal legends have not infrequently been noted,[80] and recently B. J. Van der Merwe has put forward the hypothesis that, in Genesis, Joseph is presented as succeeding Jacob as ruler.[81] He calls attention to several elements in the picture of Jacob which are found elsewhere in the Old Testament in connection with kings and in particular, with reference to the theme of the present study, he notes 'the strong resemblance between Gen. 47.29 and I Kings 2.1'.[82] The very fact that a succession narrative with so many royal characteristics appears in the case of Joseph and Jacob itself

(Philadelphia: Westminster Press, 1959 and London: SCM Press, 1960), p. 300, that, in the account of Josiah's covenant in II Kings 23, we find 'the king playing a role similar to that of Moses in Deuteronomy and Joshua in Josh. 24'.

[79] Cf. G. Fohrer, 'Der Vertrag zwischen König und Volk in Israel', *ZAW* 71 (1959), pp. 17–22, especially pp. 21f.

[80] Cf. especially the articles on the individual patriarchs in Engnell-Fridrichsen, *Svenkst Bibliskt Upplagsverk*, vols. I–II (Gävle: Skolförlaget, 1948–1952). Cf. also G. Widengren, 'Early Hebrew Myths and Their Interpretation', *Myth, Ritual and Kingship*, ed. S. H. Hooke (Oxford: Clarendon Press, 1958), pp. 183f.

[81] Cf. B. J. van der Merwe, 'Joseph as Successor of Jacob', *Studia Biblica et Semitica Theodoro Christiano Vriezen ... dedicata* (Wageningen: H. Veenman en Zonen, 1966), pp. 221–32.

[82] *Ibid.*, p. 225.

makes it not improbable that similar considerations may apply to the account of two other great figures of the past, Joshua and Moses, where there is succession of rulership. It may be possible to go even further. Genesis 48.22 seems to imply that Jacob bequeathed to Joseph, on the occasion of the latter's succession, the town of Shechem which he owned, as leader of his group, by right of conquest.[83] Involved in Joshua's succession to Moses, especially in the Deuteronomic tradition, is his conquest of the Promised Land, which Moses had failed to accomplish;[84] further, he was to divide the territory among the different tribes,[85] which implies that he had the same sort of rights over the land as did the later Israelite king.[86] It is noteworthy that on three occasions material about the succession of Joshua is closely linked with the statement that Moses was to ascend a mountain to view Palestine, and in the case of at least two of these, Num. 27.12ff. and Deut. 3.23ff., the succession of Joshua seems to be virtually the consequence of the divine command to Moses.[87] But it has been shown that the episode of Moses' ascent of the mountain to survey the land in fact enshrines an ancient legal rule for the transfer of property, by which it was intended to indicate that Moses was given full possession of Palestine before his death.[88] We seem justified in assuming then that Joshua's succeeding Moses implied his inheriting the right of full ownership of the Promised Land which his great predecessor had not been able to

---

[83] *Ibid.* For recent discussions of this difficult verse, cf. G. von Rad, *Genesis*, trans. J. H. Marks (London: SCM Press, 1961 and Philadelphia: Westminster Press), pp. 413f.; E. A. Speiser, *Genesis*. AncB (New York: Doubleday and Co., 1961), p. 358.

[84] Cf. Deut. 1.38; 3.21, 28; 31.3, 7; Josh. 1.6.

[85] Cf. Josh. 13.7.

[86] Cf. E. M. Good, *op. cit.*. p. 992.

[87] In the third example, Deut. 34.1–9, the link is perhaps not quite as close.

[88] Cf. D. Daube, *Studies in Biblical Law* (Cambridge: University Press, 1947), pp. 25–39; 'Rechtsgedanken in den Erzählungen des Pentateuchs', *Von Ugarit nach Qumran*, eds. J. Hempel and L. Rost, BZAW 77 (Berlin: Verlag Alfred Töpelmann, 1958), p. 35.

exercise. But such an absolute right was something that belonged only to the Israelite king, in sharp contrast to the older type of charismatic leader, as such a verse as I Sam. 8.14 makes clear.[89] Once more, there would appear to be a feature in the accounts of the succession of Joshua which can best be explained as a reflection from an originally royal background.[90]

IV

The preceding remarks may serve to introduce a further consideration. Kline has called attention to the influence on the book of Deuteronomy of the form of the vassal treaty, common to much of the ancient Near Eastern world, and specifically to its influence on the material dealing with the succession of Joshua, while

[89] For the full implications of Samuel's speech in I Sam. 8.10–18 for the nature of kingship in Israel, cf. I Mendelsohn, 'Samuel's denunciation of Kingship in the Light of the Akkadian Documents from Ugarit', *BASOR* 143 (1956), pp. 17–22.

[90] The foregoing argument attempts to suggest that Num. 27.12–14 and vv. 15–23 belong closely together, although most scholars consider them to be two originally distinct sections, cf. Möhlenbrink, *op. cit.*, p. 49. But even if Noth, *Numbers*, trans. James D. Martin (London: SCM Press and Philadelphia: Westminster Press, 1968), p. 213, is right in thinking that vv. 15–23 only became linked with vv. 12–14 when the Pentateuch was united with the Deuteronomic history work, and that the linking reflects the typical Deuteronomic coupling of Moses' death with Joshua's succession, this would only mean that the scheme 'Moses' ascent of a mountain/installation of Joshua' is Deuteronomic from the *literary* point of view, and we can still go on to consider what factors may have led to the formulation of this scheme. These, we have proposed, may be found in ideas connected with Israelite kingship. In any case, there are some grounds for holding, against Möhlenbrink and Noth, that the narrative of Joshua's installation is original to the Numbers narrative at this point. Möhlenbrink, *op. cit.*, p. 51, claims that vv. 18–23 are entirely unconnected with any other material in Num. 26–29. But the last verse, v. 65, of Num. 26 mentions Joshua as one of the two survivors of an earlier census. Thus the account of his succeeding Moses, now found in Num. 27.18–23, would have a certain appropriateness at this point and may even have followed 26.65 directly, if the pericope about the daughters of Zelophehad should be viewed as an independent piece of quite ancient legal tradition later added to the basic narrative, as is suggested by Noth, *Numbers*, p. 211.

Baltzer has noted a similar reflection of this treaty form in I Chron. 22: 28–29. It is noteworthy that the idea of the continuation of the overlord's dynasty figures prominently in such treaties: the vassal's oath of obedience is directed both to the reigning king and to his successors. The object of this was to secure the peaceful and orderly transmission of the royal office, since a change of ruler created a difficult situation, when disaffection and revolt might be expected to occur. This royal dynastic concern is clearly indicated in the statements, which round off the accounts of Solomon's accession, that the new king was firmly established on the throne and received the complete obedience of his subjects.[91] Very much the same kind of statements occur also in the case of Joshua. Kline refers particularly to the great vassal treaty of Esarhaddon, which had among its objects the securing of the succession of his son Ashurbanipal to the throne of Assyria, and it is not without interest to compare some of the obligations undertaken by the vassals in this treaty with what is said about the complete submission of the Israelites to Joshua. Thus,

> You will seize the perpetrators of insurrection . . .
> If you are able to seize them and put them to death,
> Then you will seize them and put them to death,[92]

may be compared with Josh. 1.18a. Again,

> You will hearken to
> Whatever he[93] says and will do whatever
> He commands,[94]

may be compared with Deut. 34.9b; Josh. 1.16f.

[91] Cf. I Kings 2.12; I Chron. 29.23f. It might be argued that the former passage, with its emphasis on Solomon's firm grip on the throne, merely reflects the fact that his succession had been disputed, cf. I Kings 1. But the narrative in Chronicles, where the people's obedience is at least equally strongly stressed, omits all reference to this struggle for power, and this suggests that something more is involved.

[92] The translation of D. J. Wiseman, 'The Vassal-Treaties of Esarhaddon', *Iraq* 20 (1958), pp. 39f. For the significance, in relation to the Old Testament, of the obligations assumed by the vassals in these treaties, cf. R. Frankena, 'The vassal-treaties of Esarhaddon and the dating of Deuteronomy', *OTS* 14 (1965), pp. 122–54, especially pp. 140–4.

[93] I.e., Ashurbanipal.   [94] Wiseman, *op. cit.*, pp. 43f.

Further, similar statements about the people's awe of the monarch and the firm establishment of his kingdom occur in connection with Solomon's dream at Gibeon:[95] here, the exceptional wisdom given to Solomon on that occasion[96] is understood as a special sign of divine favour, which creates an abnormal terror among his subjects.[97] But, in Baltzer's words, '*Der Offenbarungstraum Salomos in Gibeon ist der letzte Akt des Thronwechsels*',[98] a comment which applies as much to the narrative in Kings as to that in Chronicles. In precisely the same way, as soon as Joshua succeeds to the position of Moses, he is marked out by a sign of Yahweh's special favour, which is to make clear his continuity with his predecessor[99] and which produces awe and obedience in the people.[100] Interestingly enough, a parallel phenomenon is found in the non-Deuteronomic, and possibly earlier, tradition of Joshua's succession where it would appear that it is his possession of the רוּחַ חָכְמָה which causes the Israelites to obey Joshua.[101]

Noteworthy also is the considerable identity of language used, in the kind of statements under discussion, in the cases of Solomon and Joshua respectively.[102] The absolute obedience and the great awe which are envisaged in the passages just reviewed are surely most characteristic of the monarchy in Israel, as in the world of

[95] Cf. I Kings 3.28; II Chron. 1.1, 13b.
[96] Cf. I Kings 3.12f.; II Chron. 1.12.
[97] This is especially clear from I Kings 3.28, significantly following the story in I Kings 3.16–27, which is to be taken as the practical evidence of Solomon's remarkable wisdom.
[98] Baltzer, *op. cit.*, p. 83. The point is brought out by such passages as I Kings 3.6, 7a, 14; II Chron. 1.8, 9a.
[99] Cf. Josh. 3.7.
[100] Cf. Josh. 4.14.
[101] Cf. Deut. 34.9. Wisdom in the Old Testament is closely associated with kingship, cf. N. W. Porteous, 'Royal Wisdom', *SVT* 3 (1953), pp. 247–61, and it is never mentioned in connection with the type of leadership represented by the pre-monarchical judges.
[102] Thus שָׁמַע occurs at I Chron. 29.23 and at Deut. 34.9; Josh. 1.17f. גָּדַל occurs at I Chron. 29.25; II Chron. 1.1 and at Josh. 3.7; 4.14. יָרֵא occurs at I Kings 3.28 and at Josh. 4.14.

the ancient Near East generally,[103] and, taken together with the other evidence adduced earlier, they provide a further pointer to the original setting of the description of Joshua's succession.[104]

v

In the article referred to earlier, Lohfink demonstrates that in the Deuteronomic tradition there is in fact a double installation of Joshua in his office, on the one hand by Moses, on the other hand by Yahweh himself,[105] and that this represents a deliberately intended and carefully constructed scheme. Lohfink discusses the reason for the double installation only in the most general terms, but once again this phenomenon is best understood when we see its original home in the practice and ideology of the Israelite monarchy. For there we find not infrequently both the designation of the new king by Yahweh himself and also his installation by some human agency. In the case of the accession of Solomon in I Chronicles, where, as has been noted, the parallels with Joshua seem particularly close, David appoints Solomon king,[106] but his previous divine election is clearly referred to in the words אֶחָד בָּחַר־בּוֹ אֱלֹהִים.[107]

Nor is the picture in Samuel and Kings fundamentally different,

[103] For a recent brief account of Canaanite kingship, which particularly stresses these aspects, cf. J. L. McKenzie, *The World of the Judges* (New York: Prentice Hall, 1966 and London: Geoffrey Chapman, 1967), p. 110.

[104] In discussing the succession of Joshua, Lohfink, in line with the above discussion, notes ('Die deuteronomistische Darstellung . . .' *Scholastik* 37 [1962], p. 44): '*dass auch ein Element der Bestätigung durch den Erfolg und die Annahme der Führung durch die Untergebenen zu einem Amt gehört, steckte wohl im traditionellen Erzählungsmaterial*'. He thinks, however, that these themes belong only to Joshua as commander-in-chief and not to the other office of Joshua which he distinguishes, the divider of the land. But the two cannot be clearly distinguished, since both have a common home in the figure of the Israelite king.

[105] *Ibid.*, pp. 40, 43f.

[106] Cf. I Chron. 23.1.

[107] Cf. I Chron. 29.1. Cf. I Chron. 28.5.

for such a verse as II Sam. 7.12[108] implies that Solomon was chosen by Yahweh before his appointment by David, narrated in I Kings 1.30. The same pattern is apparent in the case of David, who in I Samuel is viewed as the successor of Saul, since the charisma of the spirit which Saul had passes to him;[109] thus, Yahweh designates David and Samuel anoints him[110] and, when the elders of Israel anoint David, it is recognized that he has already been designated by a divine oracle.[111] Very interestingly, the same feature occurs in at least two of the accounts of the accession of Saul. Saul is designated by Yahweh and then anointed by Samuel;[112] again, he is chosen by the sacred lot[113] and then accepted by the people in the cry יְחִי הַמֶּלֶךְ,[114] or perhaps 'made' king by them.[115] Further, we find the same rhythm of divine designation and human installation in the case of at least three rulers of the northern kingdom.[116]

[108] Cf. also I Kings 2.4. For the divine choice of Solomon in II Samuel, cf. now G. W. Ahlström, 'Solomon, the Chosen One', *History of Religions* 8 (1968), pp. 100f.

[109] Cf. on this point, J. L. McKenzie, 'The Four Samuels', *Biblical Research* 7 (1962), pp. 1–16, and A. Weiser, 'Die Legitimation des Königs David', *VT* 16 (1966), p. 328.

[110] Cf. I Sam. 16.1–13. That this passage forms an integral part of the narrative of David's rise to the throne in I Samuel is shown by Weiser, 'Die Legitimation des Königs David', *VT* 16 (1966), pp. 326f.

[111] Cf. II Sam. 5.1–3. For this oracle, cf. J. Alberto Soggin, *Das Königtum in Israel*, BZAW 104 (Berlin: Verlag Alfred Töpelmann, 1967), pp. 64–66, and his comment on II Sam. 5.1–3, *op. cit.*, p. 69: '*Wiederum erkennen wir das Schema: göttliche Designation – Bestätigung durch die Versammlung – Krönung.*'

[112] Cf. I Sam. 9.17; 10.1.

[113] Cf. I Sam. 10.20–23. McKenzie, *World of the Judges*, p. 172, completely misunderstands this passage when he seeks to distinguish between choice by divine election and choice by lot, for the two are the same, as I Sam. 10.24, at least in its present context, plainly shows.

[114] Cf. I. Sam. 10.24. For the implications of this expression, cf. P. A. H. de Boer, 'Vive le roi!', *VT* 5 (1955), pp. 225–31, especially p. 231: 'יחי המלך *signifie donc: le roi vit, il detient la puissance royale*'.

[115] Cf. I Sam. 11.15.

[116] Cf. I Kings 11.29–39; 14.7 and 12.20 (Jeroboam I): I Kings 19.16; II Kings 9.1–6, 13 (Jehu): I Kings 14.14; 16.2 (Baasha). We do not

That this pattern is a regular feature of royal ritual is indicated by a number of psalms which, it would now be widely accepted, formed part of an actual coronation ceremony, or the re-enactment of such a ceremony, but which also contain a reference to Yahweh's own appointment of the king. Reference may be made particularly to Pss. 2.6f.; 21.4–6; 110.1f.; 132.11f., 17f.[117] The case is strengthened when it is observed that this double appointment of the ruler, by both divine and human agency, is not confined to Israel but is commonly found throughout the ancient Near East.[118] Once more, an interesting feature in the accounts of the transmission of the leadership of the nation from Moses to Joshua seems best explained as a reflection of specifically royal ideology and practice.

The present study has been mainly concerned with the Deuteronomic tradition of the succession of Joshua, and space does not permit of any extended discussion of the alternative tradition which is found mainly in the book of Numbers. However, we have had occasion to refer more than once to this second tradition in the course of the argument, from which it is clear that it presents an understanding of Joshua's succession which is basically similar to that of the Deuteronomic outlook on this question.[119] Nor has it

---

actually read of any human installation of Baasha, but it is legitimate to suppose that it occurred. Cf. also II Kings 10.30; 15.12 (the four sons of Jehu). It may well be that the explicit mention of a divine designation only in the case of these particular rulers is dictated by the Deuteronomic editors' theological and historical conceptions, as is stressed by T. C. G. Thornton, 'Charismatic Kingship in Israel and Judah', *JTS* n.s. 14 (1963), p. 7. Thornton admits, however, that these editors may well be reflecting earlier ideas and the evidence adduced below strongly suggests that such is the case.

[117] For a representative view, which sees all these Psalms as forming part of a coronation ritual, cf. the comments *ad loc.* of H.-J. Kraus, *Psalmen*, 2nd ed. (Neukirchen: Verlag der Buchhandlung des Erziehungsvereins, 1962).

[118] Cf. the evidence summarized by Thornton, *op. cit.*, pp. 2–4.

[119] The writer may perhaps be permitted to refer to his discussion of the key-passage, Num. 27.15–23, in *Moses and Monarchy*, pp. 17–19. For the relation of this passage to the Deuteronomic traditions, cf. the remarks of R. A. Carlson, *op. cit.*, p. 241.

been possible to consider the more general question of the extent to which the figure of Joshua as a whole is depicted in royal categories in the Old Testament tradition,[120] which would again tend to confirm the view that his succession to Moses is described in terms that have a similar royal background.

One further point may be made in conclusion. Since the fundamental work of Alt and Noth, it has become widely accepted that the historical Joshua had no original connection with the historical Moses. If this is so, it must be said that the process by which Joshua came to be viewed as the 'second Moses' needs much further investigation than it has so far received. Such an investigation cannot be attempted here, but, in view of the preceding discussion, it may perhaps be suggested that the practice and ideology of the royal succession, which, as has been seen, was so vital a concern for the monarchical system in Israel and the ancient Near East, played an essential part in the entire development. Here was an existing pattern by which two great leaders of the nation could be brought together and the transfer of authority from one to the other could be explained and accounted for. It would then be no accident that the succession of Joshua to the office of Moses is most strongly emphasized, and its royal features most clearly discernible, in the scheme of the 'Deuteronomistic historical work', with its central pre-occupation with the responsibility of the Israelite king for the maintenance of the Covenant and thus for the whole religious and social well-being of the nation.

[120] Cf. e.g. E. M. Good, *op. cit.*, p. 996; Östborn, *op. cit.*, pp. 65f.; Widengren, 'King and Covenant', *JSS* 2 (1957), p. 15.

III

The Former Prophets and the Latter Prophets

7

All the King's Horses?*

A Study of the Term פרש *(I Kings 5. 6 [EVV., 4.26] etc.)*

D. R. Ap-Thomas

YEARS of close association and collaboration in the work of the British Society for Old Testament Study make it a pleasure to offer this contribution to the *Festschrift* for Principal G. Henton Davies in the hope that it may in some degree elucidate a few corners of that Book from which he has drawn and conveyed so much illumination.

King Solomon's horse trade provides a ready example of how this wide-awake monarch adopted and developed trades and practices which had existed before his day in Judah, even in Jerusalem. Not only Adonijah (I Kings 1.5) but also Absalom (II Sam. 15.1) had previously obtained and operated horse chariots.

So far as concerns the markets in which Solomon operated, we may, for present purposes, accept the view that Solomon delivered horses from a Que in Anatolia[1] to Egypt, in exchange for Egyptian-made chariots (I Kings 10.28f.).[2] The primary and limited purpose

---

* This essay was read in an abbreviated form to the Section 'Ancient Near East (Hebrew Bible)' of the Twenty-seventh International Congress of Orientalists, Ann Arbor, U.S.A., in August, 1967. An abstract thereof will appear in the *Transactions* of that Congress.

[1] But see now, H. Tadmor, 'Que and Muṣri', *IEJ* XI (1961), pp. 143–50, who denies the existence of any Cappadocian Muṣri and the reading Que in the inscription of Shalmaneser III.

[2] See W. F. Albright, *Archaeology and the Religion of Israel* (Baltimore: The Johns Hopkins Press, 1956), p. 135, for detailed elucidation. Egypt

of this paper is to investigate the origin and meaning of the Hebrew term פרש, in view of the inadequate treatment it has hitherto received.

The only detailed consideration of which the present author is aware is the article entitled 'The Word פָּרָשׁ in the Old Testament' by William R. Arnold,[3] and a section of an article by Kurt Galling.[4] Somewhat remarkably, Galling nowhere refers to Arnold's earlier treatment, though the authors show a good deal in common in their approach and their conclusions. Both prove, to their own satisfaction at any rate, that פָּרָשׁ basically means 'horse'.[5] Arnold concedes a later extension by which 'the generic פרשים *horses* is used tropically as the technical term for cavalry';[6] whereas Galling[7] considers that, by Persian times, it could and often did mean *horseman* as such.

In the opposing camp we find Wilhelm Gesenius and Ludwig Koehler who, in their respective Hebrew Lexicons,[8] make the meaning 'horseman' primary, and 'horse' secondary. Another of the same mind is Schwally[9] who goes so far as to claim, '*Die Bedeutung 'Pferd' für* פרש *ist nicht hinlänglich gesichert.*' Nearly all the ancient versions and later translations of the Old Testament follow suit, translating פָּרָשִׁים by 'horses' only where absolutely necessary – in fact AV adopts it, and almost invisibly at that, only

---

did import chariots from Syria, also leather reins, cf. A. H. Gardiner, *Egypt of the Pharaohs* (Oxford: Clarendon Press, 1964), p. 44.

[3] W. R. Arnold, 'The Word פָּרָשׁ in the Old Testament', *JBL* 24 (March, 1905), pp. 45–53.

[4] Kurt Galling, 'Der Ehrenname Elisas v.d. Entrückung Elias', *ZThK* 53 (1956), pp. 131–5; S. Mowinckel, 'Drive and/or Ride in O.T.', *VT* XII. 3 (July, 1962), pp. 278–99, was noticed too late to be used.

[5] Arnold, *op. cit.*, p. 47; Galling, *op. cit.*, p. 133.

[6] Arnold, *op. cit.*, p. 50.   [7] Galling, *op. cit.*, p. 133.

[8] W. Gesenius, *Hebrew and Chaldee Lexicon*, trans. and ed. S. P. Tregelles (London, 1846), p. 693; L. Koehler and W. Baumgartner, eds., *Lexicon in Veteris Testamenti Libros* (Leiden: E. J. Brill, 1958), p. 783.

[9] In his commentary on Jer. 46.4 – quoted from Arnold, *op. cit.*, p. 45, n. 1.

in II Sam. 1.6, where it renders בַּעֲלֵי הַפָּרָשִׁים by 'horsemen'
(LXX ἱππάρχαι).

There are two main difficulties in trying to decide not so much
whether פָּרָשׁ means 'horse' or 'horseman' but which meaning is
basic and original. The first difficulty is the date of introduction
into Israel of riding (equitation), as opposed to driving (charioteering). The second problem is to find an etymology for פרשׁ.
Neither of these specific points has yet received sufficient attention.

The horse, so we are assured by palaeozoologists, is of American
origin.[10] If so, it early on crossed over into the Old World and,
in a form recognizably similar to that of today, it was already
known to Palaeolithic Man in Europe as an object of the chase, as
evidenced by the cave paintings of Altamira, Font de Gaume and
Niaux, so often reproduced, usually after the drawings of the
Abbé Breuil.[11] The horse seems to have been domesticated first
towards the end of the Neolithic or beginning of the Bronze Age,
and how it was put to use is still not clear. J. Wiesner[12] thinks its
domestication may be as early as the Mesolithic, and that it was
used as a draught animal rather than for war in the first place. An
engraving found at Susa shows a rider on a horse, but doubts
have been cast on the ascribed date at the beginning of the third
millennium BC.[13] Apparently the description of the horse as 'the
ass of the mountains', on a tablet found north of Kish cannot,
either, be anything like as early as 3500 BC.[14] Whatever its correct
date, this tablet does indicate the generally accepted area of
origin of the horse as a domesticated animal, namely the area

[10] F. E. Zeuner, *A History of Domesticated Animals* (London:
Hutchinson, 1963 and New York: Harper and Row, 1964), p. 340.

[11] See, e.g., J. A. Hammerton, ed., *Wonders of the Past* (London:
G. P. Putnam's Sons, 1923), vol. I, p. 149, vol. II, p. 1070.

[12] J. Wiesner, 'Fahren und Reiten in Alteuropa und im Alten Orient',
AO 38 (1939), p. 7.

[13] Zeuner, *op. cit.*, p. 317.

[14] *Ibid.* Wiesner, *op. cit.*, p. 21, thinks the phrase may mean either
horse or mule; but since one parent of the mule is always a horse, the
point is of no significance here.

around the north and east of the Fertile Crescent or, still more specifically, Turkestan, east of the Caspian Sea. This attribution, it should be noted, is made more on biological grounds than from archaeological evidence.[15]

Whatever the date of the earliest record, it is indisputable that the horse, as distinct from the already long-domesticated onager or half-horse and the ass,[16] was known and used in Mesopotamia at the beginning of the second millennium BC, since 'from 2000 BC onwards the horse-drawn chariot swept across the Western world'.[17] John Gray[18] refers in this context specifically to the Aryan chariot-deploying aristocracy, the *mariannu*, exemplified also in the Homeric heroes.[19] But M. Noth[20] deduces, from references to horses at Mari,[21] 'that in Mesopotamia at any rate, the horse – at least the domesticated horse – was . . . a precious rarity' in the days of Zimri-Lim of Mari, Shamshi-Adad I and his sons Ishme-Dagan I in Assyria and Iasmakh-Adad in Mari, and this would be during the nineteenth century BC.[22] If Noth's deduction is correct, then the horse must quickly have become more familiar within the Fertile Crescent.[23]

It might seem surprising at first sight that the primary use of the

[15] Wiesner, *op. cit.*, p. 7; Zeuner, *op. cit.*, p. 315. But cf. R. Graves, *The Greek Myths* (London: Penguin Books, 1955), vol. II, p. 37, ¶109.2.
[16] On these see R. Walz, 'Gab es ein Esel-Nomadentum im Alten Orient?', *Akten der XXIV Internat. Orientalisten-Kongresses*, Munich, 1959, pp. 150f.
[17] Zeuner, *op. cit.*, p. 313.
[18] J. Gray, *The Legacy of Canaan* (Leiden: E. J. Brill, 1957), p. 167.
[19] See G. S. Kirk, 'The Homeric Poems as History', *The Cambridge Ancient History* (Cambridge: University Press, 1964), vol. II, xxxix (*b*), fascicle 22, p. 22.
[20] M. Noth, 'Remarks on the Sixth Volume of Mari Texts', *JSS* 1 (Oct., 1956), p. 331.
[21] *Archives Royales de Mari. Transcriptions et Traductions* (Paris, 1950ff.), I. 50, 9ff.; II. 123; V. 20.
[22] Chronology accepted by J.-R. Kupper, 'Northern Mesopotamia and Syria', *The Cambridge Ancient History*, vol. II, i, fascicle 14, inside back cover.
[23] Cf. H. Schmökel, *Ur, Assur und Babylon* (Stuttgart: G. Kilpper, 1955), pp. 100f.

horse within the areas of developed civilization should be for warfare. But man on the whole was a shrewd creature, very much alive to his own economic advantage. The horse is much more expensive to keep than either the ass or the camel – particularly in the areas less favoured as pasture lands, a description which applies to much of this area; its only real advantage over them is in speed and verve – qualities of prime importance only in mobile warfare. But in battle it is not only advantageous to be able to move about more speedily than one's foes, one must be able to deliver an attack and press it home. This includes the ability to control the means of transport and simultaneously to operate the weapons of aggression and indeed defence. That is why the chariot took priority over riding horseback in the military use of the horse. To ride and control a spirited horse, while at the same time effectively wielding offensive and defensive weapons, could not be easy without the aid of proper harness, and would be natural only where the horse was a familiar and constant factor in daily life. These limitations do not apply in anything like the same degree to the chariot. In the first place, the animal itself is more easily controlled; secondly, a chariot takes two or three men, sometimes four, one of whom can then give his whole attention to driving, while offensive and defensive fighting are the concern of the others in the chariot.[24] The convention on Egyptian monuments, whereby the Pharaoh is shown occupying the chariot alone, is likely to be more honorific than historical.[25]

Must we then conclude that horse-riding, as opposed to chariot-driving, was not known at all at an early period? By no means; although it has often been so implied or even asserted, e.g., E. Kautzsch[26] says, '*Reiterei ist für das ägyptische Heer nicht*

---

[24] See *ANEP* (Princeton: Princeton University Press, 1954), 165, 172; M. A. Beek, *Atlas of Mesopotamia* (London and New York: Thomas Nelson and Sons, 1962), plates 181–183, 227.

[25] E.g., *ANEP*, 190, 327; cf. Gardiner, *op. cit.*, pp. 56f.

[26] *HSAT* (Tübingen: J. C. B. Mohr [P. Siebeck], 1892) on Ex. 15.1, 21, quoted from M. Löhr, 'Aegyptische Reiterei im A.T.?', *OLZ* Nr. 11 (1928), col. 224; cf. also Kurt Galling, *Biblisches Reallexikon*,

bezeugt'. But A. R. Schulman[27] has completely refuted this view for Egypt from the sixteenth century BC on and therefore, *a fortiori*, for the Semitic Near East,[28] since it is generally conceded that Egypt derived its knowledge in matters equine from the Hyksos, i.e., ultimately from the Indo-Aryan horse-rearers of the northern highland fringing the Fertile Crescent, but mediated through the intervening Semitic populations.[29]

The evidence for horse-riding in the Near East outside Egypt is conveniently summarized by E. D. Phillips in these words:

Evidence for riding becomes more abundant late in the second millennium. For example, a Hurrian relief from Tell Halaf of the fifteenth or fourteenth century BC shows a mounted warrior. A Kassite seal of the thirteenth century from Luristan appears to show a mounted archer in fantastic form. Mycenaean potsherds from Ras Shamra (Ugarit) in Syria of the fourteenth or thirteenth centuries may show riders in formation. In the eleventh century Nebuchadnezzar I of Babylon mentions riding horses. . . . On this evidence it appears that regular riding was coming into fashion in the Near East at any rate after the fourteenth century BC, and that it spread thence through the mountain zone to the steppes.[30]

The phrase 'through the mountain zone' is very significant.

HAT (Tübingen: J. C. B. Mohr [P. Siebeck], 1937), col. 425, s.v. 'Pferd'.

[27] A. R. Schulman, 'Egyptian Representations of Horsemen and Riding in the New Kingdom', *JNES* 16 (Oct., 1957), pp. 263–71.

[28] Y. Yadin, *The Art of Warfare in Biblical Lands*, trans. M. Pearlman (London: Weidenfeld and Nicolson and New York: McGraw-Hill Book Co., 1963), p. 220, has an excellent representation of a horseman from the Amarna period and, on p. 113, quotes the envious complaint of the ruler of Byblos that the messenger of his rival of Acco has been given a horse.

[29] See B. Baentsch, *Exodus-Leviticus-Numeri*, HKAT (Göttingen: Vandenhoeck & Ruprecht, 1903), on Ex. 14.9, quoted in Löhr, *op. cit.*, p. 263; J. A. Thompson, *IDB*, vol. E–J, p. 646, s.v. 'Horse'; Zeuner, *op. cit.*, pp. 318, 320f., 337; Gardiner, *op. cit.*, p. 40; J. H. Breasted, *A History of Egypt* (New York: Bantam Books, 1964), p. 193; W. Cullican, 'The First Merchant Venturers', *The Dawn of Civilization*, ed. S. Piggott (London: Thames and Hudson and New York: McGraw-Hill Book Co., 1961), p. 152. For a different view, see I. C. Gelb, 'The Early History of the West Semitic Peoples', *JCS* 15 (1961), p. 41, n. 45.

[30] E. D. Phillips, 'The Royal Hordes', *The Dawn of Civilization*, p. 322; cf. Schmökel, *op. cit.*, p. 116.

The Assyrian records show that a chariot was more of a liability than an asset in mountainous regions. Illustrations show that in mountainous country, even where progress was possible with chariots, the horses could not be driven, they had to be led; in still rougher terrain soldiers had to carry the chariots bodily.[31] In the campaigns of Shalmaneser III to the north of Assyria 'a passage for the chariots could be made only by much labour on the part of the pioneers';[32] and it is instructive to note that Tiglath Pileser I, where the going was too rough for charioteering, fought not on horseback but on foot.[33] Shalmaneser III, though, is depicted as riding on horseback, even though Olmstead[34] comments, 'his sad lack of horsemanship is indicated by his riding straight-legged and with huge stirrups tied to the horse-blanket, not, in the only fashion known to the oriental expert, with hunched up knees and bareback'. We may question, however, whether Shalmaneser's posture is lack of horsemanship, as averred, and not rather an attempt to retain royal dignity. To quote from the letter of the official Baḫdi-Lim to his lord Zimri-Lim king of Mari, 'Let my lord honour his royal status. You are the king of the Haneans, but you are likewise the king of the Akkadians. My lord should not ride on a horse. Let my lord ride on a chariot or indeed on a mule, and let him honour his royal status.'[35] Clearly, horse-riding – perhaps until the advent of trousers or breeches – endangered the royal dignity. The bare-back rider's crouch might be

[31] Yadin, *op. cit.*, pp. 273, 284 and illustrations on pp. 426, 454.

[32] A. T. Olmstead, *A History of Assyria* (New York: Charles Scribner's Sons, 1923), p. 112.

[33] Cylinder Inscription II, 7–11, 70–75; III, 40–47; IV, 66f. – text in E. A. Wallis-Budge and L. W. King, *The Annals of the Kings of Assyria* (London: Trustees of the British Museum, 1902), I, pp. 39, 45, 52f., 65.

[34] Olmstead, *op. cit.*, p. 116.

[35] Quoted from H. W. F. Saggs, *The Greatness that was Babylon* (London: Sidgwick and Jackson, 1962 and New York: Hawthorn Books, 1963), pp. 194f. The source is *Archives Royales de Mari*, VI, 76, 22f. M. Noth, *op. cit.*, pp. 331–3, discusses its significance and tends to the opinion that Baḫdi-Lim advises the king to use a chariot drawn by mules.

good enough for Haneans and barbarous Aryan mountain dwellers; but it would not do for the cultivated, lowland Akkadian! For the latter the proper choice was between the upright stance of the charioteer or the still dignified posture attainable on the back of the plodding mule.

This point of view seems to have been held in Israel too. Absalom and Adonijah both choose the dashing war-chariot (II Sam. 18.1; I Kings 1.5), while Solomon selects – or has selected for him – the royal she-mule of David his father when about to be anointed king (I Kings 1.33). Mule-back seems, indeed, to have been the normal mode of transport of the royal princes of the house of David (II Sam. 13.29). Perhaps this is partly the wilderness streak in David's character manifesting itself again – when in trouble David always headed for the rough out-back of Palestine[36] where the mule would, in fact, be more useful than the chariot. It is noteworthy that during the battle which ended in the Forest of Ephraim we find Absalom, too, mounted not in his chariot but on a mule (II Sam. 18.9). The main conclusion to be drawn from all this is that, since the mule was certainly used for riding in Israel at least as early as David's time,[37] it would not be long before the horse also would be so used – if not by the king, then at least in his service – and so we would have horsemen in Israel as well as horses. This brings us back to the question of the meaning of פָּרָשׁ.

W. R. Arnold argues that the Hebrew פָּרָשׁ, plural פָּרָשִׁים, never means 'horseman' *per se* in the Old Testament except in two late additions, probably under the influence of Aramaic. Here רֹכְבֵי סוּסִים 'riders of horses', so Arnold maintains, has twice been glossed with the word פָּרָשִׁים.[38] Arnold[39] will, of course, agree that פָּרָשִׁים frequently includes the riders as well as their horses, but he

---

[36] Cf. I. Sam. 23.13f.; 27.5; II Sam. 15.14, 23; 17.8f.
[37] Cf. Yadin, *op. cit.*, p. 287.
[38] Ezek. 23.6, 12, but not 23.23; cf. 38.15.
[39] Arnold, *op. cit.*, pp. 5off.

claims that, when a distinction was to be made, with stress on the man rather than on the horse, then the Hebrew writer had to use an expression such as בַּעֲלֵי הַפָּרָשִׁים (II Sam. 1.6). As meaning a man who happens to be riding on a horse, Arnold would find in Hebrew no use of פָּרָשׁ corresponding to Aramaic פָּרָשָׁא, and Arabic *fārisu*ⁿ.

Much of the confusion which has arisen on this subject is probably due to the neglect of scholars to differentiate between 'equestrian' and 'cavalry'. Arnold himself uses 'cavalry' to translate פָּרָשִׁים in passages where he considers the reference to include the riders with their horses; and A. R. Schulman[40] counters objection in these words: 'It can be argued that, since riding was done on a relatively small scale, to call the riders cavalry is inappropriate. Yet they fulfilled one of the main functions of cavalry, that of providing reconnaissance and intelligence, and for that reason, surely deserve to be called cavalry.' Understood in that rather loose way, all well and good; but, in my view, it is better to be more precise. Cavalry, as the term is usually understood, means massed formations of horse-riding combat troops. These almost certainly came into use by the nations of the Fertile Crescent first in the Assyrian army of Asshurnasirpal (884–860 BC). This monarch formed mounted divisions for operation specifically against the cavalry of his opponents in the Zagros mountains. As Ghirshman[41] says, 'To fight against cavalry, cavalry had to be created.' But horse-*riding* had already been known and practiced for centuries before that.

In agreement with both Arnold and Galling it should, I think, be taken as established that the primary meaning of פָּרָשׁ is 'horse'. These two scholars, however, disagree in regard to what sort of

---

[40] Schulman, *op. cit.*, esp. p. 271, n. 52.
[41] R. Ghirshman, *Iran* (London: Penguin Books, 1954), p. 89; cf. Roland de Vaux, *Ancient Israel*, trans. John McHugh (London: Darton, Longman and Todd and New York: McGraw-Hill Book Co., 1961), p. 224; Wiesner, *op. cit.*, pp. 70, 79; Schmökel, *op. cit.*, p. 126.

horse is meant. Arnold[42] maintains that 'סוס is the name of the animal as such; employed as a riding horse, he becomes פָרָשׁ'. Gesenius[43] agrees with this distinction; he says of פָּרָשׁ, 'It is manifestly distinguished from סוּסִים common horses which draw chariots.' Koehler[44] allies himself with this by translating פָּרָשׁ as *'Reitpferd'*.

Galling, on the other hand, very possibly influenced by his own stated belief that 'the Assyrians in the eighth century were the first to form massed cavalry detachments, afterwards further developed by the Persians',[45] asserts[46] quite categorically that פָּרָשִׁים, *'die Streitrosse vor dem Kriegswagen . . . meint'*, i.e., they are chariot-horses, not cavalry horses. Why Hebrew should use two words for horses used for the same purpose he seeks to explain by claiming that פָּרָשִׁים is a technical term derived from the Aramaean area in North Syria. Whether there is anything in this or not, it is true to say that the expression *l r k b [w] l p r s* occurs in the ZKR stele.[47] Fr Rosenthal[48] translates it 'charioteer and horseman', but M. Black[49] renders it 'chariot and horse', and H. Gressmann[50] offers *'Streitwagen und Rosse'*. In their comment on the inscription, Donner and Röllig[51] conclude that, although Galling has made the meaning *'Gespanrosse am Streitwagen'* probable for פָּרָשׁ, it seems unlikely that it is so used on this stele,

---

[42] Arnold, *op. cit.*, p. 51.   [43] Gesenius, *op. cit.*, p. 693.
[44] Koehler and Baumgartner, *op. cit.*, p. 783.
[45] Galling, *Biblisches Reallexikon*, col. 420.
[46] Galling, 'Der Ehrenname Elisas v. d. Entrückung Elias', *ZThK* 53 (1956), p. 132.
[47] H. Donner and W. Röllig, *Kanaanäische und Aramäische Inschriften* (Wiesbaden: Otto Harrassowitz, 1962), vol. I, p. 37, Nr. 202, B. 2.
[48] *ANET*, 2nd ed. (Princeton: Princeton University Press, 1955), p. 502.
[49] M. Black, 'The Zakir Stele', *DOTT* (London and New York: Thomas Nelson and Sons, 1958), p. 247.
[50] *AOT* (Tübingen, 1909), p. 444.
[51] Donner and Röllig, *op. cit.*, vol. II, pp. 209f.

and they favour the translation 'riding horses', in contrast with 'spanhorses'. Their argument does not affect Galling's suggestion that פָּרָשׁ is a North Syrian technical term, but unfortunately this cannot be substantiated since our only evidence is this ZKR stele, generally agreed to date from as late as *ca.* 755 BC.[52]

Can we get any further in an attempt to fathom the true origin of the word פָּרָשׁ? Arnold[53] roundly declares that 'there is no known Semitic root from which they [sc. *pārāš* and *parrāš*] can be derived'. He claims the support of Th. Nöldeke[54] who rejects F. Delitzsch's attempted derivation from Assyrian *parâšu* 'he fled'.[55]

If there is no Semitic root – a question to which we shall return – is there a possible non-Semitic derivation? It would not be surprising to find an Indo-Aryan name borrowed along with the animal. Though there has recently been found in Sumerian a word which may be the same as the Semitic סוּס/סָס/סִיס 'horse',[56] the hitherto accepted derivation for it has been Indo-European, in spite of the difficulty – some would say, impossibility – of equating it with the Aryan *śu*, Vedic *áśva*, Old Persian *ass* – 'horse'.[57] Koehler,[58] among others, has tried to circumvent the difficulty by deriving Semitic סוּס/סָס/סִיס from Indo-Germanic *śiśu*, 'young animal'.

For our purpose it is irrelevant to pursue the derivation and affinity of Hebrew סוּס further, after showing the possibility, even probability, of its having been borrowed from the same source as

[52] Black, *op. cit.*, p. 242.   [53] Arnold, *op. cit.*, p. 45.
[54] Th. Nöldeke, Review of *Prolegomena eines neuen hebräisch-aramäisches Wörterbuch z. A.T.* by F. Delitzsch, *ZDMG* 40 (1886), p. 737.
[55] F. Delitzsch, *Prolegomena eines neuen hebräisch-aramäisches Wörterbuch z. A.T.* (Leipzig, 1886), p. 95.
[56] An identification made by B. Landsberger and mentioned to me by W. F. Albright.
[57] K. Hofman, 'Altiranistik', *HdO* (Leiden: E. J. Brill, 1952), I, iv, 3.
[58] Koehler, *op. cit.*, p. 651, with a further reference to *ZAW* 51 (1933), p. 61.

the animal itself, since one of the earliest records of horse-rearing comes from Chagar Bazar.[59] And what may be true of סוּס may equally be true of פָּרָשׁ, since it is a word for the same animal. Such would not be an isolated phenomenon, for in the reverse direction of borrowing we have animals adopted by Japhet from Shem or Ham also taking with them their original names, e.g., we have Latin *asinus* and Greek ὄνος 'ass', from Hebrew אָתוֹן (or a parallel Semitic formation), and Latin *burdo* 'hinny' from Hebrew פֶּרֶד.[60]

As far as I am aware, no non-Semitic derivation for פָּרָשׁ has yet been demonstrated or even seriously discussed, but it is certainly worth consideration by linguists qualified in this field. The importance attached to the horse in daily life in the Mitannian region is underlined by the incidence of words connected with it as elements of proper names. Of the eighty personal names of Indo-Aryan origin listed and treated by P. E. Dumont,[61] no less than nine seem to be compounded with *áśva* 'horses' or *rata/ratha* 'chariot'.

J. Fuerst[62] seems to have anticipated the hypothesis that פָּרָשׁ might be connected with פָּרַס 'Persia'. Should it be so, the פָּרָשׁ would be 'the Persian (animal)', just as nowadays one may speak of 'an Arab' or 'a Clydesdale' or 'a Morgan'. In parenthesis, it is astounding to note how many different objects – dogs, cats, peaches, window-blinds, etc. – may, in various languages, be called 'Persians'. But, if to resume the argument, 'Persian' might have been used by the West-Semites for a horse, it might have been used either as a generic term or as a more technical expression for a particular class, such as 'riding horse', or for a

[59] R. T. O'Callaghan, *Aram Naharaim*, Analecta Orientalia 26 (Rome: Pontificium Institutum Biblicum, 1948), p. 28.

[60] C. T. Lewis and C. Short, *A Latin Dictionary* (Oxford: Clarendon Press, 1933), pp. 173, 255.

[61] In an Appendix to O'Callaghan, *op. cit.*, pp. 149–53.

[62] J. Fuerst, *Librorum Sacrorum Veteris Testamenti Concordantiae Hebraicae atque Chaldaicae* (Leipzig, 1840), p. 927.

specific breed. Without any reference to an etymology or any supporting evidence at all, Montgomery[63] does indeed assert, 'The word *p r š* denoted a distinct breed of the genus *sûs*.'

Be that as it may, the connection of פָּרָשׁ with פָּרָס 'Persia' seems to break down over the difficulty if not impossibility of getting the Persians to the right place at the right time. The earliest mention of Parsua, Persians, seems to be in the days of Shalmaneser III, *ca.* 844 BC. At that time they were in an area west and south-west of Lake Urmia,[64] or maybe south and south-east thereof.[65] Later the Persians continued their migration until they occupied the area east of the Persian Gulf. Another difficulty in the way of accepting this derivation is that, if the case had been so, we would have expected the word to be found in Akkadian also – there were Persian horse-breeders in the Elamite highlands fairly early.[66] But, whatever the reason, פָּרָשׁ 'horse' or, for that matter, 'horseman' is confined to Hebrew, Aramaic/Syriac, Arabic and Ethiopic; that is, it is West-Semitic. It could therefore be argued that, if we are to seek an etymology for פָּרָשׁ outside the Semitic languages, we should look to Anatolia, which was a famous producer of horses. R. T. O'Callaghan[67] states 'that the early Hittites may also have introduced the horse is not impossible. A cylinder impression from Cappadocia represents a chariot drawn by four

[63] James A. Montgomery, *A Critical and Exegetical Commentary on the Books of Kings*, ed. H. S. Gehman, ICC (Edinburgh: T. & T. Clark, 1951), p. 83.

[64] Ghirshman, *op. cit.*, p. 90.

[65] E. F. Weidner, 'Die Feldzüge Šamši-Adads V gegen Babylonien', *AFO* 9, 3 (1934), p. 103, n. 98. He agrees with G. G. Cameron, Abstract of a Paper: 'New Light on Ancient Persia', in the Proceedings of the Sixth Session of the American Oriental Society, Chicago, 1932 (*JAOS* 52 (1932), p. 304) in distinguishing northern Parsuaš from Cyrus' Parsumaš farther south.

[66] See W. Hinz, 'Persia *c.* 2400–1800 BC', *The Cambridge Ancient History*, vol. I, xxiii, fascicle 19, p. 4.

[67] O'Callaghan, *op. cit.*, p. 69, n. 2; cf. E. Meyer, *Geschichte des Altertums*, 2nd ed. (Stuttgart, 1907ff.), vol. II, 1, p. 23.

horses.' J.-R. Kupper[68] likewise tells us that 'Carchemish . . . sent to Mari . . . horses bred in Anatolia'. Furthermore, since we are dealing specifically with the background to King Solomon's horse trade, it should not be overlooked that we are told that he obtained his horses (סוּסִים) from Cilicia.[69]

To seek a non-Semitic etymology should, though, be a last resort. We may ask whether all the resources of Semitic philology have really been exhausted. BDB[70] lists four different roots under פרשׁ, giving two verbs and two nouns: (1) to make distinct, declare; (2) to pierce, sting; (3) פֶּרֶשׁ 'faecal matter'; (4) פָּרָשׁ 'horse, horseman'. But it would be unwise to overlook the closely associated root פרש with a שׂ, which means basically 'to spread out'.

Akkadian uses both *parāsu* and *parāšu*, basically 'to divide', with the more specific meaning 'to fly'; and in Arabic we find *faraša* 'to spread (the wings)' and 'to open (the legs) wide'. The latter meaning attaches also to the quadriliteralized forms *faršada* or *faršaṭa* and *faršaḥa*.[71]

Is the פָּרָשׁ then the 'leg-stretcher', i.e., 'galloper'? Or, in view of the appearance and swiftness of a galloping horse, it might well be the 'flyer'. Not only are terms appropriate to airborne flight often applied to the movement of the horse, with or without a rider, it might not be irrelevant to draw attention to the very popular theme in mythology of the winged horse, known to the Greek world as Pegasos and, much earlier, frequently depicted as drawing the chariot of the sun across the sky.

There seems to be still another possibility, etymologically. Instead of taking פָּרָשׁ from the Akkadian *parāsu/parāšu*, Arabic

---

[68] Kupper, *op. cit.*, p. 18.

[69] I Kings 10.28, as now usually interpreted. See further J. A. Montgomery, 'The New Sources of Knowledge', *Record and Revelation*, ed. H. Wheeler Robinson (Oxford: Clarendon Press, 1938), p. 12.

[70] BDB (Oxford: Clarendon Press, 1907), pp. 831f.

[71] G. W. Freytag, *Lexicon Arabico-Latinum* (Halle, 1835), vol. III, p. 334.

faraša, in the derived, secondary sense 'to fly', we might enquire whether the more basic meaning 'to divide, split, straddle' might not yield a plausible explanation which would be in line with the use of the verb in Hebrew.

Akkadian has a well-established term *pet-ḫallu* meaning 'horse', specifically a 'riding-horse'[72] and this is also used for 'horse-rider', exactly like פָּרָשׁ in Hebrew.[73] This compound Akkadian expression consists of the verb *pata(ḫ)* 'to open' and *ḫallu* 'crotch (human), hind legs of animals (dual)',[74] or, '*Ober-schenkel*'.[75] Such would be a very graphic description of a horse-rider – he is a 'crotch-opener'! This agrees very well with the Hebrew lexicography of Gesenius and Koehler, previously mentioned, who both make 'horseman' the primary meaning of פָּרָשׁ, deriving it from the verb פָּרַשׁ 'to spread (the legs)'. However, even if פָּרָשׁ did originally mean '(crotch) opener', the application to the horse could as well be the primary one, since it opens its rider's crotch. And this would give a rational basis for its being specifically a riding horse, if the restriction is valid.

Bearing this in mind, attention may be drawn to a peculiar phenomenon or, rather, non-phenomenon of biblical Hebrew. When all the words used for horse in the Old Testament are listed, the surprising result is that, whereas all the other domestic animals have clearly differentiated terms for male and female, the horse to all appearance forms an exception. Apart from the very late trope בְּנֵי הָרַמָּכִים (Esth. 8.10) and the similarly unique לְסֻסָתִי (Cant. 1.9), which may well be collective, we may well ask, where is there a word for 'mare'? W. R. Arnold[76] seems to have

[72] *ANET*, 2nd ed., p. 281, n. 3.

[73] A. Leo Oppenheim, ed., *The Assyrian Dictionary* (Chicago: The Oriental Institute of the University of Chicago, 1956), vol. VI, p. 45, 'Ḥ'.

[74] *Ibid.*

[75] W. von Soden, *Akkadishes Handwörterbuch*, I (Wiesbaden: Otto Harrassowitz, 1965), p. 312.

[76] Arnold, *op. cit.*, p. 50.

realized this lack, but seeks to supply it by giving the phrase צֶמֶד פָּרָשִׁים (Isa. 21.7) the impossible translation 'mare'. He need not have looked so far. Arabic *farasuⁿ*, as is well known,[77] although it can be used as a generic term for 'horse' irrespective of sex, is specifically the 'mare', as opposed to the *ḥiṣānuⁿ* 'stallion'. At the very minimum, there is therefore a strong probability that פָּרָשׁ in Hebrew meant primarily 'mare', though of course it could well have been used generically when sex was not a consideration.

This explanation supplies a very satisfactory solution to the problem of סוּסִים and פָּרָשִׁים occurring pleonastically;[78] and it does not leave us out of reach of a possible further clarification of the etymology already proposed, namely from פָּרַשׁ 'to divide, split', with its Akkadian parallel in *pet-ḥallu*.

The objection to this line of derivation so far is that, if correct, it would mean that horse-riding antedated the coining of the word; and of course it has no apparent reference to the sex of the animal. In view of this and the reasonable assumption that the name is older among the West-Semites than their adoption of equitation, another application of the root meaning of the verb is not far to seek. Anyone who has compared the rear-end view of a stallion with that of a mare will realize the aptness of calling the latter פָּרָשׁ 'cleft' (cf. Hebrew נְקֵבָה 'female' from √נקב).[79]

It might further be argued that if פָּרָשׁ means specifically 'riding horse', then this word took on that meaning because the mare, being by nature less obstreperous than the stallion, was more commonly chosen for riding in the earliest period. King David

[77] E. W. Lane, *An Arabic-English Lexicon* (London, 1863), p. 2367; M. Noth, *Die Welt des Alten Testaments* (Berlin: A. Töpelmann, 1964), p. 33; ET: *The Old Testament World*, trans. V. I. Gruhn (London: A. & C. Black, 1966), p. 39.
[78] As in I Kings 5.6 (EVV, 4.26); 20.20; Ezek. 27.14; 38.4; Hos. 1.7.
[79] It has been suggested to me by W. E. Needler that 'cleft' might here be used in the sense of 'gelded'. So far I have not found evidence to support this.

certainly rode a she-mule (I Kings 1.33), but the pictorial representations of mounted horses – being in any case mainly late – do
not seem to afford much positive support.

To sum up: although a non-Semitic etymology cannot yet be
ruled out, Hebrew פָּרָשׁ, like the Arabic *farasu*ⁿ is probably to be
derived from the root פרשׁ 'to divide, split', and means specifically
'mare'. It is also used generically to indicate 'horse' in general,
but with the tendency to indicate 'riding-horse' rather than draught
animal, and from this there was a natural development to Hebrew
פָּרָ(שׁ), Arabic *fārisu*ⁿ, meaning 'horseman'. In Hebrew the latter
meaning eventually so overshadowed the earlier one that the
Massoretes never reduce the vowel under the first consonant.

Evidence has been adduced to show that at least as early as
Solomon's reign it was quite feasible that horse-riding was
practised in Israel, but when we are told that King Solomon had
'forty thousand אֻרְוֹת סוּסִים for his chariots and twelve thousand
פָּרָשִׁים', it is unlikely that the latter were horsemen or even riding
horses; it is much more probable that they were mares.

8

Elijah at Horeb: Reflections on
I Kings 19.9-18[1]

Ernst Würthwein

WITHIN the complicated chapter I Kings 19,[2] the section vv.
9–18 in particular abounds in difficulties both of a textual and a
theological nature. On the one hand, the passage describing the
events at Horeb (vv. 9–14) is clearly not in order. On the other
hand, exegetes have been faced time and again with the question
of how the content of the theophany depicted there accords with
the tasks which are set for Elijah in vv. 15–18. Such is the diversity
of the answers that have been given that considerable doubt arises
as to whether there was ever any intention at all of a real link between the two, or whether it is not possible that a much more
radical disturbance of the text has taken place. Recently, several
studies have been concerned with these difficulties. But these, too,
in my view, have not led to a satisfactory conclusion. I feel therefore that it might be of value to contribute some thoughts and
observations on the much discussed problem posed by this sec-

[1] Apart from the various commentaries on the books of Kings, I
should like to mention G. Fohrer, *Elia*, AThANT 31 (Zurich: Zwingli
Verlag, 1957); R. M. Frank, 'A Note on I Kings 19.10, 14', *CBQ* 25
(1963), pp. 410–14; Jörg Jeremias, *Theophanie. Die Geschichte einer
alttestamentlichen Gattung* (Neukirchen: Verlag des Erziehungsvereins,
1965); J. J. Stamm, 'Elia am Horeb', *Studia Biblica et Semitica*
(Wageningen: H. Veenman and Zonen N.V., 1966), pp. 327–34; O. H.
Steck, *Überlieferung und Zeitgeschichte in den Elia-Erzählungen* (Neukirchen: Verlag des Erziehungsvereins, 1968).
[2] Steck, *op. cit.*, pp. 20f., provides a perceptive analysis of the chapter.

tion. It is in this form that I should like to make my contribution to this volume in honour of one who has done so much for Old Testament study.

I

I should like first of all to discuss vv. 9–14. It is clear, at the first glance, that the text can scarcely be said to be in order. In v. 9, Yahweh asks Elijah the question 'What are you doing here, Elijah?', and in v. 10 there follows Elijah's complaint. After the description of the theophany and Elijah's reaction to it in vv. 11–13a, we have in vv. 13b–14 an almost identical repetition of vv. 9b–10. It is only after this that Yahweh turns to the complaint of the prophet. Thus, in the text as we have it, vv. 11-13a interrupt the course of the narrative, which is resumed in v. 13b by the repetition of vv. 9b–10.

Wellhausen tried to restore the original text by leaving out vv. 9b–11a[3] and many people have followed him here. More recently, Steck has proposed that we should consider the words of 9bβf., up to and including וַיֹּאמֶר] at the beginning of v. 11, as a gloss.

According to Fohrer, vv. 9b–11aα are 'an extended dogmatic gloss' which is meant 'to reduce the significance of, or even to replace, the description of the theophany'[4] – an explanation of the doublet which is not particularly enlightening. Volz attempts a different explanation of the problem. He suggests that from the similarity of the wording we may 'conclude that originally something else followed v. 13a; but this dropped out at an early period and the gap was filled by some words from the immediate context, i.e. vv. 9b–10, in accordance with scribal usage. Thus we no longer know what originally followed v. 13a'.[5]

In all these treatments of the text, the theophany itself (vv. 11f.),

[3] J. Wellhausen, *Die Composition des Hexateuchs und der historischen Bücher des AT*, 3rd ed. (Berlin: Georg Reimer, 1899), p. 280.
[4] Fohrer, *op. cit.*, p. 19.
[5] P. Volz, *Prophetengestalten des Alten Testaments* (Stuttgart: Calwer Verlag, 1949), p. 121.

where the series of negations is so striking, remained untouched and in the main attention was concentrated on what in fact this negative formulation signifies. Broadly speaking, three kinds of answer have been given to this question. These have recently been outlined by Jörg Jeremias in the book mentioned above.[6] Jeremias makes the following distinctions: (1) a natural or aesthetic interpretation which sees the theophany purely in sensuous and pictorial terms (Wellhausen) or sees it as expressing the divine majesty of God released from all natural phenomena (Gressmann); (2) a moralizing explanation, according to which Elijah is told to fight with inner weapons (Volz); (3) a far-reaching spiritualizing interpretation which finds, among other things, various indications in the theophany of Yahweh's true spiritual nature.[7] All these explanations are unsatisfactory and are rightly rejected by Jeremias. The narrator at this point is certainly not concerned with an aesthetic description. Again, Volz himself saw that on his interpretation the following verses (vv. 15–17) 'cause some difficulty',[8] while the understanding of the passage as a spiritualization of the concept of God eventually gives it 'a dubious symbolical meaning',[9] which is not in accordance with Old Testament thought.

II

Jeremias attempts his own explanation. He regards vv. 11f. as polemical and asks:

[6] Jeremias, *op. cit.*, pp. 113f. Cf. also the discussion of older attitudes in Volz, *op. cit.*, pp. 119f.

[7] Cf., e.g., Fohrer, *op. cit.*, p. 89: 'The being of Yahweh is not depicted with symbols of storm, earthquake and fire, which symbolize the sudden and frightening power of the holy and unapproachable God that scorns all efforts of self-defence by man. The divine being is rather described by the gentle stillness of the breeze.' Thus, 'there is a turning from the God of war and battles to the God whose being is not revealed in terrifying outbursts, but who can be compared to the gentle stillness of the breeze'.

[8] Volz, *op. cit.*, p. 121.

[9] G. von Rad, *Old Testament Theology*, vol. II, trans. D. Stalker (Edinburgh: Oliver and Boyd and New York: Harper and Row, 1965), p. 20.

Were there circles in Israel which spoke of the coming of Yahweh in the 'still small voice (of the wind)', and which rejected the link, often made in Israel, between Yahweh and the destructive forces of nature, because, in Israel's religious environment, the manifestation of the gods was usually just so linked with them? In this case it was not a more refined conception of God which characterized these circles, but their opposition to equating the religion of Yahweh with the religions of the world around. The polemic against the world around would necessarily lead to a polemic against Israel's own religious tradition. At the time of Elijah such a polemic would have been quite conceivable.[10]

Jeremias does not go into the textual problems of vv. 9–14, nor does he ask how his interpretation fits into the context. The polemic at this point seems to be introduced more or less by chance, which is remarkable if it belongs to the original text. Somehow or other we should have expected the narrator to have made clear the significance of such a polemic in this context. Stamm rightly asks whether it is probable 'that such a pragmatic story, centring on the concrete task of Elijah, contains a piece of theology which has nothing directly to do with the prophet's business'. In addition Stamm points out that even in post-exilic, indeed in post-Old Testament times, the destructive forces of nature kept their place in accounts of the theophany.[11]

Finally, it must not be overlooked that the theophany of I Kings 19 still remains linked to the natural phenomena of storm, fire and earthquake. They remain, as Jeremias himself says, as 'accompanying phenomena'. A polemic which sought to maintain the purity of the Yahweh cult would have had to differentiate much more sharply.[12] Thus Jeremias' solution is as unsatisfactory as those which he himself rejects.

[10] Jeremias, *op. cit.*, p. 115.   [11] Stamm, *op. cit.*, p. 333.
[12] The linking of the theophany with natural forces was apparently so firmly a part of the tradition that these accompanying phenomena could not simply be left aside. That 'Yahweh was not in the storm, the fire, the earthquake' should really be understood in the sense: 'he was not (yet) in them'. Thus, for example, in Ps. 97.2f. we have: 'Clouds and thick darkness are round about him ... fire goes before him and burns up his adversaries round about.' Here, too, as in other passages, Yahweh is not identified with the natural forces.

III

Stamm himself who, like Jeremias, does not go into the textual problems, is particularly concerned to show an inner connection of the theophany with the task described in vv. 15f. and the pronouncements of vv. 17f. Just as storm, earthquake and fire represent forces of destruction, so the three anointings which Elijah is to perform have a brutally destructive effect because all those anointed 'are appointed to take up the sword and set in motion political upheavals with horrifying consequences'. In contrast to the destructive forces of nature the 'sound of a gentle breeze' is certainly an uncanny phenomenon but nevertheless it does not bring destruction; it is something insignificant and scarcely perceptible in which, however, Yahweh draws near. Stamm believes that this fourth phenomenon corresponds to the fourth pronouncement to Elijah, according to which Yahweh would leave seven thousand who had not bowed to Baal.

> The continued existence of the people of God depends on these seven thousand. Therefore they represent the real object of Yahweh's activity, the sphere where he is present. By contrast, Elijah's spectacular tasks represent only transitional stages, acts of judgment which forward this aim. Yahweh is also the originator of these, but they are not the sphere of his actual presence. Thus the encounter with God, with its four elements, is a preparation for the future career of the prophet, particularly with regard to the seven thousand whom he himself can neither bring together nor protect. He must simply believe that they will be there and the fourth element of the theophany is a guarantee of this. [13]

Stamm's endeavour to bring out again the inner connection between the description of the theophany and the statements connected with it in vv. 15f. is to be welcomed. One cannot avoid the impression, however, that Stamm finds far more 'intellectual construction'[14] behind the story than one can really attribute to a legend of this kind and thereby comes close to that kind of symbolism which vitiates the moral and spiritual interpretations.[15]

[13] Stamm, *op. cit.*, p. 334. [14] Steck, *op. cit.*, p. 118.
[15] Cf. above p. 154.

Certainly it is right, in my view, to say that the description of the theophany sets out to distinguish between the direct and the indirect presence of God. But here clearly there is a very carefully thought out differentiation which must be understood from the standpoint of particular presuppositions.

It is moreover important to ask whether it is in keeping with the faith of the Old Testament to find these distinctions in *history*, as though Yahweh were not present in judgment as truly as in salvation. If I am right, then vv. 15–17 answer the doubts and questionings about what Israel experienced at the hands of Hazael, Jehu and Elisha. The answer is that what takes place occurs not just by permission of Yahweh, but is in fact set in motion by Yahweh. He is therefore wholly and intrinsically involved in it, just as clearly as he is in the salvation of the seven thousand. The sentence, 'Yahweh is also the originator of these (i.e. the acts of judgment) but they are not the sphere of his actual presence',[16] does not seem to me to take this into account; it is challenged by the whole Old Testament view of history.[17]

IV

Steck, to whom we are indebted for the most recent examination of the Elijah stories, partly follows Jeremias' view of the episode. '*Yahweh*,' he writes, '*is set against the deities of the world around and against the ways in which they manifest themselves – Yahweh, who manifests himself in his word to the prophets, and who works through them* (vv. 15–18)!'[18] In his view, however, Jeremias fails to grasp this latter point because of 'an impossible derivation of דְּמָמָה from

---

[16] Stamm, *op. cit.*, p. 334.

[17] Cf. also Steck's criticism of Stamm's interpretation, *op. cit.*, p. 118: 'Quite apart from the theological premises and the intellectual system behind them, Yahweh's acts of judgment and his preservation of a remnant cannot be taken as indications respectively of his indirect and direct presence, nor does the text permit us to interpret this judgment as a transitional stage having as its goal the preservation of the remnant.'

[18] *Ibid.*, Italics his.

157

the cultic sphere with the aid of Qumran texts which are scarcely enlightening here'. I intend to come back to this problem later. At this point, we need only concern ourselves with the question whether we can see in the theophany the contrast which Steck finds between the manifestation of the deities of the world around in the natural elements and the manifestation of Yahweh in the word. In my view, this question must be answered in the negative. If such a contrast had been intended, it is impossible to understand why the natural elements are mentioned at all as phenomena which accompany the appearance of Yahweh. In the outlook of the author to whom this description goes back, whoever he may have been, they belong to Yahweh, even though he is not (yet) present in them. Since Yahweh's theophany is also frequently linked with the natural elements elsewhere,[19] their mention in this passage stands in the way of Steck's view of a polemical intent in the account of Yahweh's confrontation with Elijah.

The contrast between Yahweh's manifestation in the *word* to the prophets and the manifestation of the deities of the world around in natural forces is also unhelpful because, in many descriptions of Yahweh-theophanies, the natural elements are intimately linked with Yahweh's word, c.f., e.g., Ps. 50, where Yahweh's word immediately follows the description of the theophany. Even where such a connection is not expressly mentioned, the idea of Yahweh's word may still be present. When, for example, in the Accession psalms, it is said that Yahweh is coming to judge the earth, the concept includes his word of judgment. In Ps. 95, which should be included among the Accession psalms, the warning word of Yahweh is preserved in vv. 8–11, and is to be considered as belonging to the theophany on the occasion of the accession to the throne. Thus our conclusion about Steck's modification of Jeremias' thesis must be that an intentional polemic would have had to be formulated much more plainly, if it were to be clear to the reader.

[19] Cf. the evidence in Jeremias, *op. cit.*, pp. 7ff.

V

Thus it is impossible to consider as successful either the older or the more recent attempts to interpret the theophany theologically and to relate it to its context. The fact that these attempts fail repeatedly seems to me to show that we are dealing here with a profound disturbance of the narrative and that we must use more radical means to recover the original course of the story. Steck himself seems to envisage going further when he writes: 'Of course v. 13aα could also be linked directly with the command in v. 11a.' However, he then goes on, 'but stylistic grounds for omitting the theophany are lacking'.[20] It is strange that Steck, who otherwise in general shows keen insight, has not observed the stylistic arguments in favour of leaving out the account of the theophany. For they are clearly present.

1. Such a subtle and careful description of the theophany, which with its negative statements clearly aims at precise delineation, would stylistically only signify no break within the story if its striking individuality were borne out in what followed or were even demanded by the context. This is not the case, as we have seen from the fact that the commentators have succeeded only in making a link between the theophany and its context by means of interpretations more or less forced. Hempel observed as early as 1926 that I Kings 19.10ff. is at odds with the general character of the story of Elijah and with the picture of Elijah in later tradition (cf. Luke 9.54). He suggests that vv. 10–14 'distort the outlook of a theophany, which accords rather with vv. 17ff. . . . Their author is related in spirit to the writer of the little book of Jonah'.[21] This last sentence suggests that Hempel finds in the existing theophany a theological view of Yahweh as acting not in natural catastrophes but peaceably.

Jepsen sees the genesis of the present text in a more complicated

[20] Steck, *op. cit.*, p. 22.
[21] J. Hempel, *Gott und Mensch im Alten Testament*, 1926, p. 42; 2nd ed. (Stuttgart: Verlag von W. Kohlhammer, 1936), p. 57.

light. He assumes two versions, one of which was introduced later and implies a transformation of the concept of God, 'whereas the other belongs to an older period, with its picture of Elijah being given the task of anointing Hazael, Jehu and Elisha for the destruction of Israel'. Jepsen agrees with Hempel's view of vv. 10–12, according to which these verses betray a later concept of Yahweh. Also he asks the question 'is it perhaps the case that there was once something quite different here which has later been suppressed by the two extant versions of the theophany?'[22]

But is it inevitable that there must have been in the original text something as different as Hempel and Jepsen think? Does a gap occur in the course of the narrative and, in particular, does the theological message of the story, which at any rate must be seen in the words of Yahweh in vv. 15–18, become incomprehensible if the theophany is left out? The opposite is the case. This is a strong stylistic reason which speaks for the secondary nature of the account of the theophany.

2. In the present text of vv. 9–14, it is particularly striking that vv. 9b–11a are repeated verbally in vv. 13b–14. The efforts made since Wellhausen to remove this doublet have been discussed above. But the origin of the doublet has so far not been satisfactorily explained. The solution of this problem is in my view to be found by means of literary criticism. In his article 'Die "Wiederaufnahme" – ein literarkritisches Prinzip?',[23] C. Kuhl gives examples to support the view that the repetition of whole sentences or parts of sentences is the result of the fact that 'in the original text there has been an interpolation and after the interpolation the original thread of the story is resumed by the repetition of the last words, indeed of whole sentences and sometimes even longer sections'.[24] One may well disagree with Kuhl's interpretation of specific passages, but nevertheless in my view he has proved 'the theory and the fact of resumption'. It seems here that a common

[22] A. Jepsen, *Nabi* (Munich: C. H. Beck'sche Verlagsbuchhandlung, 1934), p. 63.
[23] In *ZAW* 64 (1952), pp. 1–11.　　　　[24] *Ibid.*, p. 2.

practice of antiquity has been followed. In a note to Kuhl's article, Hempel quotes a remark of E. Hirsch:[25] 'This stylistic device can be illustrated by the practice, found also in the Hellenistic period, of ending an insertion with the same words: the interpolation ends with a statement which often corresponds word for word with that which occurs at the point where the original text is interrupted.'[26]

Clearly I Kings 19.13b–14 reproduce exactly the words of vv. 9b–10. If the resumption is to be understood as a literary device of the kind just mentioned, then vv. 11–13a must be viewed as a subsequent interpolation, and vv. 13b–14 as a resumption made necessary by it. We are therefore justified in holding vv. 11–14 to be alien to the original story. The text of the scene at Horeb then reads in its original form:

[9]And there he came to a cave, and lodged there; and behold [a voice][27] came to him and said to him, 'What are you doing here, Elijah?' [10]He said, 'I have been very jealous for Yahweh, the God of hosts; for the people of Israel have forsaken [thee],[28] thrown down thy altars, and slain thy prophets with the sword; and I, even I only, am left; and they seek my life, to take it away.' . . . [15]And Yahweh said to him, 'Go, return on your way [. . .];[29] and when you arrive, you shall anoint Hazael to be king over Syria; [16]and Jehu the son of Nimshi you shall anoint to be king over Israel; and Elisha the son of Shaphat of Abel-meholah you shall anoint to be prophet in your place. [17]And him who escapes from the sword of Hazael shall Jehu slay; and him who escapes from the sword of

---

[25] E. Hirsch, 'Stilkritik und Literaranalyse im vierten Evangelium', *ZNW* 43 (1950/51), p. 133.

[26] *Loc. cit., ZAW* 64 (1952), p. 11.

[27] Read קוֹל instead of דְּבַר־יהוה with v. 13, which has preserved the original text; the formula 'the word of Yahweh came to him and he said' is unsuitable as an introduction to the question 'What are you doing here?' or to the command in v. 11, 'Go forth, and stand upon the mount before Yahweh.' Further considerations are against the formula 'the word of Yahweh came to him': it is never followed by 'and he said' and it is not used where one would expect it, i.e., at the beginning of v. 15.

[28] Read, with some LXX evidence, עֲזָבוּךָ.

[29] מִדְבָּרָה דַּמֶּשֶׂק is an obvious gloss.

Jehu shall Elisha slay. [18]Yet I will leave seven thousand in Israel, all the knees that have not bowed to Baal, and every mouth that has not kissed him.'

We thus obtain a text which hangs together and is complete in itself. Yahweh replies to the complaint of the prophet by giving him a new task, by an announcement of judgment and by a word of promise. Elijah's assertion that he is alone is corrected. Seven thousand have not gone over to the worship of Baal. The others will face Yahweh's judgment through the agency of Hazael, Jehu and Elisha, and Elijah himself will set this judgment in motion by anointing them.

VI

The conclusion which results from our observations for the understanding of this scene can only be indicated briefly in what follows.

Obviously the description of the theophany cannot be taken into account in interpreting the original story. As we saw, it has always caused difficulties and has led to dubious speculations and reconstructions. If it is left out of account it then becomes clear that the pivot and the real point of the story lie in the words of Yahweh in vv. 15–18. These words arise from the situation presupposed in v. 17. The historical events referred to there must be dated in the period after Elijah, which makes it clear that we are not dealing with a biographical story about Elijah; the question of its historical reliability is therefore not relevant. What we have before us is similar to what, in the case of the Gospels, has been called 'a creation of the community'. It represents the preaching of a circle which, in the face of the great crisis in which Israel finds itself, a crisis which seems to be leading to her total destruction,[30] poses the question: why is this happening and how will it end? The answer is: the suffering of Israel in this crisis is part of

[30] Steck, *op. cit.*, pp. 91ff., thinks the struggle with the Arameans is in view here.

Yahweh's purpose. He himself has brought it about through the agency of Elijah, and it is to be understood as his judgment on the behaviour of his people, described in v. 10. He has, however, also given a promise: a remnant will remain, a remnant of faithful worshippers of Yahweh, who have withstood the temptation of falling away to the cult of Baal. But only these will remain, and here one can see a clear paranetic motif: Resist apostasy!

Thus in the words of Yahweh in vv. 15–18, three motifs are interwoven: the real significance of the present crisis, a promise, and a warning. Israel, which formerly at Horeb/Sinai had become the people of Yahweh, is smitten by Yahweh's judgment because of its back-sliding: but it will continue in so far as it remains the people of Yahweh.[31] This is the new message of Horeb which is put back into the mouth of Elijah.

VII

Those who see vv. 11–13 as an addition should not be satisfied merely with arguments on formal and stylistic grounds, but should try also to indicate the motives which led to this addition. One reason could well be that it was desired to associate Elijah with a theophany, since Elijah and Moses are often put in parallel, as Fohrer, for example, has stressed.[32] So Yahweh passes by Elijah as he passed by Moses (Ex. 33.19, 22).

But how are the remarkable and unique features in the description of this theophany to be explained? Here I can only venture a tentative suggestion. These features admittedly do not stand in complete contrast to other theophany descriptions, but the statement that Yahweh is not (yet) in them is very striking. Jeremias and Steck have suggested that the negations are to be

---

[31] Steck asks (*ibid.*, p. 129): 'Is there not expressed – and this goes beyond the contemporary situation – the conviction that, wherever Yahweh exists, there Israel will remain also?' But this does not seem to bring out the full sense of v. 18, since it ignores the note of warning.

[32] Fohrer, *op. cit.*, pp. 48f.

understood as a polemic against Canaanite ideas, a suggestion about which we have already expressed our doubts. We should not see a polemic here but rather some very subtle reflections on the part of the author. Their natural elements which are mentioned are met with elsewhere as the accompanying phenomena of a Yahweh-theophany and cannot be understood in any other way here. But the theophany was not only a literary convention; it was experienced as a cultic event, as is widely accepted.[33]

[33] The question whether a theophany existed in the Israelite cult has frequently been discussed in the last few years. It is only possible here to touch briefly on the question. Mowinckel, Johnson, Weiser and others have put forward weighty arguments for a dramatic celebration of the theophany. With reference to Weiser's essay 'Zur Frage nach den Beziehungen der Psalmen zum Kult: Die Darstellung der Theophanie in den Psalmen und im Festkult', *Festschrift Alfred Bertholet* (Tübingen: J. C. B. Mohr, 1950), pp. 513ff., reprinted in *Glaube und Geschichte im Alten Testament* (Göttingen: Vandenhoeck & Ruprecht, 1961), pp. 303ff., K. Koch, for example, concludes: 'Precisely how the theophany is to be envisaged within the framework of the Jerusalem cult is still not entirely clear but one can scarcely dispute that some sort of divine appearance took place within the framework of the autumn festival', 'Wesen und Ursprung der "Gemeinschaftstreue" im Israel der Königszeit', *ZevE* 5 (1961), p. 87. On the other hand, there has been some opposition to the thesis of a theophany in the cult, most recently from Jeremias, *op. cit.*, pp. 118ff. But Jeremias limits the concept of the theophany too rigidly and discusses only one tradition. It is probable that, in the Israelite cult, dramatic representations played a role indicating a divine appearance. Support may be found for this in such texts as Lev. 9.23–24b, which, according to K. Elliger, *Leviticus* (Tübingen: J. C. B. Mohr, 1966), p. 131, 'preserves an actual piece of ritual.... Yahweh's epiphany, which was expected in every act of worship and received with humble prostration, took place in the first act of worship at the time of Moses. On that occasion, the people shouted, entranced by the glory of Yahweh, only to fall on their faces at the next moment before his majesty.' There are therefore in the Old Testament other ideas that those of Lev. 16.2, on the basis of which Jeremias argues against Weiser. The problem demands the consideration of all the relevant texts, including, for example, Ex. 33 as understood by von Rad, in '"Righteousness" and "Life" in the Cultic Language of the Psalms', *The Problem of the Hexateuch and Other Essays*, trans. E. W. Trueman Dicken (Edinburgh: Oliver and Boyd and New York: McGraw-Hill Book Co., 1966), p. 258. Jeremias himself holds the view that 'from time immemorial דממה implied the cultic presence of Yahweh', *op. cit.*,

When, however, a theophany was celebrated in the cult, thoughtful spirits might well ask how the individual features in the dramatic representation were actually related to Yahweh himself. In the passage under discussion, a very discriminating answer is given: Yahweh is not present in what is seen and heard but in the 'sound of a gentle (wind) stillness',[34] which occurs after the fury of the natural elements. Here Yahweh is speaking with his prophet. Steck therefore is quite right when he suggests that קוֹל דְּמָמָה דַקָּה shows Yahweh 'as the prophet hears him when receiving his word'.[35] This view is not contradicted, as Steck maintains,[36] but is in fact underlined by Jeremias' conclusion from the appearance of the expression דממה in 4QSl 40.24 in a cultic context, 'that from time immemorial דממה implied the cultic presence of Yahweh and so, in these circles, the coming of Yahweh to Elijah was described in the same way as one spoke of his presence in the cult'.[37]

As far as the details of the theophany are concerned, it has been pointed out that Ex. 33.18, 21–23, in spite of its completely different language, is reminiscent of 1 Kings 19.9a, 11–13a.[38] Concerning the passage in Exodus, von Rad has remarked:

It seems to me certain, therefore, that the passage at Exod. 33.18ff., as well as the other *pericopae* in this chapter, formerly performed a function in the aetiology of the cultus, providing the justification for a ritual which was understood as a theophany, or perhaps even as a substitute for a theophany. The congregation would call upon Yahweh, Yahweh would pass by and declare his name and his attributes, and the congregation would prostrate themselves. Evidently it was only the cultic ministers, and perhaps only certain groups of them, who were privileged to take part in these cultic occasions.[39]

---

p. 115. Is it not likely therefore that we should think of a cultic reality in the case of the 'accompanying phenomena' also?

[34] On this, cf. Jeremias, *op. cit.*, p. 114.

[35] Steck, *op. cit.*, p. 117, n. 5.

[36] *Ibid.*, p. 118.   [37] Jeremias, *op. cit.*, p. 115.

[38] Cf. M. Noth, *Exodus*, trans. J. S. Bowden (London: SCM Press and Philadelphia: Westminster Press, 1962), p. 258.

[39] von Rad, *op. cit.*, p. 258.

Von Rad goes on: 'It is difficult to say how we ought to imagine the cultic process by which Yahweh "passed by".' In view of the Assyrian expression 'the passing by of the gods', he believes that 'cultic emblems were carried past'.[40] Such or similar cultic acts, with which a prophetic announcement was linked, are clearly presupposed by the subtle reflections on the nature of Yahweh's presence which we find in 1 Kings 19.11–13a. This passage is far removed in time from the original story, and further research would be necessary to decide in which particular circles it originated.

However one views these final suggestions, the secondary character of the theophany of vv. 11–13a seems certain in view of the arguments I have outlined above.

[40] von Rad, *op. cit.*, p. 258, n. 22.

9

Prophet and Covenant: Observations on the Exegesis of Isaiah

Walther Eichrodt

THERE has of late been a good deal of renewed discussion concerning the age and significance of the idea of the covenant in Israel and the far-reaching historical and theological researches which, during the last decades, have sought to work out the central significance of the divine covenant from various points of view, have been subjected to sharp criticism. This criticism revives, in a certain sense, the position of the Wellhausen school on this question, and denies the possibility of our speaking of a definitive formulation of the idea of the covenant in the religious thought of Israel before the sixth century BC. To be sure, the information brought together from previously unknown or unconsidered ancient oriental material is still far from really calling in question that unique form of early Israelite faith. Rather could one ask whether the role of the covenant in the message of the pre-exilic prophets does not suggest that this particular Israelite relationship with God took only superficial root and rapidly exhausted its effectiveness. It is above all the prophet Isaiah whose message seems to justify the considerable doubt about a more profound influence on the religious life in Judah of the Sinai tradition. It is at this point that criticism has begun time and time again.

Accordingly, L. Rost has stressed the antithesis between the theology of Isaiah and what is known of the faith of Northern

Israel.[1] It was above all G. von Rad who worked out, in a most interesting way, the consequences of this for the position of early prophecy with regard to the ancient Israelite theology of the covenant. The question he asked in 1949 – 'whether Isaiah knew this "theology" at all in the sense of its classical formulation in the source documents of the Hexateuch'[2] – has become the pivot of the understanding of this prophet.[3] With rather more caution, Bright[4] follows a similar line in accepting that the Sinai covenant had in fact been forgotten in the official cult and in seeing Isaiah as essentially determined by Davidic covenant theology, though leaving open a certain influence on him of the old covenant tradition.

Recently this thesis has been used by those critics who deny altogether the central significance of the idea of the covenant. Thus C. F. Whitley felt able to maintain that the prophets of the eighth and seventh centuries had little or no knowledge of a covenant of Israel with Yahweh but that they conceived the relationship of God to his people as a natural family relationship, and used the images of such a relationship to express this.[5] G. Fohrer agrees with this in his wide-ranging attack on the over-estimation of the covenant in present-day theology, even though he maintains that the Sinai בְּרִית is a well-documented historical event.[6] He sees a 'century-long gap' between the time of the Judges and the time of

---

[1] L. Rost, 'Sinaibund und Davidsbund', *ThLZ* 72 (1947), pp. 129–34.

[2] G. von Rad, 'The City on the Hill', *The Problem of the Hexateuch and other Essays*, trans. E. W. Trueman Dicken (Edinburgh: Oliver and Boyd and New York: McGraw-Hill Book Co., 1966), pp. 232–42.

[3] G. von Rad, *Theologie des Alten Testaments* (Munich: Chr. Kaiser Verlag), vol. I, 4th ed. (1962), pp. 57, 80, 350; vol. II (1960), pp. 158ff. ET: *Theology of the Old Testament*, trans. D. M. G. Stalker (Edinburgh: Oliver and Boyd and New York: Harper and Row), vol. I (1962), pp. 47, 66, 362; vol. II (1965), pp. 147ff.

[4] J. Bright, *A History of Israel* (Philadelphia: Westminster Press, 1959 and London: SCM Press, 1960), pp. 272, 278f.

[5] C. F. Whitley, 'Covenant and Commandment in Israel', *JNES* 22 (1963), pp. 37ff.

[6] G. Fohrer, 'Altes Testament – "Amphiktyonie" und "Bund"', *ThLZ* 91 (1966), pp. 801ff., 893ff.

Deuteronomy, during which the whole institution of the Covenant was forgotten. Thus D. J. McCarthy,[7] in a very cautious and pertinent analysis of the difficulties that still exist in explaining the idea of the covenant in Israel, says: 'Still the troubling question remains, why do the prophets avoid the word "covenant"?'

In the following discussion, the message of Isaiah will be examined to see whether it contains evidence which directly or indirectly gives information about its position with regard to the Sinai covenant and the sacral community of the tribes who were bound by it, and to see how this information is to be understood.

I

To begin with, the designation of God as 'the Holy One of Israel', which is characteristic of Isaiah and carries for him a special meaning, may well be of significance here. It can be found in ten well-attested passages, 1.4; 5.19, 24; 10.17; 29.19; 30.11f., 15; 31.1; 37.23.[8] The critical objections to some passages[9] are not so important that we need dwell on them here; indeed, the remaining occurrences of the name are sufficient for our purpose. As 5.19 and 30.11 make clear, it was precisely this divine name which, for the opponents of the prophet, summarized all they disliked in his message. The name must therefore have had a distinct significance for them, even though its appearances are not now particularly numerous, if they were moved to deny it so vigorously.

In fact, two things make this name unforgettable. First, the use of קָדוֹשׁ in place of the divine name. Admittedly there were also current in Israel other appellatives in place of God's own name, such as 'the Light of Israel', 'the Rock of Israel', 'the Mighty One of

---

[7] D. J. McCarthy, 'Covenant in the Old Testament', *CBQ* 27 (1965), pp. 217ff.

[8] In addition to these, in a wider sense 5.16 and 6.3 should be taken into account. Here, however, the link of the holy God with Israel is not explicit.

[9] Cf. L. Rost, *Israel bei den Propheten*, BWANT IV, 19 (Stuttgart: W. Kohlhammer Verlag, 1937), pp. 37ff.

Israel', etc. These three can also be found in Isaiah at 10.17, 30.29 and 1.24, though the first two are attributed – in my view wrongly – to a later revision of the text. It is quite clear that these names designate Israel's God as the strong helper and supporter of his people, and consequently they enjoyed considerable popularity. The title 'the Holy One' is something quite different. Originally used as a cult name to characterize the unapproachable Majesty, which meant for man awesome mystery and super-human power, and which could be made visible in the earthly world in its כָּבוֹד, that is, its shining brilliance, it becomes for Isaiah in the hour of his call an expression of the moral power of God above the world. As such, it indeed annihilates the sinner but draws the penitent into its sphere through its absolution, in order to make him the herald of its coming rule over the world.

When Isaiah links this highly significant term with 'Israel', the name for the sacral community established by Yahweh himself, he makes clear with *one* word the tremendous privilege, but also the tremendous threat, which every member of this community had taken upon himself. To stand in close relationship with this God as his people means to be in the direct proximity to the 'devouring fire' and the 'everlasting burnings'. The nation thus chosen is protected by a power above all other powers in the world, but is constantly answerable to its demands in the world and must follow them unconditionally. It is clearly impossible for the people to find comfort by resorting to the Holy One who has chosen Israel as his instrument without also following his commandments, which seek to re-make the whole life of the world. It is little wonder that the proclamation of this divine name, in all its harsh severity, aroused the powerful opposition of the self-confident authorities who fell under its sentence.

For the present discussion, however, it is of particular significance that Isaiah has created this effective weapon for his attack on a race alienated from God with the aid of the name 'Israel'. He uses the name of the sacral tribal confederacy quite naturally for the people of Judah and Jerusalem, knowing full well that he is here on a firmly established base, against which there can be no opposition. It would be pointless to date his linking of this name with Judah only after the fall of Samaria, since the relevant passages cannot be dated in most cases with any certainty and some more probably suggest an early stage in the prophet's activity, e.g., 5.19; 1.24; 5.24. It was not because the name 'Israel' had become available after the fall of Samaria that the prophet could venture to claim it for Judah, but because this name also had, as well as its political significance as a designation for the Northern Kingdom, a religious and theocratic significance, going back before the creation of the state, as the description of the people of Yahweh to whom Judah also belonged.[10]

This can further be seen in the ways Isaiah uses the name 'Israel' in other places. He knows and uses it also in its political sense, e.g., 9.7, 11,13; 17.3f., perhaps also 7.1. But in his threatening word against the Northern Kingdom, along with יְהוָה צְבָאוֹת (17.3), which was also the great name of God current in Judah, he uses the other term אֱלֹהֵי יִשְׂרָאֵל, (17.6), in order to characterize the coming annihilation expressly as the work of the God who does not spare, on grounds of favouritism, the people chosen and sanctified by him, but delivers them to ruin because of their complete estrangement from him. Even those critics who see this passage as suspect must admit that the use of the name 'Israel' for Judah is already clearly attested in the pronouncements of the early period of the prophet; cf. 5.7; 8.18. The fact that the two kingdoms are called 'both houses of Israel' in 8.14, which comes from the beginning of the prophet's ministry, is striking. There it

---

[10] 'The people is not the sum of its members, it is not a mathematical quantity. On the contrary it is represented in any group of members you like, even in individuals; but the individual is never alone where the Covenant is concerned. Always, whether by himself or in a number, he is *pars pro toto*.' L. Koehler, *Old Testament Theology*, trans. A. S. Todd (London: Lutterworth Press, 1957 and Philadelphia: Westminster Press, 1958), p. 65.

is strongly emphasized that the separated parts of the nation belong together as members of that same people of Yahweh who were originally chosen to be redeemed but are now equally to be abandoned to hostile forces. The fact that the expression is unique suggests that we should not prefer the easier reading of the LXX: 'the house of Jacob'.[11]

The conscious appeal to the same religious position of honour possessed by the two parts of the nation, which is conveyed by the use of this name here, clearly proves how alive for Isaiah was the religious bond which united the two and summoned them both to the same promise and responsibility, from the hour of the birth of God's people in the establishment of the covenant. The rare expression 'God of Jacob', which we meet in 2.3, is known from the 'Songs of Zion' where it indicates, as stemming from the old amphictyonic heritage, the legitimacy of the sanctuary of Zion for the whole nation.

II

But does this contradict the way in which Isaiah elsewhere speaks of the close relationship of God with Judah? Nowadays it is often pointed out that the pre-exilic prophets, whenever they speak of this subject, do not choose the covenant idea but use expressions denoting a family relationship.[12] Isaiah uses, for example, the father-son relationship or the relationship of the lover to the beloved (cf. 1.2, 4; 30.9; 5.1ff.). Hosea preceded him and Jeremiah followed him in this, except that the former speaks of husband rather than lover and the latter speaks of bridegroom and husband; cf. Hos. 11.1ff.; Jer. 2.27; 3.19f., 22; 4.22 and Hos. 2.2, 7, 16; 3.1; Jer. 2.2; 3.1, 6, 11. However, E. Gerstenberger[13]

[11] Thus also Rost, *Israel bei den Propheten*, pp. 34f.

[12] See Whitley, *op. cit.*, and, with reference to Whitley, Fohrer, *op. cit.*, pp. 894ff.

[13] E. Gerstenberger, 'Covenant and Commandment', *JBL* 84 (March, 1965), pp. 38ff.

and D. J. McCarthy[14] have already pointed out that outside Israel also, the community constituted by a treaty is frequently characterized by terms implying family relationships; the unity thus guaranteed is equated with the firmness of the blood bond. The expression 'brotherhood' plays here an important role, while the sovereign is also frequently referred to as 'father', as in the Amarna letters. This is therefore an illustration of how the close relationship established by treaty can be perfectly consistent with a legal agreement.

The same holds good also for the terms implying family relationships in the prophets: their purpose is to stigmatize the utter loathsomeness of apostasy, which is nothing less than the deliberate destruction of the most intimate human relationships. If on the other hand they had made use of, and thereby accepted, the idea of a physical relationship with the Godhead current among the people, the moral perfection of their God would have been precluded. So throughout Israel's traditions we find the consciousness that the whole relationship of the people to Yahweh dates from the moment when the formerly alien God involves himself directly with the destiny of the tribes by leading them to freedom and thus proclaiming them as his possession. Perhaps in the patriarchal sagas and in the old personal names compounded with עַם, we can glimpse the idea of a God who was known to the wandering nomads as himself a member of the tribe. But, in any case, this idea disappears completely in the whole of later tradition.

In order to understand the imagery of kinship used by Isaiah, it is important to interpret it in relation to the accompanying titles of God. In these the absolute power of the God of Israel over his people and the exact accomplishment of his sovereign will against all opposition is expressed. At his call Isaiah recognizes that he faces the Lord of Hosts, the enthroned king (6.5). God's being is so opposed to the sinful creature that it is not the consciousness of kinship, but its annihilating opposite, which inexorably

[14] McCarthy, *op. cit.*, pp. 234f.

overcomes the man who faces him. In the seraphs' antiphonal song of praise the Holy One, the king whose glory fills the world, is exalted as the ruler whose absolute power throws into clear light the profound abasement and tireless quest for assurance of his people. By means of this power he, like a father, has brought up his sons through a long process of education (1.2, 4,) or, like a lover wooing his bride, has sought to have his love returned (5.1). It is not Isaiah who first uses the title 'king', which belongs rather to the much older Temple hymns; but the name makes it plain that this relationship of ruler and people is an essential component of Israel's relationship with God and leads directly to the idea of the Covenant. The Hittite Vassal Treaties of the fourteenth and thirteenth centuries have illuminated the whole structure of the covenant in a most striking manner, and in particular have enabled us to understand how inextricably its commandments are connected with the sovereign's act of grace.[15]

In this connection, the question has arisen time and again whether the prophetic speech of judgment does not also bear the marks of a background in the covenant relationship. E. Würthwein has suggested that it did in fact originate there[16] and other scholars have drawn out the connection in several different ways. In a very instructive study, W. Beyerlin pointed out this connection in the case of Micah.[17] His idea was then developed in a

---

[15] See the study by the present author, 'Bund und Gesetz', *Gottes Wort und Gottes Land*, H. W. Hertzberg *Festschrift*, ed. H. Graf Reventlow (Göttingen: Vandenhoeck and Ruprecht, 1965), pp. 30ff. It is not necessary here to give further details of the literature, which is generally well known on the whole question. One aspect of the problem which has received little attention is the essential unity between the prevenient divine grace and the obedient human response. An impressive discussion of this is given by N. W. Porteous, 'Actualization and the Prophetic Criticism of the Cult', *Living the Mystery* (Oxford: Basil Blackwell, 1967), pp. 139ff.

[16] E. Würthwein, 'Der Ursprung der prophetischen Gerichtsrede', *ZThK* 49 (1952), pp. 1ff.

[17] W. Beyerlin, *Die Kulttraditionen Israels in der Verkündigung des Propheten Micha* (Göttingen: Vandenhoeck and Ruprecht, 1959).

highly individual way by Reventlow.[18] Recently R. E. Clements[19] has carefully examined these different attempts and in essence confirmed their conclusions, while quite rightly denying, however, that it is possible to trace back to the commandments of the Covenant the style of the prophetic speech of judgment. It is equally questionable whether we are on sure ground when the calling of heaven and earth as witnesses or judges (as in Isa. 1.2 but also in Micah 6.1f.; Jer. 2.12; Deut. 32.1; Ps. 50.4) is taken to be a regular part of the covenant formula on the basis of similar appeals in the Hittite treaties,[20] or when the origin of the pattern of weal and woe, so central to the prophetic message, is seen in the similar features of the curse and blessing formulae of covenant treaties in both the ancient Near East and the Old Testament.[21] Here it is possible to touch only briefly on this whole question, which requires a much fuller examination.

III

Knowledge of a regular enunciation of divine justice, which is fundamental to the relationship of Israel with God, is further shown in Isaiah at the point where he incorporates the 'Zion-Jerusalem tradition' into his message.

In 1.21–26, the fall of the faithful city, with its great tradition of justice, is proclaimed in the well-known rhythm of the dirge. By wickedly turning from its original destiny, it has become instead

[18] H. Graf Reventlow, *Das Amt des Propheten bei Amos*, FRLANT 80 (Göttingen: Vandenhoeck and Ruprecht, 1962), pp. 89ff., together with similar studies on Ezekiel and Jeremiah.

[19] R. E. Clements, *Prophecy and Covenant*, SBT 43 (London: SCM Press, 1965), pp. 77ff.

[20] Thus H. B. Huffmon, 'The Covenant Lawsuit in the Prophets', *JBL* 78 (Dec., 1959), pp. 285–95.

[21] Charles Fensham, 'Malediction and Benediction in Ancient Near Eastern Vassal-Treaties and the Old Testament', *ZAW* 74 (1962), pp. 1ff. and 'Common Trends in Curses of the Near Eastern Treaties and *Kudurru* – Inscriptions compared with Maledictions of Amos and Isaiah', *ZAW* 75 (1963), pp. 155ff.

of a bastion of justice a refuge for law breakers and robbers who no longer serve the God of justice but the God Mammon. Thus it must fall to the avenging judgment of God, who established here the ideal law embodying his holy will, although now his gift has been contaminated and desecrated. The officials appointed as judges are in open rebellion: they have failed to observe the *magna carta* which enshrines the divine sovereignty and, as little tyrants, have exploited and subjected to their own will the people entrusted to them. These his 'enemies' and 'foes' will fall to his revenge and the three names of power, 'the Lord', 'Yahweh of hosts' and 'the Mighty One of Israel' bear witness to this.

The praise of Jerusalem as the bastion of justice and as the faithful city reflects, as has long been accepted, the distinctive cultic traditions of Zion, which extolled, in the festival hymns, the Temple and city as the seat of the King-God. Over against these hymns, the prophet's dirge makes abundantly clear the discrepancy between this beautiful ideal image and the present degeneration, which brings all renown to nothing and calls forth a fearful reprisal. It is not necessary here to go into the remarkable change of tone which occurs in what follows and introduces a new age of salvation through a purifying judgment. However, the three names of God in v. 24 provide further valuable information concerning the prophet's attitude to the past which he celebrates. For the title אָדוֹן, which is also used outside Israel for the deity in his position as the ruling power, is here linked with the genuinely Israelite יהוה צְבָאוֹת, the name given to the God of the holy Ark.

This name gives to the Yahweh-symbol of the tribes who entered Canaan a meaning which is valid also for Zion, the new sanctuary of the royal city, where it had been taken by David as a guarantee of the presence of God. The religious traditions of Israel's old tribal confederacy are thus taken over by the Zion sanctuary and so are able to make effective their unifying power, by which Judah and the Northern tribes realize their unity as the one people of God, even under the new circumstances of the Davidic empire.

And as if to emphasize this, Isaiah adds the divine title 'the Mighty One of Israel', which likewise belongs to the time of the undivided sacral confederacy of the tribes.[22]

This means, however, that the cultic tradition of Zion, which Isaiah takes up here, remains closely linked to the Northern Israelite traditions, a fact which is confirmed by a whole series of festival psalms which have their home in the Zion cult (cf. Pss. 24 and 132, which centre on the Ark, and also Pss. 48, 76, 81, etc.). Here the traditions which spoke of the tribes united in the Sinai covenant and of Yahweh's saving acts lived on in the cult legends of the great festivals, thereby keeping alive the awareness of relationship to Yahweh's covenant people. These traditions clearly also formed an important component of Isaiah's thought, causing him to see the judgment and restoration of Jerusalem, the faithful city, in the perspective of the whole people of God, a people to whom Yahweh's justice and judgment were granted as the great gifts of its God. It is not the God of Jerusalem who executes judgment on the city, but the Mighty One of Israel: faithfully carrying out here his plan of salvation, he does not allow the highest gifts of his sovereignty to be sullied and contaminated through human guilt.

Of course, Isaiah feels called to announce more than merely the re-establishment of the earlier system of divine justice. Confident as he is of God's choice of Zion, where for Yahweh a furnace and a fire burn (31.9), where after the judgment he lays the foundation stone of a new divine building (28.16), where he inflicts a humiliating defeat on those who enter the field against Jerusalem (29.8), and where the whole work planned by him is brought to its conclusion (10.12), he nevertheless links with all this other hopes which are even more far-reaching. They are directed towards the great plan and decree of his God, by which he sets up his sovereignty. Living in a century of great political upheavals, when his

[22] For the relation of this title to the parallel name 'the Mighty One of Jacob', cf. H. Wildberger, *Jesaja*, BKAT (Neukirchen-Vluyn: Verlag der Buchhandlung des Erziehungsvereins, 1965), pp. 63f.

homeland was torn and destroyed by the fierce onrush of destructive forces, Isaiah saw Yahweh's hidden but victorious power bending the fury of the nations to his own purposes (8.5–10). While the godless self-will of its king was drawing Jerusalem into the whirlpool, he himself stood before the incomprehensible silence of his Lord, and was satisfied to wait, knowing himself to be powerless yet firm in faith (8.17f.). In this outward defeat, in which he felt Yahweh's hand resting heavily upon him (8.11), the certainty was strengthened in him that the constantly increasing power of the world empire was only the tool used by the divine Lord of the world in order, precisely by means of their apparently destructive power, to lay the nations at his feet. Tirelessly he called both friends and enemies alike to pay heed to this long premeditated work of God, and not to be held captive or be deceived by the immediate happenings on the world's stage; cf. 5.12, 19; 10.5ff.; 28.11, 23ff.; 22.11. As the danger grew, he depicted this, in verses of moving passion, as the kernel of all that was happening [28.11, 23ff.] (14.24–27; 17.12–14).

Even though he here goes far beyond all Zion ideology, and sees the Temple as only the tool which serves the divine plan for the whole world, Isaiah nevertheless makes use of it as a means of depicting the coming new epoch and of finding understanding with his people. The magnificent image of Zion as the centre of God's universal dominion, whence his law goes forth to be taught to the nations (2.2–4), is like a majestic paean of victory to the God of justice. After all the battles and catastrophes, which time and again seem to throw doubt on the possibility of carrying out his will for the world, God has nevertheless successfully achieved his long-planned work. The description of the position in the world of his sanctuary, in which the announcement of the divine triumph finds its concrete manifestation, is rooted deep in historical reality and the proud traditions of Zion.

In view of the basic researches of the last few years,[23] it is only

[23] See particularly H. Wildberger, 'Die Völkerwallfahrt zum Zion, Jes. ii, 1–5', *VT* 7 (1957), pp. 62–81. The antiquity of the motif of the

necessary here to mention briefly the extensive use Isaiah makes of characteristic expressions from the Temple liturgies. The idea of Zion as the highest of mountains, which, because of Yahweh's choice, is unshakable, impregnable to every adversary and the goal of pilgrims from all over the world, bringing their sacrifices, singing their songs of praise, and asking for God's arbitration, derives from the ancient cultic songs of the Temple feasts. The name 'God of Jacob', which is otherwise rare in Isaiah, belongs, as we have seen already, to cultic poetry. The vain attack by the nations on God's chosen sanctuary, which is taken up in the prophet's message in 17.12–14; 29.7f.; 14.25, may also have played a part in the traditional material of the Zion feasts. What matters, however, is the use the prophet makes of this. What was announced on Mount Zion as a claim guaranteed by God in the present now serves for a future self-glorification of Yahweh. It is no longer the imposing Temple building with its brilliant festivals that stands in the centre, but the God who reveals himself here and so directs the attention of the nations to himself. They stream past, not to increase the splendour of God's house with their gifts, but to hear in this place the announcement of the divine judgment in Yahweh's law and to bow to his decree. No bloody vengeance have they to fear, but their heart is transformed through the influence of the teaching they receive, so that they freely destroy all their weapons. This signifies a raising of the original Paradise myth to the level of moral and religious renewal, and brings out clearly the spiritual force which recasts the old traditional elements into the language of a new divine message.

This in turn means that behind the Temple service of his time, which he judges so harshly, Isaiah sees a higher reality. Even though it may in the present be distorted and covered by the rubble of the Canaanite nature religion, this is nevertheless not

---

pilgrimage of the nations in the Zion tradition has recently been rightly stressed by H. Junker, cf. his 'Sancta Civitas, Jerusalem Nova. Eine formkritische und überlieferungsgeschichtliche Studie zu Jes. 2', *Trierer ThSt* 15 (1962), p. 28.

such an obstacle that God's powerful intervention cannot bring it back again to its original purpose. Isaiah's radical rejection of the existing Temple and its worship, which amounts even to a threat of destruction (28.16ff.; 29.2b, 4; 32.13f.), as well as his relentless condemnation of the cult practised in it (1.10ff. and many other passages), need not be taken as implying that in the future all outward forms of worship will disappear. But certainly, the time for the present Temple service has run out, and if any hope at all is to remain this can only be found in God's eschatological[24] activity. This, however, maintains continuity with the past by carrying on the previous revelation, which now sets in at the same point, and leads to its goal the original divine intention.

The question has been asked where, in Isaiah, is to be found 'the germ of a hope for Zion that could be historically realized'. S. Herrmann[25] quite rightly points to 28.16, 17a, where the possibility of a belief in Yahweh centred on Zion appears, corresponding to Isaiah's ideal of 'justice and righteousness'. The passage shows that Isaiah has taken up Zion into his thought, though admittedly not in the sense of a universalism which transcends all boundaries. Rather, his thought is narrowly limited to the idea of a continuation of the existence of the city of Jerusalem, which was historically quite conceivable. Nevertheless, the attempt to separate a limited Zion hope from a universal hope, and to see the former alone as an organic part of Isaiah's thought, is rendered dubious in view of all that we said above about Yahweh's plan and work as these appear in Isaiah's message. In ch. 28, too, the idea of a universal divine judgment appears as one of the mysterious and incalculable terrors that come with the threatened appearance of God (28.17b–22). To separate, on form-critical grounds, vv. 16, 17a from their

[24] That this disputed term is quite appropriate, wherever the prophetic hope is of a decisive re-ordering of the world, has been clearly shown by J. Lindblom, *Prophecy in Ancient Israel* (Oxford: Basil Blackwell and Philadelphia: Fortress Press, 1962), pp. 360ff.
[25] S. Herrmann, *Die prophetischen Heilswartungen im Alten Testament. Ursprung und Gestaltwandel*, BWANT V, 5 (Stuttgart: W. Kohlhammer Verlag, 1965), pp. 141ff.

context because there is no legitimate place for a promise of weal in the middle of a promise of woe, is to miss Isaiah's intention. Certainly vv. 16, 17a speak of a promise to those who believe, but this promise is quite clearly subject to Yahweh's threat of destruction: it demonstrates, in the new building of Yahweh, the insuperable obstacle which, by the norms of his law, dooms to utter ruin all that is built on mere human sagacity and in disregard of the divine commandments (vv. 15, 18). The germ of the universal Zion hope, therefore, is to be sought wholly in the mysterious plan and work of Yahweh, in which also weal and woe can be closely linked together.

This is confirmed in a striking manner by the description of the theophany in Isa. 30.27–34,[26] the bold language of which has for the most part not been properly understood. The grandiose appearance of the war God, approaching in a thunderstorm to annihilate the Assyrians, reminiscent of very early theophany descriptions in the Old Testament (Judg. 5.4f.), steadily progresses to the climax of the divine victory (vv. 31, 32a). At this point, it suddenly breaks off and moves directly to a quite different scene, the festive procession of the congregation to the mountain of God during the night vigil, accompanied by dancing to the sound of tambourines, harps and flutes. Alongside the fear of God there is joy in God: faith discerns security amidst the turmoil of the judgment itself (cf. Ps. 46). The final strophe, v. 33, establishes, however, the inner connection of these two opposing images through the great ritual of sacrifice, that essential part of every festival. The frightening and gigantic imagery of this verse, which has given rise to many misinterpretations, can only be seen in the right light if one recognizes that its purpose is to present a definite conclusion which reconciles all the contradictory scenes. This is the encounter of Israel with the God who judges and who saves at the feast of Tabernacles, in which, from ancient times, the

[26] For a full analysis of this passage, which can only be outlined here, cf. my commentary on Isaiah, *Der Herr der Geschichte* (Stuttgart: Calwer Verlag, 1967), pp. 182ff.

making of the covenant was ritually recalled. This renewal of the divine basis of the people's existence becomes the direct experience of those taking part in the feast through the offering of the covenant sacrifice. But now they stand at the unique point of time when the Lord of the world himself consummates the covenant sacrifice of the feast of Tabernacles by killing the great enemy of God. God's gracious gift can only be understood and accepted in the context of this universal reckoning with all his enemies.[27] What had always been contained in the proclamation at the covenant festival of the newly confirmed divine covenant, that is, the announcement of judgment upon the enemies of the divine covenant-partner, takes on here such tremendous proportions that it can only be borne by a congregation firm in faith; a congregation which, even when God acts mysteriously and terrifyingly and even under the very execution of his sentence, continues to trust in his promised grace.

Thus Isaiah uses a cultic act known, in its amphictyonic form, to every Israelite, to interpret a divine action that far transcends the significance of the old covenant festival and points to the secret of the Lord of the world.

IV

Less fruitful for the question under discussion is that other great theme in Isaiah's expectation for the future, the hope of the coming saviour-king.[28] Admittedly the same use of the old conventional cultic style can also be perceived in chs. 9 and 11,

[27] The defeat of the Assyrian is to be understood in this way in all anti-Assyrian prophecies. A horrifying description of the judgment as a sacrificial feast prepared by God himself recurs in Zeph. 1.7 and Ezek. 39.17–20.

[28] Fohrer asks how we can attribute to Isaiah the juxtaposition of the two unconnected ideas of the promise about Zion and the promise of the Messiah. This question has now been answered by von Rad, who sees the prophets as men who regarded themselves as 'the spokesmen of old and well-known traditions', cf. his *Old Testament Theology*, vol. II, p. 185 (ET, p. 175).

where the influence of the songs for the enthronement of the king, as found in the Royal Psalms, can be felt.[29] And again the prophet reveals his complete freedom in the assimilation of these traditional elements, by using them to depict a coming saviour who will carry out the divinely willed duty of the rulers, at which the Davidic monarchy had failed. It is the charismatic bearer of the spirit who appears, in the place of David and his house, and he places the absolute power granted to him by God wholly in the service of his divine lord. He does not have the name of king or have anything to do with universal imperial aspirations, but he remains God's representative in Israel. The question whether Isaiah knew the tradition of an eternal Covenant of God with David must be answered in the affirmative in view of the Royal Psalms, such as Ps. 132, and II Sam. 23.1–5, the pre-Isaianic origin of which can scarely be disputed.

In view of the clear adoption of the stylistic forms of the national cult-traditions in Isaiah's prophecy, it can no longer be claimed that the prophet knew nothing of a covenant relationship of Israel with its God or that he rejected it as a misunderstanding of this God. Our discussion has thus led us to the point where the question arises most acutely, why the word בְּרִית, which plays such an important part in the prophetic message a hundred years later, is avoided by Isaiah.

V

One can doubtless try to answer this question by pointing to the misunderstanding prevalent in the monarchical period, by which the covenant was seen in terms of the ordinary legal system: the fact that it had consolidated and hardened into a statutory relationship, providing mutual benefits for two equal partners, stood

[29] That the Covenant with David presupposed here does not exclude the Sinai Covenant has been convincingly shown by A. R. Johnson, *Sacral Kingship in Ancient Israel*, 2nd ed. (Cardiff: University of Wales Press, 1967), pp. 136ff.

in sharp contrast to the struggle of the prophets for an inward submission of the people to Yahweh in personal love and trust. This led to an avoidance of the concept as an unsuitable description of the true relationship with God, for it showed itself useless in the struggle against the Canaanite religious system, which drew its strength from the proliferation of the sacrificial cult at the state sanctuaries and from the support it enjoyed from the despotic monarchy.[30]

Admittedly this does not answer the question completely. It is possible to doubt the necessity of this conclusion and to point, as a strong objection to it, to the total absence of any struggle against such misinterpretation of the בְּרִית in the eighth-century prophets.

One could, however, still take refuge in the theory of a Levitical reform movement in the Northern Kingdom, which was strengthened by the prophetic activity of Hosea and which prevented the demise of the covenant tradition after the fall of Samaria by transferring its literary heritage to Judah.[31]

Thus one will have to probe more deeply in order to understand why Isaiah did not use the word בְּרִית. In the first place it is important to keep in mind the *actual situation of the prophet* in the midst of a congregation in whose worship the saving fact of the covenant played an important, indeed a vital, role and where it was represented or explicitly referred to by such expressions as 'the people chosen by God', 'Yahweh's own possession', etc. For it can scarcely be seriously doubted today that these concepts were not in the first instance created and given currency only by the Deuteronomic school, but were used earlier in the language of the cult. Even though the Zion tradition or the saving significance of

[30] See W. Eichrodt, *Theologie des Alten Testaments*, vol. I, 7th ed. (Stuttgart: E. Klotz Verlag, 1962), pp. 19ff., 251; ET: Theology of the Old Testament, trans. J. A. Baker (London: SCM Press and Philadelphia: Westminster Press, 1961), pp. 51ff., 374. The same conception is found in Clements, *op. cit.*, p. 55, and Lindblom, *op. cit.*, pp. 329f.

[31] Thus particularly H. W. Wolff, 'Hoseas geistige Heimat', *ThLZ* 81 (1956), cols. 83–94, and J. Muilenburg, 'The Form and Structure of the Covenantal Formulations', *VT* 9 (1959), p. 347.

the anointed of Yahweh came more and more into prominence and the covenant with David began to colour the covenant with Israel, there was nevertheless no question of replacing the latter, as the Temple hymns show. Now, as earlier, it remained familiar to the language of the cult, by which the new saving facts of the time of David were able to find a place in the old covenant.[32] The Temple feasts, and particularly the covenant festival, had in this way the firmest guarantee of belief in Jerusalem, the indestructible city of God, and in the future salvation of Israel.[33] Though Isaiah without hesitation made use of the forms of speech that originated here, yet he did not use the word בְּרִית.

In considering the dispute as to how this fact should be interpreted, it may well be asked whether the explanations thus far given have not inevitably reached a faulty conclusion, because they start from the wrong point. For if one starts from the notion of a belief which is understood quite differently by the people and by the prophet and takes it as obvious that from both sides there would arise a bitter argument about the concept, as soon as the prophets began to attack the popular religion, then one is led immediately into error by an abstract theological reflection. One is thereby prevented from appreciating fully both the real motive, and the content, of the prophetic message. When Isaiah appeared in Jerusalem to launch a strong attack on the people's whole way of life, the first and most important reason for this was not a faulty covenant theology which had to be corrected, but an encounter with the holy God, which was granted unsolicited to the prophet and which brought with it a particular task: he was to announce the irresistible approach of a horrifying reality which would sweep

[32] Cf. H. J. Kraus, *Die Königsherrschaft Gottes im Alten Testament* (Tübingen: J. C. B. Mohr, 1951); *Worship in Israel*, 2nd ed., trans. G. Buswell (Oxford: Basil Blackwell and Richmond: John Knox Press, 1966), pp. 189f.; Porteous, *op. cit.*, p. 131.

[33] For the presence of the amphicytonic covenant tradition in the Jerusalem Temple feasts, cf., particularly, A. Weiser, *The Psalms*, trans. H. Hartwell (London: SCM Press and Philadelphia: Westminster Press, 1962).

away, in a storm of destruction, the whole well-ordered world of Israel and the other nations. It was not his task to question a belief, though important as it was, but to bear witness to a reversal of the whole existing situation in the world: and this was much more than just a theological idea. The king יְהוָה צְבָאוֹת, a power too long forgotten and shut out from practical life, but in the last analysis the sole decisive power, was to enter devastatingly into the present order and destroy it from top to bottom.

This is proclaimed in one of the greatest speeches of judgment from Isaiah's initial period, the speech about the approaching day of Yahweh (2.6ff.), where the incomprehensible holy God, whose being cannot be grasped through any human image or symbol, breaks the pride of man and destroys all sacred institutions which seek to make his hidden glory serve the demands of human self-will. The abyss which thus opens up before all conventional piety is so frightful that even the prophet himself, when he looks into it for the first time, can only shrink back with a despairing question (cf. 6.11). For he hears the goal of his mission described as a complete hardening of his people until they are ripe for full judgment, which leaves no place for hope. And while during his long career his threats change according to the changing political situation, he yet never ceases to speak, again and again, of the mysterious, even incomprehensible, working of his God which goes beyond all human understanding (cf. 18.4; 19.12; 28.11–13, 19b–21; 29.9ff., 14, 16; 31.2, and cf. also in this light 5.20f.; 8.12–14, 21f.; 10.15a; 17.11).

Here there was clearly no room for disputes about theological concepts. It was simply a question of a threatened attack by the divine power on this earthly world, one which had been revealed to the eye of the prophet in fearful clarity and which had to be proclaimed to the people with such power that they would be forced to submit to the immediate certainty of the divine presence and the decision that was now demanded. But where this shocking news is opposed by confidence in an existence secured by earlier acts of divine salvation, then, because of real crimes, a severe indictment falls like a hammer-blow on this self-confidence. Ordinary life cannot but be utterly destroyed by such an opposition to God's clear commands. Knowledge of the divine commandments is here taken for granted and does not need to be mentioned. This is the common ground of faith which allows the prophet to conduct his argument from agreed premises. He can count on awakening such knowledge, even though it is hidden under the confusion of pious practices, through the direct impact of the threatened appearance of the God who strides on to vengeance; and he knows that this in turn will lead to profound terror. Only in the context of this fundamental questioning of the whole present condition of the chosen people can there follow new and clearly formulated statements about the being and purpose of the God who comes in judgment.[34]

Is it too bold to suggest that, in the face of just such a congregation, whose religious life was dominated by the celebration of the covenant between Israel and its God, the way taken by Isaiah corresponds exactly with his commission and avoids the temptation of getting lost in the intricacies of a dispute about a concept so rich, but also so variegated, as that of the covenant? The dispute would have become all the more difficult because the prophet himself could not simply have rejected this concept, since essential elements of his own faith were contained in it. This scarcely needs to be emphasized again, in view of Isaiah's unhesitating use of amphictyonic cult-language to express his own hope for the future, encountered in our earlier discussion. Undoubtedly he saw the covenant idea in a completely new light as a result of his experience of God, and the confusion caused in it by the introduction of alien elements became a heavy burden for him. But the ambivalence of his preaching, as a message at one and the same time of both weal and woe, springs from the fact that his thought is rooted in Yahweh's covenant. Even his unqualified and explicit certainty of the obduracy of his people cannot alter this.

[34] For a fuller discussion of this short outline, cf. my earlier remarks, *Theologie des Alten Testaments*, vol. I, pp. 230–6 (Eng. trans., pp. 345–53).

We do not mean that Isaiah's avoidance of the word בְּרִית is to
be understood as his solution to a harrassing division within
himself, which sprang from his own spiritual conflict. Not only is
the evidence for this lacking, but such a view runs the risk of
distorting the relationship of the prophet to his message. But, in
view of the commission given to him, this much seems certain: he
saw that his first and most important task as a prophet was not to
argue about the correct understanding of a basic concept of belief,
but to show forth the God who had appeared to him and would
appear to all people. The message with which he was charged was
to be this God's witness to Israel and, as such, to pose decisive
questions which would illuminate his people's life and worship,
their politics and their society. He had to keep clear of all conceptual
debates, which might have drawn attention from the real matter
in hand. But when he made the decisive moment of God's relationship with Israel the centre of his message, he also destroyed the
impulse behind the false interpretation of the covenant and
cleared the way for a purification of the covenant idea from all
heathen admixtures and impurities.

Finished April 16th 1968.

10

Jeremiah's Complaints: Liturgy, or Expressions of Personal Distress?

John Bright

THOSE laments and complaints which we are accustomed, none too aptly, to call Jeremiah's 'Confessions' are a unique feature in the Jeremiah book. No other prophetic book offers us anything comparable. Here the prophet speaks in his own name rather than God's and gives vent to his anguish, complaining of the abuse the prophetic office has brought him, bitterly cursing his enemies and crying out for his own vindication, and even accusing his God of having deceived him and failed him. One would naturally suppose, as readers always have, that these pieces reflect actual experiences in the prophet's life and afford glimpses of his innermost feelings. Because of them, and because of the wealth of biographical material that his book contains, Jeremiah has always been regarded as both the best known and the most 'human' of all the prophets.

A relationship between the Confessions and certain of the Psalms, specifically the Psalms of Individual Lament, has of course long been recognized. In an earlier day it was widely supposed that Jeremiah had simply imitated the Psalms of the Psalter.[1] Later, when criticism had assigned most of the Psalms to the post-exilic period, it was commonly believed that Jeremiah's

---

[1] We cannot trace the history of the discussion here. See W. Baumgartner, *Die Klagegedichte des Jeremia*, BZAW 32 (Giessen: A. Töpelmann, 1917), pp. 1–5, for a summary of older opinion.

complaints had served as models for Psalms of similar character.[2] But when, thanks to the work of H. Gunkel and others, it was realized that the Psalm types had a long history behind them, and that many of the Psalms were far older than Jeremiah, it became wellnigh the consensus that Jeremiah had composed in the form of the Pss. Lam. (we shall use this abbreviation hereafter), adapting the form for his purpose. The important monograph of W. Baumgartner, *Die Klagegedichte des Jeremia*,[3] did much to establish this view as the generally accepted one – a position that it retains until today. To be sure, as a result of the work of S. Mowinckel and others, the cultic *Sitz im Leben* of perhaps most of the Psalms has been increasingly recognized; and the realization that the Confessions employ conventional forms of address has made recent scholars far more cautious in extracting psychological and biographical details from these pieces than some of their predecessors were. Nevertheless, it has remained wellnigh the consensus among scholars that the Confessions do in some way relate to specific experiences in the life of the prophet.

In recent years, however, this consensus has been attacked, notably by E. Gerstenberger[4] and H. Graf Reventlow,[5] though in quite different ways. The former would have it that the Confessions are the product of later reflection on the part of exilic Deuteronomists, while the latter argues that they are liturgical pieces uttered by the prophet in the context of the cult. It would be interesting to attempt a critical comparison of these two scholars,

---

[2] For a recent expression of a similar view, see P. E. Bonnard, *Le Psautier selon Jérémie* (Paris: Éditions du Cerf, 1960). It should be added that a few scholars, the most radical of whom was N. Schmidt (*Encylopedia Biblica* II [1901], pp. 2388f.), went so far as to regard the Confessions as later additions to the book; but their views gained little following, either at the time or later.

[3] Baumgartner, however, regarded the Pss. Lam. in the Psalter as later than Jeremiah, *op. cit.*, p. 91.

[4] E. Gerstenberger, 'Jeremiah's Complaints: Observations on Jer. 15.10–21', *JBL* 82 (Dec., 1963), pp. 393–408.

[5] H. Graf Reventlow, *Liturgie und prophetisches Ich bei Jeremia* (Gütersloh: Gütersloher Verlagshaus Gerd Mohn, 1963).

for although both would forbid us to see anything of Jeremiah's personal struggle in the Confessions, they arrive at this result while travelling in quite opposite directions. This does not, of course, mean that neither of them can be right. But it is certain that both cannot be: Jeremiah cannot be dissolved into anonymity in two such mutually exclusive ways.

Since it is impossible to do justice to both these approaches within the space at our disposal, we shall confine ourselves to that of Reventlow here.[6] Even so we must limit ourselves. We shall first offer a few observations of a general nature regarding Reventlow's thesis and the presuppositions that underlie it, and then proceed to the Confessions themselves, to ask if his cultic-liturgical interpretation of these pieces can be maintained.

I

It must be kept in mind that Reventlow's understanding of the Confessions is but an aspect of his understanding of the prophetic office in general. This last he has developed in two earlier works dealing with Amos[7] and with Ezekiel,[8] as well as in his most recent volume on Jeremiah. We cannot attempt to present Reventlow's position in detail. Suffice it to say that he sees the prophet as one who discharged an official cultic function, that of mediator (*Mittler*) between God and people. By its very nature, his office was a two-sided one; it was his task to bring the divine word to the people and, equally, to present their plaints and prayers before God as their official intercessor (*Fürbitter, Vorbeter*). Reventlow interprets Jeremiah's laments and complaints in the light of this understanding of the prophetic office. In these pieces we see the prophet as he discharges the latter half of his function, namely, as he addresses God on behalf of the people.

Reventlow bases himself throughout on the assumption that in the ancient Orient all forms of address have their origin in some

[6] I hope to discuss Gerstenberger's approach elsewhere.

[7] H. Graf Reventlow, *Das Amt des Propheten bei Amos*, FRLANT 80 (Göttingen: Vandenhoeck and Ruprecht, 1962).

[8] H. Graf Reventlow, *Wächter über Israel: Ezechiel und seine Tradition*, BZAW 82 (Berlin: A. Töpelmann, 1962).

specific *Sitz im Leben* and, unless broken or corrupted, remain bound to that *Sitz im Leben*.[9] Since the Confessions are in the form of the Pss. Lam., and since this last is a liturgical form designed for use in the cult, it is *a priori* unlikely that the Confessions should represent free adaptations, loosed from the cultic setting. Reventlow argues that they in fact do not. He therefore interprets them as liturgical pieces uttered in the context of the cult. As such, they reveal nothing of the prophet as a person: the 'I' is in each case collective. In these pieces the prophet speaks in the name of the people, or the 'righteous' segment of them, in his official capacity as cultic mediator, laying their plaints and petitions before God and interceding for them. The Confessions are thus as much a part of the prophet's public ministry as is the proclamation of the word itself. Indeed, says Reventlow, if this is not so it is hard to see why they should have been included in the book at all, since the prophetic books otherwise display little or no interest in the prophet as a person: 'the preached word represents the sole principle of selection for the transmission of prophetic material'.[10]

Reventlow's approach is essentially exegetical, based upon a painstaking examination of selected texts. Its validity will, in the final analysis, have to be determined exegetically. Nevertheless, certain of its features, and certain of the assumptions upon which it is based, are on the surface of it open to question.

1. The assumption that forms of address must remain anchored to the institution in which they have their original setting has already been attacked by G. Fohrer.[11] Reventlow warmly protests this,[12] but it seems to me that Fohrer is entirely correct. As Fohrer

---

[9] Reventlow, *Liturgie und prophetisches Ich bei Jeremia*, pp. 14f. All subsequent references to Reventlow in this article will be to this book, hereinafter listed simply as *Liturgie*.

[10] *Ibid.*, p. 208.

[11] Cf. G. Fohrer, 'Remarks on Modern Interpretation of the Prophets', *JBL* 80 (Dec., 1961), pp. 309–12; also H. W. Wolff, *Amos' geistige Heimat* (Neukirchen-Vluyn: Neukirchener Verlag des Erziehungsvereins, 1964), pp. 1–4. [12] Reventlow, *Liturgie*, p. 15.

points out, the prophets adapted all sorts of forms, and it is absurd to suppose that they employed each in some official institutional capacity. Fohrer also disputes the notion that the form of a piece and its content are necessarily congruent and gives various examples where it is not – to which others could easily be added. We are certainly not required in advance to understand Jeremiah's complaints, because they are cast in a cultic form (that of the Pss. Lam.), as liturgical pieces uttered in the context of the cult. Exegesis alone can determine whether or not they can so be understood. But it need not *a priori* be so.

2. Reventlow's understanding of the prophets as official cultic intercessors has likewise been disputed by H. W. Hertzberg.[13] Though I feel that Hertzberg goes too far in denying that intercession was a characteristic activity of the prophets (there is too much evidence that it was), he is certainly correct that intercession is not depicted as a specifically prophetic function: the *specifically* prophetic function was to receive and transmit the divine word. Narrative texts that tell of the activity of prophets confirm this. These yield countless examples of prophets bringing a word from God; but although one finds various examples of prophets making intercession, seldom is the setting depicted as cultic, and never is the prophet clearly represented as acting as an official of the cult. We do have examples from narrative texts of prayer made in behalf of the people in settings that are clearly cultic, and in these the following act as intercessors: Moses (Num. 14.13–19; cf. Ex. 32.11–14), Joshua and the elders (Josh. 7.6–9), Samuel (I Sam. 7.5–11; 12.19, 23), David (II Sam. 24.17), Solomon (I Kings 8.22–53); Hezekiah (II Kings 19.14–19 = Isa. 37.14–20), and Ezra (Ezra 9.6–15; also Neh. 9.6–37 [LXX]). Of all these – aside from Moses, who is scarcely typical – only one (Samuel) is ever spoken of as a prophet. And Samuel, as is well known, is depicted as discharging various functions: prophet, seer, priest, charismatic

[13] H. W. Hertzberg, 'Sind die Propheten Fürbitter?', *Tradition und Situation*, A. Weiser *Festschrift*, eds. E. Würthwein and O. Kaiser (Göttingen: Vandenhoeck and Ruprecht, 1963), pp. 63–74.

judge and judge in a more restricted sense. It is probable that in the above passages he is thought of as the last of the judges, rather than specifically as a prophet. If the making of cultic intercession was an integral part of the prophetic office, it is remarkable that narrative texts of the Old Testament do not provide us with clear and frequent examples of prophets discharging that function.[14]

The case of Hezekiah's prayer in II Kings 19 (= Isa. 37) is particularly instructive, for here a prophet is involved. We are told that Hezekiah (v. 1) on hearing of the Rabshakeh's threats went into the Temple (presumably to pray) and, at the same time, sent a message to Isaiah asking him also to pray (vv. 2–4). But the narrative says nothing of Isaiah's actually doing so. Rather, it has him, as soon as the messengers come to him, sending back a *Heilsorakel* (vv. 5–7). In the parallel account in vv. 14–20, Hezekiah goes to the temple and prays (and his prayer is recorded); whereupon, Isaiah sends a message to the king again giving a *Heilsorakel*. It is, of course, not excluded that Isaiah *did* intercede for the people; but the narrator says nothing about it, still less does he depict Isaiah as going to the Temple to do so cultically.[15]

In the case of Jeremiah, we are fortunate in having a wealth of biographical accounts telling of that prophet's activity. Now Jeremiah himself repeatedly indicates that he interceded for the people (7.16; 11.14; 14.11f.; 18.20; 15.11 [?]). But it is interesting that the biographer, although he again and again tells how Jeremiah proclaimed the divine word, never once depicts him as acting as a cultic intercessor. True, he tells of two occasions when the prophet was asked to pray for the people (37.3;

[14] One might also mention Deut. 21.1–9, where it is the village elders who are to make intercession; Joel 2.17, where the priests are called upon to do so; and Job 42.8, where Job is deemed the appropriate person to offer such prayer. In each case a cultic ceremony is involved, but in none is it suggested that prophets must play a part.

[15] The account in II Chron. 32.20 does depict both king and prophet as praying – at a place not specified.

42.2f.).[16] The first of these (37.3–10) is fully parallel to Hezekiah's request of Isaiah, just discussed. In each of these cases the king asks the prophet to 'pray'. But though we may assume that the prophet did so, in neither case does the narrative say anything of it, still less of his proceeding to the Temple to do so as a cultic official. Rather, in both cases, the prophet is depicted as simply returning a word (in one case a *Heilsorakel*, in the other an *Unheilsorakel*).

In the second instance (ch. 42), the military leaders (vv. 2f.) request Jeremiah to 'pray' for them and (cf. v. 9) to present their supplication before God; a wish that he intercede is clearly implied. The scene is not that of the normal cult, but is in a camp near Bethlehem. But too much ought not to be made of this, for the Temple has been destroyed, and it is an emergency situation. In this case, Jeremiah replies (v. 4) that he will pray. The content of the prayer is not given. But, although we may assume that it included intercession, the wording of v. 4 indicates that we are intended to see it primarily as a prayer for a word from God – which word was ultimately received. Nothing in the narrative suggests a ritual of intercession carried out in a cultic context. The fact that the word was received only after ten days (v. 7) makes it unlikely in the extreme. In short, nothing in this, or in any other, narrative text supports the thesis that the prophet functioned as a cultic mediator-intercessor; here, as elsewhere, the specifically prophetic function is to receive and transmit the divine word.

3. In view of the foregoing, Reventlow's interpretation of the Confessions as liturgical pieces, uttered in the context of the cult, seems on the surface highly dubious. To be sure, he argues that it is difficult to see why these pieces should have been included in the book if they do not in some way relate to the prophet's public ministry, since the collectors of the prophetic books were interested

---

[16] Reventlow, *Liturgie*, pp. 143–9, attempts to use both of these in support of his thesis. The account in 21.1–7, to which Reventlow also appeals, is not relevant, for here Jeremiah is asked to 'enquire' of Yahweh (for a word); and he returns a word.

only in the preached word, and not in the prophet's personal feelings.[17] There is an element of truth in this, of course, but it seems to me that the argument cuts two ways. Far from supporting Reventlow's position, it might be regarded as extremely damaging to it. It leaves us asking why such material should be found *only* in Jeremiah. If these complaints represent the prophet as he discharged one of his official functions – a function, so Reventlow argues, that was a part of the prophetic office generally – then why do we not find similar pieces in every prophetic book? One would expect to do so if all the prophets discharged a similar function. Yet the fact is that, if they did so, they left no trace of this supposedly typical activity in their books. The Confessions are peculiar to Jeremiah, without real parallel in any other prophetic book. Could it be that they are so because expressive of that prophet's peculiar personal struggle? One is at least entitled to ask the question.

Certainly it is not in itself surprising that a prophet should have addressed personal complaints to God. The prophets were not quite the disembodied voices Reventlow would have them to be, but men of passions similar to our own. Many of them to our knowledge suffered scorn, abuse, and even physical persecution because of the word they preached; on occasion they found themselves in tension with the word, and with God's dealings. It would be strange indeed if they had never lashed out in bitter complaint to God. And, indeed, various narrative texts – which, as we have said, never depict the prophet as a cultic intercessor – remember them as doing so. Space does not allow us to review all the evidence. But one thinks of Jonah who, 'angry' because of the outcome of his preaching in Nineveh (4.1), launches bitter complaint against God, including the wish (4.3, 8) that he might die; or of Elijah who (I Kings 17.20) reproaches his God for 'slaying' the Sidonian woman's son; or of Samuel who (I Sam. 15.10f.), when he received God's word of Saul's rejection, was 'angry' and

[17] Reventlow, *Liturgie*, p. 208.

'cried'[18] to God all night. But the closest parallel to the Jeremiah of the Confessions is surely the Elijah of I Kings 19. Fleeing from Jezebel's wrath, Elijah first falls exhausted under a tree in the desert and (v. 4) prays that he might die;[19] he then goes on to Horeb where, in a cave, he utters lament (vv. 10, 14). In this lament he protests his own faithfulness (as frequently in the Pss. Lam.), bewails the nation's apostasy and the fate of the prophets, and (cf. Jer. 15.16f.) his own isolation ('I, even I only, am left'). Though Horeb is a holy place, the setting is not cultic: Elijah is quite alone. He utters a personal lament regarding his plight, a plight that he is in because of his faithfulness to his calling.[20]

Most instructive of all, however, is the prayer of Jeremiah in Jer. 32.16–25. This is one of two places in the biographical sections of the book where Jeremiah is said to have prayed (the other is ch. 42, where it is clearly indicated that he did), and the only one where tradition has preserved the content of the prayer.[21] The setting is anything but cultic: Jeremiah is in jail. He has purchased the field at Anathoth at God's command (vv. 6–15) and, having completed the transaction, he addresses his God in prayer. The prayer is a complaint; Jeremiah, in effect, protests that he has been made to do a foolish thing. Moreover, although we have but a prose summary of it, the prayer contains reminiscences of the vocabulary of the Lament.[22] The fact that the only

[18] The verb is זָעַק; this verb and צָעַק are standard in the vocabulary of the Lament.

[19] The wish to die is paralleled in Jer. 20.14–18, Job 3 and in Jonah 4.

[20] It might be added that in I Kings 19.15–18 Elijah receives an answering word from God which, in effect, dismisses his complaints and tells him to get back to his prophetic duties (cf. Jer. 15.19–21).

[21] The nucleus of the prayer is found in vv. 16–17aα, 24f. The remainder, which consists of a loose series of conventional liturgical expressions, is probably an expansion.

[22] 'Ah, Lord Yahweh' occurs frequently in the context of lament-complaint (Jer. 1.6; 4.10; Ezek. 4.14; 9.8; 11.13; 21.5; Josh. 7.7; Judg. 6.22, cf. 11.35). 'Behold, thou seest' (Jer. 32.24) is likewise characteristic; cf. 'thou knowest' (Pss. 40.10; 69.20; Jer. 15.15), 'thou hast seen' (Pss. 10.14; 35.22; Lam. 3.59f.).

recorded prayer of Jeremiah in a narrative context is a private complaint to God regarding his word, uttered in a non-cultic setting, at least shows that Jeremiah was remembered as addressing his God in this way. It would therefore seem more reasonable to regard the Confessions as the texts of just such complaints rather than as the utterances of a liturgical mediator, a function the biographer never depicts Jeremiah as performing.

II

But as was said above, the matter can finally be settled only exegetically, by an examination of the Confessions themselves. Let us therefore turn to them, taking them up in the order followed by Reventlow. It is not our intention to present a complete exegesis of each of these passages. That close similarities, both formal and verbal, exist between them and the Pss. Lam. is not in question, and will be taken for granted here. That the Pss. Lam. have a cultic *Sitz im Leben* is likewise taken for granted. But do the Confessions exhibit the cultic form without modification, or is there evidence of a private adaptation of the form by a prophetic individual? The ground has been covered by Baumgartner, though of course long before Reventlow advanced his cultic interpretation. We shall try as far as possible not to repeat Baumgartner's arguments, or to bog down in unessential detail. Rather, we shall focus upon one single question: Can these passages, without forcing, really be interpreted as liturgical pieces uttered in the context of the cult? It is my conviction that an unbiased examination will show that they cannot be.

1. *Jeremiah 15.10–21.* Reventlow sees the piece as a unit which has the form of a liturgy.[23] It opens with a complaint (v. 10). But this is not to be taken as an expression of the prophet's personal anguish, for the 'I' is corporate: the prophet speaks in the name of the people. In vv. 11–14 (Reventlow retains vv. 12–14 in context)

[23] Reventlow, *Liturgie*, pp. 210–28.

198

the complaint is answered by an oracle which is addressed to the people collectively: the nation is to be destroyed at the hands of 'the foe from the north'.[24] The lament is then resumed with the prophet again speaking as intercessor for the people. He cries for their deliverance from the 'godless' among them (v. 15), protests their innocence (vv. 16–17a), laments their misery (vv. 17b–18a), and concludes with a bitter reproach against God (v. 18b). All is liturgical: the prophet nowhere speaks of his personal suffering. This complaint is then answered by a further oracle (vv. 19–21). It is not a private rebuke to Jeremiah, but a word that is proclaimed to the people. It rejects their *Klage*, both their protestations of innocence and their complaints, as 'worthless': prophet and people alike must repent. The oracle does relate to the prophetic office, but not as usually understood. As cultic mediator, the prophet was both representative of the people before God, and of God to the people. He is now told to speak as God's representative, and to stop trying one-sidedly to excuse the people: his continuance in office depends upon this.

(*a*) This interpretation might at first glance seem plausible, especially when one recalls how frequently the 'I' of the Psalms is corporate. But how can vv. 16f. be fitted into it? Do not these verses clearly express the anguish of a prophetic *individual* who, because of the divine word which he must speak, suffers isolation and loneliness? They are usually understood so. Reventlow, however, is able so to interpret them that, here too, the figure of the prophetic individual disappears behind that of the anonymous liturgist. Since these verses are the crux of the matter, let us examine Reventlow's exegesis more narrowly at the point.

As for v. 16, Reventlow denies that the expression, 'Thy words were found, and I ate them', has anything to do with the reception

---

[24] Reventlow (*ibid.*, p. 216) reads v. 11a generally following MT: 'Yahweh said, "Truly, I have helped (?) you for good; (but now) truly I will cause to fall upon you – the enemy."' We shall not discuss Reventlow's exegesis of vv. 11–14, since the text is so corrupt that any interpretation must rest on extensive emendation. In view of his general thesis, Reventlow's is defensible.

of the prophetic word.[25] Rather, 'words' has here the force of God's commandments, as frequently in the Psalms:[26] the complainant protests that he has received God's commands and gladly obeyed them. The further protestation, 'I am called by thy name', must, says Reventlow, be understood as corporate (i.e. spoken in the name of the people), since the expression is not otherwise used of God's claim upon an individual. In v. 17a Reventlow sees the continuation of the community's declaration of innocence, rather than a personal lament of Jeremiah over his lonely, joyless life.[27] He argues that the roots שָׂחַק ('merrymakers') and עָלַז ('rejoice') have a predominantly unpleasant connotation, the former with the force of 'laugh at, mock, make fun of', the latter with that of 'triumph, exult over'; v. 17a is thus the protest of the 'righteous' that they did not 'sit in the seat of the scoffers' (cf. Pss. 1.1; 26.4f.), but kept apart from godless men. Verse 17b then begins the lament of the 'righteous'.[28] God's 'hand' does not refer to the divine inspiration or compulsion, but to God's chastisement, as in certain Psalms (e.g., Pss. 32.4; 38.3; 39.11). As is shown by Lev. 13.46 (where the leper must 'dwell alone' outside the camp), 'I sat alone' suggests sickness – and sickness is a standard motif in the Pss. Lam. The 'indignation' (זַעַם) with which the complainant is filled is not the divine wrath with which God has filled his prophet, but a 'curse', '*Unheil*', which has been laid upon him. In other words, the 'righteous' complain that while the 'godless' – with whom they did not associate – exult, they are smitten with 'sickness', 'a curse', an 'incurable wound' (v. 18a) by the chastising hand of God.

If we had only v. 16, Reventlow's interpretation might just possibly be maintained. It is true that the expression, 'Thy words were found, and I ate them', is most naturally taken as referring

---

[25] It is not necessary to discuss the variant reading of LXX, since Reventlow – quite rightly, I believe – sticks with MT.

[26] He cites Pss. 17.4; 33.4; 56.5, 11; 105.8; 107.20; 130.5; 147.15ff.; 148.8, and Ps. 119 *passim* (*Liturgie*, p. 220).

[27] *Ibid.*, pp. 221–4.   [28] *Ibid.*, pp. 224f.

to the reception of the prophetic word – as when Ezekiel (2.8–3.3) 'ate' the scroll at his call. But the expression itself has no parallel;[29] and 'word' does have the force of God's commands in at least some of the Psalm references cited by Reventlow above. Reventlow's interpretation cannot be proved to be wrong. We shall have to wait to see if it does justice to other places in the Confessions where God's 'word' is mentioned. As for the expression 'I am called by thy name', the most we can say is that there is no reason why it might not have been used with reference to a single individual. The expression (lit: 'thy name is called over me') has a legal background,[30] and means 'to lay (legal) claim to something, to claim possession of something'. It is true that it is not elsewhere used of God's laying claim to a single individual.[31] But, as a legal term, it could quite properly be applied to anything a person might claim title to: land, property, a city (cf. II Sam. 12.28), or persons (in Isa. 4.1 it is used of persons, with men as the possessors). Since the expression was early taken over into a theological context (II Sam. 6.2), it could in principle at any time have been applied to anything God might claim to possess, including persons. The fact that it is not used elsewhere of a single individual may be no more than an accident of the sources (it is used only once of the ark [II Sam. 6.2], and of conquered peoples [Amos 9.12]). A corporate interpretation is not excluded, but it is certainly not required.

It is when we come to v. 17 that Reventlow's interpretation

---

[29] The closest parallel is Lam. 2.9, 'Her prophets did not *find* a vision (חָזוֹן) from Yahweh' – as Reventlow also notes (*ibid.*, p. 220).

[30] And so Reventlow (*ibid.*, p. 220f.).

[31] Except for II Sam. 12.28 and Isa. 4.1, the expression is always used with God as the possessor. It is applied to the ark (II Sam. 6.2 paralleled by I Chron. 13.6), the Temple (I Kings 8.43 paralleled by II Chron. 6.33; Jer. 7.10f., 14, 30; 32.34; 34.15), Israel (Deut. 28.10; Jer. 14.9; Isa. 63.19; II Chron. 7.14; Dan. 9.19), Jerusalem (Jer. 25.29; Dan. 9.18f.), and to conquered foreign nations (Amos 9.12). In Isa. 43.7 a very similar expression is applied to unspecified individuals who belong to God's people.

appears as decidedly forced. An examination of the roots שָׂחַק and
עָלַז does not support his contention that v. 17a refers to the
godless 'scoffers' with whom the 'righteous' did not 'sit'. In the
first place, the root שָׂחַק is *never* used in the Psalm literature to
describe the 'scoffers', while עָלַז is so used only *once* (Ps. 94.3)
out of seven occurrences there. It is true that שָׂחַק when used in
the *Qal* has, in the majority of instances, an unpleasant connotation ('laugh at', 'mock', etc.). But in the *Piel*, which is what
we have here (מְשַׂחֲקִים: 'merrymakers'), the reverse is the case. It
is not permissible to evade this, as Reventlow attempts to do, by
finding a supposed basic force of the root (to exult over a defeated
foe) in virtually every occurrence, for the vast majority of occurrences in the *Piel* (really all except Judg. 16.25; II Sam. 2.14) have
the perfectly harmless connotation of 'being glad, making merry,
rejoicing'.[32] As for עָלַז (which occurs only in *Qal*), it does at times
have an unpleasant connotation ('triumph', 'exult over'), as
Reventlow says. But it is most frequently used of exulting,
rejoicing in God and his deliverance,[33] and here it occurs in
parallelism with such roots as רָנַן, גִּיל, בָּטַח, זָמַר, שִׁיר, הֵרִיחַ,
שָׂמַח – all of which surely cannot be loaded with a jeering connotation.[34] The truth is that words such as the above, like the
English word 'laugh' (he laughed for joy; he laughed at me), can
have either a pleasant or an unpleasant connotation, and only the
context can determine which is intended. To freight them with

---

[32] The reader can easily check this. For example, מְשַׂחֲקִים is used in
Zech. 8.5 of children playing; in Prov. 8.30f. the fem. sing. is used of
Wisdom rejoicing before God at creation. In Jer. 30.19; 31.4 (*contra*
Reventlow, *Liturgie*, p. 223) only simple joy and merrymaking is intended.

[33] Cf. Hab. 3.18; Zeph. 3.14; Pss. 28.7; 68.5; 96.12; 149.5.

[34] In Prov. 23.16 עָלַז is used of the simple joy of a father who says to
his son, 'My soul (lit: 'kidneys') will *rejoice* when your lips speak what is
right.'

some supposed basic meaning at every occurrence is forced in the extreme.

Next, 'I sat alone because thy hand was upon me' (lit: 'because of thy hand'). To see 'I sat alone' (בָדָד יָשַׁבְתִּי) as a corporate lament over the 'sickness' which the divine chastisement ('thy hand') has brought, is again extremely forced. True, a similar expression (בָדָד יֵשֵׁב) is used of the leper in Lev. 13.46 – and the motif of sickness is standard in the *Klage*. But the verb יָשַׁב with בָדָד *never* appears as a figure for illness in the Psalms, and is *never* connected with leprosy – or sickness of any kind – save in Lev. 13.46; and here it is no more than the simple statement that an unclean person must stay by himself. Indeed, יֵשֵׁב occurs in connection with בָדָד (or לְבַד) only *once* in the entire Psalter (Ps. 4.9), where it is not in a *Klage* and has nothing to do with sickness.[35] Aside from the Psalms (and Jer. 15.17; Lev. 13.46), there are five occurrences of יֵשֵׁב with בָדָד or לְבַד; and if we add to these occurrences with the verb שָׁכַן, we have a grand total of nine. Four of these refer to individuals who sit by themselves, or who wish to live by themselves;[36] four others refer to peoples who live apart from others, in isolation.[37] The remaining occurrence (Lam. 1.1) is in a lament and is the closest parallel of all to Jer. 15.17: 'How she sits alone (אֵיכָה יָשְׁבָה בָדָד), the city (once) full of people! (How) she has become like a widow . . .' In short, in

[35] In fact, except for Ps. 102.8 ('a lonely bird on the roof'), all occurrences of בָדָד or לְבַד in the Psalms refer to God (Pss. 4.9; 51.6; 71.16; 72.18; 83.19; 86.10; 136.4; 148.13).
[36] Ex. 18.14 (Moses is the only one who sits): Judg. 3.20 (Eglon sits alone in his roof chamber); Isa. 5.8 ('dwell alone . . .'). Lam. 3.28 ('Let him sit alone in silence') must likewise be taken as meaning what it seems to mean.
[37] Num. 23.9; Deut. 33.28; Micah 7.14 (all Israel); Jer. 49.31 (desert dwellers: note that in this verse both יֵשֵׁב and שָׁכַן appear).

none of its occurrences does the verb יָשַׁב with בָּדָד carry the force that Reventlow assigns to it. There is nothing to suggest that it was ever used, in the *Klage* or elsewhere, as an allusion to sickness, and nothing to suggest that it ever meant (not even in Lev. 13.46) anything but 'to sit (or dwell) by one's self'.

Since this is so, it is very difficult to understand God's 'hand' as his chastisement. Rather, it must refer to the divine compulsion that is laid on the prophet – a force the word frequently has when used in connection with prophets.[38] In like manner the 'indignation' with which the speaker is filled cannot be understood as a 'curse', '*Unheil*', which God has laid on him. Regardless of what the *Urbedeutung* of זַעַם may have been, its actual usage supports Baumgartner, who says that it denotes 'always the divine wrath, which expresses itself in a *Strafgericht*'.[39] Aside from two occurrences in Daniel, the noun occurs only in the prophetic books (fourteen times aside from Jer. 15.17), and Psalms (four times) and Lamentations (once) – a total of nineteen times. *All* of these texts have to do with Yahweh's coming in wrath to judge either Israel or the nations. In fourteen of them זַעַם is used in parallelism with, or close promixity to, such words as חֲרוֹן אַף, אַף, עֶבְרָה, קֶצֶף. The prophet is filled with God's own wrath, which he must proclaim, and this makes it impossible for him to sit with his fellows and participate in their joys (as in Jer. 16.8).[40] To interpret the verse otherwise is forced.

(*b*) But even aside from vv. 16f., it is impossible to understand 15.10–21 as a liturgical text. One thinks especially of v. 18b. The sentence is to be read as an emphatic statement (inf. abs. followed

[38] Cf. I Kings 18.46; II Kings 3.15 (RSV, 'power'); Ezek. 1.3; 3.14, 22; 8.1; 33.22; 37.1; 40.1. Note especially Ezek. 3.14f., where Ezekiel, with God's 'hand' strong upon him, went to the exiles and 'sat' among them overwhelmed.

[39] Baumgartner, *op. cit.*, p. 37.

[40] There is an excellent parallel in Jer. 6.11, 'I am full of the wrath of Yahweh (חֲמַת יְהוָה) – Pour it out – !' Reventlow (*Liturgie*, pp. 233f.) too hastily brushes this verse and 16.8 aside.

by finite verb): 'You are indeed to me like a deceitful brook . . .'[41]
This is no less than an accusation against God. Such an accusation
is unthinkable in a liturgy: it would be today, and it was then.
The Pss. Lam. never include such a thing. The psalmist frequently
cries out, 'Why hast thou forsaken me?' or, 'Why art thou far from
me?' (for surely there must be a reason); he asks, 'Wilt thou forget
me forever?' (ah, surely not!) or, 'How long, O Lord?' (for it
cannot be for ever). Sometimes, indeed, his lament heightens in
intensity until it becomes a reproach (notably in Pss. 44; 88).
Yet even here reproach is uttered in the context of fervent appeal
to God, and the confidence that he can even yet save. *Never* do we
hear the flat accusation: 'God, you have failed me!' An anguished
individual might use such words – but a liturgical text, never!

Even more damaging are the opening words of the piece (v. 10):
אוֹי־לִי אִמִּי. The expression occurs only here; the prophet
apostrophizes his (presumably) long-dead mother. Such words
could not possibly introduce a liturgical text, or even be used in
the course of it. In a prayer uttered publicly in the cult, by a cultic
official, address must *always* be to God – as in fact it invariably is
in the Pss. Lam. A distressed individual might cry out, 'O mother,
why did you bring me into the world?' but a liturgist making
public intercession for the people would never do so. A lament
that 'my mother bore me' has in fact no parallel in the Old Testament save in Jeremiah's Confessions (20.14–18) and in Job (ch. 3),
and certainly none in the Psalm literature.[42]

2. *Jeremiah 17.12–18.* We can proceed more rapidly here. We
shall not delay upon Reventlow's interpretation of vv. 12f., which,

[41] This is the most natural reading and is followed by LXX; הָיוֹ is
not to be emended into the interrogative particle (so EVV), nor into הוֹי
(so BH³ and various commentators) – which is grammatically without
parallel.
[42] It might also be argued that the remainder of v. 10, especially the
complaint of being an אִישׁ רִיב and an אִישׁ מָדוֹן to the whole land, is
appropriate to a prophetic individual, but not to a corporate lament. But
space fails; see Baumgartner, *op. cit.*, pp. 60–62 on the verse.

as others have done (Baumgartner, Weiser), he connects with vv. 14–18. It is with vv. 14–18 that the problem lies. Reventlow sees these verses as a typical Pss. Lam. like those in the Psalter, uttered by the prophet in his capacity as cultic *Vorbeter*: the 'I' is again corporate, with the prophet speaking in the name of the people and laying their plaint before God.[43] Now if it were not for v. 15 (and if we had no other Confessions) this interpretation might pass. The piece has all the earmarks of the Pss. Lam.: its form corresponds perfectly, and most of its vocabulary and many of its locutions have parallels there. But v. 15 reads like the complaint of one who has spoken God's word and has been twitted because it has not come to pass – thus a prophet. Reventlow, however, says that 'the word of Yahweh' has nothing to do with the prophetic word, but rather refers to God's helping and saving power, as in certain Psalms (Pss. 33.4; 56.5, 11; 107.20; 130.5); 'Where is the word of Yahweh?' has the force of the taunt, 'Where is your God?' in Ps. 42.4, 11.[44] The verse is thus the scornful reply of the evildoers to the cry for help of v. 14: When is your God ever coming to your aid?

Let us concentrate on this, for it is the crucial point. And it seems to me that Reventlow's argument breaks down on it. It is not merely that most of the passages in Psalms adduced above do not have quite the force of God's saving power which Reventlow wishes to see here (really, only Ps. 107.20 does). It is rather that he has failed to examine the force of 'Let it come' (יְבוֹא נָא),

when used in this connection. As far as I can discover, on *every occasion* when the verb בּוֹא is used of God's word or purpose, or of a prophetic word, it has the force of 'come to pass', 'come true', 'happen'. I find no exception to this. We have a classic example in Jer. 28.9, where it is said that if a prophet prophesies of peace, it is 'when the word of that prophet comes to pass' (בְּבֹא דְּבַר הַנָּבִיא)

that one can know that Yahweh sent him. This points back to the

---

[43] Cf. *Liturgie*, pp. 234–40 for Reventlow's interpretation of these verses.

[44] *Ibid.*, p. 237.

equally classic example in Deut. 18.22, 'When a prophet speaks in the name of Yahweh, if the word does not come to pass (לֹא־יִהְיֶה) or come true (לֹא יָבוֹא), it is a word which Yahweh did not speak.' But there are many others.[45] At no place does בּוֹא when used with 'the word' ever have the force Reventlow wishes to find here. Verse 15 means what it seems to mean: Jeremiah's foes taunt him with the fact that his dire predictions have not come true. The verse is fully parallel to Isa. 5.19, where the scoffers say, 'Let him make haste, let him speed his work that we may see it; let the purpose of the Holy One of Israel draw near, and let it *come*, that we may know it!' The speaker in v. 15 has to be a prophetic individual. But if in v. 15, then throughout the entire lament.

3. *Jeremiah 11.18–12.6*. Reventlow correctly regards 11.18–23 and 12.1–6 as two formally independent and originally separate units.[46] Unlike various scholars (Volz, Rudolph, Weiser) who, assuming extensive dislocations in the text, transfer 12.6 into conjunction with 11.18 and make deletions and/or transpositions in the case of 12.3f., Reventlow (with an exception to be noted) seeks to interpret the text as it lies before us. And for this he is to be commended.

(a) *12.1–6* Reventlow regards vv. 1–4 as a complaint in the form of a legal process.[47] Its form is as follows: appeal to the judge (v. 1a), statement of complaint (v. 1b–2), protestation of innocence and plea that the guilty be punished (v. 3), and lament, plus basis upon which judgment is demanded (v. 4). Though the piece looks like the lament of an individual, it is 'a *Volksklagelied*

---

[45] I count at least fifteen aside from the two mentioned here, and there may be more (to check בּוֹא or דָּבָר in Mandelkern is a fearsome undertaking!): cf. Deut. 13.3; Josh. 21.45; 23.14; Judg. 13.12, 17; I Sam. 9.6; 10.9; Isa. 5.19; 42.9; 48.3, 5; Ezek. 24.14; 33.33; Hab. 2.3; Ps. 105.19.

[46] Reventlow, *Liturgie*, pp. 240–2. Apart from formal considerations, it is logically impossible to read 11.18–12.6 as a continuous unit, for in 12.6 Jeremiah is informed of what he already knew in 11.18; namely, that a plot against him existed.

[47] Cf. *ibid.*, pp. 240–51, 255–7, for Reventlow's interpretation of vv. 1–6.

in individual dress'.⁴⁸ What is at stake is no mere academic question, but the health of the land: there is a drought (v. 4), and this has been brought on by the wickedness of godless men. The *Klage* thus has a twofold aim: the 'righteous' protest their innocence and at the same time seek to have the guilty punished, thereby removing the curse from the land. Here again, the prophet does not speak as a 'pious' individual, but as the cultic representation of the 'pious' people.⁴⁹

Reventlow's interpretation of these verses (if studied in isolation) is not in itself implausible, and might be defended. We shall not pause upon it. It is with vv. 5f. that serious questions arise. In v. 5, says Reventlow, the divine answer to the complaint is given. As the complaint was collective, so the answering oracle concerns the whole people and is to be delivered to them. It is 'a scarcely veiled announcement of judgment':⁵⁰ their *Klage* is rejected, and worse than drought is coming upon them, namely, 'the foe from the north'. The 'horses' with which they must race are the horses of that foe (4.13; 6.23), while the 'jungle of Jordan' would call to mind the lions that lurk there (49.19; 50.44; Zech. 11.3); and 'the foe from the north' has been likened to a 'lion' (4.7). Reventlow is of course aware that v. 6 contradicts this interpretation completely, for this verse makes it quite clear that Jeremiah is addressed privately. But, says he, v. 6 does not belong here. It belongs in some other, unknown context, and has been secondarily added on – apparently by someone who wished to give the piece an individual interpretation.

One is forced to protest this. One can have no confidence in an interpretation that requires such desperate measures if it is to be maintained. There is not the slightest form-critical ground for removing v. 6 (either to put it at 11.18 or elsewhere). Moreover, some explanation of the metaphors of v. 5 is logically required; without it, v. 5 is as cryptic as a Delphic oracle (and the prophetic oracle is characteristically *not* cryptic). If there is an allusion to 'the foe from the north' in v. 5, it is so veiled that not one in a

⁴⁸ Reventlow, *Liturgie*, p. 249.   ⁴⁹ *Ibid.*, p. 244.   ⁵⁰ *Ibid.*, p. 250.

hundred of Jeremiah's hearers would have taken the point. A clarifying statement is both logically necessary and formally to be expected. The natural interpretation of vv. 5f. is the only defensible one: it is a word addressed to Jeremiah personally.[51]

(b) *11.18–23.*[52] In vv. 18–20 Reventlow sees a fragment of a Pss. Lam. which, as elsewhere, he interprets collectively. Verses 21–23, which would seem to contradict this, he regards as secondarily connected by a redactor; the verses do refer to an experience of Jeremiah, but they belong in some other context. As for v. 18, it cannot be the beginning of the piece, for it clearly points back to some divine word that has been received. But Reventlow will not allow that this was a private revelation to Jeremiah. Rather, it was the cultic *Heilsorakel* which, in the form of Pss. Lam., would have been preceded by the *Klage* itself. This part of the piece (*Klage* and *Heilsorakel*) must once have stood before v. 18, but has now been lost. The *Heilsorakel* must have contained some reference to the reason for the lament, plus assurance of divine aid.[53] Verses 18–20 are then interpreted as the *Danklied* that follows upon the *Heilsorakel* and (as so often in the Pss. Lam.) brings the piece to a conclusion.

Though I cannot agree with Reventlow's dismissal of vv. 21–23 from the context, he can at least (as he could not at 12.6) base himself on form-critical grounds. This is a formally separate piece, and it may once have been transmitted separately (the explanatory expansion in v. 21, which is superfluous in the present context, may argue that it was), and been bonded on to vv. 18–20 editorially because the situation was believed to be the same. The question then would be: Is the redactional connection factually correct? That, of course, is a question that cannot be finally settled. But the

---

[51] As a further argument against removing v. 6, note the apparently intentional link between בָּגְדוּ ('dealt treacherously', v. 6) and בֹּגְדֵי בָגֶד ('treacherous', v. 1).

[52] For Reventlow's interpretation of these verses, cf. *Liturgie*, pp. 251–7.

[53] *Ibid.*, p. 254.

possibility of correctness ought not to be ruled out: tradition is not always wrong![54] After all, vv. 21–23 are no more formally separate from what precedes them than is the case with 15.19–21, which Reventlow retains in position, presumably because it accords with his theory to do so.

But can vv. 18–20 properly be understood as a liturgical *Danklied* in response to a *Heilsorakel*? Verse 18 clearly does reach back to some divine oracle that has been displaced; it is equally clear from the wording that this included a revelation to the supplicant of a plot against him. If we suppose that it also included assurance of divine aid, we might regard it as a *Heilsorakel* answering a lament; we might then interpret vv. 18–20 as a thanksgiving, with a note of assurance (if we read 'I will see thy vengeance . . .' in v. 20).[55] But it is more natural to read, 'Let me see . . .' (so EVV; cf. Ps. 7.10), and to see the verse as a cry for vindication. In fact, the note of assurance and praise characteristic of the *Danklied* is absent from vv. 18–20. Rather, we have here complaint and protestation of innocence (vv. 19–20a), plus a cry for vengeance (v. 20b) that still *awaits* a divine answer.

Another thing, however, is still more puzzling. We know little of the *Heilsorakel* from the Psalms; it is often presupposed, but seldom given (Pss. 12.6; cf. 60.8–11; 91.14–16). Certainly it brought assurance of divine help. But it is difficult to think of a *Heilsorakel* (!) bringing the supplicant news that he is being plotted against, as is clearly the case here (cf. vv. 18f.). Moreover, if – as Reventlow believes – the lost *Heilsorakel* was itself preceded by a *Klage*, we have to suppose that this last related to something entirely different from the plot alluded to in vv.18f., or that the supplicant was complaining of troubles of which he had not yet been informed! In fact, no Psalm presupposes an oracle telling the complainant that he is in trouble. On the contrary, he utters his

[54] We have a redactional connection of formally disparate pieces in chs. 27f. which is certainly correct; in 19.1–20.6 we have another which is in all likelihood correct.

[55] As Baumgartner does; *op. cit.*, p. 29.

lament because he *is* in trouble, and knows it very well. Never is there a suggestion that he has had to be informed of that fact. A divine word to the prophet is clearly presupposed by vv. 18f. But, in view of the context, this can only be understood as a private revelation informing the prophet that a plot had been made to kill him.

III

Reventlow's interpretation of the foregoing passages seems decidedly forced. But, what is far more serious, he fails to discuss three further Confessions where it would seem that his thesis cannot be maintained at any price. Of course, he could not be expected to discuss every passage in the book. But since his argument concerns the prophetic 'I', all important first-person passages should have been considered. A thesis cannot stand if relevant evidence is ignored. Let us look at these passages briefly.

1. *Jeremiah 18.18–23*. We have to guess how Reventlow would deal with this and the following passages. But if he cannot interpret all the Confessions in the same way, his thesis is to be dismissed as invalid. One presumes that he would regard v. 18 as secondarily linked to vv. 19–23, for v. 18 clearly relates the passage to a personal experience of Jeremiah. In this, he could base himself on form-critical grounds (as at 11.21–23), for v. 18 is not formally a part of the *Klage*.[56] He would then, if he is consistent, interpret vv. 19–23 as a liturgical lament uttered by the prophet in the name of the people in his role as cultic mediator.

Now the piece clearly follows the form of the Pss. Lam., and has verbal similarities so numerous and obvious that we need not trouble to list them.[57] Yet it is just here – specifically at v. 20 – that Reventlow's interpretation breaks down. How are we to

---

[56] I believe that Baumgartner (*ibid.*, pp. 45f.) is in error at this point.
[57] Cf. Baumgartner (*ibid.*, pp. 44–48) on the point. Though few Psalms have a curse so bitter, there are parallels (cf. Ps. 109.7–20). Note also the parallel between v. 20 and Ps. 109.4–6 (also Ps. 35.7, 12).

interpret this verse? If we take the 'I' as corporate, as Reventlow has done elsewhere (i.e. the prophet liturgically voices the complaint of the community), then the *entire righteous community* is represented as the cultic intercessor! Otherwise, we have to take the verse as a personal plaint of the intercessor himself, a private expression of anger at abuse he had himself received. In other words, even if we understand the prophet as a cultic functionary, it is still impossible to dissolve the prophetic 'I' into a collective. The obvious interpretation is the natural one: Jeremiah who, as we know, did intercede for the people, complains that they have repaid him evil for good.

2. *Jeremiah 20.7–13*. Here again, parallels with the Pss. Lam., both formal and verbal, are numerous and evident[58] – even including a verbal one between v. 10 and Ps. 31.14. But it is quite impossible to interpret the piece as a liturgy. To begin with, the word translated 'deceived' in v. 7a (פָּתָה) most naturally suggests 'seduction' (Ex. 22.15; Judg. 16.5; Job 31.9), which is unthinkable in a liturgical text. No liturgist could possibly *accuse* the God to whom his prayer is directed in such rough language. Even if we translate 'deceive, trick', as is possible, the point still holds, for it is still an accusation.

Even more awkward is 'the word of Yahweh' in vv. 8ff. This can only be the prophetic word, the speaking of which has brought the prophet abuse. Reventlow has elsewhere (at 15.16f.) interpreted the 'word' as God's commandments, which the speaker has obeyed; or (at 17.15) as God's saving help, which he awaits. Neither will do here. The prophet (v. 8) 'speaks'; he 'cries out, חָמָס וָשֹׁד'. In all other occurrences of this expression (Jer. 6.7; Ezek. 45.9; Amos 3.10; Hab. 1.3) it refers to deeds of violence done to the helpless. Here the prophet says that he has spoken out accusing men of 'violence and robbery', and has been laughed at for his pains. In v. 9 he tells us that he had decided not to 'speak

[58] Cf. Baumgartner (*ibid.*, pp. 48–51, 63–66; but one ought not to divide the piece as he does).

any more in his name' (i.e. in God's), but he found that he could
not hold back the word, which was like a fire in his bones. These
could only be the words of a prophet, for the prophet was the one
who was called to speak in God's name.[59] A liturgist speaking in
the name of the community would never express himself in this
way. We see in the passage just what we seem to see: a prophet's
personal struggle with the word.

3. *Jeremiah 20.14–18.* We need say little here, for this passage
could not by any stretch of the imagination be interpreted as a
liturgy. Unlike the other Confessions, it has none of the earmarks
of the Pss. Lam. and, except for a few words in v. 18, none of their
characteristic vocabulary.[60] The piece is not addressed to God
(who is not even mentioned, save indirectly in v. 16); there is no
complaint against wicked and godless men, no protestation of
innocence or plea for divine aid, no assurance of being heard – just
unrelieved despair. The piece is actually a self-curse. There is
nothing remotely resembling it in the Psalm-literature; its only
real parallel in the Bible is Job 3, which is certainly not a liturgical
text.[61]

To interpret 20.14–18 as a collective lament, uttered by a cultic
mediator, would be absurd. I cannot imagine that Reventlow
himself would wish to do so. If we take the 'I' as representing the
community, then we have a self-curse on the part of Israel, a
lament that the Israelite people ever came into existence. If we

---

[59] Some (e.g., Hölscher) have tried to evade this by translating לֹא־
אֲדַבֵּר עוֹד בִּשְׁמוֹ as 'I will utter his name no more' – something that any
Israelite might say. But, as Baumgartner (*ibid.*, p. 65) points out, this is
impossible: דִּבֶּר (or נִבָּא) with בְּשֵׁם always means to 'speak in the name
of ——'.

[60] Only יָגוֹן, עָמָל and the interrogative לָמָּה; cf. Baumgartner, *op. cit.*,
p. 67.

[61] Even here, the parallel is more one of subject matter and mood;
verbal parallels are surprisingly few. The two texts certainly reflect a
common tradition; but it is probably futile to talk of literary dependence,
one way or the other.

take it as representing the 'righteous' in the community, then the despairing righteous collectively regret their several births – which is a mood quite opposite to that of the lamenting, but ultimately confident, 'righteous' of the Psalms. The only reasonable way to understand the passage – unless we refuse to relate it to Jeremiah altogether – is to see in it an expression of the prophet's personal anguish and despair.

We conclude, then, that Reventlow's interpretation of the Confessions, and of the prophetic 'I' generally, is to be rejected. His study is based on a painstaking examination of the text, together with a rigid application of form-critical principles, and it contains many valuable insights – which for reasons of space (and this is to be regretted) we have been unable to single out. But he has proceeded on the indefensible assumption that the cultic form necessarily remains bound to, and reflects, the cultic institution; and he arrives at his conclusions only by forcing or ignoring evidence. To be sure, Reventlow has reminded us afresh that we must take with full seriousness the cultic form in which the Confessions are cast. The fact that they employ conventional forms and conventional locutions warns us against too quickly finding biographical or psychological details, or marks of poetic genius, in each turn of phrase. But conventional forms *can* be expressive of real experiences and real emotion. In this case, we are forced to see behind the conventional forms a prophetic individual, persecuted because of the word, suffering mental and physical anguish, and lashing out at his persecutors – and God. That leaves only the question: Is that prophetic individual Jeremiah, or 'look we for another'? But that would bring us into debate with Gerstenberger, which cannot be attempted here.

11

Baruch the Scribe
James Muilenburg

THE historical period extending from the reign of Ashurbanipal, the last of the great Assyrian monarchs (663–627 BC), to the accession of Cyrus as ruler over the Persian Empire in the year 538 BC is one of the most amply documented as it is one of the most culturally significant in the history of the ancient Near East. It is also one of the most literate and articulate. Thanks chiefly to the discovery of the library of Ashurbanipal by Hormuzd Rassam in 1853, we have at our disposal today a wealth and variety of literary works and inscriptional remains to which it would be difficult to adduce a parallel. The long period of Assyrian hegemony over Western Asia was slowly drawing to a close, and forces of great vitality were challenging not only the structures of Assyrian imperial organization, but also the mentalities and interior dispositions of the peoples of the Near East. New ideas were beginning to stir in that world, and everywhere men were animated by historical forces and psychological drives more potent than anything that had been known since the period of 'the first internationalism' seven centuries earlier.[1] The perplexities and dishevelments of the age, its fears and forebodings,

---

[1] The phrase is Breasted's. Compare S. A. Cook, 'The Fall and Rise of Judah', *The Cambridge Ancient History*, eds. J. B. Bury, S. A. Cook and F. E. Adcock (Cambridge: at the University Press, 1929), vol. III, p. 394: 'There was an interconnection of peoples, for a parallel to which we must go back to the Amarna Age.'

its malaise and nostalgia for tradition are reflected in one fashion or another in the literature of the times, not only in Assyria, but also throughout the vaster ranges of its empire.[2] Ashurbanipal was a scholar and a scribe, and boasts of his proficiency as copyist and decipherer of the ancient Sumerian and Akkadian records.[3] His reign marks the zenith of Assyrian art and literature, and it is to him more than to any other that we owe our knowledge of the age.[4] He dispatched royal scribes throughout Assyria and Babylonia in order that they might assemble the ancient texts, copy and translate them, and prepare them for deposit in the library. Business texts and letters appear in profusion, but also omen texts, reflecting the distraughtness and insecurity of the men of that age,[5] lengthy chronicles or

---

[2] W. F. Albright, *From the Stone Age to Christianity* (Baltimore: The Johns Hopkins Press, 1940), pp. 240–55. 'It is not surprising that this age of growing insecurity, when the very foundations of life were trembling, should give rise to an earnest effort to find a cure for the increasing *malaise* of the social organism' (pp. 240f.). 'The question of theodicy always comes to the fore during prolonged times of crisis, when human emotions are winnowed and purified by a sustained catharsis' (p. 252).

[3] Jack Finegan, *Light from the Ancient Past* (Princeton: Princeton University Press, 1946). Note the following words of Ashurbanipal: 'I received the revelation of the wise Adapa, the hidden treasure of the art of writing . . . I read the beautiful clay tablets from Sumer and the obscure Akkadian writing which is hard to master. I had my joy in the reading of inscriptions on stone from the time before the flood' (p. 181). See also E. Speiser, 'Mesopotamia Up to the Assyrian Period: Scribal Concepts of Education', in *City Invincible*, eds. Carl H. Kraeling and Robert M. Adams (Chicago: The University of Chicago Press, 1960), p. 107 and B. Landsberger, *ibid.*, pp. 110f., for an estimate of Ashurbanipal's claims.

[4] A. T. Olmstead, *History of Assyria* (New York: Charles Scribner's Sons, 1923), pp. 489ff.

[5] *The Reports of the Magicians and Astrologers of Nineveh and Babylon in the British Museum*, ed. R. Campbell Thompson (London: Luzac & Co., 1900), vol. II; François Thureau-Dangin, *Rituels accadiens* (Paris: Ernest Leroux, 1921); *ANET*, 2nd ed. (Princeton: Princeton University Press, 1955), pp. 334–8, 349–52. Note the comment of Campbell Thompson, *op. cit.*, p. xv: 'The astrologer or the prophet who could

annals,[6] administrative documents of different kinds, treaties and rituals and much else. It was a period of *Sturm und Drang* in which men sought to overcome the incoherence and uncertainty of the times by appealing to astrologists and magicians to discern the signs of the times, or by recourse to the ancient texts, whether cosmological or mythological, to encounter the end of one age and the beginning of another, or by reflecting upon the great cultural deposits of the remote past to discover resources for the present. It was a scribal age, an age of many scribes, in which the monarch himself played a central role and provided an impetus to learning and education which extended far and wide throughout his realm.

It should occasion no surprise that the corrosive forces at work throughout Western Asia during this period should exact their toll from the kingdom of Judah, the last buffer state between Assyria and Egypt, the ultimate goal of Assyrian imperialist aggression, not only politically and economically, but also psychologically and culturally. From an early period Israel's faith was governed by the conviction that the sequences of history were embraced by an all-controlling purpose and an ultimate sovereignty. It is significant, therefore, that a substantial part of the Old Testament was composed during this period of the decline and fall of one empire and

---

foretell fair things for the nation, or disasters and calamities for their enemies, was a man whose words were regarded with reverence and awe ... The soothsayer was as much a politician as the statesman, and he was not slow in using the indications of political changes to point the moral of his astrological observations.'

[6] D. D. Luckenbill, *Ancient Records of Assyria and Babylonia* (Chicago: University of Chicago Press, 1927), vol. II, pp. 290ff.; D. J. Wiseman, *Chronicles of Chaldean Kings, 626–556 BC* (London: Trustees of the British Museum, 1956). Note Luckenbill's comment, *op. cit.*, p. 290: 'In the reign of Ashurbanipal (668–626 BC) we reach the high-water mark of Assyrian historical writing – as regards quantity and literary merit ... Furthermore, the great literary activity of Ashurbanipal seems to have come in the second part of his reign, after the overthrow of Shamash-shum-ukîn in 648 BC, and even when our documents are dated by eponyms we are in doubt as to their sequence, since the order of the eponymous years from 648 on is in doubt.' See also Olmstead, *loc. cit.*

the emergence and rise of another.[7] Even if we make full allowance for later accretions and supplementations, the amount of the literary precipitate is very impressive.[8] There was, first of all, the so-called great Deuteronomic work, extending from Deuteronomy through II Kings, a work which sought to explain why it was that the two kingdoms of Israel and Judah were destroyed, why the Lord of history had decreed his judgment upon the historical people κατ᾽ ἐξοχήν.[9] The great prophetic books of Jeremiah, Ezekiel, and Second Isaiah also come from this time, as do the smaller prophetic works of Zephaniah, Nahum, Habakkuk and Malachi.[10] The book of Lamentations too must be assigned to the period shortly after the downfall of Judah and the end of the monarchy.[11] If the book of Job belongs to this time, as some scholars hold, the situation becomes even more impressive.[12] Just

[7] Compare Hermann Gunkel, in 'Kultur der Gegenwart', *Die orientalischen Literaturen*, herausgegeben von Paul Hinneberg (Leipzig and Berlin, 1925), Teil I, Abteilung vii, p. 96: '*Die Literatur hatte vor den grossen Katastrophen ihre klassische Zeit erlebt. Das geistige Leben stand demals fast auf allen Gebieten, die Israel überhaupt gepflegt hat, in höchster Blüte.*' See also John L. McKenzie, s.j., 'Reflections on Wisdom', *JBL* 86 (March, 1967), p. 8: 'The scribes of Israel who were also the sages of Israel were not the first to collect in writing the memories of their people. The libraries of Nippur and of Ashurbanipal were obviously deliberate efforts to collect entire literary traditions. It is not without interest that both collections were made shortly before political collapse; and one wonders how much scribal activity was instigated by Josiah, who attempted a revival of the Davidic monarchy.' For an authoritative account of the latter, see *inter alia* R. de Vaux, 'Titres et fonctionnaires egyptiens a la cour de David et de Salomon', *RB* 48 (1939), pp. 394–405.

[8] If one undertakes to count the pages in Kittel's edition of the Masoretic Text, it will be recognized that almost four hundred pages out of the 1,434 may well come from our period.

[9] Gerhard von Rad, *Studies in Deuteronomy*, SBT 9, trans. David Stalker (London: SCM Press, 1953), pp. 74–91.

[10] Bruce T. Dahlberg, 'Studies in the Book of Malachi' (Dissertation, Union Theological Seminary, New York, 1963).

[11] Norman K. Gottwald, *Studies in the Book of Lamentations*, SBT 14 (London: SCM Press, 1954).

[12] R. H. Pfeiffer, *Introduction to the Old Testament* (New York: Harper & Brothers, 1941), p. 677; S. L. Terrien, 'Introduction to Job',

as Ashurbanipal and later Nabonidus sought to find in the past some threshold into the inchoate future, some ποῦ στῶ from which to withstand the agitation of stormy political seasons, so the composers of Deuteronomy had sought to comprehend the turbulence of the present within the context of the age of Moses and the words attributed to him. It has too long been our practice to speak of Deuteronomists, traditionists, and redactors. But such terms are nondescript. In all probability it is in not a few instances with scribes with whom we have to do, scribes who were not only copyists, but also and more particularly composers who gave to their works their form and structure, and determined to a considerable degree their wording and terminology.[13] In Judah as in Assyria we are living in a scribal age, an age of scribes who occupied a strategic position in the royal house of David and were entrusted with the archives of both palace and Temple.[14] The names of most of the scribes during the history of the monarchy are unknown to us, but it is not without significance that they appear more conspicuously and frequently in the latter part of the seventh century and the beginning of the sixth than they do

---

IB 3, pp. 884–91; 'Quelques remarques sur les affinités de Job avec le Deutéro-Isaïe', *SVT* 15, Congrès de Genève (Leiden: E. J. Brill, 1966), pp. 295–310.

[13] McKenzie, *loc. cit.*: 'The Israelite wise men who were the scribes of Deuteronomy knew that the past is not meaningful unless it is continuous with the present ...' Moshe Weinfeld, 'Deuteronomy – the Present State of Inquiry', *JBL* 86 (Sept., 1967), pp. 249–62, especially p. 254, where Weinfeld attributes the crystallization of Deuteronomy to the scribes of Hezekiah and Josiah. See also his article on 'The Origin of the Humanism in Deuteronomy', *JBL* 80 (Sept., 1961), pp. 241–7.

[14] Salo W. Baron, *A Social and Religious History of the Jews*, vol. I, 2nd rev. ed. (New York: Columbia University Press, 1952), p. 153: 'We would know few priests or scribes by name were it not for their accidental appearance in the political arena, but their anonymous contributions, however slow and imperceptible, were as vital and lasting as the more spectacular contributions of the others. There is no means of measuring human greatness. Would one venture to decide who was greater, the anonymous author of Deuteronomy, or Jeremiah, the prophet, the tragic grandeur of whose life has been so rich a source of inspiration? As it happened, both these men were priests.'

either during the United Monarchy of David and Solomon, or, for that matter, at any other time in the history of the monarchy. It seems probable that Josiah's policy of reviving the United Monarchy also involved the restoration of the officials of the royal court.[15]

If we leave the book of Job out of account, since its date is still much controverted, there are two books which occupy a position of pre-eminence above all others. Ever since the publication of Duhm's commentary on Jeremiah in 1901, it has been recognized that Jeremiah contains not a few passages which are closely related in style, terminology, and representation to Deuteronomy.[16] The affinities are not limited to these passages, however, but are to be recognized in other prose narratives as well. The best explanation for these affinities is that we are dealing in both works with a conventional mode of composition.[17] We encounter much the same style in the Deuteronomic history as we do in Deuteronomy, though there are differences in representation and theology. It has been suggested by more than one scholar that it is to the scribal family of Shaphan that we are to turn for the authorship of the Deuteronomistic history,[18] and while this can be little more than

[15] See *inter alia* de Vaux, *loc. cit.*; Joachim Begrich, 'Sōfēr und Mazkīr; ein Beitrag zur inneren Geschichte des davidischalomonischen Grossreiches und des Königreiches Juda', *ZAW* 58 (1940–41), pp. 1–29.

[16] See above all Sigmund Mowinckel, *Zur Komposition des Buches Jeremia*, Videnskapsselskapets Skrifter II. Hist.-Filos, Klasse, 1913, No. 5, Kristiania, 1914 and *Prophecy and Tradition*, Avhandlinger Utgitt av Det Norske Videnskaps-Akademi in Oslo, II. Hist.-Filos. Klasse, 1946, No. 3.

[17] John Bright, 'The Date of the Prose Sermons of Jeremiah', *JBL* 70 (March, 1951), pp. 15–35.

[18] A. Jepsen, *Die Quellen des Königsbuches* (Halle: Max Niemeyer Verlag, 1956), pp. 94f.; Weinfeld, 'Deuteronomy – the Present State of Inquiry', *JBL* 86 (Sept., 1967), p. 255, n. 35. Weinfeld rightly points out that a distinction should be made between Deuteronomy and the historiography of the Deuteronomic history and the 'editorial part of Jeremiah. But these three literary strands have a common theological outlook and identical stylistic features and therefore must be considered as a product of a continuous scribal school. In my opinion this school is to be connected with the family of Shaphan the scribe who took an active part in the discovery of the book in the time of Josiah'.

a conjecture it has much to commend it. That is to say, in both instances we are dealing with scribal style and with a scribal *modus scribendi*. What is more, it has been frequently pointed out that Jeremiah is to be understood as a second Moses or that he performs the functions of the Mosaic office (compare Deut. 18.15ff. and Jer. 1.4–10).[19]

The importance of Jeremiah in the history of Israel's religion and more especially of Israel's prophecy is generally recognized. It is often pointed out that we know Jeremiah more intimately than any other of the prophets. But this has often led to the mistaken conclusion that it is his interior self disclosures that mark his uniqueness. On the other hand, we are frequently informed today that he is only following conventional and traditional literary forms derived from the cult.[20] That Jeremiah was indeed an important person in his age cannot be legitimately questioned, indeed far more important than we are wont to think. Once we have recognized wherein his true importance lies we are on our way to solving some of the most contended and controversial issues which the man and his book pose for us. We must view the prophet first of all and above all as a major figure in the political, cultural, religious, and indeed international life of the period. His call to be a prophet does not overstate matters. He is appointed to be a prophet over the nations, and this was how he was meant to be understood. If we may trust our text, as I think we may, then

[19] H. J. Kraus, *Die prophetische Verkündigung des Rechts in Israel*, ThSt 51 (Zurich: Evangelischer Verlag AG, 1957); P. B. Broughton, 'The Call of Jeremiah: the Relation of Deut. 18.9–22 to the Call of Jeremiah', *ABR* 6 (1958), pp. 37–46; James Muilenburg, 'The "Office" of the Prophet in Ancient Israel', *The Bible in Modern Scholarship*, ed. J. Philip Hyatt (Nashville: Abingdon Press, 1965), pp. 74–97; Norman Habel, 'The Form and Significance of the Call Narratives', *ZAW* 77 (1965), pp. 297–323; W. L. Holladay, 'The Background of Jeremiah's Self-Understanding', *JBL* 83 (June, 1964), pp. 154ff. See also W. Zimmerli, *Ezechiel*, BKAT XIII (Neukirken-Vluyn: Verlag der Buchhandlung des Erziehungsvereins, 1955), pp. 13–37.

[20] Henning Graf Reventlow, *Liturgie und prophetisches Ich bei Jeremia* (Gütersloh: Gütersloher Verlagshaus Gerd Mohn, 1963).

Jeremiah was summoned to be Yahweh's covenant mediator, the royal emissary from the heavenly court, the divinely accredited spokesman to an age in radical ferment.[21] He is to address his nation and other nations with the word that has been committed to him to proclaim. He is endowed with the charismatic gift and is given authority and power over kingdoms and nations to pluck up and tear down, to build and to plant. The awareness of this great commission animates the prophet's mind throughout his career. Precisely because he was ordained for such a destiny he incurred the wrath of all those in high places he dared to oppose. Precisely because he is representative of the divine sovereignty or government he ventures to attack the corruption of all the venerable institutions by which his contemporaries sought to order their lives.

The cultural milieu of Jeremiah's ministry is international. The confusion and chaos within the kingdom of Judah have their source in remote lands, and Jeremiah finds himself destined to speak to that situation. The threat or actual presence of war persists throughout the ancient Near East during the period of his ministry. The book throughout bears witness to the precariousness of the international crisis, most notably in the year of the Battle of

[21] G. Ernest Wright, 'The Fruit of a Lifetime', *Interpretation* 18 (July, 1964), p. 362: 'The prophet was an officer of the heavenly government whose function, comparable to that of the royal herald in both Egypt and Israel, was to be the line of direct communication between the divine Suzerain and his vassal, Israel ... In other words, it is most important in our attempt to understand the office to stress not simply the psychology of ecstasy but the Israelite understanding of God's government of Israel and the manner in which the human phenomenon of ecstasy was taken up and transformed in that government.' Compare Georg Fohrer, 'Remarks on Modern Interpretation of the Prophets', *JBL* 80 (Dec., 1961), p. 310: 'The herald's message is originally not prophetic but typical for the royal messenger. Prophecy did not create it, but borrowed it from that source – probably by way of the prophets of the royal court, as we know them from Mari and Byblos ... The basic form of the prophetic oracles was certainly not exclusively bound to the cult or to the law, but could be sought and given everywhere and in all contexts.'

Carchemish in 605 BC (25.1–13; 36; 45; 46) and during the long period between the two deportations of 597 and 587. Jeremiah appears in the Temple at the beginning of Jehoiakim's reign and delivers his great sermon (7.1–15; 26.1–24); he confronts the envoys as they leave a plenary session of the emissaries of the nations surrounding Judah at the beginning of Zedekiah's reign (so the true text of 27.1); again and again he excoriates the delinquencies of Jehoiakim, and engages in bitter polemic against the leaders of the nation and Temple. He contends with other prophets and denies their accreditation since they have not stood in the heavenly council (23.18). Most significantly he is recognized by Nebuchadnezzar and the Chaldean commander after the fall of Jerusalem, is shown extraordinary preferential treatment, and is given the choice of determining his own future either by accompanying Nebuzaradan, the captain of the guard, personally (note *with me* in 40.4) to Chaldea, or by joining his fellow-countrymen at Mizpeh (39.11ff.; 40.1ff.; 42.1ff.). Nothing could illustrate better the importance of Jeremiah in the politics of his age or the dominating position that he held, whether in the royal councils or in the affairs of state. Unfortunately, the prestige of the prophet's office is obscured for us in the *ipsissima verba* of chs. 1–25, for here chronological and biographical data are all but wanting, and we are left in the dark as to the occasions when his words were spoken, as, for example, in connection with the oracles on the foe from the north or the lawsuits or the self-disclosures. It is when we pass from these chapters to those that follow that the situation changes strikingly, for here the mode of reporting is of quite a different order. We turn, therefore, to ch. 36, the single chapter in the book which casts light upon the history of its composition.

The thirty-sixth chapter of the book of Jeremiah brings to a culmination the sequence of prose narratives beginning with ch. 26.[22] That the two accounts are designed to form the beginning

[22] Martin Kessler, 'Form-Critical Suggestions on Jer. 36', *CBQ* 28 (Oct., 1966), pp. 389–401.

and ending of the literary complex is demonstrated by the many stylistic and linguistic features they share in common. Both chapters begin with a superscription, the occasion of both is a popular assembly in a time of great national crisis, in both we listen to the prophet's solemn and public indictments, and the motivation of repentance and forgiveness is common to both. In both the prophet's life is imperilled, in both the princes are favourably disposed to Jeremiah, in both the members of the house of Shaphan play a significant role, and throughout both the stress is constantly upon speaking and hearing.

In the fourth year of Jehoiakim Jeremiah receives a command from Yahweh to take a scroll and to write upon it all the words he had spoken to him from the time of his call in the reign of Josiah, presumably 627 BC (25.3) to the present. It was in that year that the armies of Chaldea under Nebuchadnezzar had delivered a decisive defeat to the Egyptian foe under Pharaoh Neco. The turning-point in the history of the Near East thus coincides with what was doubtless a turning-point in the prophet's career. It is not too much to suppose that the two events were closely related. If so, it is a remarkable witness to the fatefulness of the issues which were involved for Judah and for the other peoples of the Near East.

Jeremiah summons Baruch, the son of Neriah, and he writes at the prophet's dictation. Thereupon Jeremiah informs Baruch that he has been debarred from the Temple, but that he is to go and read there all the words he had written. Baruch complies with the prophet's demand. In December of the following year a fast is proclaimed. Precisely what it was that motivated the event we are not told, but it may well be that it was related to the victory of Chaldea at Carchemish and to the prophet's conviction that his oracles on the foe from the north had at long last been fulfilled. In the hearing of all the people and then the princes, Baruch reads from the scroll in the לִשְׁכָּה or cabinet room of Gemariah, the son of Shaphan, the secretary of state, perhaps in exactly the same place where Jeremiah had delivered the Temple speech some years previous (26.10, cf. 7.2).[23] The presence of all these princes more than suggests that they were quite aware of the impending crisis. The atmosphere was doubtless electric. When Micaiah, the grandson of Shaphan, heard all the words of Jeremiah from the mouth of Baruch, he goes to the cabinet room of the secretary in the royal palace to report to the princes who were gathered there. The latter order a certain Jehudi whose genealogy is traced back to the third generation to command Baruch to come to them. The words here are ironically much the same as those which Yahweh has employed in his command to Jeremiah (cf. v. 2). So Baruch comes, scroll in hand. The narrative at this point is dramatic. The princes say to Baruch, 'Sit down and read it' (*sic!*). Baruch accedes to their demands, and the princes turn to each other in fear and tell Baruch that they will have to report what has happened to the king. Significantly they enquire, 'Was it at his dictation?' and Baruch acknowledges that it was he! The princes then counsel Baruch that he and Jeremiah should go into hiding so that no one may know where they are. It is obvious that Baruch has fallen into friendly hands and it may be assumed that they were friendly to Jeremiah too. But what is more they recognize the validity of their credentials.

We are informed that the scroll was placed in the cabinet room of Elishama the secretary. It is not improbable that it was the repository of other documents. The princes report to the king, who orders Jehudi to procure the scroll, and the latter brings it to the king. Again the narrative is graphic and extraordinarily compressed, without any show of emotion. It is winter, and the king is seated before the open hearth. As Jehudi reads, the king cuts with a pen knife every three or four columns and consigns them to the flames. There is no terror or show of grief, in striking contrast to the time when Josiah had listened to the Book of the Covenant (II Kings 22). The supporters of Jeremiah of whom we

[23] Kurt Galling, 'Die Halle des Schreibers', *Palästinajahrbuch des Deutschen evangelischen Instituts* 27 (1931), pp. 51–58.

have heard previously – Elnathan and Delaiah and Gemariah – urge the king not to burn the scroll, but to no avail. Jehoiakim gives orders that Baruch the secretary and Jeremiah the prophet be seized, but his designs are thwarted because 'Yahweh had hid them' (cf. 26.24).

The account is notable for several reasons. Nowhere else in the Old Testament do we have a comparable report of a prophet dictating all his prophecies over a period of many years, nowhere else do we hear of a prophet employing an amanuensis for the purpose of transcription, nowhere else do we have a narrative so rich in graphic and circumstantial detail. The book is addressed to Israel, Judah, and all the nations. Since several manuscripts of the Greek (see *BH ad loc.*) read *Jerusalem* for Israel, many scholars emend the text accordingly, but the procedure is unwise since the whole phrase is meant to mark the momentousness of the event – an event, as we have seen, which is commensurate to the solemnity and gravity of the national and international crisis. We are informed that the book was read three times in the course of a single day, so it cannot have been very long (compare the similar case in II Kings 22). It may have been a summary or condensation of the prophet's utterances. The question naturally arises why such a document needed to be put to writing at all. Why could not a single utterance or speech have sufficed for the particular purpose in view? The fact that the words were addressed to Israel, Judah, and all the nations when Assyrian power had come to an end and Chaldea was now in ascendant – a circumstance of which the prophet could not but be aware – may offer some explanation. But there is a deeper reason. The words of Yahweh are for the particular hour, to be sure, but they are more. They are at once a witness to the fulfilment of past predictions, notably the oracles on the foe from the north,[24] and a witness

[24] Douglas Jones, 'The Traditio of the Oracles of Isaiah of Jerusalem', *ZAW* 67 (1955), p. 229: 'There can be little doubt that the motive which led Jeremiah to dictate the oracles of his life's ministry was to demonstrate how old predictions were on the point of fulfilment. The foe from the North could now be identified.'

for the future, the time that is still to come (Isa. 30.8; 55.10f.; Jer. 32.14).[25]

The momentousness of the event is further demonstrated by another consideration of the first importance. Jeremiah summons to his service a scribe or secretary by the name of Baruch, the son of Neriah. Speculations are numerous as to why the prophet needed someone to whom he could dictate his prophecies. Was it that he could not write, as some have supposed, or that his handwriting was poor, as has been suggested by others? We are not informed how it was that Jeremiah came to know Baruch, how long and in what capacity he had known him previously, or anything about his past history. But we are plainly told that Baruch was a scribe or secretary. On the face of it, of course, the designation could indicate that he was only an amanuensis or private secretary. But a careful inspection of our narrative and the fact that Baruch appears in other notable contexts of the prose narratives suggest that he was a man of some importance and was well known and highly regarded by his confreres and peers. The most plausible explanation for Jeremiah's summoning of Baruch is precisely that the occasion called for one who could represent him in the Temple, one who would have ready access to the chamber of

[25] Johannes Pedersen, *Israel: Its Life and Culture* I–II, trans. Aslaug Møller (London: Oxford University Press, 1926), pp. 167f.; H. Wheeler Robinson, *Inspiration and Revelation in the Old Testament* (Oxford: Clarendon Press, 1946), pp. 170f.; Aubrey R. Johnson, *The One and the Many in the Israelite Conception of God*, 2nd ed. (Cardiff: University of Wales Press, 1961), pp. 1ff.; *The Vitality of the Individual in the Thought of Ancient Israel*, 2nd ed. (Cardiff: University of Wales Press, 1964), pp. 87f.; Isaac Rabbinowitz, 'Towards a Valid Theory of Biblical Hebrew Literature', *The Classical Tradition: Literary and Historical Studies in Honor of Harry Caplan*, ed. Luitpold Wallach (Ithaca: Cornell University Press, 1966). Note p. 324: 'The utterance of prophetic words, in fine, is for the purpose of getting them into the world so that they may act upon that world; as such they are conceived as transcending the limits of communication, and do not necessarily require an audience.' In the present context, the words of Jeremiah do indeed have an audience, but their range of meaning extends far beyond it into the history of the time.

Gemariah, son of Shaphan,[26] to whom Jeremiah was bound by many years of friendship, esteem, and mutuality of respect. That is to say, Baruch was more than a private secretary. He was a person of some eminence, one who was favourably known to his professional colleagues. The cabinet room would be an advantageous locale from which he could address the assembled throng in the outer court.

We are singularly fortunate in having the twofold reference to the cabinet room of the scribe, in the first instance in the Jerusalem Temple (36.10) and in the second in the royal palace (36.21). The two were closely connected, and we may be confident, quite intentionally.[27] The men who are gathered in the chambers are in both cases שָׂרִים or royal officials. To be sure we hear elsewhere

---

[26] G. G. Findlay, 'Baruch', *Dictionary of the Bible*, ed. James Hastings, rev. ed. Frederick C. Grant and H. H. Rowley, eds. (London: Thomas Nelson and Sons and New York: Charles Scribner's Sons, 1963), p. 91: 'He belonged to the order of "princes", among whom Jeremiah had influential friends (26.16; 36.25); Baruch's rank probably secured for Jeremiah's objectionable "roll" (ch. 36) the hearing that was refused to his spoken words.'

[27] Galling, *op. cit.*, pp. 51–56. See especially the excellent chart on p. 53. Cf. Adolf Erman, *The Literature of the Ancient Egyptians*, trans. M. Blackman (London: Methuen & Co., 1927), p. 185: 'It [the scribal school] was attached to the temple which Ramesses II built for Amūn on the west bank of Thebes, the so-called Ramesseum.' See also C. F. A. Schaeffer, *The Cuneiform Texts of Ras Shamra-Ugarit*. The Schweich Lectures of the British Academy, 1936 (London: Oxford University Press, 1939), pp. 34–35: 'The library was housed in a building situated between the two great temples of Ugarit, one dedicated to Baal and the other to Dagon. . . . As was usual at this time, a school of scribes was attached to the library. Here the young priests were set to copy documents and were instructed in liturgical and sacred literature.' For its royal connections, see p. 34. Cf. S. Mowinckel, 'Psalms and Wisdom', *Wisdom in Israel and in the Ancient Near East*, H. H. Rowley *Festschrift*, eds. M. Noth and D. W. Thomas, *SVT* 3 (Leiden: E. J. Brill, 1955), p. 207: 'There is every reason to believe that the school for scribes in Jerusalem, as elsewhere in the Orient, was closely connected with the temple; this is apparent from the very fact that the "wisdom literature" of Israel was considered to belong to the canonical writings.' Aage Bentzen, *Introduction to the Old Testament* (Copenhagen: G. E. C. Gad, 1948), vol. I, p. 171, refers also to a temple school at Mari.

of chambers or rooms belonging to private persons or eminent families (35.4), and they are also referred to later in Ezekiel, Ezra, Nehemiah, and I–II Chronicles. But the לִשְׁכָּה of the scribe referred to in 36.10 is certainly to be distinguished from these, in the first place because it was immediately connected with the royal palace and in the second because it bore the title of a distinctive office.[28] Among the other peoples of the Near East from ancient times the training of the scribe was connected with the Temple and his service associated with the royal house. We hear frequently of scribal schools and of the training that was received there.[29] Such training was closely related to what falls under the general category of wisdom, at least as it was understood in Egypt and Mesopotamia.[30] That is, the scribes were wise men

[28] Galling, *op. cit.*, p. 54.

[29] In addition to the foregoing, see Lorenz Dürr, *Das Erziehungswesen im Alten Testament und im Antiken Orient*. Mitteilungen der Vorder-asiatischen-Aegyptischen Gesellschaft (E.F.) 36 Band, 2 Heft (Leipzig, 1932); de Vaux, *op. cit.*, pp. 394–405; Millar Burrows, *What Mean These Stones?* (New Haven: American Schools of Oriental Research, 1941), p. 183; R. de Langhe, *Les textes de Ras Shamra-Ugarit et leurs rapports avec le milieu biblique de l'Ancien Testament* (Paris: Desclée de Brouwer, 1945), vol. I, pp. 332ff.; Samuel N. Kramer, *The Sumerians; Their History, Culture, and Character* (Chicago: University of Chicago Press, 1963), pp. 230f.; A. Leo Oppenheim, 'A Note on the Scribes in Mesopotamia', *Studies in Honor of Benno Landsberger on his Seventieth Birthday*, Assyriological Studies No. 16 (Chicago: The Oriental Institute of the University of Chicago, 1965), pp. 253–6; William McKane, *Prophets and Wise Men*, SBT 44 (London: SCM Press, 1965), pp. 36f.; John Gray, *Archaeology and the Old Testament World* (London and New York: Thomas Nelson and Sons, 1962), pp. 80ff. See also W. G. Lambert, *Babylonian Wisdom Literature* (Oxford: Clarendon Press, 1960), p. 8: 'One point of organization on which we are regrettably ill-informed is the relation of the scribes to the temple. General considerations would lead us to suppose that the scribal schools were attached to a temple, but we are in no position either to affirm or to deny if all scribes were *ipso facto* priests.'

[30] McKenzie, *op. cit.*, p. 4: 'We know that wisdom literature is associated with scribal schools in Egypt and Mesopotamia, and we can assume that the same association existed in Israel.' Cf. G. Fohrer, *Introduction to the Old Testament*. Initiated by E. Sellin, trans. D. E. Green (New York: Abingdon Press, 1968), p. 315: 'Baruch, Jeremiah's scribe and biographer, was at least educated in the wisdom school.'

because they had been reared in the wisdom school and had mastered its curriculum, not only in calligraphy, though this was to be sure of the first importance, but in other disciplines associated with governmental administration and finance as well. That the United Monarchy under David and Solomon was profoundly influenced by the organization of the Egyptian court is now well known,[31] and there is every reason to believe that the same is true of the period with which we are concerned. Egyptian influence is doubtless primary, but it is probable that Mesopotamian influence also made itself felt, particularly in the period of Assyrian domination. It could scarcely have been otherwise when one takes into account the international character of the age and, indeed, the international character of wisdom. In any event, it is clear that the office of the scribe was one of distinction. He was the most eminent and influential of the royal officials and was charged with governmental affairs as well as many other functions.

It is not exceeding the limits of evidence to contend that both the northern and southern kingdoms had scribal schools similar to those among the other peoples of the Near East,[32] and one may venture to assert with some confidence that they were associated with the royal house and the national sanctuaries.[33] Sigmund Mowinckel maintains that Solomon founded a school for scribes in Jerusalem and there introduced the international poetry of wisdom of the Orient.[34] I am inclined to support this contention as a real possibility, but would go somewhat farther perhaps by contending that wisdom in this case should be construed as broadly as it was among other Near Eastern peoples, to include such works as the Yahwist and the court history which teems with wisdom motifs. The training in the scribal schools was of a diversified kind. There were doubtless, too, many different kinds of

[31] de Vaux, *loc. cit.*; Begrich, *loc. cit.*

[32] So de Vaux, Mowinckel, and others.

[33] Cf. *inter alia* R. B. Y. Scott, 'Priesthood, Prophecy, Wisdom, and the Knowledge of God', *JBL* 80 (March, 1961), p. 10.

[34] Mowinckel, 'Psalms and Wisdom', *Wisdom in Israel and in the Ancient Near East*, p. 206.

scribes as there were different kinds of priests and prophets in Israel.

As we have already had occasion to observe, it was with the scribal family of Shaphan that Jeremiah was on intimate terms. The former were among the central figures associated with the Reform of Josiah,[35] and it is likely that in the early period of his ministry Jeremiah was favourably disposed to the movement.[36] Both Shaphan and his son Ahikam are members of the delegation sent to Huldah (II Kings 22.11–13), and Elasah, another son of Shaphan, serves as an agent in connection with the letter to the exiles (29.3). Finally, it was a grandson of Shaphan with whom Jeremiah was on friendly terms during the trying period after the fall of Jerusalem (43.1–7). What relationship Baruch may have had to Shaphan and his family we do not know, but it is not unlikely that it was similarly intimate. Baruch could enter the cabinet room of the scribe because he had a rightful place there and was himself a member of the royal officials who had come together on the crucial occasion of the public reading of the scroll. He was among colleagues.

Many attempts have been made to reconstruct the scroll which Jeremiah dictated to Baruch.[37] We are not left without some clues as to its probable content. It must have contained the oracles of judgment preserved in 1.1–25.13 from the thirteenth year of

[35] H. J. Katzenstein, 'The "'Asher 'al ha-bayith" from the Days of the United Kingdom to the Downfall of Samaria', *Memorial Volume to Eliezer Shamir, Sdeh Elijahu*, 1957, pp. 120–8; 'The Royal Steward Asher 'al ha-Bayith', *IEJ* 10 (1960), pp. 149–54; 'The House of Eliakim, a Family of Royal Stewards', *Eretz Israel* 5 (Jerusalem: Israel Exploration Society and the Hebrew University, 1958), pp. 108–10 (in Hebrew). Katzenstein maintains that the position was hereditary in one family and that there was a direct line of succession from Hilkiah (Isa. 22.20–24; II Kings 18.18; 19.2) to Gedaliah.

[36] H. H. Rowley, 'The Early Prophecies of Jeremiah in their Setting', *BJRL* 45 (1962–63), pp. 225ff. or *Men of God: Studies in Old Testament History and Prophecy* (London and New York: Thomas Nelson and Sons Ltd., 1963), pp. 158ff.

[37] Note, for example, Otto Eissfeldt, *The Old Testament: an Introduction*, trans. Peter R. Ackroyd (New York: Harper and Row and Oxford: Basil Blackwell, 1965), p. 351.

Josiah to the year 604 when the scroll was dictated. But what are we to say of the prose narratives? While absolute certainty is in the nature of the case excluded, the probabilities strongly favour the assumption that they are the work of Baruch.[38] It is certain that Baruch continued to be the companion of Jeremiah until after the fall of the nation in 587. It is in these narratives, if anywhere, that we have an authentic exhibit of the scribal mode of composition. They open with the accession of Jehoiakim to the throne of Judah in 608, the occasion for the Temple speech (26.1). The account merits careful inspection because we can compare it with the report given in 7.1–15. The scribe gives the speech in his own way, abridging it by omitting details, but adding others such as the exact temporal locus, transforming the probably poetic form of the original into prose, and above all by recounting the sequence of episodes which followed upon its delivery. There is every reason to believe that he composed the other speeches or proclamations of Jeremiah in the same way. We move from the prophet's poetic formulations to the scribe's prose. It is noteworthy that all the speeches reported by Baruch, whether Jeremiah's or those of others, have the same style and terminology.[39] Following the practice of ancient historians, he reports what was spoken in his own style and language. We are fortunately not at a loss to learn whence he derives this manner of speaking. We encounter the same style elsewhere in Deuteronomistic contexts; the manner of Baruch is the manner of the scribes, not only of his own time, but long before.[40]

[38] For reconstructions of Baruch's work, see T. H. Robinson, 'Baruch's Roll', *ZAW*, Neue Folge Erster Band, 1924, pp. 209–21; Pfeiffer, *op. cit.*, p. 502; Mowinckel, *Prophecy and Tradition*, pp. 61f.; Norman K. Gottwald, *A Light to the Nations: an Introduction to the Old Testament* (New York: Harper and Brothers, 1959), p. 353; Fohrer, *Introduction to the Old Testament*, p. 436.

[39] Leonhard Rost, 'Zur Problematik der Jeremiabiographie Baruchs', *Viva Vox Evangelii, Festschrift für Landesbischof D. Hans Meiser* (Munich: Claudius-Verlag, Oskar Koch and Co., 1951), pp. 241–5.

[40] Mowinckel, *Prophecy and Tradition*, p. 63: 'Baruch was a "scribe" and belonged to "the learned": that the "Deuteronomists" are also

It is probable that Baruch and his professional confreres have been influenced by the official state or temple archives. The numerous superscriptions (26.1; 27.1; 28.1; 29.1–3; 32.1; 34.1; 36.1; 39.2; 40.1; 41.1, etc.) suggest as much.[41] They are to be compared with the formal openings of the reigns of the kings of Judah and Israel reported in the books of Kings. While different literary types are to be recognized in the complex of Jer. 26–45, it is the biographical narrative that predominates.[42] These should not be confused with the legends that are reported concerning Elijah and Elisha.[43] Complaints that are often registered against Baruch that his style is monotonous or ponderous are quite beside the point as are the characterizations which speak of his 'popular narrative art'.[44] To be sure there is considerable diversity in the style of the narration, but nowhere is it alien to the scribal manner of reporting. Notable among its features is the proclivity to cite words of the participants in the events (26.2–6, 13–15; 27.5b–11,

---

associated with the learned circles of the scribes, is obvious; already Jeremiah offers us a piece of evidence that "the law", the *tora*-tradition, and the pursuit of it, belongs to the "scribes" (Jer. 8.8).'

[41] Hans Schmidt, *Die grossen Propheten übersetzt und erklärt* in Die Schriften des Alten Testaments, Zweite Abteilung, Zweiter Band (Göttingen: Vandenhoeck & Ruprecht, 1915), p. 377: '*Als Vorbild für sein biographisches Werk haben dem Baruch wahrscheinlich offizielle Staats – oder Tempelchroniken gedient. Die Art, wie er jedes Ereignis mit einem Datum versieht, die in solchen öffentlichen Urkundenführung zu Hause ist, legt diese Vermutung nahe.*'

[42] For a form-critical study of the narratives, see Martin Kessler, 'A Prophetic Biography: A Form-critical Study of Jeremiah: chs. 26–29, 32–45' (Dissertation, Brandeis University, Boston, 1965), ch. II.

[43] *Contra* Klaus Koch, *Was ist Formgeschichte?* (Neukirchen: Neukirchener Verlag des Erziehungsvereins, 1964), pp. 224ff.

[44] So Johannes Hempel, *Die Althebräische Literatur und ihr hellenistisch-jüdisches Nachleben* (Wildpark-Potsdam: Akademische Verlagsgesellschaft Athenaion M.B.H., 1930), p. 155: '*Stilistische Vorzüge weist dies Buch nur in beschränktem Masse auf. Seine Darstellung ist oft reichlich schwerfällig.*' But note Hempel's comment on the same page: '*Überragend in ihrer Wahrhaftigkeit, einzigartig in ihrer Verbindung tiefster-menschlich-persönlicher Anteilnahme mit einer sicheren Erfassung sachlich entscheidender Züge am Werk des dargestellten Meisters, stehen die Erzählungen Baruchs von Leben und Leiden des Jeremia in der altorientalischen Literatur ...*'

233

12b–15, 16b–22; 28.2–4; 29.4–23, 24b–28; 32.17–25, 27–44; 33.2–17, etc.). Even more striking and more central to the narrator's interest is his profound interest in the person of Jeremiah. Nevertheless, despite his intimate association with the prophet and his affection for him, he nowhere indulges in subjective words of sympathy. Jeremiah does not appear as a hero or saint. The events that are recorded tell their own story. It was a long career of suffering and apparent defeat.[45] Dramatic elements are not wanting. Note the finales of 26.6, 24; 27.22c; 28.9, 16c, 17; 29.9b, 23d; 32.5b, 8d, 15b, 25; 35.19b; 36.19, 26b, 31d, etc.). The canvas upon which the scribe portrays the events of the prophet's career is crowded with many *dramatis personae*. Kings, princes, priests, prophets, scribes, and others appear upon the stage, and Jeremiah moves in the midst of them, a solitary and often tragic figure. From our modern point of view, it is amazing that Baruch makes his appearance so seldom in the narratives, though where he does appear, it is clear that he must have played a not insignificant role.[46]

But there are other features in Baruch's prose narratives that demand our attention. While we have insisted that he writes in the characteristic manner of the scribe, there are a number of indications that he is deeply immersed in the ancient traditions and formulations of the covenant. He is a faithful reporter of his master's covenant-faith. He employs the classical messenger's formula כֹּה אָמַר יהוה with very great frequency as he does the formula for the reception of the divine word, *The Word of Yahweh came to me saying*. He follows the schemata of the revelatory forms with consistency, and employs the characteristic phrase נְאֻם יהוה

---

[45] Heinz Kremers, 'Leidensgemeinschaft mit Gott im Alten Testament: Eine Untersuchung der "biographischen" Berichte im Jeremiabuch', *EvTh* 13 (Aug., 1953), pp. 122–40.

[46] Note the central role that Baruch plays in the account of the purchase of the field in 32.6–25 and in the crisis after the city's fall in 43.1–7 where he is censored for having influenced Jeremiah in his counsel to the people. On the former passage see Jones, *op. cit.*, pp. 227–9.

and more especially the strategic and characteristic transitional phrase וְעַתָּה precisely in the manner of Jeremiah's *ipsissima verba*.

His profuse use of the terminology of hearing is very striking. But dominating all else are the frequent conditionals, so crucial and central to the covenantal and legal formulation, most notably in the book of Deuteronomy. Nowhere are the affinities of Baruch with the latter more in evidence than here (compare *inter alia* Jer. 33.20f., 25f.; 37.10; 38.6, 17f.; 40.4bc, 5; 42.5, 6, 9f., 15f.).[47]

The sequence of prose narratives comes to a dramatic and moving finale in ch. 45.[48] It is probable that the Greek text has preserved the right order in placing it at 51.31–35. It is surely quite singular that an oracle should be addressed to an individual (cf., however, the divine word addressed to Ebed-melech in 39.15–18). The precise date and occasion are carefully given, the fourth year of Jehoiakim, at the time that Jeremiah dictated the scroll to Baruch. A number of scholars, offended by the sharp break in chronology here, have deleted the entire temporal reference, but there is no legitimate support for the procedure (1) because it is dominated by western views of compilation and editing and (2) because the passage as we have it makes very tolerable sense. For one thing, it may have been purposely designed as part of the framework with ch. 36. It is very probable that it was meant to be the divine word which illuminated all the foregoing narratives, the single divine disclosure to Baruch which had guided and directed him through all the travailing years, ever since the time, now many years ago, when the word of Yahweh had come to him. As he had written the terrible words of judgment upon the royal house and the people of Judah, line after line, he must have been torn with anxiety and sorrow. If he was closely related to the

[47] James Muilenburg, 'The Form and Structure of the Covenant Formulations', *VT* 9 (Oct., 1959), pp. 354–7.

[48] Kremers, *op. cit.*, pp. 128–40; Artur Weiser, 'Das Gotteswort für Baruch und die sogenannte Baruchbiographie', *Theologie als Glaubenswagnis*. Karl Heim *Festschrift* (Hamburg: Furche-Verlag, 1954), pp. 35–46.

inner circle of royal officials, as we have contended, we can readily grasp the depth of his feelings.

Those who were closest to Baruch would be the first to bear the brunt of Chaldean hostility, and he would surely himself be among them. The oracle opens with unusual solemnity: 'Thus says Yahweh, the God of Israel, to you, O Baruch.' Interestingly, Yahweh cites Baruch's own words of lamentation. The oracle is at once a rebuke and a word of comfort. In a supremely moving divine self-disclosure Yahweh tells Baruch what he is doing in the earth, breaking down what he has planted and plucking up the whole land. It is highly revealing that the last words to which we are to listen echo the words of Jeremiah's call (1.10, cf. 31.28). The sorrows and griefs of Baruch are here mastered by the sorrows of God.[49] It was not a time in Judah for one to expect the realization of his ambitions and aspirations. Baruch was not to seek vindication for himself; he is to rest only in the assurance that there was an agony deeper than his own and that his life would be spared. The words accompanied him from the hour that he had read the scroll aloud before the members of the royal cabinet and the gathered crowd of Judeans. Throughout all the vicissitudes of the years he had been upheld by the momentous word from God.[50] It is surely clear why he placed the chapter at the close. It belonged with ch. 36 certainly, but it belonged even more profoundly at the point where he had completed the record of Jeremiah's trials and rejections, the end of the *via dolorosa* he had been fated to walk with the prophet. It tells us much about Baruch. In the rest of the narratives we hear of him but seldom; here a flash of unexpected light illumines the page.

It has been the purpose of the foregoing account to call attention

[49] Cf. G. von Rad, *Old Testament Theology*, vol. II, trans. D. M. G. Stalker (Edinburgh: Oliver and Boyd and New York: Harper and Row, 1965), p. 208: '. . . here a human being has in a unique fashion borne a part in the divine suffering.' See also Abraham J. Heschel, *The Prophets* (New York: Harper and Row, 1962), pp. 256ff.

[50] W. Rudolph, *Jeremia*, HAT (Tübingen: J. C. B. Mohr [Paul Siebeck], 1958), p. 245.

to the importance of Baruch in the prophetic activity of Jeremiah and more particularly to set forth some of the characteristic features of scribal composition. It is very possible, indeed probable, that Baruch had a major hand in the compilation and editing of the original work extending from 1.1 to 45.5. If so, it is probably to him that we are to look for such prose additions as we find in 1.15–19, 3.6–12a, and elsewhere. It has been our contention that the so-called 'Deuteronomic additions' by no means represent a separate source, but conform to conventional scribal composition and are therefore to be assigned to Baruch. The ambitions of Baruch to which reference is made in ch. 45 suggest that he may well have been a person of some eminence, corresponding to the prestige of his master. This is confirmed by the fact that his brother Seraiah served as the royal quartermaster (51.59). But it is also confirmed, in my opinion, by a circumstance of even greater significance. The traditions associated with Baruch, brief as they are, did not end with his deportation to Egypt after the fall of the nation. It has sometimes been averred that he was Jeremiah's literary executor, and if our contentions concerning his part in the composition of the book have any force in them, then this is probably true. But Baruch was to outlive his own career. He was remembered and became the inspirer of elaborate traditions and legends. The literature connected with his name is surprisingly large.[51] He moves into the future as few others in the history of Israel's traditions. It is surprising that he should find so eminent a place in the Jewish apocalypses. It is easy to understand why such protological figures as Enoch, Noah, Abraham, and Moses should play a central role in these compositions. Not so with

---

[51] R. H. Charles and W. O. E. Oesterley, *The Apocalypse of Baruch* (London: SPCK, 1917), pp. vii–viii: 'It may be wondered why there was such a considerable Baruch-literature, for we can hardly suppose that the books mentioned represent more than a part of those written under the pseudonym of Baruch; but the fact is that, whatever may have been the reason, a good deal of legend clustered round the name of Baruch in ancient times among the Jews, and it was one which evidently enjoyed much popularity.'

Baruch. It is indeed true that he had survived the destruction of the Temple, the end of the Davidic monarchy, and the fall of the nation, but this can hardly suffice as an explanation of his continuing importance in the history of tradition. Rather, if I am not mistaken, we are to see in these ancient compositions an authentic witness to the importance of Baruch during his own lifetime. His distinction, all but suppressed in the biblical records, is recovered in legend and apocalypse and wisdom. This is not to credit these narratives with historical authenticity, though there are indeed many authentic echoes which derive from historical memory. The perplexities which seared his heart, the griefs which laid him low, the search for a wisdom that could withstand the threat and torment of inchoate times, the wrestlings with the demands of the *Torah* upon his people's life, all these have their source in Baruch's own life, a life that was lived courageously and often agonizingly in company with the prophet Jeremiah.

12

Shiloh, the Customary Laws and the Return of the Ancient Kings

Henri Cazelles

ON the occasion of the publication of the *Hethitische Totenrituale* of H. Otten,[1] M. Vieyra has recently drawn attention to a text of Hurrian origin.[2] It has to do with a ritual against family feuds, ascribed to the wise woman Mastigga of Kizzuwatna or of Kummani. At the end of the magical rites, she pours water into a horn of an ox, she affixes a seal and exclaims: 'If the ancient kings should return and occupy themselves anew with the country and with its customary laws, then only will this seal be broken.'

Such a formula is exceptional, for in the Mesopotamian world he who is dead has departed to the realm 'from which one does not return'.[3] But we must not forget that the king of Jerusalem

---

[1] (Berlin: Akademie Verlag, 1958.)

[2] M. Vieyra, 'Ciel et Enfers hittites', *RA* 59 (1965), p. 129. The text has been published by Liane Rost, 'Ein Hethitisches Ritual gegen Familienzwist', *Mitteilungen des Institut für Orientforschung* I (1953), pp. 365-7, 376. 'Customary laws' is the translation of the Hittite *saklinna*, see J. Friedrich, 'Brauch, Sitte, Gewohnheit, Art, Ritus', *Hethitisches Wörterbuch*, ed. J. Friedrich (Heidelberg: Carl Winter Un. Verlag, 1953), p. 176. The verb has been translated '*prüfen*' by Rost but following Friedrich, *op. cit.*, p. 99, this *appan kappuwai* has a meaning sufficiently broad – '*Nachzahlen, nachrechnen, abrechnen, nachbedenken, sich kümmern um*' – to sustain the Vieyra translation.

[3] L. Rost referring to H. G. Guterbock, 'Das Siegeln bei den Hethitern', Symbolae *Paul Koschaker*, eds. J. Friedrich and others (Leiden: E. J. Brill, 1939), p. 29.

in the El Amarna age was a Hurrian[4] and that the Egyptians of that period called Palestine *Hurru*. The prophet who most stresses these pagan origins of Jerusalem is Ezekiel (16.3), even though the Hurrians had for a long time been forgotten, and Ezekiel mentions only Hittites and Amorites. This prophet also delighted in rituals and symbolic gestures.

Now it is the same prophet who tells us of the coming of an ancient king. It is not a question of his shade, such as that of Samuel called forth by the pythoness of Endor. In Ezek. 34.23f. the Lord God exclaims:

> And I will set up over them[5] one shepherd, my servant David,
> and he shall feed them (the lean sheep):
> he shall feed them and be their shepherd.
> And I, Yahweh, will be their God,
> and my servant David shall be prince among them;
> I, Yahweh, have spoken.

Therefore, Yahweh means to be the אֱלֹהִים of the fat sheep and the lean sheep, but David will be shepherd and נָשִׂיא (prince).

This declaration comes after another one (Ezek. 34.20–22) where Yahweh reproaches the shepherds or the rams (masc.) for having maltreated the lean sheep and having struck them with the horn (v. 21), and it is he himself who will judge (שָׁפַט)[6] between

[4] F. Thureau-Dangin, 'Le Nom du prince de Jérusalem au temps d'el-Amarna', *Mémorial Lagrange*, ed. L.-H. Vincent (Paris: Librairie Lecoffre, J. Gabalda et Cie, 1940), pp. 27f.

[5] There is in the text an alternation of masculine and feminine suffixes, where the masculine represents the bad shepherds and the sheep are in the feminine (v. 19); perhaps the masculine encompasses the rams and the he-goats of v. 17.

[6] On שָׁפַט see my 'Institutions et Terminologie en Deut. 1.6–17', *SVT* 15, Congrès de Genève (Leiden: E. J. Brill, 1966), pp. 108f. Add to the bibliography D. McKenzie, 'The Judge of Israel', *VT* 17 (1967), p. 118; H. C. Thompson, '*Shophet* and *Mishpat* in the Book of Judges', *Transactions of the Glasgow University Oriental Society* 19 (1961–62), ed. C. J. Mullo Weir (Leiden: E. J. Brill, 1963), pp. 74–84: '*Mishpat* would then tend to be a term used more and more for case-law decisions.' A. Gamper, *Gott als Richter in Mesopotamien und im Alten Testament*

'sheep and sheep' (v. 22), 'between the fat sheep and the lean sheep' (v. 20). We shall not discuss here the precise relationship between v. 20 and v. 22. Let us only observe that in v. 22, this exercise of the judgment of Yahweh follows upon an act of salvation (יוֹשִׁיעַ in the *hiph'il*), an act of deliverance like that of the premonarchical judges (Judg. 2.16, 18; 6.14) and of the kings (I Sam. 9.16, etc.). This enables us to determine precisely the vocabulary of Ezekiel which is the same as that of the book of Judges. A sudden, and more or less supernatural, intervention is what is meant by the use of the verb יוֹשִׁיעַ.

It is after this act that God establishes his rule, that he judges his flock, between sheep and sheep, just as Othniel, after having delivered Israel (Judg. 3.9), 'judged' Israel (v. 10). The formula 'so-and-so judged Israel during so many years' recurs regularly, particularly for the 'minor' judges. שָׁפַט then does not designate a unique act of deliverance or of condemnation, but a series of acts of government. It is the political aspect of the שֹׁפֵט of Israel which approximates him to the Carthaginian *suffetes*.

To consider the terminology further, we know that the good shepherd, the good king, must exercise מִשְׁפָּט and צְדָקָה. This is said in Gen. 18.19, Isa. 9.6, Ps. 89.15 [EVV, v. 14], II Sam. 8.15, I Kings 10.9, and Jer. 22.15. This is entirely in line with what was demanded of the ancient near eastern king in general. The Babylonian sovereigns, in particular Hammurabi, were usually 'shepherds' and had to practice *kittu* and *mešaru* (Code V, 20–23). Our Hurrian text envisages that at the time of their return, the ancient kings will occupy themselves afresh with the 'customary laws' just as in his edict of reform Urukagina sets out to re-establish

(Innsbruck: Universitätsverlag Wagner, 1966), p. 171: '*Quelle und Ausgangspunkt des "Gerichts" ist Gott. Er führt in erster Linie das "Richten" aus; er allein kann es an den König weitergeben. Dieses "Gericht" meint zunächst den Akt des "Richtens", mišpat. Ergebnis dieses Tuns ist ṣedaqa(h), "Gerechtigkeit", d.h. der von Gott gewollte Zustand, in dem jedes Wesen und vor allem der Mensch sich an dem ihm gebührenden Platz befindet, in Harmonie mit Gott und der Welt.*'

the customary laws of former times. The Hebrew מִשְׁפָּט, as one sees it as early as the covenant code, is an ancient customary law by virtue of which the judge re-established the right. It is not a single judgment, but a principle by which judgments, and indeed numerous judgments, are made.[7]

Ezekiel also follows this terminology and uses the combination צְדָקָה/מִשְׁפָּט in order to designate justice, good and normative rules (18.5, 19, 21, 27; 33.14, 16, 19) and good government (45.9). This favourable meaning is equally clear in other texts where מִשְׁפָּט is used alone, as in 22.29; if one oppresses the poor, the destitute or the stranger, one is 'without מִשְׁפָּט (בְּלֹא מִשְׁפָּט)'. In Ezek. 11.20 Yahweh demands that one keep his מִשְׁפָּטִים, his customary laws and not his judgments, for the prophet puts them in opposition to those of the nations. But the term is in the plural and the sense is a little different from the singular as we shall see later. One finds the singular again in the chapter under considera-tion (in 34.16), which deals with the bad shepherds, God's future exercise of justice and the advent (הֲקִים) of David; here again the sense is favourable. God will feed his sheep בְּמִשְׁפָּט, '*mit Gerech-tigkeit*' (W. Zimmerli),[8] '*avec justice*' (P. Auvray),[9] 'in justice' (H. G. May).[10] Even those who believe that the literal trans-lation should be 'with judgment'[11] conclude that this judgment

---

[7] Hence the expressions מִשְׁפַּט הַמֶּלֶךְ (I Sam. 8.9, 11), מִשְׁפַּט הַכֹּהֲנִים (Deut. 18.3, etc.), do not refer to judicial acts of the king or the priests, but to the basic statute of the kings and priests.

[8] W. Zimmerli, *Ezekiel*, BKAT XIII (Neukirchen: Neukirchenen Verlag. Kreis Moers, 1963), p. 826.

[9] P. Auvray, *Ezechiel*, La Bible de Jérusalem (Paris: Éditions du Cerf, 1957), p. 34.

[10] H. G. May, 'Ezekiel', *IB* (Nashville: Abingdon Press, 1956), vol. 6, p. 253.

[11] G. A. Cooke, *Ezekiel*, ICC (Edinburgh: T. & T. Clark, 1936), p. 376; A. B. Davidson, *The Book of the Prophet Ezekiel*, CambB (Cambridge: at the University Press, 1916), p. 272.

would be favourable. But in this passage as in others as well, there is not a single act but a series of acts of governing which feed the sheep. The terminology of Ezekiel is so precise that he uses a rarer word, שְׁפָטִים, for punishments (5.10, 15; 11.9; 14.21; 16.41; 25.11; 28.22, 26; 30.14, 19).

Because of this terminology I have suggested that מִשְׁפָּט in Ezekiel means 'the order of government, the right',[12] and have defended the favourable sense usually admitted for Ezek. 21.32 (EVV, v. 27): 'until he comes whose right it is; and to him I will give it'.[13] But R. Criado[14] has criticized this translation, which is perhaps in fact imprecise and does not make it clear enough that מִשְׁפָּט includes individual acts as well as general rules. But, further R. Criado believes that it is necessary with W. L. Moran[15] to see in this verse an unfavourable meaning: it would be a question of a judgment of condemnation. In order to justify this exceptional meaning in the terminology of Ezekiel, R. Criado appeals to five passages. It is necessary for us to consider them in detail in the light of the terminology which we have just reviewed.

1. *Ezekiel 7.23*. This concerns the sins of Israel: '. . . the land is full of מִשְׁפַּט דָּמִים and the city is full of violence . . .'

The LXX did not read מִשְׁפָּט and, as Cornill before him, Zimmerli does not consider the Hebrew text trustworthy. Relying on 9.9, he sees in מִשְׁפָּט 'ein jüngeres Interpretament'. Cooke was tempted to see here a gloss and felt that the suppression of the word made the text clearer.

If we retain this uncertain text, the sense is not favourable. But the parallel with חָמָס, violence, shows that it is not a question of a

[12] H. Cazelles, 'Patriarches', supplément to *Dictionnaire de la Bible*, (Paris: Librairie Letouzay et Ané, 1961), vol. VII, p. 154.
[13] Herrmann, Knabenbauer, Fohrer, and others. See Zimmerli, *op. cit.*, p. 495.
[14] R. Criado, 'Hasta que venga Silo', *Est Bibl* 24 (1965), pp. 289–320.
[15] W. L. Moran, 'Gen. 49.10 and its use in Ez. 21.32', *Biblica* 39 (1958), pp. 405–25.

judgment. מִשְׁפַּט דָּמִים would be the same as מִשְׁפַּט־מָוֶת (Deut.
19.6; Jer. 26.11), a legal expression where מִשְׁפַּט (in the construct
state) signifies 'a case where the guilty party is exposed to death or
blood vengeance'. The city is full of such cases, and it is rather a
matter of absence of judgment than of judgment.

2. *Ezekiel 16.38.* The word here is in the plural in the Masoretic
Text, but in the singular in the LXX. Put out of patience by the
abuses of Israel and her infidelity, Yahweh proceeds to re-establish
justice by subjecting Israel to 'full punishment' (LXX ἐκδικήσει,
sing.) or to the 'customary laws' (מִשְׁפָּטֵי, plur.) which relate to
women who break wedlock and shed blood. He will bring upon
Israel 'the blood of wrath and jealousy', an expression which is
not entirely clear, but is certainly not favourable to guilty Israel.

But, in order properly to understand the thought of the prophet
it is necessary to point out that the action of God is here expressed
by the verbs שְׁפַטְתִּיךְ, נְתַתִּיךְ, and not by the substantives. The
מִשְׁפָּטִים or the מִשְׁפַּט are not the judgment of God but the ancient
customary laws by which justice had been established in the land.
The substantive signifies not so much the condemnatory judgment
of criminals as the good, old law of the land.[16]

3. *Ezekiel 23.24.* In 23.24 we have the singular and the plural
together. It is therefore necessary to see clearly the relationship
between the singular and the plural, especially as it is this text
which has led Zimmerli[17] to accept the position of Moran.

The plural מִשְׁפָּטִים occurs more than twenty times in Ezekiel,
with or without suffixes, eight times with the first person suffix, 'my
מִשְׁפָּטִים'. God never says to Israel 'your מִשְׁפָּטִים', they are 'my
מִשְׁפָּטִים', given by God to Israel; and clearly in 23.24, they are
opposed to the מִשְׁפָּטִים of the nations. The great sin of Israel is that

---

[16] The English 'common law' conveys the biblical concept better than
French concepts. It is at one and the same time the traditional law and the
manner in which it is applied.

[17] Zimmerli, *op. cit.*, p. 495.

she has not kept them (5.6ff.); she has rebelled. God gave them first of all so that man might live (20.11, 13, cf. 18.17). But finally, after the rejection of Israel, Yahweh gave them statutes (חֻקּוֹת) that were not good and מִשְׁפָּטִים by which they could not live (with allusion to the sacrifices of the first-born). This is what shows again that the term does not signify judgment but the decrees or acts of rule of the national God of Israel, who is responsible for all that the nation thinks itself obliged to do. The sense may perhaps then be unfavourable, but it is clear that the מִשְׁפָּטִים are analogous to the decrees and laws by which the nation is governed in the name of the national God.

This is precisely the situation in 23.24. The Lord brings against Israel (Oholibah) her 'lovers', the Babylonians and the rest. He abandons her to them and they will 'govern her according to their customary laws' (MT וּשְׁפָטוּךְ בְּמִשְׁפְּטֵיהֶם). This last illumines the preceding phrase, וְנָתַתִּי לִפְנֵיהֶם). It should not be translated 'I have charged them to judge you', but 'I have committed[18] to them the legislative power'. In handing over Israel, God abandons the laws by which he has governed Israel, and it is foreigners who will now govern her according to their own laws and judgments.

4. Ezekiel 39.21. God announces that he is going to manifest his glory when till that moment he had hidden his face from rebellious Israel. This is therefore a vision of restoration, *a priori* a favourable one. Israel will know that Yahweh is her God, from this day forth, 'and forever'. Is it necessary to see a judgment of condemnation against the nations (and not against Israel) when God says: 'all the nations shall see my מִשְׁפָּט'? No, for the important part of the verse is what follows: 'All the nations shall see my מִשְׁפָּט which I

---

[18] The expression נָתַן לִפְנֵי in the sense of 'commit' is well known from Deuteronomy. See Otto Plöger, *Literarkritische, Formgeschichtliche und Stilkritische Untersuchungen zum Deuteronomium*, BBB 26 (Bonn: Peter Hanstein Verlag, 1967), pp. 62f., who would translate with Nötscher '*preisgeben*'. In Ezekiel see 6.5.

have executed, and my hand which I have laid on them.' The מִשְׁפָּט

of Yahweh had not been executed in a rebellious nation, but in Ezek. 36.27 the prophet announces that through the sprinkling of clean water and through implantation of a new spirit the מִשְׁפָּטִים

will be put into effect (עָשָׂה). After having abandoned his power to the nations (23.24) Yahweh makes it known to these who are now obliged to see the מִשְׁפָּט of Yahweh realized in an Israel which has

become faithful. It is not a question of a condemnatory judgment, but of the restoration of an Israel obedient now to the statutes or customary laws sanctioned by Yahweh.

5. *Ezekiel 5.8.* Here one finds מִשְׁפָּטִים as the object of עָשָׂה.

W. Zimmerli, while translating by 'Gericht halten', remarks in his note[19] that all the parallels (v. 10, also, 5.15; 11.9; 28.22, 26; 30.19) have שְׁפָטִים. With others P. Auvray translates by 'châtiments',[20] but indicates that he has made a correction. We may retain the questionable מִשְׁפָּטִים, but in the sense of 16.38 (see above, p. 244).

You do not keep my customary laws and you live by oppression. Only in Israel (בְּתוֹכֵךְ, 'in the midst of you' and not 'against you') is Yahweh righteous and only there does he execute the מִשְׁפָּטִים in

the sight of the nations (in the sense of 39.21, see above, p. 245).

These passages then clarify the sense of the legal (and not judicial) terminology of Ezekiel. מִשְׁפָּט is not 'the right' in the sense of the right to govern – '*titulo para gobernar*', according to the expression of R. Criado;[21] it is the legislative power which is demonstrated by the customary laws already existing and in force, even if the people did not observe them and should they appear to fall into disuse.

We do not find any difference in terminology in 21.32 (EVV, v. 27). This short paragraph is parallel to ch. 23. Jerusalem has been given up to Babylon, the king is deprived of his crown and

[19] Zimmerli, *op. cit.*, p. 98.   [20] Auvray, *op. cit.*, p. 34.
[21] Criado, *op. cit.*, p. 307.

his turban, that is, the insignia of rule, what is low is exalted and vice versa: the word 'ruin' is three times repeated (עַוָּה, if this hapax ought so to be translated) and Moran[22] seems to me to be right to find here, following the root, an idea of destruction, of throwing down, in conformity to what is said in the preceding verse: '. . . and abase that which is high'. This throwing down is indicated in the same verse by זֹאת לֹא־זֹאת, 'things shall not remain as they are', זֹאת, which is taken up again *a fortiori* in v. 32. Noting with Cornill and Davidson that this זֹאת does not agree[23] with the הָיָה which follows, we can avoid emending the text by connecting this גַּם־זֹאת to the אֲשִׂימֶנָּה which precedes it, a solution which is supported by the fact that לֹא הָיָה is a formula for beginning a clause (II Kings 20.15, Jer. 52.20; with the *wāw* in Ezek. 19.14 and elsewhere). As in Josh. 10.14, the subject of this לֹא הָיָה at the beginning would be the subject implied in the expression which follows. That gives us a better balanced first stichos than is possible with the Masoretic punctuation, and we would translate:

> Overturning, overturning, overturning
> it is that which I will establish, even that;
> there will not have been (one to whom the מִשְׁפָּט belongs)
> until he comes whose right the מִשְׁפָּט is
> and to him I will have given it.

The king of Israel is seen in v. 31 (EVV, v. 26). He had lost his crown, then his power of government, then his legislative power: the מִשְׁפָּט. After this reversal, described in terms worthy of the sage Ipuwer,[24] the prophet declares that there will no longer be a king until a certain epoch. The LXX and the Targum Pseudo-

---

[22] Moran, *op. cit.*, citing עֲוָיִם from Isa. 19.14.

[23] *Ibid.* cites four passages where הָיָה is in agreement with a feminine, but not one of them is found in Ezekiel.

[24] *ANET*, 2nd ed. (Princeton: Princeton University Press, 1955), pp. 441ff.

Jonathan[25] render by a future the Hebrew perfect which we have translated 'will not have been'. The action is completed at the moment when a new element occurs.

The situation is exactly parallel to that of ch. 34. God condemns the bad shepherds, takes back into his own hands the government of his people and feeds his sheep by the מִשְׁפָּט (34.16), but he gives this to David when he raises him up (הֲקִים) to be a shepherd (vv. 23f.), which implies that he transmits to him his מִשְׁפָּט or his הָקִים. This return of David, accompanied by the mention of the traditional and just customary laws, is therefore seen not only in the case of Mastigga and Ezek. 34.23, but also in Ezek. 21.32. And this is also the usage, as Zimmerli has noted, in Jer. 30.9, which uses the same verb, הֲקִים, as does Ezek. 34.23, and only a little less clearly in Hosea 3.5, which does not have הֲקִים, but does use language which is very near that of Jeremiah.

Finally there is Gen. 49.10, which has long been compared with Ezek. 21.32, but whose full significance appears only when one recognizes in מִשְׁפָּט the sense of just government and not of judgment and when one considers it in the light of all the texts about the 'return' of David. Before translating this verse it is necessary to establish the true sense of the difficult words.

We shall not discuss the reading שִׁלֹה, which is that of the Samaritan Pentateuch, LXX, the versions of Aquila, Symmachus and Theodotion, the Targums and the Peshitta.[26] R. Criado has accepted my explanation of the שִׁילֹה of the Masoretic Text from the orthography of Qumran. S. Segert[27] had already pointed out

---

[25] The LXX manuscripts are studied by Moran, *op. cit.*, pp. 420f. For the Targum Pseudo-Jonathan, see A. Sperber, *The Bible in Aramaic*, III (Leiden: E. J. Brill, 1962), p. 312: תתקיים. The Syriac does not have לֹא הָיָה.

[26] See the table of Moran, *op. cit.*, p. 414.

[27] S. Segert, 'Zur Habakuk-Rolle aus dem Funde vom Toten Meer I', *ArOr* 21 (1953), p. 221. For the Mishnaic usage, see M. H. Segal,

at Qumran the Mishnaic practice of indicating the doubling of the consonant by preceding it with a *mater lectionis* and I am indebted to J. Carmignac for a series of examples: Genesis Apocryphon II 8, דיברה for דִּבְרָה; Rule IV 11, כיבוד for כְּבּוֹד; Pesher Habakkuk VII 13, קיצי for קִצִּי. Nor shall we discuss the interesting suggestion of Eissfeldt[28] which has to meet the objections formulated by Moran and Criado. We translate as in Ezekiel: 'he to whom it belongs'.

That which belongs is the sceptre and the מְחֹקֵק, two royal insignia like the turban and the crown of Ezek. 21.31. There is no difficulty about the sceptre. The מְחֹקֵק is a princely implement in Num. 21.18 (the song of the well), Ps. 60.9 (EVV, v. 7), etc., and in the song of Deborah (Judg. 5.9) unless this is the prince himself (cf. Judg. 5.14 and Isa. 33.22).[29] This royal staff is analogous to the *was* of the Pharaoh which he holds before him; actually the text says that this מְחֹקֵק is בֵּין רַגְלָיו, but with a מִן of separation.[30] Moreover, to this personage belongs the יְקָהַת עַמִּים and the meaning of יקה, originally וקה, is now clear from Ugaritic and South Semitic. One could translate by 'to fear' (Aistleitner), by 'to protect' (Gordon), but more simply by 'to command',[31] implying

Mishnaic Hebrew Grammar (Oxford: at the Clarendon Press, 1927), pp. 26–38. There are numerous examples in the Damascus Document, but the manuscript is much later (V 15; IX 19; etc.).

[28] O. Eissfeldt, 'Silo und Jerusalem', *SVT* 4, Congrès de Strasbourg (Leiden: E. J. Brill, 1957), pp. 138–47.

[29] So the הַחֹקְקִים (qal) of Isa. 10.1 and the מְחֹקֵק of Deut. 33.21. For the Egyptian *was*, see *ANEP* (Princeton: Princeton University Press, 1954), no. 414. But this could be the staff in the hand of Hammurabi on his stele; it is more suitable for engraving.

[30] בֵּין רַגְלָיו alone means 'before' in Judg. 5.27 and Deut. 28.57, as בֵּין עֵינֶי means the forehead and not the space between the two eyes, in Ugaritic (C. H. Gordon, *Ugaritic Textbook* (Rome: Pontificium Institutum Biblicum, 1965), Text 68.22, 25) as in Hebrew (Ex. 13.9, 16).

[31] There are few references in the Ugaritic texts (Gordon, *op. cit.*, 137; 18.34–35, cf. Glossary no. 1143), but many are now known in South

the subject's awe before his ruler (God or man) which is so frequently expressed in ancient Near Eastern texts.

We therefore translate:

> The sceptre shall not depart from Judah
> nor the ruler's staff from before his feet
> until he comes to whom it belongs
> and to him shall belong the obedience of the peoples.

Peoples, עַמִּים, could designate the clans or the nations as a whole, since the Judean monarchy laid claim to universal dominion, as did all the monarchies of the time. In II Sam. 7.19 it is said that to David belongs the תּוֹרַת הָאָדָם, corresponding to the *terit niše* of the Accadian texts:[32] that is, the decree concerning humanity in general. Hence there is in Gen. 49.10 a king in Judah, and David was the first Judean king. He has power and with מְחֹקֵק he can make חֻקּוֹת, establish decrees, a term already known to the Yahwist (Gen. 47.22, with reference to Egypt, probably also Ex. 5.14 and 15.25). The Deuteronomist assimilated this term to the מִשְׁפָּטִים and Ezekiel does the same (20.18, 25). The מְחֹקֵק, instrument of legislation in Gen. 49.10, therefore corresponds to the מִשְׁפָּט of Ezek. 21.32.

Genesis 49.10, then, is concerned with the return of David, as are Ezek. 21 and 34, Jer. 30 and Hosea. 3. The oracle could very well go back to the time of Solomon, the author expressing both his faith in the dynasty and his mistrust of the actual king. The sceptre will not depart from Judah, but he hopes for someone better than the reigning sovereign, the return to a righteous king like David, a good lawgiver, respectful of the traditional customary laws, as the Yahwist hopes for in other passages (Gen. 34.7,

---

Semitic; cf. A. Jamme, *Sabaean Inscriptions from Mahram Bilqis (Marib)* (Baltimore: Johns Hopkins Press, 1962), references listed in the index, p. 435.

[32] See E. Ebeling, *Quellen zur Kenntnis des babylonischen Religion I* (Leipzig: Vorderasiatische Gesellschaft, 1918), p. 16, line 23.

cf. II Sam. 13.12). We are still in the world of ideas represented by the Hurrian text of the wise woman Mastigga.

There is, however, the difference that the biblical texts never speak of a 'return', but of a 'coming', בוֹא in the infinitive in Ezekiel, יָבֹא in the imperfect in Gen. 49. By contrast, in Hosea it is Israel who 'comes back' to David. From this we may conclude that the Yahwist was the first to demythologize the old Hurrian text or its counterparts. He thinks less of a return of David than of the coming of a Davidic heir possessing the true royal qualities as David had, and as he retained them in the Israelite tradition up till the time of the cry, 'Hosanna, O Son of David'. It is the dynastic successor *par excellence* who is envisaged, heir to David's legitimate and legal authority, but possessing the moral qualities which were lacking in David's actual successors, whether we think of Solomon, Ahaz, Jehoakim, or Zedekiah. If not for the Yahwist, who does not and could not name David in the book of Genesis (not even in Gen. 36.31 and 38), yet clearly in Hosea, Jeremiah, the titles of the Psalms and in Ezekiel, the title 'David' corresponds to the Caesar of the Romans and Tlaberna of the Hittites. The old background and the ancient phraseology thus remain, even when the language was transformed and charged with new meanings. Ezekiel seems to evoke, as does Mastigga, the return of the ancient kings and the restoration of laws both old and good, but he forms part of a tradition which expects a new king, without the defects of his predecessors.

IV

The Psalms

13

Psalm 23 and the Household of Faith[1]

Aubrey R. Johnson

WHEN Hermann Gunkel made his now famous classification of the psalms in terms of their literary types, he added to the group which he labelled as that of the 'Individual Lament' a smaller section to which he gave the name 'Psalms of Confidence',[2] and it is to a consideration of the note of trust which Gunkel rightly discerned in this connection as the leading motif of Ps. 23 that the following short study is devoted.

The familiar words of this psalm in the rendering of the Authorized (or King James) Version of the Bible occupy so cherished a place in the devotional life of the English-speaking world that any attempt to improve upon them, not of course from the standpoint of their literary quality but purely from the standpoint of their faithfulness to the intention of the original author, may well seem to many like an act of sacrilege. Nevertheless even the most ardent

[1] In offering these pages as a small token of my regard for my old fellow-student and friend of many years' standing, I ought, perhaps, to comment upon the fact that the Hebraist will find here more than one glimpse of the obvious. The reason for this is simple. It so happens that Principal Henton Davies, in addition to his scholarly and administrative gifts, enjoys a considerable reputation as an expository preacher, and as it is conceivable that some among the many lay friends whom he has made in this connection may wish to possess a copy of this volume, I have sought to bear them in mind.

[2] See, for example, H. Gunkel and J. Begrich, *Einleitung in die Psalmen*, HKAT II Ergänzungsband (Göttingen: Vandenhoeck and Ruprecht, 1933), ¶6, 27, pp. 254-6.

admirer of the Authorized Version may find it a valuable spiritual exercise to compare what appear to have been the actual thoughts of the psalmist with those which his work has come to evoke in the mind of the English reader.

We may begin, then, by recalling the translation which is under review, i.e.:

THE LORD *is* my shepherd; I shall not want.
He maketh me to lie down in green pastures:[3] he leadeth me beside the still waters.[4]
He restoreth my soul: he leadeth me in the paths of righteousness for his name's sake.
Yea, though I walk through the valley of the shadow of death, I will fear no evil: for thou *art* with me; thy rod and thy staff they comfort me.
Thou preparest a table before me in the presence of mine enemies: thou anointest my head with oil;[5] my cup runneth over.
Surely goodness and mercy shall follow me all the days of my life: and I will dwell in the house of the LORD for ever.[6]

Strange as it may seem, part of the charm of the foregoing translation is due to the sheer simplicity of its almost literal rendering of the Hebrew, and this also makes it a simple matter to draw attention to a number of expressions which require comment before one may attempt a somewhat freer translation in the hope of recovering for the modern English reader just what the author had in mind when he gave such pictorial expression to his faith.

He restoreth my soul: It must be borne in mind that the word נֶפֶשׁ may not be translated by the English term 'soul', if the latter is understood to imply such a dichotomy of 'body' and 'soul' as is found, for example, in Orphic myth and Platonic philosophy.[7] It is used, rather, in such a context as this with reference to the vital principle in both man and beast which experiences a kind of ebb and flow as it is felt to drain away through, say, the purely

---

[3] Hebrew, *pastures of tender grass.*   [4] Hebrew, *waters of quietness.*
[5] Hebrew, *makest fat.*   [6] Hebrew, *to length of days.*
[7] Cf. A. R. Johnson, *The Vitality of the Individual in the Thought of Ancient Israel*, 2nd rev. ed. (Cardiff: University of Wales Press, 1964), pp. 3ff.

physical conditions of starvation or under some form of emotional strain and to 'return' (שׁוּב) to normal vigour when circumstances improve. Both of these aspects find ready illustration in the work of a poet who, speaking in the name of Jerusalem, thus laments the scenes of famine and misery in the city after it had fallen to the Babylonians in 587 BC:[8]

> All her people are groaning,
> are seeking bread;
> they barter their treasures for food
> to bring back the נֶפֶשׁ.
>
> . . . .
> This is why I keep weeping,
> why mine eyes run with tears;
> for I have no comforter at hand,
> no one to bring back my נֶפֶשׁ.

In both of these cases the bringing back of the נֶפֶשׁ is expressed by the *Hiph'îl* or so-called causal form of שׁוּב, 'to return'; so that, up to a point, we may regard them as offering close parallels to the 'restoring' of the 'soul' which is referred to in our psalm. However, the parallel is not exact, for the verbal form which lies behind the familiar words 'He restoreth my soul' is not that of the *Hiph'îl* but that of the *Pôlēl*, and we must be careful, so far as we can, to reproduce its exact force. This may be done by comparing our verb with the corresponding forms of the similar verb מוּת, 'to die', which is used in the *Hiph'îl* with the force 'to put to death' and so, quite simply, 'to kill', whereas the *Pôlēl* has the force 'to kill' with the further implication of giving the *coup de grâce* and thus finishing off what has been begun.[9] Similarly in the case before us, as with other examples of the *Pôlēl* of שׁוּב,[10] the emphasis lies upon finishing off what one has set out to do, so that it is not just a matter of 'restoring the soul' but, rather, one

---

[8] Lam. 1.11, 16.

[9] Cf. T. H. Robinson, 'Note on Psalm xxxiv. 21', *ExpT* 52 (Dec., 1940), p. 117.

[10] Cf. Ps. 60.3 (EVV, v. 1); Isa. 49.5, 58.12; Jer. 50.19; Ezek. 38.4, 39.2, 27.

of completing successfully the task in question. Moreover, in this instance the metrical structure of the psalm reveals just what the finishing touches were thought to be; for this stichos must be construed closely with what precedes, and the implication is that by leading his charge to the spot where restful water may also be found the shepherd completes his task of satisfying its need.

the paths of righteousness: In this context the term צֶ֫דֶק which lies behind the word 'righteousness', is clearly used to define the type of track (מַעְגָּל) which possesses the quality of being rightly related to the goal at which one is aiming, just as it may be used in a forensic context to denote scales, weights, and measures which possess the quality of leading to a right result at the conclusion of a business transaction;[11] and in the circumstances it seems necessary to render the expression under discussion by 'the right tracks', i.e. as leading, under the direction of the shepherd, to the required end of meeting his charge's need. Nevertheless it must be borne in mind that the motive behind the resultant word-picture is the religious one which insists that man does not live by bread alone,[12] and the author's approach is thus wholly in line with the common practice in ancient Israel of representing man's conduct or behaviour in relation to both God and men by employing the metaphors of the right 'way' which leads to life and the wrong 'way' which leads to death.[13] Accordingly, if the translators of the Authorized Version leave one with the impression of confusing the task of the exegete with that of the translator, there is nothing essentially misleading in what they have done.

[11] Cf. Lev. 19.36 (H); Deut. 25.15; Job 31.6; Ezek. 45.10.
[12] Cf. Deut. 8.3.
[13] Cf., for example, Deut. 30.15–20; Ps. 16.11; Prov. 4.10–19, 12.26, 28. See further, for example, J. Muilenburg, *The Way of Israel: Biblical Faith and Ethics* (New York: Harper and Brothers, 1961 and London: Routledge and Kegan Paul, 1962), pp. 33ff.; also, for the significance of 'life' and 'death' in this connection, Johnson, *op. cit.*, pp. 87–109, esp. pp. 106ff.

for his name's sake: Both etymologically and in practice לְמַעַן,
as the introductory expression which lies behind these words,
implies an answer of some kind; and, indeed, it is often used as a
conjunction to indicate the securing of a specific result as the
response to a particular action.[14] The recognition of this fact is
important for understanding the use of this expression in connection with Israel's worship, which, significantly enough, could
be referred to idiomatically as 'calling *with* the "Name" of
Yahweh'.[15] Accordingly one may be tempted at a first glance to
think that its occurrence in psalms of a petitionary character simply
reflects the thought of worship as providing the established means
for securing the desired response to one's needs.[16] However,
apart from the fact that such calling *with* the divine 'Name' could
imply the thought of proclaiming as well as that of petitioning,[17]
it must also be borne in mind that the personal 'Name' by which
the God of Israel was known both to his own worshippers and to
the world at large served to distinguish him from the gods of
other nations and peoples, and, therefore, in appropriate circumstances would be evocative of his character as made known in his
dealings with his people. Thus the expected response to the
prayer of the penitent believer is basically an answering to the
'Name' of Yahweh in the sense of its being in keeping with his
character; and we may compare the way in which a psalmist,
whose work was composed in praise of the God of Israel and thus,
in principle, is an example of proclaiming Yahweh's 'Name'
rather than petitioning him, could refer to the way in which
Yahweh forgave the rebellious behaviour of his followers at the
Red Sea and saved them from the pursuing Egyptians – 'for his
"Name's" sake'.[18] That is to say, in each case Yahweh is thought

[14] E.g., Deut. 5.16, as cited below, p. 263, n. 30.
[15] E.g., Gen. 4.26 (J), Jer. 10.25.
[16] Cf. I Kings 8.41ff. in relation to Pss. 25.11, 31.4 (EVV, v. 3), 79.9,
143.11.
[17] Cf. A. R. Johnson, *The Cultic Prophet in Ancient Israel*, 2nd rev. ed.
(Cardiff: The University of Wales Press, 1962), pp. 54–60.
[18] Ps. 106.8.

of as acting in keeping with his character as a compassionate and forgiving God,[19] just as he is found to do elsewhere from a recognition of his responsibility to his covenant obligations or even towards the maintenance of his own standing among the nations.[20] Now in principle it is the same thought of 'answering to one's name' in the sense of behaving in accordance with one's character which is present in the passage before us; but in this case the point is that Yahweh, in leading his protégé along the right tracks, is answering to what is expected of him in the character of a shepherd.

the valley of the shadow of death: The translation 'shadow of death' is in keeping with the reading of the Masoretes and the renderings of the Ancient Versions, the word in question being vocalized as צַלְמָוֶת on the assumption that it is derived from a combination of צֵל, 'shadow', and מָוֶת 'death'. However, as such compounds are not commonly found in Hebrew save in the case of proper names, it is frequently held that one should think, rather, of a possible derivation from a single root recognizable from parallels in Accadian, Arabic, and Ethiopic, and should vocalize the consonantal text accordingly as צַלְמוּת, 'deep darkness'.

Further, even if one accepts the traditional etymology, there is no justification for interpreting 'the valley of the shadow of death' in so narrow a way as to limit it to the thought of death as the complete cessation of life; for in Israelite thought the expression would suggest quite simply a valley so dark as to conceal that which might offer any kind of threat to one's well-being.[21] In short, therefore, if we would do justice to what the author of the psalm had in mind at this point, we ought to think primarily of a valley deep in shadow, leaving any possible implications to the imagination.[22]

[19] Cf. Ex. 34.6f. (J); Pss. 78.38, 86.5, 15, 103.8ff.
[20] E.g., Isa. 48.9; Jer. 14.7, 21; Ezek. 20.9, 14, 22, 44.
[21] Cf. again Johnson, *The Vitality of the Individual*, pp. 87–109.
[22] For the Hebrew term under discussion, see in general D. W. Thomas, 'A Consideration of Some Unusual Ways of Expressing the

goodness and mercy: As is generally recognized, the dominant meaning of the term חֶסֶד, which is rendered here by 'mercy', is that of loyalty; and we may compare the way in which Absalom, at the time of his revolt against David, felt constrained to say to his father's old friend Hushai when he found that the latter had not joined the king in flight, 'Is this thy loyalty to thy friend?'[23] Accordingly this term is found in frequent use with reference to the keeping of one's promise and, notably, of keeping faith with regard to one's commitments in respect of a formal promise or covenant which was guaranteed under oath.[24] This fact, coupled with the term's further quite close association with the thought of sympathy or compassion (√רחם),[25] suggests that the word 'devotion' is most suitable for conveying to the English reader the full force of the Hebrew term.[26] However, in the passage before us we have an example of hendiadys, the second term thus serving to underline the fact that the goodness referred to has a permanent quality upon which one may rely; and the result is that the expression as a whole conveys the thought of something more akin to what we should call 'unfailing kindness'.

and I will dwell: The consonantal text has been vocalized by the Masoretes as וְשַׁבְתִּי, and was thus evidently regarded as an example of the *Qal* perfect of שׁוּב, 'to return', preceded by the *wāw* consecutive and thus yielding the meaning 'and I shall

---

Superlative in Hebrew', *VT* 3 (July, 1953), pp. 219–22; 'צַלְמָוֶת in the Old Testament', *JSS* 7 (Autumn, 1962), pp. 191–203; and, in summary fashion, *Understanding the Old Testament* (London: Athlone Press, 1967), pp. 17f.; but note also the words of caution which are offered by the present writer, *The Vitality of the Individual*, p. 9, n. 8.

[23] II Sam. 16.17.
[24] Cf. Gen. 47.29 (J); Josh. 2.12–14; I Sam. 18.3, 20.8, 12–17, 42; II Sam. 9.1–7, 21.7.
[25] Cf. Ps. 103.4; Jer. 16.5; Hos. 2.21 (EVV, v. 19).
[26] See further the present writer's essay, 'ḤESED and ḤĀSÎD', *Interpretationes ad Vetus Testamentum pertinentes*, S. Mowinckel *Festschrift* (Oslo: Forlaget Land og Kirke, 1955), pp. 100–12.

return'. On the other hand, one may follow the Septuagint and vocalize the text so as to read וְשִׁבְתִּי, i.e. the *Qal* infinitive construct of יָשַׁב, 'to dwell', followed by the first singular suffix; and the rendering of the Authorized Version may be justified in this way as representing the thought 'and my dwelling will be'. There is no good reason to doubt that this was the way in which the author wished the form to be understood, for the fact is that we have here a construction which corresponds to that of a circumstantial clause in prose and thus serves to stress the thought of contemporaneity with the ideas expressed in the preceding metrical line.[27] In other words, the author is reinforcing what he has just said about the experience of unfailing kindness throughout his life by adding that his dwelling in Yahweh's house, which is the guarantee of this good fortune, will be of long duration – in fact, according to the Authorized Version, 'for ever'.

for ever: literally 'for length of days', which is a Hebrew way of saying 'for a long time' but not necessarily 'for ever'. For example, the expression 'length of days' may be used quite simply to imply what we should describe as a long life; and we may compare Job's dictum:[28]

> Wisdom is with the aged,
> and understanding in length of days. (RSV)

This is also in keeping with the use of the corresponding verbal expressions, which are to be found in the *Qal*[29] and especially the *Hiph'îl*, with its inwardly transitive and its fully transitive force, to denote either the 'growing long' or the 'prolonging' of one's days. Indeed this use of the *Hiph'îl* is one of the stylistic features of the book of Deuteronomy with its emphasis upon obedience to Yahweh's commands as enabling one to live long

---

[27] Cf. E. Kautzsch, ed., *Gesenius' Hebrew Grammar*, 2nd rev. ed. by A. E. Cowley (Oxford: Clarendon Press, 1910), ¶156, with special reference to ¶141e.

[28] 12.12; cf. Deut. 30.20; Prov. 3.2, 16.   [29] Gen. 26.8 (J).

in the Promised Land.[30] On the other hand, the Psalter offers two examples of this expression which seem to imply the thought of far more than the reaching of what would be, from the human standpoint, an advanced age. Thus on one occasion it is said of the Davidic king or 'Messiah':[31]

> Life, which he asked of thee, thou hast given him,
> length of days for ever and ever.

Again, in our second passage from the Psalter, which belongs to those psalms which celebrate the kingship of Yahweh, the expression 'for length of days' appears to be used without any such elaboration to denote his eternal being as the creator and sustainer of the world.[32]

> Thy testimonies are strongly supported;
> it is seemly that thy house should be holy,
> O Yahweh, who abidest throughout the years (*lit.* for length of days).

On the whole, however, these cases must be regarded as exceptional; for one must beware of taking at its face value the seeming parallel at the ordinary human level which appears to be offered by Lam. 5.20:

> Why dost thou forget us for ever,
> why dost thou so long forsake us? (RSV)

Here the Hebrew expression which is rendered by the words 'for ever' should not be taken too literally as corresponding to the expression 'so long' (i.e. 'for the length of days') in the parallel stichos, for it merely emphasizes the thought of continuity, and

[30] Cf. (*a*), for the inwardly transitive use, Deut. 5.16 (cf. Ex. 20.12), 6.2, 25.15; (*b*), for the fully transitive use, Deut. 4.26, 40, 5.33, 11.9, 17.20, 22.7, 30.18, 32.47; also I Kings 3.14. See also in the latter connection (i) Prov. 28.16; Isa. 53.10; Eccles. 8.13; and (ii) Josh. 24.31 = Judg. 2.7, where the expression is used of the elders who 'outlived' Joshua.

[31] Ps. 21.5 (EVV, v. 4); cf. A. R. Johnson, *Sacral Kingship in Ancient Israel*, 2nd rev. ed. (Cardiff: The University of Wales Press, 1967), pp. 132ff.

[32] Ps. 93.5; cf. *ibid.*, pp. 65ff., esp. p. 66, n. 2.

the present writer cannot resist comparing the language of a once popular song which, if one's memory serves one aright, began with the words 'I'm for ever blowing bubbles'!

We are now left with the problem of what exactly the psalmist meant by his reference to the 'House' of Yahweh. Of course, for most commentators of recent years the psalmist's use of this expression offers no problem at all, because it is taken for granted that he had in mind the sanctuary and indeed, quite specifically, Solomon's Temple. On such a view the psalmist's expression of trust in Yahweh is thought to have been prompted by his actual participation in worship, for example, his own enjoyment of the communal sacrifices or his happiness at being freed in the sanctuary from some threat to his well-being, notably at finding asylum and even, perhaps, permanent asylum within its hallowed confines. By contrast it is only very rarely that one comes across the suggestion that the author's language is as figurative in his reference to the 'House' of Yahweh as it is elsewhere in the psalm; but, as we shall see, there is good reason to believe that here again the language is indeed figurative. Nevertheless this does not cancel out all thought of a sanctuary or even of Solomon's Temple, for we must not overlook the possibility that from the author's standpoint the fellowship which he enjoyed in virtue of the cultus and its privileges was eloquent of that wider fellowship which he was permitted to enjoy any and every day through his finding a place in the 'Household' of Yahweh.[33]

An excellent example of the relationship between the somewhat restricted conception of Yahweh's 'House' which was supplied by the Temple (or, no doubt, any other sanctuary consecrated to the

[33] No doubt this symbolic aspect of the Temple *vis-à-vis* the 'Household' of Yahweh was linked in some way with the thought of the Holy Land (cf. Hos. 8.1, 9.15; Jer. 12.7); but this is far too difficult a question to be dealt with here. Cf., for example, R. E. Clements, *God and Temple: The Idea of the Divine Presence in Ancient Israel* (Oxford: Basil Blackwell, 1965), with much of which I agree, although I am unable to accept his argument (pp. 5off.) with regard to the historical factors in the development of this link.

service of Yahweh) and, on the other hand, the wider conception of Yahweh's 'House' as embodying all those who placed their trust in him may be seen in Ps. 27. In this case we have to think of a suppliant whose plea for Yahweh's aid is centred in the thought that the privilege of belonging to the 'Household' of Yahweh brings with it the right to make use of the means provided by the Temple for securing Yahweh's help in time of need; and it is to be observed that at this point the psalmist's words are closely reminiscent of Ps. 23, and, what is more, that this conception of Yahweh's 'Household' may be expressed equally well in terms of his 'Tent'.[34]

> There is one thing that I have asked of Yahweh,
>   one thing that I seek;
> that I may dwell in the House of Yahweh
>   all the days of my life,
> enjoying Yahweh's favour
>   and enquiring in his Temple.
> For he will shelter me in hiding
>   at such time as trouble cometh.
> He will conceal me in his Tent;
>   he will set me high upon a rock.

It may well be that the author of Ps. 23 would have regarded his own place in the divine 'Household' as a somewhat lowly one; and in that case we could compare the author of Ps. 84. Indeed this psalm is particularly interesting in that, like Ps. 27, it illustrates quite clearly the way in which one's thought of the 'House' of Yahweh in its restricted application to the Temple might pass over simply and naturally into that of the 'Household' of Yahweh and indeed, as one may see from the last line of the psalm, that of the 'Household of Faith'. In the earlier part of this psalm the author evidently has in mind a contrast between the happy experience of the pilgrim who is able to visit the Temple for one or another of the recurrent festivals and, on the other hand, the still happier lot of those followers of Yahweh who enjoy the privilege of living within the precincts of the Temple, *qua* 'House' of Yahweh, and being engaged regularly in praising him there.[35]

[34] Verses 4f.   [35] Verse 5 (EVV, v. 4).

> How happy are they who dwell in thy House,
>   who can always be praising thee!

In the latter part of the psalm, however, the author's thought passes beyond the temporary pleasure of the pilgrim on his occasional visit to the Temple, and touches upon the lasting pleasures which are in store even for one who occupies only a subordinate position in this society of believers; for here, quite significantly, the comparison which he makes between the 'House' of Yahweh and the 'tents of wickedness', coupled with the emphasis which is laid upon trusting Yahweh, serves to show that he has passed beyond the thought of the Temple to this wider conception of what may justifiably be described as the 'Household of Faith'.[36]

> For I prefer a day in thy courts
>   to a thousand elsewhere,
> hovering on the threshold in the House of my God
>   to dwelling in the tents of wickedness.
> For Yahweh (*or* God) is both sun and shield;
>   he bestoweth grace and glory.
> Yahweh doth not withhold what is good
>   from those who walk in integrity.
> O Yahweh of Hosts,
>   how happy mankind who trust in Thee!

Such words find a striking contrast in those of the early oracle, preserved in Num. 12.7ff. (JE), which stresses the outstanding role of Moses as an intermediary between Yahweh and his people when compared with that of the typical prophet; for Yahweh, after saying that he reveals himself to the latter in visions and dreams, continues with the picturesque statement:

> My servant Moses is not like that;
>   *he* can be trusted anywhere within my House!
> It is mouth to mouth that I speak with him,
>   in plain view and not in riddles;
> yea, he may see the very Figure of Yahweh!

Perhaps, however, the most colourful picture of the benefits which

[36] Verses 11–13 (EVV, vv. 10–12). For the treatment of the text, see Johnson, *Sacral Kingship in Ancient Israel*, pp. 105f.

were enjoyed by those who sought Yahweh's protection and enjoyed the hospitality of his 'House' is furnished by the psalmist who says:[37]

> How precious is thy devotion, O God,
>> when men find refuge in the shadow of thy Wings!
> They are regaled with the rich food of thy House,
>> and thou givest them to drink of thy delightful Stream;
> For the Spring of Life is in thy keeping;[38]
>> it is through thy Light that we see light.

The simile which governs this imagery is, of course, the same as that which is normally recognized by commentators in their exposition of the final lines of Ps. 23. In short, it is provided by the figure of the גֵּר or תּוֹשָׁב, i.e. the 'sojourner', whether passing guest or more permanently resident alien; and comparison is frequently and rightly made with the claim to hospitality which is still enjoyed by the corresponding figure of the *jār* among the Bedawin of the present day. For our immediate purpose the most picturesque references to the figure of the sojourner are to be found, not in the prose narratives or legal codes,[39] but in the poetical books of the Old Testament. Thus on one occasion, when drought had reached the scale of a national disaster, Jeremiah could go so far as to reverse the normal procedure and apply this simile to Yahweh himself; for, speaking on behalf of his compatriots, he thus appeals to Yahweh not to forsake his people in their need despite the widespread corruption which is so clearly present in the nation's life:[40]

> Thou Hope of Israel,
>> his Saviour in time of trouble!

[37] Ps. 36.8–10 (EVV, vv. 7–9). Cf. Johnson, *The Vitality of the Individual*, pp. 103ff., esp. p. 105.

[38] *Lit.* 'with Thee'; but in this context the Hebrew is used idiomatically with reference to that which is to be found at one's home. Cf., for example, the Latin *apud* and the French *chez*; and see below, p. 270, n. 51, with further reference to Ps. 39.13 (EVV, v. 12).

[39] E.g., (*a*) Gen. 12.10ff. (J), 19.1–28 (J), 20.1ff. (E), 23.1ff. (P), 26.1ff. (J), 47.1–4 (J); Judg. 17.7ff., 19; II Kings 8.1–6; (*b*) Ex. 12.19, 45, 48f. (all P), 23.12 (E); Lev. 16.29 (P), 17.8ff., 18.26, 19.33f., 22.10, 24.16, 25.6, 39ff., 45ff. (all H); Num. 9.14, 15.14ff., 30, 35.15 (all P); Deut. 5.14 (cf. Ex. 20.10 [RᴰP ?]). [40] 14.8.

Why be like a גֵּר in the land,

like a traveller who turned aside for a night?

A similar picture is offered by Job, when he seeks to defend himself by an appeal to the way in which he has tried to live in accordance with the standard of behaviour required by Yahweh, and cites among the many examples of his conduct the fact that:[41]

No גֵּר ever spent the night in the street;

I kept open door for the traveller.[42]

Further, when this imagery is used of the hospitality and protection which was enjoyed by the follower of Yahweh, the governing thought, as one might imagine, appears to be that of the resident alien rather than that of the passing guest; and in the nature of the case such a member of the divine 'Household' was not without certain responsibilities of his own. This finds most forcible expression in the words of Isaiah who, picturing the righteous anger of Yahweh in terms of a consuming fire, makes repeated play with the corresponding verb along the following lines:[43]

In Zion the sinners are filled with dread,
　the godless have been seized with trembling.
'Who among us may sojourn (יָגוּר) with consuming fire?

Who among us may sojourn (יָגוּר) with ceaseless flame!'

The answer which Isaiah gives to this rhetorical question is unequivocal:

He that walketh in righteousness and speaketh the truth,
　that despiseth gain through extortion,
he that keepeth his hands from the taking of a bribe,
　that shutteth his ears to the suggestion of bloodshed,
that closeth his eyes to the attractions of evil,
　such a man shall settle on the heights,
with a fortress among the crags as his lofty stronghold,
　his bread always on hand, his water unfailing.

In this connection the reader who knows his Old Testament can hardly fail to be reminded of Ps. 15, which is now commonly

[41] 31.32.　　[42] Vocalizing the Hebrew term as above in Jer. 14.8.
[43] 33.14–16.

thought to deal with the question of admission to the Temple on Mount Zion, its liturgical setting being furnished by one of Israel's regular pilgrim festivals; for it offers a similar pattern of question and answer.

O Yahweh, who may sojourn (יָגוּר) in thy Tent?

Who may settle on thy Holy Hill?

'He that walketh in integrity and acteth with righteousness,
and speaketh truth from the heart.
He that hath no slander on his tongue,
that doeth no evil to his fellow,
and bringeth no ridicule upon his neighbour.
He that looketh with scorn upon the reprobate
and honoureth those who fear Yahweh.
He that keepeth his oath though it be to his hurt,
that lendeth not his money at interest,
and taketh no bribe against the innocent.
He that doeth these things shall never be dislodged.'

It is to be noticed, however, that the final line reads somewhat oddly, if one tries to understand the psalm as being concerned only with the Temple on Mount Zion; and, while the author's immediate concern may well have been with the question of admission to the Temple area,[44] he must have had far more in view than this. The simple fact which needs to be borne in mind is that in Israelite thought Mount Zion was the equivalent of the divine Mount of Assembly, the Temple itself being the early counterpart of Yahweh's heavenly Palace.[45] What is more, as a centre of worship it was not merely a significant part of the Holy Land; on the familiar principle of synecdoche (*pars pro toto*) it was virtually identified with it.[46] Accordingly, when the psalmist speaks of sojourning in Yahweh's 'Tent' and settling on his 'Holy Hill', he has in mind the thought of enjoying Yahweh's hospitality and protection as an inhabitant of the Holy Land; and, like Isaiah, he is

[44] Cf. Ps. 24, as discussed by Johnson, *Sacral Kingship in Ancient Israel*, pp. 72ff.   [45] Cf. *ibid.*, p. 75, n. 2.
[46] Cf. Clements, *loc. cit.*; and for the importance of recognizing the part played by synecdoche in Israelite thinking, see Johnson, *The Vitality of the Individual, passim*.

269

really insisting that obedience to Yahweh's ethical requirements is the condition or *sine qua non* of one's being able to live there in security and prosperity.

Correspondingly, when any worshipper came to the sanctuary to enquire of Yahweh and seek healing or protection along the established lines, this was but a typical example of the succour or, it might be, the right of asylum which any of his protégés might claim. This comes out quite clearly in the case of Ps. 61, where the suppliant prays:[47]

> Set me[48] on a cliff which I could not scale for myself,[49]
> for I have found in thee a refuge,
> a strong tower in the face of the enemy.
> I would sojourn (אָגוּרָה) for ever in thy Tent,
> finding refuge in the shadow of thy Wings.

Here again, however, the thought of enjoying Yahweh's protection 'for ever' is to be understood as implying no more than continuity throughout a long life; and, by way of a final comparison with the figurative language of Ps. 23, we may note that the temporary nature of this relationship between Yahweh and his follower comes strongly to the fore in Ps. 39. In this case we have the prayer of a suppliant who is forced to acknowledge that the troubles from which he seeks to be delivered are due to his own rebellious nature; but, despite this confessional aspect, the whole psalm is carefully designed to arouse Yahweh's compassion and forgiveness by dwelling upon the comparative brevity of human life, and it is rounded off with a pathetic appeal to the fact that the suppliant is no more than an alien figure who must presently lose for ever his privileged place in the divine Household.[50]

> O hear my prayer, Yahweh, and pay heed to my cry;
> do not meet my tears with silence.
> For I am but a גֵּר in thy keeping,[51]
> a תוֹשָׁב as all my fathers were.

[47] Verses 3c–5 (EVV, vv. 2c–4).
[48] Vocalizing the consonantal text as תַּנְּחֵנִי.

[49] *Lit.* 'which would be too high for me'.
[50] Verses 13f. (EVV, vv. 12f.).   [51] See above, p. 267, n. 38.

Let me be, that I may find happiness
before I depart and am no more.

We are now in a position to look again at Ps. 23 in the hope that
the foregoing discussion may enable one to appreciate more fully
just what the author was trying to say in describing his relationship with Yahweh in terms of his being both Shepherd and Host.

> With Yahweh as my Shepherd there is nothing that I lack;
>   he seeth that I lie down where there is grass for pasture.
> He leadeth me where restful water may be found,
>   satisfying my need to the full.
> He guideth me along the right tracks,
>   thus answering to his name.
> Even if my way lieth through a valley deep in shadow,
>   I dread no evil;
> for thou art with me,
>   my fears allayed by thy club and thy staff.
> Thou dost show mine enemies
>   that I am welcome at thy table,
> pouring oil upon my head,
>   my cup filled to overflowing.
> Yea, I shall be pursued by unfailing kindness
>   every day of my life,
> finding a home in the Household of Yahweh
>   for many a long year.

Finally, if the familiar words of the Authorized Version convey
more to the reader than the psalmist himself appears to have
intended, it should be a valuable spiritual discipline to ask oneself
just what this semantic change involves and how it came to be.[52]

[52] As for the original author, it must remain uncertain whether or not
this psalm was composed by David; and the reader may be referred to
what I have to say on the question of Davidic psalms in J. Hastings, ed.,
Dictionary of the Bible, 2nd rev. ed. by F. C. Grant and H. H. Rowley
(London: Thomas Nelson and Sons and New York: Charles Scribner's
Sons, 1963), p. 819. At the same time it should be borne in mind that,
since the language of the last metrical line is as metaphorical as the rest
of the psalm and, despite the *double entendre* which we have found
possible in other psalms, need have no immediate reference to any specific
sanctuary, there is no justification for the frequent claim that the mention
of Yahweh's 'House' must point to the existence of Solomon's Temple,
and that, as a result, David cannot have been the author.

14

שָׁלוֹם and the Presence of God

John I Durham

IT has frequently been pointed out that the Hebrew word שָׁלוֹם, in its Old Testament usage at any rate, has a significance which is basically religious. This significance, further, has often been described as a very complex one, difficult to represent in English. שָׁלוֹם is usually rendered in the English versions by the word 'peace', and such a translation has been criticized as inadequate and even misleading – though these criticisms have so far had little effect on the translators,[1] who are undoubtedly awaiting some better suggestion. It is not the purpose of this essay to provide such a suggestion – that would require an examination of the etymology of שָׁלוֹם and the usage of its cognates in Hebrew and related languages, and this cannot be accomplished here. The present intention is, rather, to study the usage in the Hebrew Old Testament of שָׁלוֹם with special emphasis upon its relation to the Old Testament concept of the PRESENCE of God.

I

The standard lexicons are in general agreement in their definitions of שָׁלוֹם. So Brown, Driver and Briggs give 'completeness,

---

[1] So, for example, RSV, Moffatt and Jerus, Bible render 'peace' in a large majority of the occurrences.

soundness, welfare, tranquility, friendship, peace';[2] Koehler, *'Unbefangenheit, Gedeihen, Unversehrtheit, Wohlergehen, Befinden, gedeihliche Beziehung = Friede, Freundlichkeit, Heil'*;[3] and Gesenius, 'wholeness, safety, health, peace, concord, friendship'.[4]

Von Rad, in his excellent article in *TWNT*, comments that the root meaning of שָׁלוֹם is '"well-being" with a strong emphasis on the material side', and adds that it signifies 'bodily health', 'prosperity' of a group, and very often, 'stability of relationship' rather than a state as such.[5] E. M. Good makes a somewhat arbitrary division in his definition of שָׁלוֹם and its cognates 'for analytic purposes', and speaks of 'secular peace' and 'religious peace'. This involves, on the one hand, 'health and the good life' for the individual, 'prosperity and security' for the family or the nation, and on the other hand 'obedience to God', 'wholeness of relationship to God', which is both 'blessing' and 'salvation'. Good would apparently render שָׁלוֹם nearly always by 'peace', with the understanding that more is involved than quietness and absence of conflict. All the same, his division of שָׁלוֹם into 'secular' and 'religious' is a misleading interpretation of the biblical usage of שָׁלוֹם.[6]

Pedersen considers the 'fundamental meaning' of שָׁלוֹם to be 'totality'.[7] 'Comprehensive and positive' in meaning, שָׁלוֹם

[2] Francis Brown, S. R. Driver and C. A. Briggs, eds., *A Hebrew and English Lexicon of the Old Testament* (Oxford: at the Clarendon Press, 1952), pp. 1022f.

[3] Ludwig Koehler and Walter Baumgartner, eds., *Lexicon in Veteris Testamenti Libros* (Leiden: E. J. Brill, 1958), pp. 973f.

[4] S. P. Tregelles, trans. and ed., *Gesenius' Hebrew and Chaldee Lexicon to the Old Testament Scriptures* (Grand Rapids: Wm. B. Eerdmans Publishing Co., 1949), p. 825.

[5] G. von Rad, 'שָׁלוֹם in the OT', *TDNT* (Grand Rapids: Wm. B. Eerdmans Publishing Co., 1964), vol. II, p. 402.

[6] E. M. Good, 'Peace in the OT', *IDB* (New York: Abingdon Press, 1962), vol, K–Q, pp. 704–6.

[7] J. Pedersen, *Israel, Its Life and Culture*, I–II, tr. A. Møller (London: Geoffrey Cumberlege, O.U.P., 1959), p. 263.

'expresses every form of happiness and free expansion, but the kernel in it is the community with others, the foundation of life'.[8] So, says Pedersen, שָׁלוֹם 'itself says that it denotes harmony, agreement and psychic community. . . .'[9] Closely influenced by Pedersen, C. F. Evans gives the basic meaning of שָׁלוֹם as '"totality", "well-being", "harmony", with stress on material prosperity untouched by violence or misfortune'.[10] So also G. G. Findlay – J. Mauchline, 'wholeness, health (i.e. hale-th), security',[11] though M. S. and J. L. Miller seem to limit their definition almost completely to the idea of peace as tranquility and freedom from conflict.[12]

The translators of the LXX most often rendered שָׁלוֹם by εἰρήνη, which in classical Greek, according to Liddell and Scott, refers primarily to a state of being from which conflict is absent.[13] Werner Foerster concludes, from the usage of εἰρήνη by the LXX, that 'the thought of well-being or salvation' inherent in שָׁלוֹם must have 'penetrated into the Greek'.[14] In those passages where some word other than εἰρήνη has been used for שָׁלוֹם,[15] Foerster notes

[8] J. Pedersen, *op. cit.*, p. 313. [9] *Ibid.*, p. 265.
[10] C. F. Evans, 'Peace', *A Theological Word Book of the Bible*, ed., Alan Richardson (London: SCM Press and New York: Macmillan Co., 1957), p. 165.
[11] G. G. Findlay and J. Mauchline, 'Peace', *Dictionary of the Bible*, ed., James Hastings, rev. ed. by F. C. Grant and H. H. Rowley (London: Thomas Nelson and Sons and New York: Charles Scribner's Sons, 1963), p. 742. Cf. also W. Adams Brown, 'Peace', *Dictionary of the Bible*, ed., James Hastings (New York: Charles Scribner's Sons, 1911), vol. III, pp. 732f.
[12] 'Peace', *Harper's Bible Dictionary*, M. S. and J. L. Miller (New York: Harper and Brothers, Publishers, 1954), p. 534.
[13] H. G. Liddell and R. Scott, *A Greek-English Lexicon*, new ed., rev. by H. J. Jones and R. McKenzie (Oxford: at the Clarendon Press, 1940), p. 490.
[14] W. Foerster, 'εἰρήνη in the LXX', *TDNT*, vol. II, p. 406. Cf. also Liddell and Scott, *op. cit.*, who note that the use of εἰρήνη in LXX to refer to health, etc., is a Hebraism.
[15] As, for example, Gen. 26.31, 37.14, Ex. 18.7, Josh. 10.21 and Isa. 57.21.

that 'external welfare', 'greetings', or 'coming and going' are 'almost exclusively' the concern.[16] In only a few instances, however, is εἰρήνη used to translate Hebrew words other than שָׁלוֹם.[17]

H. S. Gehman, who has for some years been at work on a dictionary of Septuagintal Greek, has concluded that in the LXX εἰρήνη has taken on the meanings of שָׁלוֹם 'which go beyond those referring to the absence of strife or war'. Thus εἰρήνη comes in the LXX to mean 'completeness', 'the satisfaction of having lived a full life', 'inner satisfaction', and is 'closely allied to salvation'. So the LXX '. . . translators appropriated all the meanings of שלום for εἰρήνη'.[18]

II

שָׁלֵם/שָׁלוֹם occurs more than 250 times in the Old Testament,[19] in over 200 separate verses.[20] In about 10 per cent of its Old Testament usages, שָׁלוֹם is a word of greeting[21] or farewell.[22] As such, it may have been simply a formal term, with no special

[16] Foerster, *op. cit.*, p. 408.

[17] Foerster (*ibid.*) lists שֶׁקֶט in I Chron. 4.40; בֶּטַח in, for example, Isa. 14.30, Ezek. 34.27, Prov. 3.23; שַׁלְוָה in Prov. 17.1. Evans must be corrected at this point, as he apparently overlooked these and similar usages and wrote of εἰρήνη 'only shalom so rendered' (*op. cit.*, p. 165).

[18] H. S. Gehman, 'Adventures in Septuagint Lexicography', *Textus V*, ed., S. Talmon (Jerusalem: at the Magnes Press, 1966), pp. 130f.

[19] The word count varies slightly – Brown, Driver and Briggs (*op. cit.*, p. 1022) say there are 237 occurrences, Koehler-Baumgartner (*op. cit.*, p. 972) say 236 occurrences, probably because of strong critical evidence against the occurrence in Jer. 13.19. The present writer has counted some 259 unquestioned occurrences of שָׁלוֹם in the Old Testament.

[20] Both Solomon Mandelkern, *Veteris Testamenti Concordantiae, Hebraicae atque Chaldaicae* (Lipsiae: Veit. et. Comp., 1896), pp. 1182f., and Gerhard Lisowsky, *Konkordanz zum Hebräischen Alten Testament* (Stuttgart: Privileg. Württ. Bibelanstalt, 1958), pp. 1436–8, list the same 213 separate verses.

[21] As in Judg. 19.20, I Sam. 25.6, II Kings 5.21f.

[22] As in I Sam. 25.35; 29.7; II Sam. 15.9; II Kings 5.19.

content. While it is impossible to say whether it was more, the usage of שָׁלוֹם in the Old Testament as a whole, plus the fact that it is not mentioned more frequently in the greeting/farewell category may at least imply that it was a special and loaded term even in these contexts.[23]

In an additional 25 per cent of its total Old Testament occurrences, שָׁלוֹם is used to describe a condition or state from which conflict, either physical or mental, is absent. Thus שָׁלוֹם may mean 'peace' in contrast to hostilities between nations,[24] cities[25] or clans.[26] It may refer to the mind free of vexation[27] or distress.[28] It may describe the condition of a people after a treaty has been successfully ratified[29] or the situation of victorious soldiers just after a battle.[30] Quite often, it depicts good will or the lack of it between individuals,[31] and it can even refer to harmony between Yahweh and his creatures.[32]

In far the majority of the Old Testament passages in which שָׁלוֹם occurs, however, indeed in virtually 65 per cent of the usage-pattern, the reference is not to 'peace' but rather to 'fulfilment'. Here שָׁלוֹם describes a completeness, a success, a maturity, a situation which is both prosperous and secure – withal, a state of well-being which is a direct result of the beneficent PRESENCE of

[23] Note in particular Ex. 4.18; I Sam. 1.17; 20.42; II Sam. 15.27 (cf. unemended MT), where a religious blessing is probably involved; cf. I Kings 2.6, where withholding a benediction of שָׁלוֹם amounts to a curse.

[24] As in Judg. 4.17; I Kings 5.4 and 26 [EVV, 4.25 and 5.12]; Eccles. 3.8b; Isa. 33.7.

[25] As in Deut. 20.10f.; Judg. 8.9; I Kings 20.18.

[26] As in Josh. 9.15; Judg. 21.13; I Sam. 7.14.

[27] As in Ex. 18.23; cf. Gen. 41.16.

[28] As in Gen. 43.23; 44.17; cf. Isa. 38.17; Judg. 6.23; Dan. 10.19.

[29] As in I Sam. 16.4f.; cf. Gen. 26.29, 31 and Josh. 9.15.

[30] As in Josh. 10.21; Judg. 11.31; I Kings 22.27; cf. II Sam. 11.7.

[31] As in Gen. 37.4; II Sam. 3.21f.; I Kings 2.13; II Kings 9.17ff.; Ps. 120.6; Jer. 9.7 [EVV, v. 8].

[32] Isa. 27.5; Job 5.24; Ezek. 34.25.

God. This beneficent PRESENCE is at the very least either assumed or implied in the context of each of these usages of שָׁלוֹם, and it is mentioned in some specific way in nearly fifty separate passages.

There is not sufficient space here to consider all the references – well over 125 verses – upon which these suggestions are based. Representative occurrences may, however, be set forth, and the additional passages which have been examined in the preparation of this essay will be listed in the accompanying footnotes. The contention is that in these passages, שָׁלוֹם refers to more than 'peace and contentment', indeed to an active condition, 'completion and fulfilment', which comes not as a result of man's efforts alone, but is the result of the blessing of God. This definition of the word will be considered first, and its usage in connection with the PRESENCE of God will then be taken up.

III

In a considerable number of passages, שָׁלוֹם becomes a term by which the general welfare of persons, animals, things or situations is inquired after or described. In such cases, it is altogether possible that the term has a stylized usage, and that the application to it of too profound or extensive a content is both misleading and eisegetical. This of course is one of the basic hazards of word-study in a collection of literature so diverse and varied in origin and context as the Old Testament. But even as a stylized term, שָׁלוֹם carries a meaning which clearly transcends the ordinary categories of greeting and social amenity.

So in the passages where שָׁלוֹם becomes a part of an enquiry or an answer concerning another's welfare, more than just health or just prosperity or just peace of mind is involved. All these are involved, for the inquiry literally means 'Is it all right and well and coming up to the highest expectation?' When Yahweh

277

promises Abram[33] 'As for yourself, you shall go to your fathers בְּשָׁלוֹם', he is promising the patriarch that he will join his fathers a success – that he will have fulfilled the divine purpose, and so be a 'complete' and 'accomplished' servant. Note the parallel statement, תִּקָּבֵר בְּשֵׂיבָה טוֹבָה. Thus when Jacob asks about the שָׁלוֹם of Laban,[34] or Joseph about the שָׁלוֹם of his brothers and his father,[35] or Moses about Jethro's שָׁלוֹם,[36] it is possible to suggest that the concern being manifested was a wide-ranging one, involving the totality of life and being.[37] So it is that David instructs his young men to ask after the שָׁלוֹם of Nabal in his name,[38] and then to state his concern for the totality of Nabal's person, family and possessions.[39] Similarly, the Danite spies ask Micah's young Levite, with the intention of luring him away, how everything is

---

[33] Gen. 15.15. The complexity of the literary analysis of this chapter is well known – cf. the recent work by R. E. Clements, *Abraham and David*, SBT 2nd series 5 (London: SCM Press, 1967) and the list of studies cited in n. 7, pp. 16f. H. Gunkel assigned v. 15 to a redactor (*Genesis*, HKAT, 6th ed. [Göttingen: Vandenhoeck and Ruprecht, 1964], pp. 177–84), and G. von Rad describes it as part of 'a cabinet piece of Old Testament theology of history' (*Genesis*, trans. J. H. Marks [London: SCM Press and Philadelphia: Westminster Press, 1961], p. 183). If this verse is later than the undoubtedly more ancient material of vv. 7–12, 17–18ab, this is not detrimental to the present argument; if anything, it enhances it.

[34] Gen. 29.6.   [35] Gen. 43.27f.   [36] Ex. 18.7.

[37] So also Gen. 37.14; Deut. 23.7 [EVV, v. 6]; I Sam. 17.18, 22; 20.7, etc.

[38] I Sam. 25.5; RSV's translation, 'and greet him' is much too weak. Cf. RSV's reading of II Sam. 11.7, where David enquires of Uriah about the שָׁלוֹם of the מִלְחָמָה: 'David asked . . . how the war prospered.'

[39] I Sam. 25.6; this interpretation of שָׁלוֹם may help to interpret the difficult usage of לֶחָי in this verse: could David not be saying to his emissaries 'And you must speak this concerning [his] life [i.e., his whole existence] . . .'? On לֶחָי, see S. R. Driver, *Notes on the Hebrew Text and the Topography of the Books of Samuel* (Oxford: at the Clarendon Press, 1960), pp. 196f.

going for him: וַיִּשְׁאֲלוּ־לוֹ לְשָׁלוֹם;[40] and Ahimaaz, running to tell
David that Yahweh has vindicated (√שׁפט) him from the power
of his enemies, i.e., that the king's person and rule are now safe,
exclaims: שָׁלוֹם;[41] and the covenant of Phinehas, the perpetual
legitimization of the Aaronic priestly line, is called by Yahweh 'my
completion covenant' or 'my covenant of fufilment': בְּרִיתִי
שָׁלוֹם.[42]

When Ahab orders Micaiah thrown into solitary confinement
until he returns from the battle with the Syrians בְשָׁלוֹם,[43] he is
surely saying 'until my victorious return', i.e. 'until I return with
my purpose accomplished' – an eventuality which would give the
lie to Micaiah's prophecy.[44] When Josiah sends a delegation to
Huldah the prophetess to 'inquire of Yahweh' (דִּרְשׁוּ אֶת־יְהוָה)
concerning his fate,[45] Yahweh sends word that Josiah is to be
gathered to his fathers and his grave בְשָׁלוֹם – not 'in peace', as
RSV has it, but 'in success', i.e., 'having achieved his calling'.[46]
Had his people only obeyed his commandments, their שָׁלוֹם
would have been like a river (כַנָּהָר), writes the great poet of Isa.
40–55.[47] That is, they would have been completely fulfilled and

---

[40] Judg. 18.15.
[41] II Sam. 18.28. It should be borne in mind that Ahimaaz does not
mention that Absalom has been killed (v. 29) – this knowledge would have
prevented David's receiving his report of שָׁלוֹם, for he had named his
son 'Father's fulfilment', אַבְשָׁלוֹם. Note RSV's correct rendering of שָׁלוֹם
in v. 28: 'All is well.'
[42] Num. 25.12; cf. Isa. 54.10; Ezek. 34.25; Mal. 2.5.
[43] I Kings 22.27.
[44] As Micaiah clearly recognizes: אִם־שׁוֹב תָּשׁוּב בְּשָׁלוֹם לֹא־דִבֶּר יְהוָה בִּי
(v. 28).   [45] II Kings 22.11–13.
[46] II Kings 22.20; note the entire speech of Yahweh concerning
Josiah, vv. 18–20.
[47] Isa. 48.18; cf. Num. 24.6; Pss. 1.3, 65.10 [EVV, v. 9]; and esp.
Isa. 66.12.

totally cared for – the river is a well-known figure in the Old Testament of 'abundance' and 'of the favour of God',[48] of 'the prosperity of a region over which God's power extends'.[49] And the parallel member, וְצִדְקָתְךָ כְּגַלֵּי הַיָּם makes it plain that this שָׁלוֹם would have included cultic perfection as well as material and domestic fulfilment.[50] By contrast, however, there is אֵין שָׁלוֹם for the wicked.[51] Similarly, the sons who are schooled (לִמּוּדֵי) by Yahweh shall have רַב שָׁלוֹם, 'complete fulfilment'.[52] Indeed, the covenant of Yahweh's שָׁלוֹם, the 'promise of his completion' for his people, will not 'come to nothing'.[53]

The examples could easily be multiplied, but perhaps enough have been cited to suggest that שָׁלוֹם is often indicative, in Old Testament usage, of a comprehensive kind of fulfilment or completion, indeed of a perfection in life and spirit which quite transcends any success which man alone, even under the best of circumstances, is able to attain. It may be contended, indeed, that שָׁלוֹם in these contexts refers to man's realization, under the blessing of God, of the plan which God has for him and the potential with which God has endowed him. As such, it would be

[48] W. Ewing and D. R. Ap-Thomas, 'River', *Dictionary of the Bible*, ed. J. Hastings, rev. ed. F. C. Grant and H. H. Rowley, pp. 853f.

[49] W. L. Reed, 'River', *IDB*, vol. R–Z, pp. 100f.

[50] Cf. the comments of G. von Rad, '"Righteousness" and "Life" in the Cultic Language of the Psalms', *The Problem of the Hexateuch and Other Essays*, trans. E. W. Trueman Dicken (Edinburgh: Oliver and Boyd and New York: McGraw-Hill Book Co., 1966), pp. 243–66. Cf. also Isa. 55.12, 57.19. [51] Isa. 48.22; cf. also 57.21; 59.8.

[52] Isa. 54.13; note also v. 14a, and cf. Prov. 3.2, which adjures the student to remember תּוֹרָה and commandments for they will bring length of days, years of life, and שָׁלוֹם יוֹסִיפוּ לָךְ.

[53] Isa. 54.10; note that the phrase here is בְּרִית שְׁלוֹמִי as compared with בְּרִיתִי שָׁלוֹם in Num. 25.12. C. R. North renders here 'my covenanted peace' – *The Second Isaiah* (Oxford: at the Clarendon Press, 1967), p. 67, cf. pp. 248, 118. Cf. also Ezek. 34.25, 37.26, Mal. 2.5.

the perfection towards which God has directed man and to which he alone can draw man.

IV

Further and more direct support for such an interpretation of the deeper meaning of שָׁלוֹם may be found in those passages which describe שָׁלוֹם as a gift of God and those passages which refer to שָׁלוֹם as a blessing specially connected to theophany or the immanent PRESENCE of God.

In a considerable number of places in the Old Testament, God is described, either directly or by implication, as the source of שָׁלוֹם. So Jacob, following the dream-theophany of Bethel, says 'If God will be with me [near me, beside me, עִמָּדִי], ... I will return to my father's house a success [בְשָׁלוֹם].'[54] Solomon, piously justifying the execution of Joab and absolving the Davidic dynasty of any responsibility in the matter, exclaims, '... to David, and to his descendants, and to his house, and to his throne, there shall be fulfilment (success) עַד־עוֹלָם מֵעִם יְהוָה.'[55] Isaiah of Jerusalem declares 'Yahweh keeps on giving success [שָׁלוֹם] to us, for "thou also have accomplished for us all our undertakings"'.[56] Deutero-Isaiah has Yahweh saying, in the commission to Cyrus, 'Forming (יוֹצֵר) light and ... manufacturing (עֹשֶׂה) fulfilment (שָׁלוֹם) ..., I am Yahweh, doing all these things.'[57]

[54] Gen. 28.21; cf. Judg. 18.6 and Gen. 41.16.
[55] I Kings 2.33; cf. Isa. 9.5f. [EVV, vv. 6f.]; Ezek. 37.26.
[56] Isa. 26.12; cf. the problematic v. 3 and note also Lev. 26.6.
[57] Isa. 45.7; this prophet speaks several times of Yahweh as the source of שָׁלוֹם – cf. 48.18, 22; 54.10 and 13; 55.12 and 53.5c, which can be rendered 'the punishment which has effected *our* שָׁלוֹם was upon *him*!' Note also 41.3, and the references to שָׁלוֹם in Isa. 56–66, similar to those cited already: 57.2, 19, 21; 60.17; 66.12.

281

Jeremiah similarly describes Yahweh declaring that he will make (√עָשָׂה) both good (טוֹב) and maturity (שָׁלוֹם) for his people,[58] and will disclose to them 'abundance of שָׁלוֹם and אֱמֶת (fulfilment and security)'.[59] Yahweh's purposes for those who are in Babylonian exile are described as מַחְשְׁבוֹת שָׁלוֹם, to give them a future and a hope.[60] Indeed, Jeremiah binds שָׁלוֹם to the authentic commission of God, making it the mark of prophetic authenticity – prophets who announce שָׁלוֹם when there is none do not come from God and are liars.[61] For sometimes, after all, Yahweh withdraws (√אָסַף) his שָׁלוֹם from near (מֵאֵת) the people, in judgment.[62]

So also among the prophets Ezekiel,[63] Micah,[64] Nahum,[65] Haggai,[66] Zechariah,[67] and Malachi,[68] either imply or say directly that Yahweh is the source of שָׁלוֹם. It is in the Psalter in particular, however, that Yahweh/Elohim is most frequently and directly described as the giver of שָׁלוֹם – a fact which is not difficult to understand in view of the cultic purpose and use of at least a majority of the Psalms. So Ps. 29.11:

> Yahweh strength to his people keeps on giving!
> Yahweh keeps on blessing[69] his people with שָׁלוֹם!

Indeed, Yahweh is 'the one who takes pleasure in' or even 'wills' (הֶחָפֵץ) the שָׁלוֹם of his servant,[70] and the one who 'ransoms' or 'redeems' the soul of his beleaguered devotee בְשָׁלוֹם.[71]

---

[58] Jer. 33.9.   [59] Jer. 33.6.   [60] Jer. 29.11.
[61] Jer. 14.13; 23.17; 28.9; cf. 6.14; 8.11, 15; Micah 3.5; so also Ezek. 13.10 and 16 – note in this latter verse the usage חֲזוֹן שָׁלֵם, though חֲזוֹן is lacking in the LXX.
[62] Jer. 16.5; cf. 14.19; 12.12 and 25.37.   [63] Ezek. 34.25; 37.26.
[64] Micah 5.4 [EVV, v. 5].   [65] Nahum 2.1 [EVV, 1.15]; cf. Isa. 52.7.
[66] Hag. 2.9.   [67] Zech. 6.13; 8.12; cf. 8.10 and 9.10.   [68] Mal. 2.5f.
[69] Note that both verbs in this verse are *Pi'el* imperfect; cf. GesK ¶ 52f.   [70] Ps. 35.27.
[71] Ps. 55.19a [EVV, v. 18], reading יִפְדֶּה instead of פָּדָה in accord with the LXX and the Vulgate of Jerome.

שָׁלוֹם and the Presence of God

The Psalmist longs to hear what Yahweh keeps saying, 'For he is always saying שָׁלוֹם to his people and to his loyal servants. . . .'[72] In fact, 'abundant שָׁלוֹם' belongs to those who love Yahweh's instruction (תּוֹרָה), and 'nothing can make them fail'.[73] One reason Yahweh is to be praised, finally, is that 'he is the one who makes your territory complete (שָׁלוֹם)'.[74]

There are additional occurrences of שָׁלוֹם in the Psalms which at least imply that שָׁלוֹם comes from God,[75] and the book of Proverbs[76] and the book of Job[77] sound a similar note. The Chronicler depicts Amasai, under the influence of רוּחַ, saying to David:

[We are] for you David, and with you, son of Jesse! שָׁלוֹם שָׁלוֹם to you and שָׁלוֹם to those helping you, because (כִּי) your helper is your God![78]

And it is Yahweh, says the Chronicler, who told David, that during his son's reign, 'I will give fulfilment (שָׁלוֹם) and quietness (שֶׁקֶט) to Israel.'[79] This latter verse is significant not only for its designation of Yahweh as the giver of שָׁלוֹם, but for its use of הֲנִחוֹתִי, מְנוּחָה and שֶׁקֶט in context with שָׁלוֹם. It may at least be suggested that the wider significance of שָׁלוֹם as 'fulfilment' is

---

[72] Ps. 85.9 [EVV, v. 8]; note *Pi'el* imperfect יְדַבֵּר in v. 9a and 9b, and see note 69, above. Cf. also vv. 11 and 13 [EVV, vv. 10 and 12].

[73] Ps. 119.165; cf. Prov. 3.2. [74] Ps. 147.14.

[75] Cf. Pss. 4.9 [EVV, v. 8]; 34.15 [EVV, v. 14]; 37.11 and 37; 69.23 [EVV, v. 22], though note a critical problem; 72.3 and 7; 73.3, in the context of vv. 16f. and 27f.; 122.6, 7, 8; and 125.5 (see *BH* app. crit.) and 128.6, as benedictions.

[76] Prov. 3.2 and 17.

[77] Job 25.2; cf. also 5.24; 15.21 ('in fulfilment'?), rather than '"in peace", i.e. when all is quiet' as E. Dhorme renders – *A Commentary on the Book of Job*, trans. H. Knight [London: Thomas Nelson and Sons Ltd., 1967], p. 216.

[78] I Chron. 12.19 [EVV, v. 18]. [79] I Chron. 22.9.

here attested by these words, whose basic meaning is 'peace and quiet', 'absence of turmoil'.[80] Indeed it may be argued that שָׁלוֹם has this special meaning in each of the passages where it is mentioned as the special gift of God.

While it may be noted that the immanent PRESENCE of God is at the very least implied in all the passages which refer to שָׁלוֹם as his beneficent gift, there is a smaller group of passages which undeniably connect the gift of שָׁלוֹם to this real PRESENCE. In so doing, these passages justify this conclusion for the larger collection of references which imply such a PRESENCE only, and suggest that שָׁלוֹם, as a cultic term, is related specifically to the PRESENCE-theology recurrent in the Old Testament.

It is in the aftermath of the dream-theophany in which Jacob experienced Yahweh's real PRESENCE at Bethel that Jacob first comes to know what this PRESENCE can mean, and so says in his vow, that the condition of שָׁלוֹם is dependent upon the PRESENCE of Elohim.[81] Following the theophany which authenticates his call to generalship, Gideon declares with understandable fright, 'Woe, Lord Yahweh, for indeed I have seen (רָאִיתִי) Yahweh's messenger face to face!'[82] But it is Yahweh himself who replies to

---

[80] Cf. Brown, Driver and Briggs, *op. cit.*, pp. 628–30, 1052f. and Koehler-Baumgartner, pp. 537, 601f., 1007f. Cf. also 1 Chron. 23.25, הֵנִיחַ. Though it may also be argued that שָׁלוֹם here is intended as synonymous with these other terms, שָׁלוֹם in such a sense would be considered no less a result of God's active blessing.

[81] Gen. 28.10–22; cf. esp. vv. 19–22, and note above, p. 281. Compare the statement of Micah's Levite, Judg. 18.6, who enquires of Elohim (שָׁאַל־נָא בֵאלֹהִם, v. 5) for the Danites, who wish to know whether their journey (or 'course of action', דֶּרֶךְ) will 'lead to success' (הֲתַצְלִיחַ, cf. the הַתִצְלַח of *BH* app. crit.), then says 'Go in success (לְשָׁלוֹם) – your journey which you are undertaking there is in Yahweh's PRESENCE' (lit., 'just in front of Yahweh', נֹכַח יְהוָה).

[82] Judg. 6.22.

Gideon:[83] 'שָׁלוֹם to you[84] – do not be fearful, you shall not die!'
It is indeed from this moment that Gideon seems fit for the first time for the work to which he has been called, and when he builds an altar in commemoration of Yahweh's appearance, he calls it 'Yahweh is fulfilment'.[85]

The theophanic language of Ps. 29 is well known,[86] with its dramatic trip-hammer repetition of the phrase קוֹל־יְהוָה, and its culminating cultic shout, כָּבוֹד. The psalm concludes with a declaration of the kingship of Yahweh (v. 10) and with the assertion (v. 11) that Yahweh will continue to strengthen his people and bless them 'with fulfilment' (בְשָׁלוֹם).[87] There is in Deutero-Isaiah[88] a comparable statement: the herald of Yahweh's return to Zion (בְּשׁוּב יְהוָה צִיּוֹן, v. 8) brings the welcome news of 'fulfilment' to a shattered nation and a frustrated people. While the context here is not so clearly theophanic as in the case of Ps. 29,

---

[83] Judg. 6.23.

[84] It is probable that more than 'peace' as 'relax' is meant, esp. in view of the אַל־תִּירָא לֹא תָמוּת which follows. Perhaps שָׁלוֹם לְךָ may here be rendered 'It is fulfilment for you', i.e., 'this is a part of your preparation'.

[85] יְהוָה שָׁלוֹם, Judg. 6.24; cf. Ps. 120.7, where the poet declares אֲנִי־שָׁלוֹם 'I am peace itself!' (as opposed to war).

[86] So Artur Weiser, *The Psalms*, trans. H. Hartwell (London: SCM Press and Philadelphia: Westminster Press, 1962), p. 261 ('The psalm is a theophany psalm . . .') and H. J. Kraus, *Psalmen* I, BKAT (Neukirchen: Neukirchener Verlag/Kreis Moers, 1960), pp. 233ff. ('*Die Machtvolle Erscheinung Jahwes im Gewitter*'), to cite two representative commentaries.

[87] Weiser renders בְשָׁלוֹם here 'with salvation', and makes this interesting comment (*op. cit.*, p. 265, cf. p. 261): 'The vital energy of the Old Testament belief in God springs from the very fact that the people know what it means to encounter such a mighty God and enjoy the privilege of continually receiving from his hand in a time of festival his strength, blessing and salvation.'

[88] Isa. 52.7; cf. Nahum 2.1 [EVV, 1.15]; Ps. 85.9, 11 [EVV, vv. 8, 10], which von Rad, 'שָׁלוֹם in the OT', *TDNT*, pp. 403f., following W. Caspari, 'Vorstellung und Wort "Friede" im AT', *BFChrTh* 14, 4 (1910), p. 161, considers 'a climax in the OT use of the term שָׁלוֹם'.

there is at least the plain suggestion of a cultic theophany in the words מֶלֶךְ אֱלֹהָיִךְ,[89] and it is obvious that it is the returning Yahweh who will bring the much needed שָׁלוֹם.

There are additional passages which at least suggest an association of the gift of שָׁלוֹם with the cult theophany: II Sam. 15.24ff., for example, where Zadok and his fellow priests, who are bearing the ark of Elohim, are told by David to return with the ark to Jerusalem בְּשָׁלוֹם,[90] or Ps. 4, with its 'certainly of a hearing' theology[91] and the words נְסָא־עָלֵינוּ אוֹר פָּנֶיךָ יְהוָה[92] declaring,

Satisfied (בְּשָׁלוֹם) I will both lie down and fall asleep, because you alone, Yahweh, keep causing me to rest secure (לָבֶטַח).[93]

But one passage, above all others, brings שָׁלוֹם and the cultic theology of the PRESENCE of God together: it is the familiar Aaronic benediction, the so-called 'priestly blessing' of Num. 6.24ff.

V

While no one has yet advanced a satisfactory date for Num. 6.24–26, there is general agreement among most scholars that it is considerably more antiquated than its immediate context. Curt Kuhl attributes the passage to the 'Pre-Mosaic and Mosaic

[89] See Ivan Engnell, 'The 'Ebed Yahweh Songs and the Suffering Messiah in Deutero-Isaiah', *BJRL* 31 (1948), pp. 54–93; note also the comments of North, *op. cit.*, pp. 221f.

[90] David himself thus chooses to leave the ark in its proper place and discover what his fate is to be on his own merit alone – vv. 25f., 29.

[91] Verse 4 [EVV, v. 3]; cf. H. Gunkel, *Einleitung in die Psalmen*, HKAT (Gottingen: Vandenhoeck & Ruprecht, 1933), ¶ 23, pp. 243–7.

[92] Verse 7 [EVV, v. 6]; note *BH* app. crit., and see below, pp. 291ff.

[93] Verse 9 [EVV, v. 8]; note also the references which promise שָׁלוֹם and the PRESENCE of God to the Davidic dynasty – so, for example, I Kings 2.33; Isa. 9.5f. [EVV, vv. 6f.]; Ezek. 37.26; cf. also Jer. 33.6, 9; Hag. 2.9; Ps. 122.6–8; and note, without שָׁלוֹם, the language of Ps. 20.

period',[94] and though few scholars have been willing to go that far, few would argue for a date later than the seventh century BC. So G. B. Gray suggested, well over fifty years ago, that 'the blessing . . . was not composed by P' and that it is 'of earlier origin than the date of its incorporation in P'.[95] A. H. McNeile assigned the verse to P, but proposed that it is out of context and that it 'probably dates from a time anterior to P'.[96] H. Holzinger, in his source-analysis of Numbers, assigned both 6.1–21 and 6.22–26 to 'Pˢ', but comments on the latter, '*darin v. 24–26 älter, nicht Konzeption von P*'.[97]

Some commentators have suggested the relocation of Num. 6.24–26 at contexts more congenial to it, such as following Lev. 9.22.[98] Similarities to the language or content of the passage have been discovered in extra-biblical literature[99] and within the Old

[94] C. Kuhl, *The Old Testament, Its Origins and Composition*, trans. C. T. M. Herriott (Edinburgh: Oliver and Boyd, 1960 and Richmond: John Knox Press, 1961), p. 312.

[95] G. B. Gray, *A Critical and Exegetical Commentary on Numbers*, ICC (Edinburgh: T. & T. Clark, 1903), p. 71. Gray goes on to suggest (p. 72) that Num. 6.22–24 may 'probably' have been 'a blessing actually used in the Temple at Jerusalem before the Exile', and adds that it 'would have been a natural product of the period of the Josianic Reformation'. Cf. also Gray's remarks on pp. xxiif., xxxvi–xxxviii and l–li.

[96] A. H. McNeile, *The Book of Numbers*, CambB (Cambridge: at the University Press, 1931), pp. 36f. So also L. Elliott Binns, *The Book of Numbers*, WC (London: Methuen & Co. Ltd., 1927), pp. xviii, xxvii, 41f.

[97] H. Holzinger, *Numeri*, KHC (Tübingen: J. C. B. Mohr [P. Siebeck] 1903), p. xiv, note also pp. 28f.

[98] So Gray, *op. cit.*, p. 71; Binns, *op. cit.*, pp. 41f.; cf. A. Dillmann, *Die Bücher Numeri, Deuteronomium und Josua*, KeH (Leipzig: Verlag von s. Hirzel, 1886), p. 38.

[99] See A. Jeremias, *The Old Testament in the Light of the Ancient East*, trans. C. L. Beaumont and C. H. W. Johns (London: Williams and Norgate, 1911), vol. I, pp. 105f.; E. G. Gulin, 'Das Antlitz Jahwes im Alten Testament', *Annales Academiae Scientarum Fennicae*, series B, vol. XVII, 3 (1923), pp. 15f.; F. Delitzsch, *Babel and Bible* (London: Williams and Norgate, 1903), pp. 32f., 94–96. Note also the wording of the Ugaritic letter listed by Gordon as 'text 117': Cyrus H. Gordon, *Ugaritic Literature* (Rome: Pontificium Institutum Biblicum, 1949), pp. 116f., text 117.5–7 and *Ugaritic Textbook* (Rome: Pontifical Biblical Institute, 1965), pp. 490f., glossary no. 2424.

Testament itself,[100] most particularly in the Psalms.[101] Buchanan Gray felt that 'linguistic affinities' and 'general tenor and feeling' relate the 'blessing' to the Psalms,[102] a connection which has at the very least been intimated by many scholars. One writer indeed has advanced the view, in what will appear to many as too clever a proposal, that Psalms 120–134 ('the Songs of Ascents') 'contain an elaboration upon four key words of the Priestly Blessing'.[103] The 'Blessing' itself, 'tersely formulated and couched in general terms', is said to be interpreted by 'the Songs of Ascents', which have as their 'unifying principle ... their verbal connection with the Priestly Blessing'.[104]

While such a view as this seems too fanciful for the available evidence, the relation of the poem of Num. 6.24–26 to the cultic milieu of which the Psalms are the cardinal Old Testament example is hardly questionable. Scholars who have commented on the passage recently have espoused such a view, and have considered the 'blessing' to be both early and influential.[105]

[100] Note, for example, in addition to the many שָׁלוֹם-passages cited already, the following passages which omit שָׁלוֹם: Gen. 43.29; Ex. 33.19 and 34.5; Deut. 28.10; Dan. 9.17; and I Chron. 23.25, where David says הֵנִיחַ יְהוָה אֱלֹהֵי־יִשְׂרָאֵל לְעַמּוֹ וַיִּשְׁכֹּן בִּירוּשָׁלַם עַד־לְעוֹלָם.

[101] Note especially the following passages from the Psalms: 4.7b [EVV, v. 6b]; 31.17 [EVV, v. 16]; 44.4 [EVV, v. 3]; 63.3 [EVV, v. 2]; 67.2 [EVV, v. 1]; 80.2, 4, 8, 20 [EVV, vv. 1, 3, 7, 19]; 89.16 [EVV, v. 15]; 119.135; 121.8; 128.5; 129.8; and 134.3. Cf. 17.15; 24.6; 74.7; 118.25f.; and 122.6–8.

[102] Gray, *op. cit.*, p. 71.

[103] Leon J. Liebreich, 'The Songs of Ascents and the Priestly Blessing', *JBL* 74 (March, 1955), pp. 33–36. The 'four key words' are held to be שלום and ויחנן, וישמרך, יברכך (p. 33).

[104] *Ibid.*, pp. 34 and 36. Liebreich gets around the Psalms within this group which really cannot be connected with the 'four key words' (Pss. 124, 126, 131) by proposing that they were added to make the number of Psalms in the group equivalent to the total number of words in Num. 6.24–26 (p. 36).

[105] See, e.g., Otto Eissfeldt, *The Old Testament: An Introduction*, trans. P. Ackroyd (New York: Harper & Row and Oxford: Basil Blackwell, 1965), pp. 73–75, who considers the 'blessing' a 'priestly saying',

In the light of its usage in the passages which have been discussed already,[106] and upon the basis of its association with such other terms which play an important role in the cultic vocabulary as חֶסֶד,[113] בָּרַךְ,[107] בְּרִית,[108] טוֹב,[109] צֶדֶק,[110] תּוֹרָה,[111] שֵׁם,[112] מִשְׁפָּט,[119] מִישׁוֹר,[118] אֱמֶת,[117] כָּבוֹד,[116] יְשׁוּעָה,[115] בֶּטַח,[114] חַטָּאת,[120] and רַע/רָשָׁע/רָעָה,[121] it can hardly be denied that שָׁלוֹם has a significant use as a cultic term. It may be suggested that the occurrence in Num. 6.26 is its ultimate usage in this sense.[122]

and reconstructs its setting in cultic ceremony; or George Fohrer, *Introduction to the Old Testament*, trans. D. E. Green (New York: Abingdon Press, 1968), pp. 181f., who considers the 'blessing' a part of the early, previously independent material incorporated by P. So also James Muilenburg, writing on Old Testament literary forms in H. H. Rowley, ed., *A Companion to the Bible*, 2nd ed. (Edinburgh: T. & T. Clark, 1963), pp. 131f., classes the blessing among 'the most ancient formulations', and Rowley himself (*ibid.*, pp. 35f.) suggests that the 'blessing' is one of 'the poetical passages in the Pentateuch' which 'may have been taken over from oral tradition'.

[106] In particular on pp. 281–6.
[107] Num. 6.24; II Sam. 8.10; Ps. 29.11.
[108] Num. 25.12; I Kings 5.26 [EVV 5.12]; Isa. 54.10; Ps. 55.21 [EVV, v. 20].
[109] Deut. 23.7 [EVV, v. 6]; Jer. 8.15, 14.19, 33.9; Pss. 34.15 [EVV, v. 14], 122.8f.; Esth. 10.3; Lam. 3.17; Ezra 9.12.
[110] Isa. 32.17, 48.18, 57.2, 60.17; Ps. 85.11 [EVV, v. 10], cf. Ps. 72.3, צְדָקָה.
[111] Ps. 119.165; Prov. 3.2.
[112] Num. 6.27; cf. LXX v. 23; I Sam. 20.42.
[113] Jer. 16.5 (including also רַחַם); Ps. 85.11 [EVV, v. 10].
[114] Ps. 4.9 [EVV, v. 8]. [115] Isa. 52.7. [116] Isa. 66.12.
[117] Jer. 14.13, 28.9, 33.6; Ps. 85.11 [EVV, v. 10]; Zech. 8.19; Esth. 9.30.
[118] Mal. 2.6. [119] Isa. 59.8. [120] Ps. 38.4 [EVV, v. 3].
[121] רַע, Ps. 34.15 [EVV, v. 14]; רָעָה, Jer. 29.11; רָשָׁע, Ps. 73.3 and Job. 15.21.
[122] Cf. the comment on the 'blessing', for example, of A. Murtonen, 'The Use and Meaning of the Words L°BÅREK and B°RÅKÅ^h in the Old Testament', *VT* 9 (April, 1959), p. 162: '*šmr* may have the normal meaning "to guard, keep safe", while the two following mean favour and grace, the "lifting up of his face" perhaps a little more strongly = active love, and the whole is crowned by the wish of *šālom*, the perfect "peace"

Furthermore, the ancient poem of Num. 6.24–26 makes what may be considered the ultimate association of שָׁלוֹם with the PRESENCE of God. Artur Weiser has argued persuasively the case for theophanic representation within the Israelite cult.[123] While his position is not without its critics,[124] and while Weiser does at times press his evidence perhaps too enthusiastically, his basic contention is undoubtedly a correct one.[125] The concept of the PRESENCE of God was certainly of vital importance to the Old Testament cult, and theophanic representation within the cult was one, though only one, important means of promulgating this concept.

Weiser holds Num. 6.24ff. to be an 'ancient liturgical blessing' which had an 'original association with the cultic theophany' – an association, indeed, which is preserved in the usage of certain

---

or condition where all things function in harmony and nothing is wanting.' Note also Walther Eichrodt's comment on 'the terminology in which *natural and spiritual goods can be combined in a great unity*. One of these terms is *šālōm*, 'well-being', 'peace', which as early as Num. 6.26 is used in the widest sense to include every divine blessing, and which now combines the supreme good of fellowship with God with the blessings of earthly life . . .' – *Theology of the Old Testament*, vol. II, trans. J. A. Baker (London: SCM Press and Philadelphia: Westminster Press, 1967), p. 358.

[123] A. Weiser, 'Zur Frage nach den Beziehungen der Psalmen zum Kult: Die Darstellung der Theophanie in den Psalmen und im Festkult', *Festschrift Alfred Bertholet*, eds. W. Baumgartner, O. Eissfeldt, K. Elliger, L. Rost (Tübingen: J. C. B. Mohr [P. Siebeck], 1950), pp. 513–31; *The Psalms: A Commentary*, trans. H. Hartwell (London: SCM Press and Philadelphia: Westminster Press, 1962), *passim*, but esp. pp. 28–52.

[124] So, for example, Claus Westermann, *The Praise of God in the Psalms*, trans. K. R. Crim (Richmond: John Knox Press, 1965), pp. 98–101; Kraus, *op. cit.*, on Ps. 18, esp. pp. 143–6; *Worship in Israel*, trans. G. Buswell (Oxford: Basil Blackwell and Richmond: John Knox Press, 1966), pp. 213–18; and most recently Jörg Jeremias, *Theophanie: Die Geschichte einer alttestamentlichen Gattung* (Neukirchen-Vluyn: Neukirchener Verlag, 1965), pp. 118–64, who would separate theophany from the cult in source and representation.

[125] Cf. J. K. Kuntz, *The Self-Revelation of God* (Philadelphia: The Westminster Press, 1967), *passim*, but esp. pp. 169–231, and note the comments of Ernst Würthwein, above, pp. 164ff., n. 33.

Psalms.[126] '*Der Zusammenhang der Formel des aaronitischen Segens mit der Kulttheophanie ist besonders greifbar in Ps 80.2, 4, wo der kultische Terminus für die Epiphanie Gottes im himmlischen Lichtglanz* .(=kabôd *vgl. Ex 33.14, 18; 1 Kön 8.11; Jes 6.3; Ps 96.6 usw.)* hôphî'a *(vgl. Deut 33.2; Ps 50.2; 94.1) in synonymem Parallelismus steht zur Bitte "lass leuchten dein Angesicht!"*'[127]

Walter Beyerlin, a pupil of Weiser, follows his mentor's basic approach to the question of the cultic role of theophany, and places particular stress upon the use of the term פָּנִים in the 'blessing' and similarly elsewhere.[128] Drawing attention to the fact that פָּנִים in reference to Yahweh nearly always occurs in cultic contexts, a point for which he is in part indebted to the work of Gulin cited earlier in this essay,[129] Beyerlin posits a distinctively Israelite connection between the פָּנִים of Yahweh and Yahweh's cultic theophany, adducing many examples to establish his case,[130] and comments on the passage under consideration as follows: 'The liturgical formula of the Aaronite

---

[126] A. Weiser, *The Psalms*, p. 39.

[127] A. Weiser, 'Zur Frage . . .' *Festschrift Alfred Bertholet*, p. 519, n. 1.

[128] Walter Beyerlin, *Origins and History of the Oldest Sinaitic Traditions*, trans. S. Rudman (Oxford: Basil Blackwell and New York: Humanities Press, 1965), pp. 98–112.

[129] See above, p. 287, n. 99. Gulin's study is done in the *religiongeschichtliche* vein of the Wellhausen school, and proposes three possible conceptions of 'Face of Yahweh' which underlie the Old Testament usage: a cultic concept (pp. 3–13), an astral concept (pp. 13–17), and an anthropomorphic concept (pp. 17–29). '*Bisweilen ist es schwer zu bestimmen*,' concludes Gulin (p. 30), '*ob die betreffende Stelle zur kultischen, astralen oder anthropomorphistischen Kategorie gehört.*' Cf. also the interesting article of A. R. Johnson, 'Aspects of the Use of the Term פָּנִים in the Old Testament', *Festschrift Otto Eissfeldt zum 60 Geburtstage*, ed. Johann Fück (Halle: Max Niemeyer Verlag, 1947), pp. 155–9. Johnson does not refer to the article by Gulin.

[130] See Beyerlin, *op. cit.*, pp. 103–11, and note particularly two remarks: '. . . the cultic worship of Yahweh, which presupposes his personal presence, is a practical reality' (p. 107), and 'Without Yahweh's *pānîm* no cult of Yahweh in Canaan would be possible' (p. 111).

blessing in Num. vi. 24f. also makes clear the connection between Yahweh's face and his theophany.'[131]

While it seems reasonably clear that Num. 6.27 was not originally a part of the 'blessing' or even perhaps, a part of its original context,[132] it now follows the blessing in the MT and precedes it in the LXX. This verse includes the phrase וְשָׂמוּ אֶת־שְׁמִי עַל־בְּנֵי יִשְׂרָאֵל, and the equation of the שֵׁם of God and his PRESENCE is far too well known to require repetition here.[133] Whatever the original setting of Num. 6.24–26, it is plain that the editors who placed these verses where they now stand gave strong support to the interpretation being maintained here.

It may thus be said that this ancient blessing effectively sums up a basic contention of this essay: that שָׁלוֹם is the gift of God, and can be received only in his PRESENCE. But the use of שָׁלוֹם in the blessing also lends credence to the view that שָׁלוֹם serves as a cultic term and possesses a meaning far more comprehensive than the one usually given to it in the translations and by many commentators. For שָׁלוֹם in Num. 6.24–26 is intended as a description of the man who is blessed (בָּרַךְ), guarded (שָׁמַר) and treated graciously (חָנַן) by God; the man who is doubly in God's PRESENCE;[134] the man who is 'fulfilled', and so 'complete'. Indeed

---

[131] Beyerlin, *op. cit.*, p. 106 (citing Weiser in support of the statement, n. 404).

[132] See above, pp. 287ff; note also N. H. Snaith, *Leviticus and Numbers*, CentB, new ed. (London: Thomas Nelson and Sons, 1967), p. 207.

[133] Cf., for example, Eichrodt, *op. cit.*, vol. I, pp. 206–10; A. R. Johnson, *The One and the Many in the Israelite Conception of God*, 2nd ed. (Cardiff: University of Wales Press, 1961), pp. 17–19: having set forth Num. 6.24–26 as 'the official priestly blessing', Johnson says of 6.27: 'Yahweh's emphatic comment upon this, as recorded by the P Code, is to be noted: "So, when they (i.e. the priests) put my 'Name' upon the children of Israel, then 'tis *I* (וַאֲנִי) will bless them"' (p. 18);

and John Wm. Wevers, 'A Study in the Form Criticism of Individual Complaint Psalms', *VT* 6 (Jan., 1956), pp. 83–85.

[134] Verse 25, יָאֵר יְהוָה פָּנָיו אֵלֶיךָ and v. 26, יִשָּׂא יְהוָה פָּנָיו אֵלֶיךָ.

שָׁלוֹם *and the Presence of God*

has such a man answered the New Testament commandment which is attributed to our Lord: *"Εσεσθε οὖν ὑμεῖς τέλειοι ὡς ὁ πατὴρ ὑμῶν ὁ οὐράνιος τέλειός ἐστιν.*[135]

[135] Matt. 5.48. Cf. the interesting remarks of Gerhard Barth on τέλειος in Günther Bornkamm, Gerhard Barth, Heinz Joachim Held, *Tradition and Interpretation in Matthew* (London: SCM Press and Philadelphia: Westminster Press, 1963), pp. 95–105. Note esp. pp. 97–99; n. 1 on p. 98 on the LXX use of τέλειος to reproduce 'words of the stems שלם and תמם'; and the comment on p. 101: '. . . Matthew does not use τέλειος in the Greek sense of the perfect ethical personality, but in the Old Testament sense of the wholeness of consecration to God, as the close relationship with the use of תמים in I QS shows. That discipleship itself is "perfection" and not merely the way to it follows above all from the fact that the necessity of imitation in suffering is not grounded primarily on a goal envisaged in the future but on belonging to the Son of man.'

INDEX OF BIBLICAL PASSAGES

OLD TESTAMENT

Index of Biblical Passages

APOCRYPHA

NEW TESTAMENT

INDEX OF AUTHORS

INDEX OF HEBREW WORDS DISCUSSED

MUP PROCLAMATION AND PRESENCE

Production specifications:
    text paper—60 pound Warren's Olde Style
    end papers—75 pound Strathmore Brigadoon, Ancient Red
    cover (on .088 boards)—Holliston Roxite B (51507)
    and jacket—75 pound Strathmore Brigadoon, Ancient Red,
    printed (PMS 492)

Printing (offset lithography) by Omnipress of Macon, Inc.,
    Macon, Georgia
Binding by John H. Dekker and Sons, Inc., Grand Rapids, Michigan